Postcolonial Audiences

ROUTLEDGE RESEARCH IN POSTCOLONIAL LITERATURES

Edited in collaboration with the Centre for Colonial and Postcolonial Studies, University of Kent at Canterbury, this series presents a wide range of research into postcolonial literatures by specialists in the field. Volumes will concentrate on writers and writing originating in previously (or presently) colonized areas, and will include material from non-anglophone as well as anglophone colonies and literatures. Series editors: Donna Landry and Caroline Rooney.

Postcolonial Audiences

Readers, Viewers and Reception

Edited by Bethan Benwell, James Procter and Gemma Robinson

 Routledge
Taylor & Francis Group
NEW YORK AND LONDON

First published 2012
by Routledge
711 Third Avenue, New York, NY 10017

Simultaneously published in the UK
by Routledge
2 Park Square, Milton Park, Abingdon, Oxon OX14 4RN

Routledge is an imprint of the Taylor & Francis Group, an informa business

© 2012 Taylor & Francis

The right of Bethan Benwell, James Procter and Gemma Robinson to be identified as the authors of the editorial material, and of the authors for their individual chapters, has been asserted by them in accordance with sections 77 and 78 of the Copyright, Designs and Patents Act 1988.

Library of Congress Cataloging-in-Publication Data

Postcolonial audiences : readers, viewers and reception / edited by Bethan Benwell, James Procter and Gemma Robinson.
   p. cm. — (Routledge research in postcolonial literatures ; 37.)
   Includes bibliographical references and index.
  1. Commonwealth literature (English)—History and criticism.   2. English literature—Developing countries—History and criticism.   3. Postcolonialism—English-speaking countries.   4. Postcolonialism—Commonwealth countries.   5. Intercultural communication.   6. Postcolonialism.   I. Benwell, Bethan.   II. Procter, James.   III. Robinson, Gemma.
   PR9080.P54 2011
   820.9'3581—dc23
   2011036138

ISBN13: 978-0-415-88871-4 (hbk)
ISBN13: 978-0-203-12616-5 (ebk)

Typeset in Baskerville by IBT Global.

Printed and bound in the United States of America on acid-free paper by IBT Global.

Contents

PART III
Reading in Representation

PART IV
Reading and Nationalism

PART V
Reading and Postcolonial Ethics

Figures

Acknowledgements

The editors would like to acknowledge the AHRC, who funded the conference which inspired the genesis of the collection and most of the chapters. Grateful thanks go to Grove Press for their permission to use the image of the front cover of Robert Antoni's *My Grandmother's Erotic Folktales*, Firehouse Films for their kind permission to use stills from *bro'Town* and to Random House for allowing the use of quoted material from their archives.

A Preface[1]

Reflections on The Postcolonial Exotic

Graham Huggan, University of Leeds

Back in 2001, I called *The Postcolonial Exotic* "a speculative prolegomenon to the sociology of postcolonial cultural production" (xvi), partly in the knowledge that my own methodology was insufficiently rigorous to merit the admittedly capacious term "sociological" and partly in the hope that others might go on to produce the kinds of empirical work that were needed to flesh out a field in which textual analysis continues to predominate over studies of the material conditions of production and consumption—studies often seen as not belonging to the remit of traditional literary studies and as falling, rather, into the separate domain of literary publishing or the history of the book. Needless to say, I found—still find—this separation of the spheres to be naïve, and over the last ten years or so it has been gratifying to see a number of studies that look in much more detail than I was able to at various aspects of local literary industries and the global markets that increasingly sustain them (examples here might include the research of David Carter and Mark Davis (2007) on changing patterns of literary publishing in Australia, or an excellent 2007 book on Canadian literary celebrity by Lorraine York). As Lynn Innes says in her *Cambridge Introduction to Postcolonial Literary Studies*, also published in 2007, much more work is needed on the different ways in which postcolonial literary works are read in a variety of contexts that are as much local or regional as they are global, and which –in keeping with the dictates of an increasingly global literary marketplace—may end up being local, regional and global at once. Innes warns, and rightly so, that globalisation must not be used as an excuse to "de-differentiate" local readers, or to create the fiction of a "global market reader" who is addressed, explicitly or implicitly, in a wide range of market-conscious postcolonial literary texts (2007, Ch. 11).

This point is also taken up, but in more detail, in Sarah Brouillette's combative study *Postcolonial Writers in the Global Literary Marketplace* (2007), which seems unsure whether to pay tribute to what she calls my "innovative materialist assessment [of] postcoloniality [as] a form of industrial commodification that serves the interests of privileged audiences", or whether to spike my guns by including me among the ranks of the privileged, thereby implicitly accusing me of practising the same bad faith as the largely mythic figure of the "global market reader" I seem so eager to denounce (15, 21). *The Postcolonial Exotic*, claims Brouillette, is as much a symptom of postco-loniality as a critical assessment of it, and is motivated by an amateurish "ethnography of reading" that smacks alternately of academic elitism and postcolonial stricken conscience; moreover, it performs the same metropoli-tan commodity fetishism of which it complains by assuming that postcolonial literature "exists only as evidence of the Western fetishization of the rest of human experience, or that the reception of postcolonial texts is always or only a kind of market colonization" (22–24). For Brouillette, the book thus ignores the basic fact that the "material organization of the current literary marketplace does not reveal a single market, but rather a fragmenting and proliferating series of niche audiences, which are admittedly united by a set of general rules dictated by the major transnational corporations" (24). Unsurprisingly, I find the criticism unfair: not only does my book not ignore this last fact, but it is largely predicated on it, and I am actually in full agree-ment with her that few researchers, least of all myself, have performed what she calls "the detailed analyses of reading practices that might justify the identification of a characteristic mode of cosmopolitan consumption that is dehistoricizing and depoliticizing" (24)—hence my insistence on the largely speculative nature of my work. Certainly, as Brouillette suggests, there is an urgent need for more work on the geographical and historical *particularities* of audience and reception in postcolonial literary studies, the kind of situ-ated work to which this volume usefully contributes; and perhaps less now needs to be said about postcolonialism within the context of global commod-ity culture—postcolonialism *as* a global cultural commodity—than about the wide range of empirically verifiable reading practices that obtain within a literary field that is probably not even recognised as postcolonial by many of its readers, and the academic institutionalisation of which has been much more varied—and often significantly less Western-oriented—in its effects than some of its practitioners seem ready to admit.

There are a number of good reasons, of course, why postcolonial literary scholars have tended to ignore issues of audience and reception. These reasons are partly historical. Until recently, there have been few obvious models to turn to in either reception theory, which has European and American roots, or postcolonial theory, which, when it has used literature at all, has either done so illustratively (Homi Bhabha) or symptomatically as a means of reading culture or assessing the political instrumentality of literary and other cultural texts (Gayatri Spivak, Edward Said). At the same time, the remarkable "celebrity effect" of these three thinkers, while commented on often enough, has not led to any sustained treatment of celebrity in postcolonial studies—celebrity is often alluded to, and occasionally studied in individual instances, e.g., the "global brand" that is Salman Rushdie (Ommundsen 2009), but there is still no full-length work that I am aware of that offers a comparative analysis of postcolonial writing—and postcolonialism itself—as a reciprocal effect of the actions of global celebrity on a culturally commodified literary field. Brennan's important earlier work (e.g., Brennan 1989) continues to be referred to, but mostly to be dismissed, while there still seems to be residual suspicion that the study of celebrity, arguably one of the most significant cultural phenomena of our era, is either inherently trivialising or somehow unsuitable for the serious analysis of literary texts (see, however, Moran 2000).

There are also practical reasons. Most postcolonial literary scholars –or those who designate themselves as such –have little training in the social science techniques needed to undertake either qualitative or quantitative forms of audience analysis, and though there have been some notable recent exceptions (e.g., Fraser 2008), there has generally been little attempt by postcolonial scholars to engage with that fascinating congeries of disciplinary methods that is the history of the book. However, lack of formal training has not held back postcolonial scholars, literary-minded and not, from foraging across a wide range of disciplines, and indeed these forms of promiscuous interdiscursivity are an integral part of what the field of postcolonial studies means for many of its practitioners today (Huggan 2008). Why, then, have these scholars—so bold in other ways—been so conspicuously reluctant to look at issues of audience and reception in the disparate literatures they study? Could snobbery about popular culture be an issue here? While there have been welcome signs in recent years that the postcolonial literary field has opened up to popular forms, the predominance of "high" literature continues, and it is surely no coincidence that some of the best recent examples of reception-based postcolonial studies stake a legitimate claim for the re-visiting of such long taken-for-granted terms as "literature", "the author", and "the text" (see, for example, Fraser 2008; Griswold 2000; Newell 2006).

Also well worth considering in this context is Chris Bongie's provocative argument that the apparent disjunction between cultural studies (which enthusiastically engages with popular culture) and postcolonial studies (which generally avoids it) is down to the latter's "foundational bias" against what many of its practitioners perceive to be the "inauthentically popular", i.e., those globalised modes of mass production and consumption which are mistakenly seen as being separate from "authentic" folk forms linked to the popular imaginaries of formerly colonised societies and cultures or to their revolutionary imperatives (2008: 7, 282–83). As Bongie sardonically enquires, "legitimate custodians of a traditional past . . . or subaltern adepts in the ethical practices of freedom . . . might be presumed to have better and more 'authentic' things to do with their time than watch *Roseanne* or read *Annie John*. In the failed dialogue between Roseanne and Kincaid, where are the 'real' people situated, presuming 'they' even exist?" (283). As Bongie rightly suggests, it is not enough to account for those ideological faultlines that have historically tended to distance postcolonial criticism from, or even to pit it against, the study of popular culture; it also needs to be shown how and why postcolonial studies— above all postcolonial *literary* studies—has been invested in marking off the middlebrow from the lowbrow, and has attempted to distinguish between the "authentically" and the "inauthentically" popular in each case (283). What the chapters that follow reveal is that one of the most effective means of exposing these ideological faultlines, and exploring the commonsense assumptions that flow from them, is a sustained attention to *reception*. For reception returns us to the vexed question of value, and the often eclipsed politics of cultural and critical evaluation, that have for too long remained concealed within the field of postcolonial studies. *The Postcolonial Exotic* might be more productively reread in this context, not in terms of what it leaves unsaid about empirical audiences, but for its attempt to initiate new conversations around the unsaid "regimes of value" (Frow 1995) that have been part and parcel of the institutionalisation of postcolonial production within the academy.

Notes

1. This preface is a shortened and edited version of a chapter: "Celebrity Conservationism, Postcolonialism, and the Commodity Form". In *Commodifying (Post) colonialisms: Othering, Reification, Commodification and the New Literatures and Cultures in English*, edited by Rainer Emig and Oliver Lindner (2010), Amsterdam: Rodopi, pp. 241–258. I am grateful to the publishers for permission to reuse some of this material.

References

Bongie, Chris. 2008. *Friends and Enemies: The Scribal Politics of Post/Colonial Literature*. Liverpool: Liverpool University Press.

Brennan, Timothy. 1989. "Cosmopolitans and Celebrities." *Race & Class* 31: 1–19.

Brouillette, Sarah. 2007. *Postcolonial Writers in the Global Literary Marketplace*. Houndmills: Palgrave Macmillan.

Carter, David, and Anne Galligan, eds. 2007. *Making Books: Contemporary Australian Publishing*. St Lucia: University of Queensland Press.

Fraser, Robert. 2008. *Book History through Postcolonial Eyes: Re-writing the Script: 1*. London: Routledge.

Frow, John. 1995. *Cultural Studies and Cultural Value*. Oxford: Clarendon Press.

Griswold, Wendy. 2000. *Bearing Witness: Readers, Writers, and the Novel in Nigeria*. Princeton: Princeton University Press.

Huggan, Graham. 2001. *The Postcolonial Exotic: Marketing the Margins*. London: Routledge.

———. 2008. *Interdisciplinary Measures: Literature and the Future of Postcolonial Studies*. Liverpool: Liverpool University Press.

Innes, Lynn. 2007. *The Cambridge Introduction to Postcolonial Literatures in English*. Cambridge: Cambridge University Press.

Moran, Joe. 2000. *Star Authors: Literary Celebrity in America*. London: Pluto Press.

Newell, Stephanie. 2006. *West African Literatures: Ways of Reading*. Oxford: Oxford University Press.

Ommundsen, Wenche. 2009. "Salman Rushdie: The Postcolonial Writer as Global Brand." In *Celebrity Colonialism: Fame, Power and Representation in Colonial and Postcolonial Cultures*, edited by Robert Clarke, 159–72. Newcastle: Cambridge Scholars Publishing.

York, Lorraine. 2007. *Literary Celebrity in Canada*. Toronto: University of Toronto Press.

Introduction

Bethan Benwell, James Procter
and Gemma Robinson

Captive Audiences

By evoking the "postcolonial audience" in the title of this book we do not mean to conjure a particular demographic that, as Ien Ang puts it in a different context "is analogous to that of 'population', 'nation' or 'the masses'" (Ang 1991, 2). Rather we use the term to think in the broadest possible way about the different theoretical and empirical consequences of reception, from ideal to real readers. Ang's reservations regarding audience as an identifiable grouping would appear magnified many times within the context of postcolonial studies, where any conception of audience is likely to be global (as well as local), where reading, viewing and listening are frequently activities involving mobile, exilic and diasporic audiences, and where the potential distances between producers and consumers place an increased emphasis on translation and mistranslation. As Gayatri Spivak writes in *Outside in the Teaching Machine*, "The audience is not an essence, the audience is a blank. An audience can be constituted by people I cannot even imagine . . . " (1993, 22).

Yet if the audience is in a sense unknowable it has also played a concrete role in the history of colonialism. Empire building involved more than the construction of roads, railways and monuments; it also entailed the production of audiences, and certain kinds of readers, listeners and viewers. Frantz Fanon observes some of the consequences of cultural imperialism in Martinique: "I am a Negro—but of course I do not know it, simply because I am one. When I am at home my mother sings me French love songs in which there is never a word about Negroes. [. . .] Somewhat later I read white books and little by little take into myself the prejudices, the myths, the folklore" (1986, 191). Colonial audiences were crucial to the manufacture of consent in the colonies where, as Stephen Slemon has argued, "the 'English' [or European] book . . . becomes the foremost machinery for forging . . . obedience" (Slemon 1989, 103). Audiences are central to the zeal and civilising mission of conversion through reading/listening to the word of God (see for example Bhabha 1994, 102–22). They are the link between "literary study" and "territorial expansion" in British India in the nineteenth century (Viswanathan

1989). They are the market for Crown and Royal Readers, which provided standard reading fare for pupils across the Commonwealth until 1907 (Fraser 2008a, 91). Elleke Boehmer has observed in this context that "Colonial spaces—from company offices to the guest-rooms of government houses to the libraries of hill-stations—became flooded with the same kinds of literature. The imaginations of readers across the British Empire were led along parallel grooves" (Boehmer 2005, 52).

Meanwhile, in the West, Edward Said estimates that the orient was the subject of around sixty thousand books between 1800 and 1950, a "school of interpretation" he names "orientalism" (Said 1978, 203–4). Joseph Bristow notes the significance of what he terms "reading for the empire" among working-class British boys: "between 1870 and 1900 narratives celebrating empire and techniques in teaching reading and writing gradually converged" (1991, 20). Bill Bell traces the often elaborate libraries Scottish emigrants took with them to imperial outposts, observing that "[c]ultural memory is in exile contingent on—even reinforced by—the continued practices of reading and writing" (1998, 87). The captivation of audience was as significant in the metropolitan centres as it was at the so-called peripheries.

Research across book history, reception and colonialism reinforces this sense of the captivation: D. F. McKenzie's work in *Bibliography and the Sociology of Texts* advocates a shift in bibliographical approaches "from questions of textual authority to those of dissemination and readership as matters of economic and political motive" (1986, 1), and is founded in his research on New Zealand colonial textual production and readerships. In Latin America emergent national and transnational circuits of publishing both shaped and were shaped by new readers (Anderson 1983; Roldán 2003). Robert Darnton's "Communications Circuit" necessarily involves reading, despite his warning that "reading remains the most difficult stage to study in the circuit that books follow" (1982, 74). For example, Isabel Hofmeyr's study of the transnational, multilingual circulation of John Bunyan's *The Pilgrim's Progress* explores the "convoluted routes that books travel and [. . .] the complex intra-African circulation that documents take" (2003, 136) but she too notes the difficulties of researching the "effects" of the circulation of "images and texts [that] travel into colonial contexts" (135; see also 2002).

If most of the foregoing research privileges readers and reading in the Anglophone world (a bias we would acknowledge characterises this collection as a whole), a more comprehensive study of postcolonial reception would reveal to the field the pervasive centrality of audiences. It would also uncover the multifaceted and multilingual character of these audiences, including spectators, viewers and listeners. Television, the Internet, cinema, a music concert, a football match, a radio programme, a magazine article, a book: all entail very different kinds of postcolonial audience (see Banaji, Evans, Keown and Stadtler, this volume, who address film, cartoon and song audiences in their chapters). Key thinkers in the field have amply illustrated the postcolonial politics of cricket spectatorship (James 1963) and the football crowd (Phillips 2001, Gilroy 2004 and McLeod 2008) and the ways in which they complicate local, national and transnational attachments. In early twentieth-century Europe, nationalist and fascist movements reinforced and reproduced their power through the performance of public spectacles (Mosley's fascist parade; The Nuremburg Rally) capable of modelling the crowd, "an inevitable and untidy diversity into an ideal and unnatural symmetry" (Gilroy 1997, 305). Away from the public sphere, Anne McClintock has illustrated how the steady stream of Victorian advertising that drew upon "colonial heroes and colonial scenes . . . from milk cartons to sauce bottles, tobacco tins to whiskey bottles, assorted biscuits to toothpaste, toffee boxes to baking powder" (1995, 515), created a fetishistic audience caught up in the domestic consumption, and the domestication, of empire.

Until relatively recently, however (and when it has discussed audiences at all), postcolonial studies has spoken about readers alone, and in isolation from the other audiences indicated earlier.[1] To be sure, reading has been the core activity of postcolonial studies as it has been reproduced within the institution over the past twenty-five years. Perhaps because of its centrality, the act has slipped into common sense, a taken-for-granted activity that very few in the field have commented upon (Procter 2009). When postcolonial books have been central to accounts of audience, they often entail expanded notions of reading and readers. For example, apartheid in South Africa created a tortuous culture of bureaucratic and legal consumption of banned texts, with proliferating judicial and government documents to support it (van der Vlies 2007a, 2007b; McDonald 2009). The divided reception of Monica Ali's *Brick Lane* was most pronounced in relation to the film, rather than the novel on which it was based (Benwell, Procter, and Robinson 2011a). Aamir Mufti has argued that the controversy over *The Satanic Verses* demands an appreciation that, for the many South Asian readers, reception of the novel was not by traditional reading, but via electronic media, faxes, and photocopies (1994). Elsewhere, Gayatri Spivak has noted how an event like the "Rushdie Affair" directs us away from traditional close reading and towards issues of audience, translation and exchange: "Literature is transactional. The point is not necessarily and exclusively the correct description of a book, but the construction of readerships" (1993, 228; see also Allington, this volume, on an analysis of the reception of *The Satanic Verses*).

Audience and Anxiety

What seems to connect many of the foregoing examples is the idea of audience as a site of control and subjection. Without wishing to underestimate the cumulative impact of these diverse instances, there is a danger that, viewed alone, they present a passive narrative of consumption in which readers, viewers and listeners are inevitably duped by colonial, postcolonial and neo-colonial ideologies. Roger Chartier, however, complicates this view of reception outlining "the founding paradox of any history of reading": that firstly "against all the reductions that cancel out the creative and inventive force of practices, [. . .] reading is never totally constrained" but that secondly "the tactics of readers [. . .] obey certain rules, logic, and models" (1992, 49). Researching cultural practices that shift between these two modes of freedom and rule characterises much of the recent work that has been done at the varying interfaces between book history, reception studies, and colonial and postcolonial studies. Stephanie Newell, for example, argues that Ghanaian popular reading tastes for writers such as Marie Corelli were devalued within prevailing educational mores, but nevertheless offered readers ways to "comprehend the moral obligations and ethical foundations of 'modern', colonial and Christian social formations" (2002, 102). Research on African, Australian, Canadian, Caribbean and Indian popular literary cultures—in both their historical and contemporary forms—continues to impress upon us that readers have never been a stable or static constituency (Carter and Galligan 2007; Gerson 1989; Gupta and Chakravorty 2004; Darnton 2001; Edmondson 2009; Joshi 2002; 2004; Kapcia and Kumaraswami 2010; Nayak, this volume; Orsini 2010).) There has always been the possibility that the production of colonial and postcolonial audiences would bring about localised readings, aspirational readings, parallel readings, judicial readings, public and private readings, misreadings, communal readings, contrary readings, resistant readings and new technologies of reading. As Michel de Certeau famously argued in another context:

> Readers are travellers; they move across lands belonging to someone else, like nomads poaching their way across fields they did not write, despoiling the wealth of Egypt to enjoy it themselves. (1984, 174)

De Certeau's contradictory model of the reader as traveller, poacher, nomad and despoiler describes a multifaceted process of consumption that at once turns on the idea of reading as a colonising enterprise, and also questions the types of possessions that are accrued through reading. Although only briefly sketched, his metaphor proposes a relationship between the ways that readers and empires consume. But as his mixed metaphor also reveals, acts of reading can be conceived both inside and outside the structures of empire: as imperialising practice (the colonising "despoiler" of text) and anti-imperial action (the tactical, marginalised "poacher" of text)—a point addressed by many of the contributors to this volume examining both the producers and consumers of Anglophone diasporic literature.

Although he has more to say about audience than is often acknowledged, one of the main criticisms of Said's *Orientalism* (1978) is that it presents the reader with a monolithic Western discourse in which resistance seems almost impossible. We would add within the context of this volume that one of the ways *Orientalism* manages this is by focusing on the text as a static object rather than as objects of reception and consumption whose meanings are always negotiable. As Ania Loomba has argued:

> Literature . . . both reflects and creates ways of seeing and modes of articulation that are central to the colonial process . . . Such complexity is not necessarily a matter of authorial intention. Plays such as *Othello* and *The Tempest* thus evoke contemporary ideas about bestiality or incivility of non-Europeans. But do they do so in order to endorse dominant attitudes to "race" and culture or to question them? . . . Both plays have been interpreted and taught in ways that endorse colonial ways of seeing, but both have also inspired anti-colonial and anti-racist movements . . . (2005, 66–67)

One of Homi Bhabha's key contributions in this context has been to emphasise that "communication is a process that is never perfectly achieved and that there is always a slippage, a gap, between what is said and what is heard" (in Loomba, 78). Orientalism becomes for Bhabha less a site of absolute textual authority or "hold" than a site of anxious repetition working to secure an object and an audience that is always capable of eluding it. It tends to be forgotten that one of Bhabha's earliest essays on colonial texts was a critique of representationalist/mimetic theories of reading published in Gloversmith's (ed.) *The Theory of Reading* (1984). Here, Bhabha argues for a greater awareness of the constitutive forces of literary critical reading within the academy, "as one of the major operators in the cultural reproduction of texts and the constitution of the order of *Literature*" (1984, 99). Readings produced by the academy are the means by which "texts are systematized, synthesized and signified", they "give us unifying [but misleading] titles such as 'Commonwealth Literature' or 'The Caribbean Tradition' (1984, 99) which may have a ring of truth, but it is only the shrill school bell that establishes a discipline and guards its boundaries defensively" (99). Failures to recognise this is what, according to Bhabha, "make our readings unwillingly collusive and profoundly uncritical" (99).

Joseph Bristow identifies another set of anxieties to Bhabha around empire and audience in his early study of Boy's Own literature. *Empire Boys* (1991) demonstrates how rising literacy rates among the British working-class created, from the 1860s, anxieties around the use and abuse of leisure time, anxieties that were essentially bound up with empire. The popular market among working-class boys for penny dreadfuls in this period was regarded as a negative consequence of teaching the poor how to read. The sense was that this new audience should be trained to read literature of an "improving" kind (12) because empire placed a particular onus on the need for the British masses to read responsibly in order to grasp their privileged place in the world: "Gradually, the imperialist knowledge supplied in school lessons would converge with the world-view laid out in what became a canon of children's literature reaching back into the colonial past of the mid-eighteenth century" (12) (see also Halsey on Macaulay's legacy, this volume). Such anxieties around readership, literacy and empire have a much longer colonial history. As early as 1660 British slave-owners were disconcerted by Charles II's decree that "the Council for Foreign Plantations should instruct natives, servants and slaves of the British empire" how to read (see Manguel, 280), whereas in nineteenth-century America, anti-literacy laws were enacted across many southern states (Rodriguez 2007, 172). D. F. McKenzie's work on literacy and William Colenso's Maori New Testament (1837) reveal a missionary culture that sought to control forms of reading by "limit[ing] the Maori to knowledge of an ancient middle-eastern culture" thus enhancing "their familiar pastoral role morally and politically as interpretative guides" (340).

The Death of the Reader

Given the centrality of audience to the establishment of power, as well as the struggle over and re-negotiation of power, it is surprising that audiences, readers and reception have not featured more prominently on the radar of postcolonial studies. Despite the growing and compelling claims for reading; as an ethical act (Attridge 2004a; Hale 2007; also see Attridge, Farrier, Hallemeier, Allington, this volume); as a means of establishing collective, quasi-political consciousness (Radway 1991; Long 2003); as identification with difference (Felski 2003; Attridge, this volume); and as a mode of resistance (Fetterley 1978), the audience in postcolonial studies persists as a marginal figure. In the field of audience studies, work on postcolonial, diasporic and global contexts is longer established and populated by empirical, ethnographic studies of actual audiences (Banaji 2006; Banaji, this volume; Dickinson, Harindranath and Linné 1998; Dudrah and Desai 2008, Gillespie 1995, Harindranath 2009, Liebes and Katz 1989, Mankekar 1999). By contrast, the few postcolonial critics who *have* sought to address the aporia around audience have tended to do so in cynical, suspicious or negative terms, even to the extent of proclaiming the "death of the reader" (Khair 2006).

Writing in 1990, at a fledgling/formative moment in the institutional history of postcolonial studies, Helen Tiffin notes the curious absence of audiences in the field:

> there has been little detailed study of the relationship between texts and their captive colonial (indeed) post-colonial audiences, and there have been few studies of the implied audience or audiences of post-colonial texts. This is a curious omission given the degree to which questions of this kind have a direct bearing on any analysis of the discursive field. (1990, 27)

Throughout the 1990s, and despite an unprecedented expansion in the field's range and coverage, little work was done that could be said to date Tiffin's early observation. In 1992, David Carter observed "there are very few studies of consumption in postcolonial criticism, few studies of the reader; perhaps there are none at all of the circulation of contemporary postcolonial texts . . . " (Carter 1992, 300). In 2003 Chris Bongie urged postcolonial studies to "take the insights of reception theory more fully into account [and] . . . place a new emphasis on consumption . . . : what sorts of pleasure, for instance, do these various audiences take from their readings . . . ?" (2003, 21). More recently, Sarah Brouillette has noted that the field's understanding of audience remains largely unsubstantiated, as "few researchers have performed . . . detailed analysis of reading practices" (2007, 24). Against this set of critical opinion, we should remember that there has been increased attention to these very practices and the cultures in which they are situated (see earlier). For example, researchers in African popular literary cultures have attended to the social spaces and formations of reading, carrying out pilot interviews and questionnaire studies to track trends in reception (Nuttall 1994; Newell 2000; Griswold 2000). Notwithstanding Karin Barber's concerns about the methodological difficulties involved in tracing "attitudes" (1997), essays in her *Africa's Hidden Histories: Everyday Literacy and Making the Self* (2006) and her own research are centrally concerned with questions of audience formation (Hofmeyr 2006; Newell 2006; Peterson 2006; Barber 2000, 2007). Yet despite instances of regionally specific studies of reception, the sort of comparative, transnational contexts that would allow a broader conception of "postcolonial" audience remain "hidden". Further, there is still a tendency to avoid questioning the methods for researching "audience" in postcolonial studies, and to avoid considering how these methodologies might affect dominant paradigms in the field.

As Tiffin notes, there has been plenty of talking *around* the subject of audiences, and postcolonial critics have been quick to challenge contemporary writers that seem to appeal to contemporary Western audiences (Brennan 1997; Khair 2006; Huggan 2001). However, these different accounts tend to project their concerns onto a "straw" audience rather than directly engaging with these consumers. The result, C. L. Innes argues, is that:

> [T]here is little differentiation between kinds of Western readers. As a result there is an implicit assumption that the texts may be read in one way, that there is a manner of homogenous or universal reading . . . Where there is diversity or ambiguity of meaning, many critics assume it to be a property of the text rather than a consequence of diverse readerships. (Innes 2007, 200)

The tendency to gesture towards, or generalise about abstract audiences, rather than engaging with them in more concrete, differentiated terms would seem to have a number of causes. On a quite practical level, empirical audience research is both costly and time-consuming and in the absence of substantial and sustained institutional funding there has been an historical neglect of this area (Hall 1994, 271). In 2009 the National Book Trust India and the National Council of Applied Economic Research carried out the first 'National Youth Readership Survey' (Shukla 2010).[2] When the recentness of this attention to contemporary markets and consumption is coupled with the global span of postcolonial audiences, it is perhaps no wonder that postcolonial studies has preferred to conjure an abstract audience rather engage with it, focusing on books rather than their readers.

Another possible reason for the apparent hedging around the actual consumers of postcolonial cultural production is implicit in the various responses outlined so far: "audience" talk quickly rounds upon concerns about Western consumption and the global literary marketplace, concerns that can seem to undermine the liberatory political project of postcolonial studies. Reception study from this perspective threatens to short-circuit a more "committed" or "resistant" mode of textual interpretation in which the postcolonial text can appear politically uncompromised (Ashcroft 2001; Cudjoe 1980). From this perspective a full account of audiences risks reducing postcoloniality to "a relatively small, Western-style, Western trained, group of writers and thinkers [and readers] who mediate the trade in cultural commodities of world capitalism at the periphery" (Appiah 1992, 149; see Loh, this volume). Arguably then, audiences have been kept at arm's length or otherwise regarded with distrust because foregrounding readers, viewers and listeners (ideal or actual) risks compromising some of the more general claims that have been made in the field around the transformative, resistant or subversive capacities of isolated postcolonial texts. The formalism that underpins such readings can work with confidence and consistency only when texts are removed from the contingent relations they share with different reading publics, at different historical moments.

How to Read

David Carter makes a similar point in his essay on taste and postcolonial studies suggesting that postcolonial critics have not only neglected other audiences, but also failed to recognise *themselves* as a constitutive audience with particular dispositions, tastes and ways of reading:

> Postcolonial criticism in the first instance is about producing new sorts of readers within the institution. Thus, besides offering an account of an institutional history, *The Empire Writes Back* by Ashcroft, Griffiths and Tiffin . . . is a "how-to" book: how to become a postcolonial reader, how to do (new) things with books. (293)

Within this context we might note the telling definition of "post-colonial reading" which appears in Ashcroft, Griffiths and Tiffin's *Post-Colonial Studies: The Key Concepts* (2000), a reference book which arguably serves the market created by the new sorts of readers David Carter mentions earlier:

Post-Colonial Reading. A way of reading and rereading texts of both metropolitan and colonial cultures to draw deliberate attention to the profound and inescapable effects of colonization on literary production; anthropological accounts; historical records; administrative and scientific writing. It is a form of deconstruction most usually applied to works emanating from the colonizers (but may be applied to works of the colonized) which demonstrates the extent to which the text contradicts its underlying assumptions (civilization, justice, aesthetics, sensibility, race) and reveals its (often unwitting) colonialist ideologies and processes. (2000, 192)

Reading according to this definition has a project and purpose (to foreground the effects of colonisation on writing), and is "a way" of interpreting that can be "applied" to literary works. This sense of "post-colonial reading" as something which has an aim/objective and which is consistent in approach, and therefore infinitely reproducible, suggests what is being described here is not any old way of reading, but an approach to texts that has been disciplined to suit the conditions and requirements of the academy (see Srivastava, this volume). "Post-colonial reading" is something which is bound by certain institutional rules and procedures adopted by professional critics.

By contrast, reading for pleasure as opposed to pedagogy might be characterised by its relative lack of purpose, and its unregulated, inconsistent or idiosyncratic approach to texts (Guillory 2000). To read *Midnight's Children* merely to pass the time would not count as "post-colonial reading" in this context; would not be "deliberate" or indeed programmatic enough. The emphasis placed in this definition on interdisciplinary modes of reading, rereading, and on deconstructive approaches which dwell on the ambivalence and aporia of texts further marks this out as a specialist approach to cultural production that is largely shaped by the "interpretive community" (in Stanley Fish's memorable phrase) of the university. The proliferation of ways of reading in the field—colonial discourse analysis, contrapuntal reading (Said 1994), patient reading (Spivak 2004), distant reading (Moretti 2005), "reading for resistance" (Slemon 1989)—is in stark contrast to studies of readers themselves, especially postcolonial critics-as-readers. This inward rather than outward direction of reading suggests the potential for exclusivity, and the transcendence of the professional critic from the world of everyday reading (see Guillory 2000, Procter 2009, and Keown, this volume, for a problematisation of the distinction between "lay" and "professional" reading).

"A Nice Little Audience"

Browsing the bookstalls at an MLA conference in the early 1980s, Edward Said asked an unsuspecting sales representative, "Who reads these books?", to which the reply was "People who write specialized, advanced . . . criticism".

10   *Bethan Benwell, James Procter and Gemma Robinson*

Said is concerned with this image of an "earnest crowd of three thousand . . . reading each other" (1985, 138). Academic criticism, he suggests, is not dissimilar to genres like cookbooks, and exercise manuals that attract "a nice little audience" of specialised, niche readers (137) The anecdote appears in Said's "Opponents, Audiences, Constituencies" (1985), an essay in which he suggests that, under Reaganism, the audiences for academic writing have become mere "clientele" rather than "constituencies", "people who use (and perhaps buy) your services because you and others belonging to your guild are certified experts" (152; see also Le Roux; Low and Squires on publishers and reading clienteles/constituencies, this volume). While Said's account is ultimately less concerned with audiences themselves than with how writers need to engage or create wider audiences, and while his focus is literary studies in general rather than postcolonial studies in particular, his question, "Who reads?", runs to the core of our collection, and connects and animates all of its chapters. The question of audience is deceptively simple, but as our contributors show, its possible answers move us towards a fuller elaboration of the sociology of reception, the pragmatics of publishing, the fictive representation of reading, nationalism's production of "fellow-readers" (Anderson 1983, 44), and the moral ambitions and limitations of postcolonial ethics.

Where Said, the public intellectual, strives to move beyond the niche audience of the academy, Gayatri Spivak has typically come at the question of audience from the other side, exploring the institutional politics of reading from the relatively privileged perspective of the university teacher. This difference of approach is best thought of, not as a retreat from public to private (a distinction that a title like *Outside in the Teaching Machine* clearly unpicks), but rather as an attempt to take seriously what an institutional training in reading literature might offer. As Mark Sanders argues, Spivak is concerned with the question of whether training in a literary habit "can give a special character to ethical and political responsibility?" (2006, 1) In her early essay 'How to Read a "Culturally Different" Book', Spivak addresses herself to the "conscientious teacher" (1996, 126) within the context of changes to canon formation and the subsequent opening up to postcolonial writing. Spivak emphasises the need for more than a vicarious reading for pleasure in this context. "Vigilance" (135), she notes, is required in order to move beyond the "aura of self-representation" (127) and to recognise that postcolonial novels (R. K. Narayan is her chosen example) are caught up in the uneven, "neo-colonial traffic" of "international cultural exchange" (127). Spivak's early essay anticipates Graham Huggan's *The Postcolonial Exotic* in this respect, turning its attention from the academic/ student audiences of postcolonial literature to the vulnerable position of this literature within the global literary marketplace.

Spivak's connection between reading, pedagogy and postcolonial politics is a consistent focus point throughout her work of the last quarter of a century, even as the values of education have shifted. Far from reading losing its critical edge following the urgent political upheavals around 9/11, for Spivak literary reading becomes if anything more valuable:

However unrealistic it may seem to you, I would not remain a teacher in the Humanities if I did not believe that at the New York end—standing metonymically for the dispensing end as such—the teacher can try to rearrange desires noncoercively . . . through an attempt to develop in the student a habit of literary reading, even just "reading," suspending oneself into the text of the other . . . A training in literary reading is a training to learn from the singular and the unverifiable. (2004, 532)

Postcolonial Audiences

So far this introduction has worked to connect just some of the scattered and isolated speculations on audiences that are available within the field of postcolonial studies in order to offer a provisional, retrospective history of reception studies for the field. When these otherwise isolated concerns with audiences are put together, a more persistent if currently unarticulated debate around audiences emerges that will, we hope, provide a useful foundation, or point of departure for scholars wishing to take this work further, and indeed the chapters that follow represent a preliminary attempt to rise to this very challenge. The projects outlined in 'The Book in the World' (Fraser and Nasta 2007) and *Books Without Borders* (Fraser and Hammond 2008) inaugurated in many ways a cross-regional postcolonial approach to book history. Our attention, then, to "postcolonial audiences" is one answer to Robert Fraser and Susheila Nasta's call for investigation of the "contours, geographies and nature" of our "reading lives" (2). Furthermore, this collection confirms Fraser's sense that this "world of readers" (2008b, 167) is constantly shifting (187), and also supports our recent suggestion that practices of "reading after empire" involve mutable notions of colonial, postcolonial and neo-colonial reception, and contrasting formulations of the empire of reading (2011b).

The chapters in this present volume approach reading, reception and audiences in a wide range of geographical locations and employ a number of different methodologies, from the gathering of empirical evidence of reading from groups of actual readers through recordings, interviews, online material and newspaper archives (Benwell, Procter and Robinson; Banaji; Keown; Srivastava; Nayak) to the study of the reading practices of a single, influential reader (Low on William Plomer; Halsey on Thomas Macaulay). Others again (Le Roux; Squires) focus on the practices of the publishing industry as it fashions and responds to trends of consumption. Many contributions consider the complex *variety* of reading positions simultaneously hailing local and cosmopolitan readers and audiences, implicitly embedded in the writing of Anglophone diasporic authors (Stadtler; Loh; Evans), while others engage with the potential practical effects of such positioning for an *ethics* of reading within the contexts of cultural and religious difference, asylum and apartheid (and its aftershocks) (Attridge; Allington; Farrier; Hallemeier).

The collection is arranged around five sections:

1. Real Readers/Actual Audiences

When readers are referred to in postcolonial criticism and theory, they are most often "ideal" readers (Culler 2006), "mock" readers (Gibson 1950), "implied" readers (Iser 1978; Booth 1961), "model" readers (Eco 1979). Such forms of critical shorthand allow for a consoling interpretive or imagined community that nevertheless conveniently conceals the local, contingent and messy work of meaning production. This section foregrounds empirical or recorded evidence from "real" readers/audiences in their reception of post-colonial and diasporic texts—a common approach in media-based audience studies, but one which has been neglected in literary reception studies of contemporary literature in particular (though see Allington and Swann 2009; Benwell 2009; Lang 2009). The three chapters are united by their focus on "actual" audiences and use a variety of data and analytical approaches in order to conceive reading, reception and consumption as a socially situated, localised activity embedded in the practices of everyday life.

Michelle Keown, in 'The Politics of Postcolonial Laughter: The International Reception of the New Zealand Animated Comedy Series *bro'Town*', analyses a range of both critical and "lay" responses to *bro'Town* by academics, journalists and fans contributing to Internet discussion forums as a means of analysing audience responses to "ethnic" or "postcolonial" comedy. Like Benwell, Procter and Robinson, she is interested in exploring the reception politics of location and the extent to which "local" and "international" viewers diverge in their responses to the show's complex comic strategies. Keown concludes that fan responses often involve "a convergence of putatively separate reading practices associated with 'lay' and 'professional' constituencies", as outlined by theorist John Guillory, and that formulations of "the Pacific 'exotic'" inform the production, marketing and reception of *bro'Town*, interacting with the location of its audiences.

Transcripts of reading group sessions from a network of transnational reading groups are analysed by Bethan Benwell, James Procter and Gemma Robinson's chapter, "'That May Be Where I Come from but That's Not How I Read': Diaspora, Location and Reading Identities'. In our chapter, we configure some of the vexed relationships between location, identity and reception, paying close discursive attention to the ways in which readers both invoke and resist the significance of place, authenticity and belonging in reading group talk about diasporic fiction. While reader location never ultimately anchors meaning-making, location nonetheless continues to matter to our readers. We show how some of these orientations operate in the practices and performance of reading and how resistance to being "located" by literary producers and markets may be viewed as the assertion of a specific and autonomous "reading identity".

In the final chapter of this section, '"Bollywood" Adolescents: Young Viewers Discuss Class, Representation and Hindi Films', Shakuntala Banaji uses original audience research carried out between 2000 and 2009 in India with young film viewers. Here, she evaluates responses to changing representations of adolescence and class in Bollywood films since the deregulation and neo-liberalisation of the Indian economy, and their possible disjuncture with the realities of audience experience. While the consistent stereotyping or erasure of the everyday lives of the poor in recent blockbusters signals a betrayal of the "integrationist postcolonial vision of numerous Hindi films in the post-independence decades", Banaji demonstrates that her young audiences call on their "distinctive experiences and shared social formations" to reflect critically, imaginatively and tactically on these representations in their everyday lives.

2. Readers and Publishers

In the second edition of *The Post-Colonial Studies Reader* (2006), Ashcroft, Griffiths and Tiffin note that "[w]ho consumes and produces the texts for the 'post-colonial' world, who canonizes them, who acquires them and has them available as physical objects is an important but neglected precondition for more abstract and theoretical discussions of the agency of the post-colonial subject" (397). In this section we turn to twentieth-century and contemporary case studies to redress the theoretical imbalance identified by Ashcroft et al. Considering the institutional and empirical relations between publishers and readers in Africa and Britain, our contributors demonstrate the industry pressures that are placed upon reception, and evaluate the singular and collective attempts to make sense of the transactional relationships between reading and book production.

Elizabeth le Roux is interested in the discrepancy between different audiences and markets in a global context. Her chapter, 'Does the North Read the South? The International Reception of South African Scholarly Texts', analyses and evaluates whether South African scholarly books find an international readership (especially in the markets of the "North") through the examination of the marketing and distribution efforts of several publishers. Her findings suggest that far from globalisation shrinking the distance between readers and publishers in the North and South, the assymetrical production/consumption of texts continues to present ongoing challenges to the contemporary publishing industry.

Based on a sustained body of archival research, Gail Low's contribution, 'William Plomer Reading: The Publisher's Reader at Jonathan Cape', looks at a very different kind of reader to the ones mainly considered elsewhere in this volume: publishers' professional readers. Examining the reader reports, letters and correspondences of one of Cape's professional readers, William Plomer, her chapter offers a unique insight into the politics of taste, prestige and consumption and how they helped to shape the postcolonial literary marketplace. Specifically, it addresses how Plomer's construction of a "cosmopolitan Englishness" informed his assessments of manuscripts (particularly South African writing) and his central role as an "advocate" for Derek Walcott's verse early in the poet's career. Like the other chapters in this section, Low overturns the commonsense assumption that production is followed by consumption: here reading and writing are mutually constitutive.

The final chapter of this section, 'Too Much Rushdie, Not Enough Romance?: The UK Publishing Industry and BME (Black Minority Ethnic) Readership', by Claire Squires, examines the UK publishing industry's concerns over and responses to the neglect of one of its particular markets: Black Minority Ethnic (BME) readers and writers. Using industry reports from the 2000s, Squires's chapter questions whether the recent critical and commercial success of diasporic literary fiction in the market has inflected the production of other genres by BME writers (specifically away from the mass market). She calls for an integrated "analysis of BME readership and literary consumption, as well as the demographics of publishers, writers and the contents of their books". Her chapter reveals the problems associated with the identificatory mapping that goes on within the industry, and evaluates the processes of devising strategies for a "properly diversified publishing industry".

3. Reading in Representation

If, in the previous two sections, the examination of readers seemed to take us closer to some kind of secure or empirical site of research, more generally, audiences and reading acts remain frustratingly elusive. Most notably, perhaps, we have access only to what Bakhtin once called the "mute perception" (1982, 3, 379) of reading as a mediated discourse. The "postcolonial audience" is not out there waiting to be discovered in all its pristine reality, but can be only partially and indirectly recovered at the level of language, text and representation. In this section, critics consider the implications of thinking about reception inside representation through the kaleidoscopic lens of cultural consumption—from cinema audiences, to bookstore popularisms, to oral storytelling and calypso songs.

Florian Stadtler's chapter, 'Rushdie's Hero as Audience: Interpreting India through Indian Popular Cinema', is animated by the observation that "Rushdie's novels are populated by a range of audiences: listeners, readers and viewers". Here Stadtler outlines key features in Salman Rushdie's national and diasporic reception, and after reviewing Rushdie's readers, compares and contrasts them with the viewing practices of his novels' characters and their reception of Indian popular cinema. Stadtler argues that "popular culture and film are transformed into important interpretative instruments" in the novels, and that cultural texts "filtered and refocused through the narrator as consuming viewer, extend the interpretative framework of the novels for Rushdie's 'implied' sub-continental and diasporic readership".

In 'The "New" India and the Politics of Reading in Pankaj Mishra's *Butter Chicken in Ludhiana*', Lucienne Loh takes up Mishra's 1995 non-fiction travel narrative to chart the author's encounters with readers and his textual assumptions about his implied readers. Contextualising Mishra's "journey through many of India's small towns" against "new forms of cultural populism", Loh identifies a central tension between Mishra's "desire to relate the fragile lives led by the powerless in this new India [and] his own efforts to secure his authorial and intellectual credibility". This analysis attends closely to Mishra's struggle to make sense of the cultural forms of a newly liberalised India (and in particular their populist literary tastes), but Loh concludes that his encounters with readers serve ultimately to reinforce Mishra's interest in "a shared cultural heritage forged through access to an elite global and cosmopolitan intellectual circle".

Lucy Evans's chapter, 'Local and Global Reading Communities in Robert Antoni's *My Grandmother's Erotic Folktales*', closes this section with an analysis of Robert Antoni's 2000 short story sequence and its integrated audience. Where Loh finds narrative failure, Evans asserts Antoni's sensitivities to the pressures of globalisation: "through its attention to overlaps between consumed and consumer cultures [. . .] *Folktales* complicates the idea [. . .] of a 'metropolitan reading public' or a 'target consumer public' which is both distinct and distant from a local audience". Paying attention to the global marketing of postcolonial cultural products, Evans identifies how Antoni's fictive concern to represent "reading communities and the reading process" is thematised through an attention to the overlapping local and global consumers of Caribbean cooking, the sexualised bodies of Caribbean women, and mid-century calypso and Carnival.

4. Reading and Nationalism

In *Imagined Communities* (1983), Benedict Anderson argues that print capitalism created new, anonymous, but intimately related, national audiences: "fellow-readers . . . connected through print, formed, in their secular, particular, visible invisibility, the embryo of the nationally imagined community" (44). Simultaneously reading the same newspapers, books, pamphlets and so on made it possible for an otherwise disconnected audience to think about themselves collectively in new ways. While scholarship has since questioned Anderson's models (e.g., Chatterjee 1986, 19–21; 1993, 3–13), questioned the ease with which audiences can be turned into communities (Robinson 2006), and questioned the necessarily nationalist implications of reading (Newell 2011), the three contributors in this section confirm the continued need to address the entwined formations of reading and nationalism.

Srila Nayak's chapter, 'Reading Gender and Social Reform in the *Indian Social Reformer*', explores the relationship between readers, newspapers and nationalism in late nineteenth-century India. Her discussion focuses on colonial readers of the periodical *Indian Social Reformer* and the ways in which reform-oriented print media opened up channels for native agency and identification with the reformist legacy of empire. She argues "Indian men and women read liberal reform journalism as a means of entry into reform-oriented public activities that fostered identities often counter to nationalism's attempt 'to make modernity consistent with the nationalist project' (Chatterjee 1989, 240)". Male and female readerships of this reformist periodical, Nayak concludes, constitute a discourse of "sovereign liberalism" that critiques "the enterprise of social reform as constitutive of a masculine public sphere".

In 'Reading after Terror: *The Reluctant Fundamentalist* as a First-World Allegory', Neelam Srivastava also challenges the relations between reading and nationalist discourses, in this case through her examination of Mohsin Hamid's 2007 novel and forms of representation. This chapter outlines how postcolonial reading has privileged a "symptomatic approach"—a mode that assumes that "texts are shaped by questions they do not themselves pose". In contrast, following Stephen Best and Sharon Marcus (2009), Srivastava mobilises a formulation of "surface reading" to critique Fredric Jameson's now canonical essay, 'Third World Literature in the Era of Multinational Capitalism' (1986). Reading Hamid's work against other fiction about 9/11, and alongside Amazon readers, Srivastava challenges us to see Hamid's novel as a "first-world allegory" and as "a form of political critique" of America that is "enabled by an allegory at the *surface* of the text".

If Nayak and Srivastava highlight the tense links between audiences and nationalism, Katie Halsey continues this line of inquiry, turning our attention to reading as it was used in imperialist discourse to contain and short-circuit an emergent national consciousness. Her chapter, '"Macaulay's Children": Thomas Babington Macaulay and the Imperialism of Reading in India', offers a fine-grained account of empire's most notorious advocate of reading. Drawing on Macaulay's marginalia as well as broader reception contexts, the chapter discusses his reading habits, in relation to the educational policies set out in his influential 'Minute of Indian Education' (1835). Halsey encourages us to view Macaulay's 'Minute' through the lens of his extensive reading of the classics during 1833 and 1834. In doing so, the chapter identifies a central tension "between Macaulay's own reading habits (resistant, oppositional, critical) and the ways in which he paternalistically conceptualised the effects of reading on Britain's Indian subjects".

5. Reading and Postcolonial Ethics

Charting an ethical turn within postcolonial studies is an imprecise business. Certainly, the foundation of South Africa's Truth and Reconciliation

Commission in 1995 was a key moment in formulating the contemporary terms of a shared practical politics and reason, while in the aftermath of 9/11 there has been a renewed interest in the terms forgiveness, responsibility, reconciliation and hospitality. What are the implications of this turn (or turns) for readers and reception? Far from signalling a retreat from the world of obligation and responsibility, critics such as Derek Attridge (2005), James Phelan (2001) and Daniel R. Schwarz (2001) have insisted reading is founded upon ethical action, even if its effects cannot easily be measured. "Reception" might be said to carry a dual significance in any consideration of the relations between reading and ethics, referring us both to questions of hermeneutics, and hospitality. As Gayatri Spivak has suggested, "patient reading" carries a particular ethical value within our terrorised world, precisely because it involves "suspending oneself into the text of the other—for which the first condition and effect is a suspension of the conviction that I am necessarily better, I am necessarily indispensable, I am necessarily the end product for which history happened, and that New York is necessarily the capital of the world . . . " (2004, 532). The following chapters attend to the pressing questions of not just "who reads?", but "how should we read?"

Daniel Allington's chapter, 'Theorising Postcolonial Reception: Writing, Reading, and Moral Agency in the *Satanic Verses* Affair', concentrates on the most notorious instance of postcolonial reading to date, examining public commentators' pronouncements on the ethics of the writing and production of Rushdie's 1988 novel. Drawing on speech act theory and ethnomethodology, this chapter conceives of *The Satanic Verses* as "a complex and unfolding history of writing, publication and reception". Allington's attention to this complex and mutable history leads him to contend that "it is a sequence of actions (real and alleged) that any work becomes—and remains—a part of the social world". Like many contributions to this volume, Allington thus highlights the productive capacity of the sphere of reception (in this instance, public commentators and their contribution to the "symbolic" production of *The Satanic Verses*).

In 'Reading before the Law: Melville's "Bartleby" and Asylum Seeker Narratives', David Farrier pursues Spivak's "suspended" or unguaranteed relationship between hermeneutics and hospitality through a contrapuntal reading of Herman Melville's 'Bartleby' (1853), legal texts and the work of the Iranian poet, Mohsen Soltany-Zand. Following Derrida and J. Hillis Miller, Farrier offers a comparative account in which reading is both "undecidable" and "parasitic". He argues that "[p]ostcolonial reading ethics are determined, largely, by the nature of the reader's response to an undecidable question: how to engage with representations of other(ed) experiences, without replicating in the reading act worldly structures of power". For Farrier, an ethical reading practice "places the reader in the position of a parasite, at a threshold between decision and indecision".

Katherine Hallemeier's 'Sympathetic Shame in J. M. Coetzee's *Disgrace* and *Diary of a Bad Year*' compares shame and sympathy as ethical modes of reading. She rereads the history of novel reading since the eighteenth and nineteenth centuries to understand its reckoning of sympathy. Hallemeier outlines how novel reading became construed as "an exercise of the sympathetic imagination" and "a means of furthering not only individual moral development, but also the common welfare". This contextualisation is central to her study of the morally freighted work of J. M. Coetzee. Here she reads *Disgrace* and *Diary of a Bad Year* in terms that show how sympathy and shame can be understood as mutually constitutive and concludes by offering "a caution against an ethics of reading that elevates shame as a productive response to legacies of empire".

Finally, Derek Attridge tackles the "question of cultural distance" when reading, asking "what would constitute a responsible reading" of the otherness of a translated text. An examination of Western responses (in the form of critical reviews) to the English translation of Alaa al Aswany's *The Yacoubian Building*—a novel which achieved significant success both within and outside its original publishing context—serves as a case history. Drawing on his formulations of the "singularity of literature" (2004b), Attridge returns us to accounts of the elusive "pleasures" of reading, with which Keown began this collection. He argues that "distance is part of what makes the work valuable, and a responsible reading is one that will take full account of it rather than one that undertakes the impossible task of abolishing it".

Notes

1. On a pragmatic level, this confines to a manageable scale what is already a bewilderingly large (global), and mobile (diasporic) constituency or imagined community: "the" postcolonial audience. More importantly, it allows us to reflect fully, and for the first time, on the paradigmatic audience of postcolonial studies: readers, and their reading acts.
2. Consider also that Nielsen BookScan, "the largest continuous book sales tracking service", has incomplete coverage of what we might consider postcolonial regions: it covers Australia, Denmark, Ireland, Italy, New Zealand, South Africa, Spain, the UK and the US, launching an Indian panel only in 2010. See http://www.nielsenbookscan.co.uk/controller.php?page=1021.

References

Allington, Daniel and Joan Swann. 2009. "Reading Groups and the Language of Literary Texts: A Case Study in Social Reading". *Language and Literature* 18(3), pp. 219–230.

Anderson, Benedict. 1983. *Imagined Communities: The Origin and Spread of Nationalism*. London: Verso.

Ang, Ien. 1991. *Desperately Seeking an Audience*. London: Routledge.

Appiah, Kwame Anthony. 1991. "Is the Post- in Postmodernism the Post- in Postcolonial?" *Critical Inquiry* 17: 336–57.

Ashcroft, Bill. 2001. *Postcolonial Transformation*. London: Routledge.

Ashcroft, Bill, Gareth Griffiths and Helen Tiffin. 2000. *Post-Colonial Studies: The Key Concepts*. London: Routledge.

———, eds. 2006. *The Post-Colonial Studies Reader*. 2nd ed. London: Routledge.

Attridge, Derek. 2004a. *J. M. Coetzee and the Ethics of Reading: Literature in the Event*. Chicago: Chicago University Press; Scottsville: KwaZulu-Natal University Press.

———. 2004b. *The Singularity of Literature*. London: Routledge.

Bakhtin, M. M. 1982. *The Dialogic Imagination: Four Essays*. Edited by Michael Holquist. Translated by Caryl Emerson and Michael Holquist. Texas: University of Texas Press.

Banaji, Shakuntala. 2006. *Reading "Bollywood": The Young Audience and Hindi Films*. Basingstoke: Palgrave Macmillan.

Barber, Karin. 1997. "Popular Reactions to the Petro-Naira." In *Readings in Popular African Culture*, edited by Karin Barber, 91–98. Oxford: James Currey. First published in *The Journal of Modern African Studies* 20(3): 431–50.

———, ed. 2006. *Africa's Hidden Histories: Everyday Literacy and Making the Self*. Bloomingdale: Indiana University Press.

———. 2007. *The Anthropology of Texts, Persons and Publics: Oral and Written Culture in Africa and Beyond*. Cambridge: Cambridge University Press.

Bell, Bill. 1998. "Print Culture in Exile: The Scottish Emigrant Reader in the Nineteenth Century." Papers of the Bibliographical Society of Canada 36(2): 87–106.

Benwell, Bethan. 2009. "'A Pathetic and Racist and Awful Character': Ethnomethodological Approaches to the Reception of Diasporic Fiction." *Language and Literature* 18(3): 300–315.

Benwell, Bethan, James Procter and Gemma Robinson. 2011a. "Not Reading *Brick Lane*." *Reading after Empire: Special Issue of New Formations* 73: 90–116.

———, eds. 2011b. *Reading after Empire: Special Issue of New Formations* 73.

Best, Stephen, and Sharon Marcus. 2009. "Surface Reading: An Introduction." *Representations* 108: 1–21.

Bhabha, Homi. 1984. "Representation and the Colonial Text: A Critical Exploration of Some Forms of Mimeticism." In *The Theory of Reading*, edited by Frank Gloversmith, 93–122. Brighton, Sussex: Harvester Press.

———. 1992. "Signs Taken for Wonders." In *The Location of Culture*, 102–22. London: Routledge.

Boehmer, Elleke. 2005. *Colonial and Postcolonial Literature*. Oxford: Oxford University Press.

Bongie, Chris. 2003. "Exiles on Main Stream: Valuing the Popularity of Postcolonial Literature." *Postmodern Culture* 14(1): n.p.

Booth, Wayne C. 1961. *The Rhetoric of Fiction*. Chicago: University of Chicago Press.

Brennan, Timothy. 1997. *At Home in the World: Cosmopolitanism Now*. Cambridge: Harvard University Press.

Bristow, Joseph. 1991. *Empire Boys: Adventures in a Man's World*. London: HarperCollins.

Brouillette, Sarah. 2007. *Postcolonial Writers in the Global Literary Marketplace*. Palgrave Macmillan.

Carter, David. 1992. "Tasteless Subjects: Postcolonial Literary Criticism, Realism and the Subject of Taste." *Southern Review* 25(3): 292–303.

Carter, David, and Anne Galligan, eds. 2007. *Making Books: Contemporary Australian Publishing.* St Lucia: University of Queensland Press.

Chartier, Roger. 1992. "Laborers and Voyagers: From the Text to the Reader." *Diacritics* 22(2): 49–61.

Chatterjee, Partha. 1986. *Nationalist Thought and the Colonial World: A Derivative Discourse?* London: Zed.

———. 1989. "The Nationalist Resolution of the Women's Question." In *Recasting Women: Essays in Indian Colonial History*, edited by Kumkum Sangari and Sudesh Vaid, 233–53. New Jersey: Rutgers University Press.

Cudjoe, Selwyn R. 1980. *Resistance and Caribbean Literature.* Athens: Ohio University Press.

Culler, Jonathan. (1981) 2006. *The Pursuit of Signs.* London: Routledge.

Darnton, Robert. 1982. "What Is the History of Books?" *Daedalus* 111(3): 65–83.

———. 2001. "Literary Surveillance in the British Raj: The Contradictions of Liberal Imperialism." *Book History* 4: 133–76.

Dickinson, Roger, Ramaswami Harindranath and Olga Linné. 1998. *Approaches to Audiences.* London: Arnold.

Dudrah, Rajinder Kumar, and Jigna Desai, eds. 2008. *The Bollywood Reader.* Berkshire: Open University Press.

Eco, Umberto. 1979. *The Role of the Reader: Explorations in the Semiotics of Texts.* Bloomington: Indiana University Press.

Edmondson, Belinda. 2009. *Caribbean Middlebrow: Leisure Culture and the Middle Class.* Ithaca: Cornell University Press.

Fanon, Frantz. (1952) 1986. *Black Skin, White Masks.* London: Pluto. [*Peau noire, Masques Blanc.* Paris: Editions de Seuil.]

Felski, Rita. 2003. *Literature after Feminism.* Chicago: Chicago University Press.

Fetterley, Judith. 1978. *The Resisting Reader: A Feminist Approach to American Fiction.* Bloomington: Indiana University Press.

Fraser, Robert. 2008a. *Book History through Postcolonial Eyes: Rewriting the Script.* London: Routledge.

Fraser, Robert. 2008b. "School Readers in the Empire and the Creation of Postcolonial Taste." In *Books without Borders: Volume 1*, edited by Robert Fraser and Elizabeth Hammond, 89–106. Palgrave Macmillan.

Fraser, Robert, and Susheila Nasta. 2007. "The Book in the World." *Wasafiri: The Book in the World* 22(3): 1–2.

Gerson, Carole. 1989. *A Purer Taste: The Writing and Reading of Fiction in English in Nineteenth-Century Canada.* Toronto: Toronto University Press.

Gibson, Walker. 1950. "Authors, Speakers, Readers, and Mock Readers." *College English* 11: 265–69.

Gillespie, Marie. 1995. *Television, Ethnicity and Cultural Change.* London: Routledge.

Gilroy, Paul. 1997. "Diaspora and the Detours of Identity." In *Identity and Difference*, edited by Kathryn Woodward, 299–343. London: Sage.

———. 2004. *After Empire: Melancholia or Convivial Culture?* London: Routledge.

Guillory, John. 2000. "The Ethical Practice of Modernity: The Example of Reading." In *The Turn to Ethics*, edited by Marjorie Garber, Beatrice Hanssen and Rebecca Walkowitz, 29–46. New York: Routledge.

Gupta, Abhibit, and Swapan Chakravorty, eds. 2004. *Print Areas: Book History in India.* New Delhi: Permanent Black.

Hale, Dorothy. 2007. "Fiction as Restriction: Self-Binding in New Ethical Theories of the Novel." *Narrative* 15(2): 187–206.

Hall, Stuart. 1994. "Reflections upon the Encoding/Decoding Model: An Interview with Stuart Hall." In *Viewing, Reading, Listening*, edited by Jon Cruz and Justin Lewis, 253–74. Boulder: Westview Press.

Harindranath, Ramaswami. 2009. *Audience-Citizens: The Media, Public Knowledge, and Interpretive Practice*. London: Sage.
Hofmeyr, Isobel. 2003. "Portable Landscapes: Thomas Mofolo and John Bunyan in the Broad and the Narrow Way." In *Disputed Territories: Land, Culture and Identity in Settler Societies*, edited by David Trigger and Gareth Griffiths, 131–54. Hong Kong: Hong Kong University Press.
———. 2004. *The Portable Bunyan: A Transnational History of* The Pilgrims Progress. Princeton: Princeton University Press.
———. 2006. "Reading Debating/Debating Reading: The Case of the Lovedale Literary Society, or Why Mandela Quotes Shakespeare." In *Hidden Histories: Everyday Literacy and Making the Self*, edited by Karin Barber, 258–77. Bloomingdale: Indiana University Press.
Huggan, Graham. 2001. *The Postcolonial Exotic: Marketing the Margins*. London: Routledge.
Innes, C. L. 2007. *The Cambridge Introduction to Postcolonial Literatures in English*. Cambridge: Cambridge University Press.
Iser, Wolfgang. 1978. *The Act of Reading: A Theory of Aesthetic Response*. Baltimore: Johns Hopkins University Press.
James, C. L. R. 1963. *Beyond a Boundary*. London: Hutchinson.
Jameson, Fredric. 1986. "Third-World Literature in the Era of Multinational Capitalism." *Social Text* 15: 65–88.
Joshi, Priya. 2002. *In Another Country: Colonialism, Culture, and the English Novel in India*. New York: Columbia University Press.
———. 2004. "Reading in the Public Eye: The Circulation of British Fiction in Indian Libraries, c. 1835–1901." In *India's Literary History: Essays on the Nineteenth Century*, edited by Stuart Blackburn and Vasudha Dalmia. New Delhi: Permanent Black.
Kapcia, Antoni, and Par Kumaraswami. 2010. "The Feria Del Libro and the Ritualisation of Cultural Belonging in Havana." In *Cultures of the City: Mediating Identities in Urban Latin/o America*, edited by Richard Young and Amanda Holmes, 167–82. Pittsburgh: University of Pennsylvania Press.
Khair, Tabish. 2006. "The Death of the Reader." *Wasafiri* 21(3): 1–5.
Lang, Anouk. 2009. "Reading race in Small Island: Discourse deviation, schemata and the textual encounter." Language and Literature. 18(3): 316–330.
Liebes, Tamar, and Elihu Katz. 1993. *The Export of Meaning: Cross-Cultural Readings of Dallas*. 2nd ed. Oxford: Oxford University Press; Cambridge: Polity.
Long, Elizabeth. 2003. *Book Clubs: Women and the Uses of Reading in Everyday Life*. Chicago: Chicago University Press.
Loomba, Ania. (1998) 2005. *Colonialism/Postcolonialism*. London: Routledge.
Manguel, Alberto. 1996. *A History of Reading*. London: HarperCollins.
Mankekar, Purnima. 1999. *Screening Culture, Viewing Politics: An Ethnography of Television, Womanhood and Nation in Postcolonial India*. Durham: Duke University Press.
McClintock, Anne. 1995. *Imperial Leather: Race, Gender and Sexuality in the Colonial Context*. London: Routledge.
McDonald, Peter D. 2009. *The Literature Police*. Oxford: Oxford University Press.
McKenzie, D. F. 1984. "The Sociology of a Text: Orality, Literacy and Print in Early New Zealand." *The Library* 6(4): 333–65.
———. 1999. *Bibliography and the Sociology of Texts*. Cambridge: Cambridge University Press.
McLeod, John. 2008. "Diaspora and Utopia: Reading the Recent Work of Paul Gilroy." In *Diasporic Literature and Theory—Where Now?*, edited by Mark Shakleton, 2–17. Newcastle: Cambridge Scholars Publishing.
Moretti, Franco. 2005. *Graphs, Maps, Trees: Abstract Models for a Literary History*. London: Verso.

Mufti, Aamir. 1994. "Reading the Rushdie Affair: 'Islam', Cultural Politics, Form." In *The Administration of Aesthetics: Censorship, Political Criticism, and the Public Sphere*, edited by Richard Burt, 307–39. Minneapolis: University of Minnesota Press.

Newell, Stephanie. 2000. *Ghanaian Popular Fiction: "Thrilling Discoveries in Conjugal Life" & Other Tales.* Oxford: James Currey.

———. 2002. *Literary Culture in Colonial Ghana.* Manchester: Manchester University Press.

———. 2006. "Entering the Territory of Elites: Literary Activity in Colonial Ghana." In *Hidden Histories: Everyday Literacy and Making the Self*, edited by Karin Barber, 211–35. Bloomingdale: Indiana University Press.

———. 2011. "Articulating Empire: Newspaper Readerships in Colonial West Africa." *New Formations.* 73.

Nuttall, Sarah. 1994. "Reading in the Lives and Writing of Black South African Women." *Journal of Southern African Studies* 20(1): 85–98.

Orsini, Francesca. 2010. *Print and Pleasure: Popular Literature and Entertaining Fictions in Colonial North India.* New Delhi: Permanent Black.

Peterson, Bhekizizwe. 2006. "The Bantu World and the World of the Book: Reading, Writing and 'Enlightenment.'" In *Hidden Histories: Everyday Literacy and Making the Self*, edited by Karin Barber, 236–57. Bloomingdale: Indiana University Press.

Phelan, James. 2001. "Sethe's Choice: *Beloved* and the Ethics of Reading." In *Mapping the Ethical Turn: A Reader in Ethics, Culture and Literary Theory*, edited by Todd F. Davis and Kenneth Womack, 93–109. Charlottesville: University of Virginia Press.

Phillips, Caryl. 2001. "Leeds United, Life and Me." In *A New World Order: Selected Essays*, 298–302. London: Secker & Warburg.

Procter, James. 2009. "Reading, Taste and Postcolonial Studies: Professional and Lay Readers of *Things Fall Apart.*" *Interventions: International Journal of Postcolonial Studies* 11(2): 180–98.

Radway, Janice. (1984) 1991. *Reading the Romance: Women, Patriarchy, and Popular Literature.* Chapel Hill: University of North Carolina Press.

Robinson, Gemma. 2006. "Guyanese Writers on the Radio." *Arts Journal* 2(2): 41–62.

Rodriguez, Junius P. 2007. *Slavery in the United States: A Social, Political and Historical Encyclopedia.* 2 vols. Santa Barbara: ABC-CLIO.

Roldán Vera, Eugenia. 2003. *The British Book Trade and Spanish American Independence: Education and Knowledge Transmission in Transcontinental Perspective.* Aldershot: Ashgate.

Said, Edward. 1978. *Orientalism.* London: Penguin Books.

———. 1985. "Opponents, Audiences, Constituencies." In *Postmodern Culture*, edited by Hal Foster, 135–59. London: Pluto Press.

———. 1994. *Culture and Imperialism.* London: Vintage.

Sanders, Mark. 2006. *Gayatri Spivak: Live Theory.* London: Continuum.

Schwarz, Daniel R. 2001. "A Humanistic Ethics of Reading." In *Mapping the Ethical Turn: A Reader in Ethics, Culture and Literary Theory*, edited by Todd F. Davis and Kenneth Womack, 3–15. Charlottesville: University of Virginia Press.

Shukla, Rajesh. 2010. *Indian Youth: Demographics and Readership. Results from the National Youth Readership Survey.* New Delhi: National Book Trust, India and National Council of Applied Economic Research. http://www.ncaer.org/downloads/Reports/NBT.pdf.

Slemon, Stephen. 1989. "Reading for Resistance in the Post-Colonial Literature." In *A Shaping of Connections: Commonwealth Literary Studies: Then and Now*, edited by Hena Maes-Jelinek, Kirsten Holst Petersen and Anna Rutherford, 100–115. Mundelstrup: Dangaroo.

Spivak, Gayatri. 1993. *Outside in the Teaching Machine.* New York: Routledge.

———. 1996. "How to Read a 'Culturally Different' Book." In *Colonial Discourse/ Postcolonial Theory*, edited by Frances Barker, Peter Hulme and Margaret Iversen, 126–50. Manchester: Manchester University Press.

———. 2004. "Righting Wrongs." *South Atlantic Quarterly* 103(2/3): 524–80.

Tiffin, Helen. 1990. "Decolonization and Audience." *SPAN* 30: 27–38.

van der Vlies, Andrew. 2007a. "Reading Banned Books." *Wasafiri* 22(3): 55–61.

———. 2007b. *South African Textual Cultures: White, Black, Read All Over.* Manchester: Manchester University Press.

Viswanathan, Gauri. 1989. *Masks of Conquest: Literary Study and British Rule in India.* Oxford: Oxford University Press.

Part I

Real Readers/ Actual Audiences

1 The Politics of Postcolonial Laughter

The International Reception of the New
Zealand Animated Comedy Series *bro'Town*[1]

Michelle Keown

This chapter takes the New Zealand animated television comedy series *bro'Town* (written and performed by Polynesian comic actors) as a case study for considering the advantages and limitations of reception theory in analysing audience responses to so-called "ethnic" or "postcolonial" comedy. In particular, the chapter draws upon the distinction reception theorists such as John Guillory have made between "lay" and "professional" interpretations of "texts" (here taken to include media productions as well as literary works). Guillory has described professional "reading" as a "disciplinary" activity, a "kind of *work*", governed by "conventions of interpretation", that "stands back from the experience of pleasure in reading" and is often targeted towards the production of "a public and publishable 'reading'". Lay reading, on the other hand, is categorised as a largely solitary leisure activity performed primarily in pursuit of pleasure (Guillory 2000, 31–32). As James Procter points out, however, the distinction between lay and professional reading can be less polarised than Guillory suggests: he discusses this dynamic in relation to book groups, which are "communal rather than solitary affairs", potentially containing "combinations of both professional and lay readers" and "in certain ways" replicating "the habits of professional reading" (2009, 183). In this chapter I will analyse a range of "professional" and "lay" responses to *bro'Town*—the former from academics and journalists, and the latter from fans contributing to various Internet discussion forums—in order to suggest that while many *bro'Town* "lay" readers foreground the show's appeal as entertainment, some of their responses involve a convergence of putatively separate reading practices associated with "lay" and "professional" constituencies.

In analysing comments posted on the fan websites, I will also evaluate the extent to which "local" and "international" viewers diverge in their responses to the show's complex comic strategies (given that *bro'Town* has achieved widespread popularity both within New Zealand and abroad).[2] Comedy often relies heavily upon cultural/racial stereotypes, and as Christiane Schlote notes, critical debates on "ethnic" comedy have commonly centred on the degree to which comedians "use their cultural and national heritages to confront and eventually subvert ethnic and racial stereotypes, or whether their, although satirical, incorporation of these stereotypes into their sketches does not, in fact, lead to their reinforcement" (2005, 180). Such preoccupations characterise many "professional" critical responses to *bro'Town*, but are also relevant to a comparison of "local" and "international" viewer responses on the *bro'Town* fan discussion forums. Although the series accommodates a broad spectrum of viewers by blending the conventions of "mainstream" and "ethnic" Anglo-American comedy with the specific strategies of Polynesian comic theatrical traditions, I suggest the "local" knowledge possessed by New Zealand fans often affords them deeper insights into the complexities of the racial politics (and stereotypes) explored in the show, while the responses of overseas viewers appear more in keeping with international marketing strategies that have situated the series within global popular culture while making a feature of its unique status as a "Pacific" production. As I will argue, such strategies can be analysed in terms of Graham Huggan's theories on the postcolonial "exotic", given that the international marketing, distribution and reception of the series have subjected it to a "mode of aesthetic *perception*" which "renders people, objects and places strange even as it domesticates them" (Huggan 2001, 13).

The Pacific "Exotic" and *bro'Town's* Exploration of Racial Stereotypes

Significantly, exoticising representations of the Pacific in colonial discourse strongly inflect the racial stereotypes explored in the show. Since the Enlightenment period in particular, the Pacific Islands have been romanticised and exoticised by "Western" explorers, colonial administrators, artists and authors. Although the Pacific encompasses a diverse range of cultures (commonly broken down into the geocultural categories of Polynesia, Melanesia and Micronesia), the Pacific "exotic" has become focused primarily upon the Polynesian "triangle" (from Hawai'i in the north-east to New Zealand in the south and Easter Island to the east).[3] While the myth of the Pacific as an environmental and sexual "paradise" persists in contemporary media and tourist-industry representations, the formation of substantial Polynesian diasporic communities within Australia, New Zealand and the US since the Second World War has given rise to another, largely negative set of stereotypes representing Pacific immigrants as socio-economic underachievers plagued by domestic violence and alcoholism (Keown 2007, 19 and 2008, 48). The fact that many of these immigrants originate from current or former colonies of the "Western" nations to which they travel has often resulted in a consolidation of these newer stereotypes with earlier colonial representations of the "ignoble" or "uncivilised" *sauvage*.[4]

bro'Town explores the particular inflections of these stereotypes within Aotearoa New Zealand, revealing both indigenous Māori* and Pākehā[5] resistance to Pacific Island (as well as Asian) immigrants as perceived threats to the unique bicultural relationship that has long shaped understandings of New Zealand "national" identity. Described on the official website as a "proudly suburban, non-PC satire", the series is set in Morningside, a suburb of Auckland (New Zealand's largest and most culturally diverse city, often described as "the largest Polynesian city in the world"). It centres on the experiences of five pubescent Polynesian schoolboys, including an indigenous youth known as "Jeff da Maori", three Samoans (brothers Vale and Valea Pepelo, and friend Sione Tapili), and a boy of mixed Pālagi[6] and Polynesian descent (Rodney McCorkenstein-Taifule, commonly known as "Mack"). The physiognomy and character traits of these youths (depicted in Figure 1.1)[7] are largely based on those of the "Naked Samoans", four Polynesian comic actors (including Samoan actors Oscar Kightley, David Fane and Mario Gaoa, and Niuean actor Shimpal Lelisi) who created the series (in collaboration with producer Elizabeth Mitchell) and "voice" the characters.

Exploring dominant cultural stereotypes of immigrants with a prevailing wry humour, *bro'Town* invites comparisons with other "ethnic" or "postcolonial" comedy such as *Goodness Gracious Me* (a character comedy series created by four British Asian actors), but it is also rooted in Samoan *fale aitu* (literally, "house of spirits"), a theatrical tradition in which actors perform comic sketches commonly replete with verbal punning, sexual innuendo,

Figure 1.1   *bro'Town*'s five central characters (from left to right): Mack, Sione, Valea, Vale and Jeff da Maori. Image courtesy of Firehouse Films (c) 2005.

social critique, role reversals and transvestism, with male actors often adopting exaggerated female personas (see Sinavaiana-Gabbard 1999 and Keown
2008). Although much of *bro'Town*'s humour and cultural references are
aimed at a New Zealand audience, its considerable success abroad has been
attributed to its affinity with North American animated comedy series such
as *South Park* and *The Simpsons* (Henley 2004; Wichtel 2004; Lustyik and
Smith 2010). Like its globalised counterparts, *bro'Town* features a blend of
socio-political satire, postmodernist parody and cameo performances from
various local and international celebrities and public figures (from actor Sam
Neill and New Zealand Samoan hip hop artist Scribe, to Prince Charles and
former New Zealand Prime Minister Helen Clark).

   bro'Town first aired in September 2004, with six thirty-minute episodes
screened at 8:00 p.m. on Wednesdays, reaching a large, culturally and demo-
graphically diverse "primetime" audience, and running to five series in total
(ending in 2009). The show was strategically scheduled straight after *The
Simpsons* (on commercial channel TV3) and proved popular with both adult
and young viewers: series 1, for example, attracted 33 percent of the total
viewing audience during its timeslot, and in 2005 *bro'Town* was the top rat-
ing series for 5–12-year-olds (Lustyik and Smith 2010, 343; Bannister 2008,
7). As media reception theorists (both within and beyond New Zealand)
have noted, visibly "different" ethnic minorities living in white-dominated
societies are often negatively stereotyped or excluded from representation
in mainstream media, and in this context *bro'Town* is a rare example of a
production, featuring and created by Pacific Islanders, that has achieved
widespread mainstream success (Kothari, Pearson and Zuberi 2004; Staiger
2005).[8] *bro'Town* won the "best comedy" category of the *TV Guide* "Best on
the Box"—New Zealand's largest annual "people's choice" television audience
award—for four years in a row (until 2008), and won again in 2010 following
the screening of the final series.[9] It was selected as the theme for the New
Zealand village at the 2008 Beijing Olympics, and in 2010 formed the focus
of a long-term installation at New Zealand's national museum, Te Papa.

"Professional" Critical Responses
to *bro'Town*'s Racial Politics

Alongside its considerable popularity, *bro'Town* has generated critical controversy, largely due to conflicting responses to the show's engagement
with racial stereotypes. Within New Zealand, the channelling of post-war
Pacific immigrants (as well as Māori) into low-skilled jobs and depressed
housing areas has led to widespread social deprivation, and much of the
show's humour operates by invoking and (often implicitly) satirising dominant cultural stereotypes associated with Māori and Pacific socio-economic
"problems" (including unemployment, domestic violence, alcoholism and
"broken homes"). As noted earlier, in "professional" critical circles *bro'Town*'s

irreverent comedy has sparked debate about whether the show ultimately *reinforces* cultural stereotypes even as it lampoons them, given the differences in the "horizon of expectations" (Jauss 1982) among viewers from different ethnic and demographic groups. Samoan academic Melani Anae has argued that *bro'Town* promotes the stereotype of "the happy-go-lucky funny brown coconut" that Pacific Islanders "fought against in the 70s", and that Kightley is one of a number of Pacific creative practitioners who "pick the negatives of our cultures and get rich on it by entertaining people" (Spratt 2006, 20). This argument resonates with debates among media reception theorists regarding the burden of representation placed upon ethnic minority creative practitioners (Kothari, Pearson and Zuberi 2004; Schlote 2005; Staiger 2005). As Samoan columnist Tapu Misa points out in a more sympathetic analysis of Kightley's work:

> This is the other side of being a prominent brown playwright, comedian, and entertainer . . . Everything you do is loaded with meaning and consequence. It isn't enough that you're funny and entertaining, as well as commercially successful and critically acclaimed. You have to be socially responsible, too. (2006, E1)

Concerns about *bro'Town*'s engagement with racial stereotypes have also been expressed by Pākehā/Pālagi commentators. In a review of *"bro'Town* Live on Stage", a stage documentary about the show performed at the 2008 New Zealand Arts Festival, Melody Nixon expressed reservations about *bro'Town*'s humour from a "white" point of view, remarking: "As with the TV show I felt a slight dissonance at the mass laughter at racial stereotypes, and wondered if we (we Pakeha, especially) were allowed to be laughing, really" (2008). Another Pākehā critic, Greg Dixon, similarly criticised *bro'Town*'s putative reliance on "incredibly blunt, incredibly predictable" racial stereotypes (2004).

In defending *bro'Town* against such assessments, Kightley argues that laughter is an effective way of confronting and critiquing social "flaws", and that it can also help to ameliorate the bleakness of the lives of Pacific peoples suffering socio-economic deprivation (Spratt 2006, 20). He also reminds critics of the show's grounding in *fale aitu*, which customarily serves a mediatory function, serving (like romantic comedy) to resolve "tension or conflict between major characters" (Wichtel 2006; Sinavaiana-Gabbard 1999, 188). The targets of *fale aitu* comedy—often present at performances, and representing all levels of the social spectrum, from commoner to chief—are expected to take the satire "in the spirit of fun", and a similar expectation appears to be implicit in *bro'Town* (Sinavaiana-Gabbard 1999, 186).

One of the key episodes in which this dynamic plays out is "Morningside Story" (series 2), where Vale writes and directs a musical (loosely based on Arthur Laurents's *West Side Story*) that projects a utopian social vision in which

Morningside's (and by extension, wider New Zealand's) different ethnic communities learn how to "get along". Vale is inspired to write the musical after witnessing various scenes of racial intolerance in his community, including immigrant Palestinian and Israeli customers exchanging insults while squabbling over a steak in "Tony the Tongan's Organic Halal Kosher Olde English Pacific Island Butchery", and a Pākehā customer describing a Fiji-Indian corner shop owner as a "rip-off curry muncher" after being refused a refund on a packet of crisps on the grounds that "twenty-seven years is a perfectly respectable shelf life for the potato chip". Vale's ensuing musical traces conflict between a 1960s immigrant "Polynesian" family and New Zealand's Irish community, offering a comic pastiche of various (often sobering) narratives of post-war Pacific Island immigrant experience produced by authors and dramatists such as Albert Wendt and Kightley himself (see Keown 2007, 191–93). The musical ends with Sione's sister Sina, cast as "Maria", fatally wounded in a gang brawl only to return posthumously to lead the company in the closing song "Can't we all just get along?" (depicted in Figure 1.2).

Invoking the familiar Pacific Island immigrant myth of New Zealand as "a land of milk and honey", the actors claim that "the milk was sour", but joyfully conclude that "we're all homogenised", with "honkys [whites] and Asians, horis [Māori] and curry munchers" banding together harmoniously. The ostensibly politically correct "neatness" of the musical's concluding

Figure 1.2   Finale of the musical "Morningside Story" (*bro 'Town*, series 2, episode 5). Cast members, scriptwriter Vale and Jeff da Maori appear on the right, while audience members (including Sione's mother Agnes, Vale and Valea's father Pepelo, Prince Charles, singer-songwriters Chris Knox and Scribe, and pupils Wong and "Abo" (of Hong Kong Chinese and Koori descent respectively) appear to the left. Image courtesy of Firehorse Films (c) 2005.

vision of racial tolerance is undercut, however, by scatological references within the song ("What's in a name when our poo smells the same?") and by older Pacific immigrants in the audience who contradict their children's inclusive pronouncements, reinforcing a comment made at the beginning of the episode about parents being to blame for the perpetuation of racial prejudice across generations.

A similarly complex approach to racial stereotypes is evident in other *bro'Town* episodes. "The Wong One" (series one), for example, plays on negative public reactions to large-scale east and south-east Asian immigration to New Zealand since the early 1990s, following substantial changes to immigration policy (which had previously favoured ethnically European immigrants, particularly of British origin) (see Keown 2008). The policy changes were made in order to encourage investment from "emerging" Asian economies in a new era of free-market monetarism, and the episode explores the putative socio-economic disparities between "deprived" Pacific Islander and "affluent" Asian immigrant communities, focusing on a Hong Kong Chinese student (Wong) who becomes a temporary member of the Pepelo household on a "homestay" scheme (designed primarily for visiting students wishing to improve their English, but here exploited by Wong's father, a wealthy

Figure 1.3 Wong (centre), Valea, Mack, Sione and Vale watching television in a tent outside the Pepelo house (*bro 'Town*, series 1, episode 3). Image courtesy of Firehorse Films (c) 2005

business magnate, to protect his son from business rivalries back in Hong Kong). Wong is "loaded" and spends lavishly on an "assortment of electrical appliances" for the dilapidated Pepelo home (see Figure 1.3), once Valea and his friends overcome their initial (often comically exaggerated) presuppositions about Chinese as "inscrutable" Asians who "make rockets . . . sell takeaways, wear glasses . . . bind feet, invade Tibet [and] do long division".

As I have argued elsewhere, the characteristically ambiguous (or provisional) nature of this inter-ethnic bridge-building is revealed in a later scene where, after surviving a kidnapping attempt and treating the boys to a Chinese meal, Wong announces, "I used to think Islanders were inefficient and uneconomical, but now I see that's not a bad thing!", and Sione replies "and we used to not like Asians, but now we see that your people make yummy food and you're loaded!" These backhanded compliments initially promise to overcome, but in reality comically reinscribe existing stereotypes (Keown 2008, 51–52).

Arguably, *bro'Town*'s complex but ultimately inclusive racial politics are encapsulated in the title of the show, which, in adapting the term "Motown" to a New Zealand context, may first appear deliberately to foreground the "ethnic minority" or "non-mainstream" status of its central characters and storylines (see also Lustyik and Smith 2010). However, as noted by cultural critics Teresia Teaiwa and Sean Mallon (both of Polynesian/Pacific descent), the show's title also proffers a "notion of open-ended kinship . . . [implying] you don't have to be 'blood' to be a 'bro' [brother]", thereby suggesting "the ways that art can serve as a much-needed bridge from cultural specificity to universal humanism" (2005, 223). Such a view accords not only with Kightley's views on *bro'Town*'s grounding in the "mediatory" potential of *fale aitu*, but also with co-actor Shimpal Lelisi's (partly tongue-in-cheek) description of the show as "the glue that holds all our different ethnicities together in perfect harmony" (Firehorse Films 2005, 29).

While it is likely that a large proportion of *bro'Town*'s audience would be unfamiliar with the *fale aitu* tradition, there is evidence that the show has succeeded in performing a "mediatory" function within and between various ethnic groups. Episodes from *bro'Town* have been used for training in racial tolerance and sensitivity by health professionals, the police, social workers and schoolteachers, and the Naked Samoans have made a number of school visits in order to promote harmonious race relations, also appearing at dozens of charity functions and public events attended by young fans (Firehorse Films, n.d.).

There have also been positive critical responses to the series from Pacific and Pālagi commentators alike. Teaiwa and Mallon argue that *bro'Town* consistently subverts "attempts to romanticise, exoticise, domesticate or simplify the Pacific experience in New Zealand" and demonstrates a "confident assertion of kinship" that bears witness to the increasing contribution Pacific Islanders have made to mainstream media from the 1990s (2005, 221–22).

Samoan columnist Tapu Misa applauds the show's comic energies, noting that although many Samoans she has encountered object to *bro'Town*'s representation of Polynesian men in particular (who often appear as alcoholic, violent, negligent or absent fathers), "in its optimism and humour" the show is "more truly Pacific than anything else on our screens" (2006, E1). Pākehā critic Margaret Henley describes *bro'Town* as a "text of resistance" that offers "numerous points of entry" for Pākehā as well as ethnic minority viewers (2004, C4), while Diana Wichtel (also Pākehā) praises the show's "affectionate" and "even-handed" exploration of inter-ethnic relations (2004).

"Lay" Responses to *bro'Town*: The Fan Websites

The "professional" responses to *bro'Town* discussed earlier indicate that journalists and academics tend to analyse *bro'Town* with reference to current debates about race, ethnicity and the incipient transition from bicultural to multicultural conceptualisations of New Zealand culture, assessing the degree to which the show is successful in creating a positive representation of, and point of identification for, ethnic minority groups. Such approaches are in keeping with Guillory's argument for the "disciplinary", interpretive orientation of "professional" readings, which in postcolonial contexts can translate (as Procter notes) into "exaggerated claims for the political effects" of individual "texts" (2009, 181). "Lay" responses produced by fans on various *bro'Town* Internet discussion sites, on the other hand, are often less concerned with the ideological implications of the show's representation of minority groups, and more centred on its value as entertainment. This again resonates with Guillory's arguments for the putatively pleasure-centred aims of "lay" readers, but I would argue that (like Procter's book groups) the web discussion sites (which include an official *bro'Town* website featuring a discussion forum for registered fans, as well as Myspace and Bebo fan discussion sites) facilitate "communal" patterns of identification and interpretation that complicate Guillory's distinctions.

One manifestation of "communal" activity involves interactions between Pacific Islander and Māori fans, who appear to make up the majority of those participating in the Internet discussion sites. In addition to addressing other "PI" and Māori participants, these fans commonly identify the show as a positive source of ethnic identification, a phenomenon which Janet Staiger argues is common among ethnic minority audiences (2005, 161). Staiger also notes a related trend in which media fans draw "personal associations" between characters'/performers' personalities (or experiences) and their own (99–101 *passim*). In keeping with this argument, many fans identifying as Māori express explicit affinities with "Jeff da Maori": one *bro'Town* forum participant declares his favourite character is Jeff "mainly because I'm a hori as well", and a Myspace fan reveals Jeff is his favourite "cause he resembles me a lot".[10] Similarly, fans identifying as Pacific Islanders frequently express affinity with the Pacific characters in *bro'Town*: one *bro'Town* forum member argues the show is "great" for "Islanders who can relate to the stories", and a Myspace fan claims "I coz [have] a aunty dat iz jus da same az sionez mum". Relatedly, in contrast to "professional" critics who commonly argue for *bro'Town*'s self-conscious artifice (particularly given its cartoon medium), many *bro'Town* forum and Myspace fans claim that the show's appeal lies in its realism, its putatively "truthful" depiction of Polynesian or wider New Zealand culture, which apparently allows viewers to "relate to" *bro'Town* at a personal level (a practice commonly discouraged within academia; see Carter 1992, 295).

It is of course important to acknowledge that Internet discussion forums—which typically involve "virtual" contact between participants commonly using pseudonyms—disrupts any clear sense of an "authentic" or "unmediated" viewer response (see also Procter 2009, 186), but it is notable that participants on the *bro'Town* fan sites often appear to advertise their ethnic identities by using a distinctive, "Polynesian"-inflected form of "chatspeak". Many participants use code-switching between English and Polynesian languages, often opening posts with greetings in languages such as Māori, Samoan, Tongan, Niuean and Hawai'ian—or more rarely, with longer sections of untranslated material addressed directly to the Naked Samoans. Many others use slang associated with Māori/Polynesian youth culture, such as "cher" and "choice" (nouns/adjectives expressing approval or admiration); "yous" and "u fulas" (second person plural pronouns); and "baaye" and "cuzzie bro" (meaning "friend" or "relative"). In keeping with Guillory's arguments about "lay" readers, the widespread use of predominantly non-standard, heavily abbreviated "sms language" and emoticons gives the impression of fans self-consciously distancing themselves from the "seriousness" of "professional" analyses of the show (see also Procter 2009, 185). Some deliberately foreground their non-professional status: one *bro'Town* forum fan, after arguing the "multicultural/international touches" make the show "something that all people can relate to", comically self-censors: "OMG can I just be writing a review [?]". Similarly, another *bro'Town* forum fan, after describing *bro'Town* as "culturally aware and sharp", immediately "lowers the tone" by commenting on the sexual appeal of one of the characters.

Yet there is evidence that some fans assume an "educative" role more readily associated with Guillory's "professional" reader: several expatriate New Zealand fans, for example, claim to have used the show to introduce overseas friends to the complexities of "kiwi" culture, and a heated and lengthy debate takes place on the *bro'Town* forum regarding the provenance and spelling of the tag "ow", frequently used for rhetorical emphasis by Jeff da Maori. Several different fans collectively outline an etymology that traces the word back to the Māori term "e hoa", meaning "friend", which has over time been abbreviated to "eho" and then "ow", and consensus on *bro'Town*'s spelling of the tag is achieved by reference to its appearance on branded t-shirts and posters.[11] Such interactions indicate a pseudo-"professional" attention to the "conventions of interpretation" (Guillory 31), and various other postings validate Mathew Bannister's observation that *bro'Town* is popular as a topic for academic analysis among teachers and students of English and media studies (2008, 2).

Notwithstanding these examples of "serious" engagement, however, the majority of fan responses focus on the "pleasure" principle Guillory outlines, and—in contrast to some "professional" critics—most fans appear to find *bro'Town*'s comic invocation of racial stereotypes unproblematically entertaining. A handful express concern that the show reinforces pejorative racial stereotypes: one Myspace fan using a Samoan name asks "u guys thinking of having some more positive portrayals of minorities in coming shows?", while another reports that "alot of maori take it as a put down because jeff is so dumb and it makes the rest of us look dumb" but personally expresses strong approval for the series, arguing it is "good that they finally made something for us polynesians in new zealand . . . that entertains us because there isnt alot of shows and programmes that truly include us". One *bro'Town* forum fan makes explicit an attitude expressed more obliquely by many fellow participants, observing that comedy "is very ofenceive [sic] at tyms 2 lots of ppl but is al just 4 a LAUGH don't watch it if u cant take a joke". Fans seem to be attracted to *bro'Town*'s self-consciously "non-pc" humour largely because of its transgressive or non-mainstream approach to culture, but also because globally successful precedents such as *South Park* and *The Simpsons* (to which fans frequently refer) arguably furnish fans with a reading strategy that allows them to recognise the ironic basis of many of the ostensibly "racist" attitudes expressed by characters. As Fredric Jameson argues, within the realm of globalised media culture, stereotypes commonly function as "allegorical cartoons that no longer convey the racist contempt of the older imperialism and which often . . . function as affectionate forms of inclusion and of solidarity" (2003, 107). Such a view seems validated by various comments on the *bro'Town* forum fan site: several fans, for example, use originally perjorative names for Pacific Islander immigrants (such as "coconuts" and "fobs")[12] to express admiration for the business acumen of the Naked Samoans, or to greet fellow Pacific Islander fans. A Myspace fan jokes about not being able to afford to buy one of the *bro'Town* DVDs because "lol im a poor maori", while another playfully accuses a Māori "cuzzie" of stealing her DVD, remarking "WAT a HORI" (thereby comically invoking the stereotype of the light-fingered Māori).

Exoticising Strategies in the Marketing and Reception of *bro'Town*

In contrast to the more culturally informed responses offered by the "interpretive community" of New Zealand fans, comments from non-expatriate

overseas fans on the *bro'Town* websites are predominantly less specific or
"savvy" about the show's multilayered humour, though it clearly resonates
with a number of viewers from other ethnic minority groups (including those
identifying as "African", Koori (aboriginal Australian) and Native American, as well as a range of fans from "other" Pacific Islands such as Fiji and
Hawai'i). Some of the ways in which *bro'Town* has been received beyond
New Zealand point towards the more questionable processes of exoticisation that Huggan outlines in *The Postcolonial Exotic* (2001). Dominic Redford,
marketing director for Sony in Australia, anticipated pitching the series to
Australians as "The Simpsons of the South Pacific" (a tagline first devised by
bro'Town producer Elizabeth Mitchell),[13] signalling a desire both to assimilate
the series within global popular culture, and to make a feature of its unique
status as a "Pacific" production. Similar ambiguities are evident in comments
posted by an American Myspace fan, who jokes about her boyfriend assuming that Cliff Curtis (a Māori actor who has appeared in various Hollywood
blockbusters and makes a guest appearance on *bro'Town*) was "Mexican",
thereby revealing the processes of cultural homogenisation that can accompany the global dissemination of popular culture. Curtis's cooptation into US
"ethnic minority" culture in the Myspace commentary resonates with statements made by Jean LaRose, CEO of the Canadian Aboriginal Peoples Television Network (APTN), which bought the series as an example of "creative,
Indigenous programming",[14] while Jane Roscoe, acting network programmer
for the Australian SBS network (which also bought the series), described it as
"an innovative, fun, multi-cultural animation", again implying an exoticising
valorisation of the show's ethnic "otherness".[15] Notably, *bro'Town*'s comic formula renders it easily assimilable by overseas viewers: many episodes include
"overseas" characters (from Australia, to Brazil and Canada), and the proliferation of globalised popular cultural references (from *The Sound of Music* to
Apocalypse Now) offers international viewers familiar contexts within which to
"domesticate" *bro'Town*'s exotic "foreignness" (to paraphrase Huggan).

Further, some *bro'Town* forum fans appear to resort to well-established stereotypes surrounding Polynesian sexual attractiveness and "exoticism": one
female fan, for example, issues a provocative invitation: "if your [sic] Maori
Samoan or pacific Islander please take my email address and talk to me some
time coz if u are any of these ethnicities I think your sexy and I love your skin
your lips and your nose", while an Australian fan declares "I love maoris"
because they're "hot". Regardless of whether these comments are made in
the spirit of irony, they imply a continuing exoticisation of Polynesian culture
that is also evident in comments by other white Antipodean *bro'Town* forum
fans who jokingly express a desire to become "Maori" or "Samoan". This
is an inversion of the social stigma commonly attached to urbanised Māori
and Pacific Islander immigrants in the post-war era, and one which bespeaks
a contemporary fetishisation and commodification of Polynesian youth culture as "cool" and streetwise. As media theorist Emma Earl notes, "Maori

and Pacific Island youth are the 'it kids' in the endorsement of brand identity" in contemporary New Zealand advertising culture, and she reads the conspicuous placement in *bro'Town* episodes of products by the show's commercial backers (including Vodafone, Frucor Beverages and Mars Incorporated) as part of "a marketing strategy to tap into a popular ideological shift towards multiculturalism" which offers only a token "acceptance of ethnic diversity" and privileges "the ethnic Other that assimilates" to Western capitalist "norms" (2005, 3–7 *passim*). Such a view (and the foregoing examples) accords with Huggan's observation that "the exoticist rhetoric of fetishised otherness and sympathetic identification masks the inequality of the power relations without which the discourse could not function" (14). Relatedly, Earl also argues that the positioning of the boys as conspicuous consumers (evident, for example, in their prominent use of an expensive *Vodafone Live* mobile phone in episode 3 of series 1) belies the poverty that afflicts many Pacific Island families, and conveniently assuages white guilt about the role that colonialism has played in the establishment of socio-economic inequalities between New Zealand's various ethnic groups (Earl 2005, 10).

However, it is important to note that the mobile phone used in episode three has been purchased for the boys by Wong (the wealthy Hong Kong Chinese student discussed earlier), and that throughout the series, *bro'Town* is consistently forthright in confronting Māori and Pacific Island socio-economic deprivation (while also providing characters who play against stereotype). Further, the product placement in the series should be understood within the context of the paucity of funding for "minority" media productions in New Zealand. While *bro'Town* has received substantial financial support from New Zealand On Air (a government funding agency charged with supporting local programming), a considerable proportion of the show's funding came from commercial channel TV3 (on which *bro'Town* was screened), and advertising and merchandising have been essential to the show's continued viability (Lustyik and Smith 2010, 339). Further, while "professional" critics—especially those with interests corresponding to the discipline of postcolonial studies—are trained to read media "texts" such as *bro'Town* in terms of their embeddedness within, or negotiation of, conflicted socio-cultural contexts, perhaps the most reliable index of *bro'Town*'s cultural impact lies in the responses of "lay" readers such as those on the *bro'Town* Internet fan sites. As I have indicated, the majority of "lay" responses to *bro'Town* centre on its entertainment value—a crucial prerequisite for the show's commercial and popular success both at home and abroad—but there is also evidence to suggest that lay readers (particularly those with experience of New Zealand culture) are as interested as critics in producing culturally informed readings of the show's racial politics, but are not limited by the same disciplinary protocols. As Procter suggests (with reference to his book group analysis), such responses "suggest a more open, less suspicious hermeneutics that might also bring us closer to an understanding of the popular pleasures motivated by a text, and its conspicuous global circulation and consumption in the present, than do available professional readings" (197). These fan responses also resonate with Guillory's argument for a less polarised model of interpretation in which both "professional" and "lay" readers recognise reading as an "ethical" practice governed by "self-recognition" and the potential for developing "the capabilities of private citizens" (43–44). At the very least, the various "professional" and "lay" readings of *bro'Town* I have discussed point towards the ways in which the global dissemination of electronic media has transformed "contextual literacies" (Appadurai 1996, 3) and necessitates new models of audience reception. It seems appropriate here to end with an assessment of the show from a New Zealand schoolboy, who combines an awareness of *bro'Town*'s cultural significance with an appreciation of its value as entertainment, thereby reconciling the extremes of the professional and lay readings of *bro'Town* I have outlined in this chapter:

> Who knew playing on the stereotypes in a multicultural society could be so entertaining? The good thing about *bro'Town* is that the joke isn't just on the Maori and Pacific Island people, but on everyone else as well—the Asians, Indians, but also the Pakeha or Europeans. And even if you don't belong to one of these groups, everyone in some way can relate to the themes and ideas. (Henley 2004, C4)

Notes

*   Throughout this chapter I follow the linguistic convention of placing a macron about the 'a' vowels in 'Maori' and 'Pakeha', and the first 'a' in 'Palagi', to represent the double/long vowel phoneme, except in cases where I quote from sources that do not use the macron.

1.   I wish to thank the Carnegie Trust for the Universities of Scotland for funding that supported research for this chapter. Many thanks also to Elizabeth Mitchell (*bro'Town* producer) and other staff at Firehorse Films for their generous provision of information on (and images from) the series. I am grateful also to Margaret Henley, Philippa Smith and Geoff Lealand for sending me copies of their publications on *bro'Town*/NZ television, and to David Farrier for feedback on a draft version of this chapter.

2.   *bro'Town* has been distributed in the US, Canada, Australia, Fiji, the Cook Islands, Latin America, Russia, Denmark and Portugal.

3.   This tripartite division was systematised in 1832 by the French explorer Dumont d'Urville (see Keown 2007, 13). While aware of the colonial provenance and limitations of these terms, I use "Polynesia" throughout this chapter, not least because diasporic Pacific Islanders in New Zealand are increasingly resorting to panethnic labels such as "Polynesian" and "PI" in order to express solidarity with fellow Pacific migrants as well as indigenous Māori.

4.   (Western) Samoa, the Cook Islands, Niue and Tokelau are all former New Zealand colonies, while Tonga (like Fiji and Tuvalu) has had close administrative links with New Zealand, particularly in the education sector. New Zealand

contains substantial diasporic communities originating from these countries (http://www.stats.govt.nz; Keown 2007, 190).

5. "Pākehā" is the Māori name for New Zealand's white settler culture.
6. "Pālagi" is a Samoan term referring to people of European descent.
7. *bro'Town* character profiles and promotional clips can be accessed at http://www.brotown.co.nz.
8. By the 2006 census Pacific Islanders represented 6.9 percent of New Zealand's overall population (with Europeans at 67.6 percent, Māori at 14.6 percent and Asians at 9.2 percent).
9. "Best on the box . . . Again!", bro'Town news, http://www.brotown.co.nz/news_34.html#1716.
10. To protect the privacy of fans on the *bro'Town* Internet discussion forums, I avoid using their names here, instead referring only to the *bro'Town* forum and Myspace sites from which I accessed their postings (see http://www.brotown.co.nz/forum.html, which can be accessed only by joining the *bro'Town* fan club, and http://www.myspace.com/bro_town).
11. The debate takes place under the "favourite character" section of the series 1 forum thread (http://www.brotown.co.nz/page59.html); access is restricted to fan club members.
12. "Fob", an acronym for "fresh off the boat", is commonly applied to newly arrived and putatively naive Pacific Island immigrants.
13. "bro'Town DVD in Australia", bro'Townnews, http://www.brotown.co.nz/archive_27.html#1071.
14. "bro'Town in Canada", bro'Town news, http://www.brotown.co.nz/archive_10.html#1513.
15. "bro'Town series 2 in Australia", bro'Town news, http://www.brotown.co.nz/archive_14.html#1508.

References

Appadurai, Arjun. 1996. *Modernity at Large*. Minneapolis: University of Minnesota Press.
Bannister, Mathew. 2008. "Where's Morningside? Locating *bro'Town* in the Ethnic Genealogy of New Zealand/Aotearoa." *New Zealand Journal of Media Studies* 11(1): 1–15.
Carter, D. 1992. "Tasteless Subjects: Postcolonial Literary Criticism, Realism and the Subject of Taste." *Southern Review* 25(3): 292–303.
Dixon, Greg. 2004. "Hey Bro, Is This Where I Get Off?" *New Zealand Herald*, September 29. http://www.nzherald.co.nz/lifestyle/news/article.cfm?c_id=6&objectid=3595539.
Earl, Emma. 2005. "Brand New Zealanders: The Commodification of Polynesian Youth Identity in Television Advertising." University of Canterbury. http://www.mang.canterbury.ac.nz/anzca/All%20Abstracts/18.pdf.
Firehorse Films. n.d. "*bro'Town* in the Community." PDF, 16 pp., supplied June 20 2008 via email.
———. 2005. *The bro'Town Annual*. Auckland: Random House.
Guillory, John. 2000. "The Ethical Practice of Modernity: The Example of Reading." In *The Turn to Ethics*, edited by Marjorie Garber, Beatrice Hanssen and Rebecca Walkowitz, 29–46. New York: Routledge.
Henley, Margaret. 2004. "Morningside Has Broken." *Sunday Star Times*, November 7, C4.

Huggan, Graham. 2001. *The Postcolonial Exotic*. London: Routledge.

Jameson, Fredric. 2003. "Fear and Loathing in Globalization." *New Left Review* 23: 105–14.

Jauss, Hans Robert. 1982. *Toward an Aesthetic of Reception*. Translated by Timothy Bahti. Minneapolis: University of Minnesota Press.

Keown, Michelle. 2007. *Pacific Islands Writing: The Postcolonial Literatures of Aotearoa/ New Zealand and Oceania*. Oxford: Oxford University Press.

———. 2008. "'Can't We All Just Get Along?': *bro'Town* and New Zealand's Creative Multiculturalism." *Moving Worlds* 8(2): 44–58.

Kothari, Shuchi, Sarina Pearson and Nabeel Zuberi. 2004. "Television and Multiculturalism in Aotearoa New Zealand." In *Television in New Zealand: Programming the Nation*, edited by Roger Horrocks and Nick Perry, 135–51. Auckland: Oxford University Press.

Lustyik, Katalin, and Philippa Smith. 2010. "From The Simpsons to 'The Simpsons of the South Pacific': New Zealand's First Primetime Animation, *bro'Town*." *Television New Media* 11: 331–49.

Misa, Tapu. 2006. "We Can Enjoy a Laugh at Ourselves But We're No Bad Joke." *New Zealand Herald*, September 27, E1.

Nixon, Melody. 2008. Review of "*Bro'Town* Live on Stage." *The Lumiere Reader,* March 6. http://lumiere.net.nz/reader/arts.php/item/1549.

Procter, James. 2009. "Reading, Taste and Postcolonial Studies." *Interventions* 11(2): 180–98.

Schlote, Christiane. 2005. "'The Sketch's the Thing Wherein We'll Catch the Conscience of the Audience': Strategies and Pitfalls of Ethnic TV Comedies in Britain, the United States, and Germany." In *Cheeky Fictions: Laughter and the Postcolonial*, edited by Susanne Reichl and Mark Stein, 177–90. Amsterdam: Rodopi.

Sinavaiana-Gabbard, Caroline. 1999. "Where the Spirits Laugh Last: Comic Theatre in Samoa." In *Inside Out: Literature, Cultural Politics, and Identity in the New Pacific*, edited by Vilsoni Hereniko and Rob Wilson, 183–205. Lanham, MD: Rowman and Littlefield.

Spratt, Amanda. 2006. "Bro'Town Faces Racial Flak." *The New Zealand Herald on Sunday*, August 27.

Staiger, Janet. 2005. *Media Reception Studies*. New York: New York University Press.

Teaiwa, Teresia, and Sean Mallon. 2005. "Ambivalent Kinships? Pacific Peoples in New Zealand." In *New Zealand Identities: Departures and Destinations*, edited by James H. Liu, Tim McCreanor, Tracey McIntosh and Teresia Teaiwa, 207–29. Wellington: Victoria University Press.

Wichtel, Diana. 2004. "Fat Albert and the South Park Kids." *New Zealand Listener*, October 16. http://www.listener.co.nz/entertainment/fat-albert-and-the-south-park-kids/.

———. 2006. "Funny, That." *New Zealand Listener*, December 9–15. http://www.listener.co.nz/issue/3474/features/7652

2 "That May Be Where I Come from but That's Not How I Read"

Diaspora, Location and Reading Identities

Bethan Benwell, James Procter
and Gemma Robinson

The historical neglect of readers within the field of postcolonial studies has produced what C. L. Innes suggests is a reductive and presumptuous idea of "the reader": "most critical analyses of postcolonial writing implicitly or explicitly presume that the reader is either a member of the writer's nation, as in Benedict Anderson's *Imagined Communities* (1983) . . . or, more frequently, a generalized cosmopolitan Westerner"; even in those accounts that do exist "there is little differentiation between different kinds of Western reader" (2007, 200). Much of the haziness around readers here hinges upon commonsense assumptions about the *location* of reading, whether it is conceived in terms of national affiliation or in more generalised, global and diasporic terms of cosmopolitan consumption in "the" West. In what follows we explore some of the findings of a recent project that attempted to firm up current conceptions of readership by investigating how readers in a series of geographically dispersed locations made sense of the same, or similar works of fiction associated with postcolonial or diaspora writing.[1] These works included canonical classics such as Chinua Achebe's *Things Fall Apart* (1958), as well as proto-canonical contemporary works such as Zadie Smith's *White Teeth* (2001), experimental writers like Junot Diaz and more mainstream realist novelists like Andrea Levy and Monica Ali, poetry and short fiction, as well as novels, and prescribed works as well as books selected by the individual groups themselves. By recording and transcribing a series of isolated book group readings of these texts in Africa (Lagos, Kano, Nigeria; Tetuan, Morocco), India (New Delhi), Canada (Kingston), the Caribbean (Port of Spain, Trinidad and Tobago; Kingston, Jamaica) and across the UK (from Cornwall to Glasgow), this project asked how (if at all) the reception of the same book differs according to the place in which it is read.

Drawing upon this data elsewhere, we have argued that "the vocabularies of *dislocation* wielded by professional readers (reviewers, publishers, academics, critics) to describe . . . diasporic cultural production tend to conceal the precise provenance of those vocabularies within a select series of metropolitan *locations*" (Procter 2010, 261). We have also proposed that there is a "social order" *within* reading groups, whose encounter with books is always "a socially situated, localized activity, contingent upon the context in which it is produced" (Benwell 2009, 300). However, if one of our concerns has been to provide a more manifold, situated understanding of the kind of undifferentiated postcolonial audiences identified by Innes, the project has also taught us to be increasingly suspicious around assumptions of the whereabouts of reading.

In what follows we will see there are good reasons to hesitate before prescribing *where* difference might be identified or delineated in relation to regional, transnational and global audiences. For example, we remain unconvinced that the location of readers can be accessed in any direct or transparent manner. Reader location never ultimately anchors meaning-making and therefore cannot operate as a guarantee of what Hans Robert Jauss, in a different context, refers to as a "horizon of expectations" (1982). In short, we doubt whether reading, a notoriously elusive act, can be *mapped* in a manner that is ultimately or empirically exhaustive: any attempt to generalise from the micro (an individual reader's response) to the macro (talk about the locale/ethnicity/national identity of participants) involves speculative leaps (Benwell, Procter and Robinson 2008). At the same time, we cannot overlook the fact that location continues to matter to our readers, who continually allude to place, or ritually situate themselves in spatial terms of intimacy or unfamiliarity with particular fictional narratives.

Reading, Location and Identity in Reading Group Conversation

In what follows, we do not assume that a particular *kind* of response is representative of a location, even if it appears to have a consistency or homogeneity that might seem to attach it to a particular place. In a comparative analysis such as this, it may appear that the most compelling conclusions orbit around clear and culturally determined readings that offer a point of contrast between groups, such that, for instance, reading groups in Nigeria have a special "insight" into the cultural details of Ibo society that is unlikely to be shared by readers elsewhere, and thus engenders different patterns of interpretation and evaluation of Achebe's *Things Fall Apart*. However, our findings suggest that location is more helpfully understood as the ongoing production of book group talk, rather than a fixed place that prescribes that talk (see Benwell 2009 and Procter 2009), seeking to analyse in broadly ethnomethodological terms[2] how groups understand themselves as readers in both the social situation of the group and the larger geographical location. In this context we also share Ramaswami Harindranath's concerns about treating global audiences as "ethnically self-contained groups" (Harindranath 2005, 6), and John Frow's view that, where reading formations are concerned, there is "a danger of positing imaginary social unities as the explanatory basis of cultural texts" (Frow 1995, 13).

One of the observations that arose more or less consistently from the book group recordings was the way in which readers grounded *themselves* in their "local" contexts in ways that supported, legitimised or justified their interpretations or evaluations of the texts. In a series of transcripts in which fictional texts chosen for their proximity to the culture and location of the groups were discussed, we observed how a repeated trope of belonging or proximity seemed to index a relationship of representational veracity between reader experience and the fictional worlds of books.[3] For example, in a discussion about Junot Diaz's *The Brief and Wondrous Life of Oscar Wao* (2007) (a novel narrating the inter-generational ambitions, histories and curse of a "ghetto nerd" (11) in New Jersey, Rutgers University and the Dominican Republic), one member of the Port of Spain group works up her right to evaluate the text by identifying herself in both spatial and political terms as "a diaspora person": "well no I'm just speaking as a diaspora person and reading this no I can see where he's coming from". This speaker alludes to both literal and metaphorical senses of place here, by her use of the phrase "where he's coming from", which seems to yoke location to meaning or intention. At the same time, the "just" seems to modulate this identification, perhaps as a way of naturalising its significance. Meanwhile, in the same book group, readers of Andrea Levy's bestselling Windrush fiction *Small Island* (2004), set across the UK, Jamaica and India, acknowledge the experience of those who have spent some time in England: "but Ellen you were saying it sort of reminded you of your experiences in London?" In the Kano group's discussion of Jackie Kay's *The Adoption Papers* (1991), *distance* is explicitly invoked ("being somewhere else") as a hurdle to understanding or as a lack of qualification to evaluate Kay's poetry of adoption in Glasgow across boundaries of ethnicity and geography:

S3 she went and wrote about Scotland a lot about stuff that concerned
    herself that we might not really be [able to
S5   [being somewhere else we
    might not be able we are not well informed=
S6 =of the context

Similarly, in Kingston, Ontario, a reader makes explicit the connection between spatial belonging, distance and the process of identification in the reading of Dionne Brand's *What We All Long For* (2005), a novel of the interlocking lives of twenty-somethings "born in the city from people born elsewhere" (20):

> you know there may have been something about the Toronto aspect of it that made it more familiar to me than the books that took place in London

The discussion of Diaz's *The Brief and Wondrous Life of Oscar Wao* by the Port of Spain group reveals an affiliation to the text's aesthetics and values which is explicitly premised by one member on spatial metaphors: "*I'm there I'm there* you know I feel I feel the whole you know I'm into the rhythm of the language" (our emphasis). The ability of the text to *transport* its readers in acts of translocal identifications is related in this particular book group's discussion to an ongoing debate that posits the novel as "Caribbean", and as connecting to *them*, across the region from its Dominican Republic and US topographical foundations. Their comments range from the barbed ("it was a mildly interesting primer on Dominican history") to the positive (" . . . but this was the first book [from the project's list] that said okay I can see us in it I mean can see um I can see our experience in it"). Furthermore, one reader notes that despite the profile of Junot Diaz, this Caribbeanness is a trope internal to the novel:

> in the US I mean it's like oh he's a Dominican American writer or like a young American writer with immigrant roots but he kept emphasizing he keeps using the words Caribbean and Antillean and island over and over again I thought it was really interesting that he was laying claim to that.

Later in the transcript, an exchange occurs between readers which debates the plausibility of Oscar. Described by the novel's narrator as "a fat sci-fi reading nerd" (19), two group members defend a reading of him as "authentic" by a rhetorical merging of fiction and the readers' own lives and autobiographies:

S1   so do you think that Oscar's character is not believable? I know Oscar I I know Oscar

S2   I was about to say I I've been thinking of someone I went to school who could have been Oscar

In a similar rhetorical move, the same group bestows or withholds authenticity from the Jamaican characters Gilbert and Hortense in Andrea Levy's *Small Island* (2004) (narrating the tensions between a British and a Jamaican couple living through war and immigration in the mid-century) by noting they have "met a lot of Gilberts"; and conversely that "the way Hortense speaks is not plausible" (1997, 235). These comments assume social and spatial identities that are readily understandable both in terms of a lived reality and in terms of the form of literary realism. We could say that the Caribbean operates as a shared field of *situated* knowledge that can be drawn upon by shorthand comments about masculine identity (we know what a "Gilbert" is), or about language use (we know what is implausible speech for Hortense). But we should also note how insistently varied, localised and deictic are the ways in which comments about social and spatial identity operate here. The Caribbean is clearly significant in the discussion, but it is not the only way that location and located identity get discussed here. For example, in the discussion of *Oscar Wao* (in formulations of noun and adjective), Caribbean and Dominican Republic are mentioned 34 times, Trinidad 28, America (including references to hyphenated Polish-, black-, and African-) 27, Diaspora 23, Latin America 9, Guyana 6, Grenada 4, West Indies 4, Iraq 3, Jamaica 3, England, India, South America and Cuba 2, not to mention appeals of "our society" and "our experience" that assume but do not explain the boundaries of identification.

Elizabeth Long's ethnographic study of women's book clubs has commented in detail upon the relationship between acts of reading and lived or personal experience (2003). Her study focuses particularly on the interface between a reader's own personal experience and a book's value as a realist text through a process of "self-recognition" (153) and also the quasi-therapeutic function of book group discussions in working through issues raised by novels that are embedded in their own lives: "participants speak of a process that couple reflection about literature with self-reflection in the company of others who bring similar reflectiveness, but different selves, into the process" (1997, 228). However, self-recognition is not only an act in and of itself, but also a form of social action and identity *work* in interaction: the invocation of location is used to accomplish the act of "being a reader" with all the moral rights and responsibilities that attend this identity.[4] To be a reader on this account is to engage in the discursive production of value judgements about texts. One of these responsibilities is implicitly that of producing justified and well-founded evaluations of a text—its veracity, its artistry, the sympathy of its characters, the pleasures or aversions it provokes and the plausibility of its plotting. Thus invocations of location are frequently deployed in order to give explicit credence to judgements about a text and in this way constitute and support the "moral order" of the book group. We can see this moral order being accomplished particularly at points of *disagreement* or *contestation* where readers challenge or support a text's right to be deemed "representative" of a particular location and cultural experience.

In the New Delhi group there is an explicit disagreement about the antihero of Hari Kunzru's novel *Transmission* (2004), who moves from New Delhi to California to take up a job in Silicon Valley. For one reader he is "every Indian": "I mean we can see that he . . . every Indian they can see their own character in Arjun Mehta's and their ambitions", but there is also concern about whether the book stereotypes the "Indian" experience ("this land of beggars and snake charmers") for a Western readership. In both statements the speakers appeal to a common appreciation of the national character by the use of "we" pronouns, the construction of a point of generic experience premised on nationality ("every Indian"), the use of proximal deixis ("this land") and the economical stock image of an orientalised India that triggers a shared scepticism among a local community of readers. Later a reader describes the representation of India as "shabby":

but when you look at the entire setting that he's an Indian and . . . in America so I'm not very happy about the setting you know cause again it's like an Indian coming off looking quite sorry, so for *that* that was one part and furthermore like there were two passages in which the reference to actual places in India was again quite often shabby

But this negative judgement is swiftly countered by the invocation, by another speaker, of autobiographical identification with Kunzru's description of Janpath, one of New Delhi's main roads. He asserts that "it summarised my six months of experience of living in like a dusty crowded y'know . . . ". Similarly, when one member complains that the hyper-realism of the novel which portrays the seedier side of Indian life compromises an "Asian" identity, this is countered by the slightly mocking suggestion that a globally appealing "Clark Gable Indian" would be the first speaker's preferred alternative:

S4 you wish he would have been a Clark Gable Indian uh?
Grp [laughing]
S1 *no* no I'm just saying this was again another novel in which Asians do not do good that's all I'm saying

This contestation of the veracity of group identity also arises in our Scottish groups in relation to the orthographic representation of Glaswegian speech. In the Glasgow (extract 1) and Edinburgh (extract 2) groups there is disagreement about the "authentic[ity]" of the Glaswegian script used to narrate Suhayl Saadi's 'Extra Time in Paradise', a short story of an encounter between Aamir Donovan Khan, a Celtic football apprentice, and a mysterious "auld man sittin oan the Manager's bench". Both reading groups ask whether the rendering of Glaswegian "jars"—a choice of word which is suggestive of physical dislocation from a familiar and stable position:

(1)
S1 there's some things that you think that's not the way I think that was spelled and that actually jar- it's one . . . it jars so you can't . . .
S4 but there isn't there isn't a recognised spelling I mean Margaret's right it jars because I mean I've never heard anybody saying "war are ye frae?"
(2)
S7 (waving the transcript of the story) what sort of people speak like that?
S1 sorry?
S7 (waving papers again) what sort of people speak like that?
S1 it didn't jar with me too much I have to say when I was reading it

By occupying a located identity in these discussions, readers are able to damn or defend an author's attempts to represent a location, a national character or linguistic experience faithfully, and in this way silently maintain the notion that there *are* such truthful benchmarks for a writer to set his or her art against.

In an overwhelmingly negative assessment of *Small Island*, the Port of Spain group refers to its representation of the Caribbean as focalised by an "other's" view:

> I think we all articulated it in various ways was it really was not *us* it was somebody else's perception of us

And another reader from the same group notes:

> It's a bit sad—we've all said it here—that this is all material we've seen, we've heard, but this is what will be discussed in book groups all over the world as the West Indian experience, and for us it's maybe forty years too late. And it seems to me there's a gap between what's actually happening in the Caribbean and what's getting out to the world

The speaker here takes the floor for about three minutes—a marker of the consequence of the topic—voicing an asserted collective concern about the present and future representations of the Caribbean in literature and that a single book might represent West Indian experience as singular. In this way, readers monitor the boundaries of their own locations vis à vis the wider context of literary markets in order to assert and position themselves within a global order of reading.[5] We might wonder if the voiced concern overstates the hegemonic presence of *Small Island* in a book-reading world, but given the novel's high profile, it is worth considering two reviews featured on Levy's official website:

> Andrea Levy has written one of those rare fictions that tells you things you didn't know but feel you should have known (*Sunday Herald*, Scotland)

> Andrea Levy gives us a new urgent take on our past (*Vogue*, UK)

Both the Port of Spain reading group member and the reviewers recognise belatedness and gap-filling as important in relation to *Small Island*. But for the reader in Port of Spain, the belatedness of *Small Island* refers to its status within a Caribbean tradition of writing about emigration that began at least "forty years" ago (Lamming 1954; Selvon 1956). To be late in this instance is to be clichéd and unoriginal, and *Small Island*'s popularity might be seen to reveal starkly the gap between an informed and uninformed readership of Caribbean literature. For the *Sunday Herald* and *Vogue* reviewers, it is the belatedness of their own knowledge that is being addressed. *Small Island* fills in the gaps: about West Indian emigration to Britain, the nature of the British Empire and the global nature of the Second World War. Marketing the novel as recovering a hidden history, Levy's website plays on assumptions about her general readership's UK identity and understanding of "our [unknown] past". It is a mass-market strategy that has no space to contemplate how this past of Empire and migration is already registered in Caribbean writing and history, and for the Port of Spain group, the novel's success seems simultaneously to register a failure to see "what's actually happening in the Caribbean".

All the foregoing examples focus primarily on explicit mentions of location and an assumption that location in some ways stands in productive relation to reception. But listening to these group discussions we find that there is no simple correlation between place and interpretation. As the reading group members explore their reading practices, the possibilities of *reading identities* emerge. We believe it is possible to explore how practices of reading reveal neglected forms of identity work—about how to be a reader—and to consider how these converge with or diverge from other kinds of identity formations that our group members appeal to and refuse at their meetings.

In the next section we explore further this concept of a more autonomous "reading identity" that, while not mappable or subsumed by sociological categories such as gender, ethnicity or nationality, nonetheless continues to interact in relevant ways with notions of "location".

Reading Practices and Reading Identities

Our readings of these transcripts in terms of "location" have so far attempted to illuminate the acts that are accomplished by invoking belonging and space, including identity work (e.g., "being a loyal member of a national community"), accounting for literary judgements (both positive and negative) and consolidating the social order of the book group. Locatedness (of reader and text) is valued among reading groups, and when we focus further on reading practices (such as how to choose a book to read), we see more ways of conceiving the relationship between location and interpretation:

> I read [*White Teeth*] on a plane I actually I found it was good plane reading because it wasn't too taxing (laughter) you know I always sit I find it hard to read on planes cause you're you know you're trapped in a small space.
> (Port of Spain group)

Here the physical *difficulties* of the "small space" of the plane are offset by a preference for a novel that is defined by an *easiness* to read. Matching a book to the location of its reception is one commonsense way that books circulate. We need only to turn to the UK print media's annual attention to "summer reading" to see this: "*Anna Karenina* on the beach, *The Corrections* in Patagonia, *Death in Venice* overlooking the Lido" (e.g., Hooker 2011). In these pairings the possibility of what Pascale Casanova titles "the world republic of letters"—a shared world of writers and readers lived and understood as a global reality—holds out, at least potentially, against the negative connotations that are exposed in her model of literary inequalities, and the circulation of dominant literatures (2004).

The possibility of translocated reading is reformulated in a further discussion:

> S1 who speaks to you as a writer? who has something to say to you as a writer?
> S2 from this part of the world? right now?
> S1 from any *from anywhere*
>
> (Port of Spain group, our emphasis)

Here authors being able to engage in conversation with their readers is negotiated first from within a perceived set of geographical boundaries and then corrected to mean the possibility of global literary communication. Readers of Chinua Achebe's *Things Fall Apart* in two different groups in Kano go further, to speak of the universality of texts as well as of readers' freedom to read across borders:

> (Group 1)
> S2 I think one of the reasons why it's so successful like a lot of people will relate is the fact you know of the conflict that goes on between tradition and modernity I think that's *something that is common to everyone no matter where you come from*
> (Group 2)
> S7 I am also going to add that I think probably one of the this Achebe's bringing out aspects of human nature is probably one of the reasons *why everyone you know world over is able to identify with this book* because whether you're Nigerian you're Ibo you're Jamaican you know white black whatever colour
> S5 *it's universal*
>
> (Kano groups, our emphasis)

While questions of authenticity and universality are necessarily fraught within the realms of literary representation, it is striking to note a shift in reception here from the critique of universalism that Achebe articulates in 'Colonialist Criticism' (1988).

Where Achebe feared for a "narrow" world of letters that must render African novels American in order to value them (52), these three readers in the Kano group formulate a different non-Eurocentric meaning for "universal", one imagining a readerly network that connects "Nigerian" to "Ibo" to "Jamaican" to "white" to "black" to "whatever colour". In their exchange, *Things Fall Apart* is a text that is consecrated internationally. And this ongoing process of debating the meaning of literary universality turns on their understanding of the multiplicity of sites of reception, as well as a sense that practices of reading might be shared across borders: in this instance that readers share an interest in exploring "human nature" and conflicts between tradition and modernity. This does not necessarily amount to a rejection of "located reading", nor however does it necessarily imply the same readings across the globe. It might be more accurate to see these invocations of universality as hopeful that some consensus about readerly interest in a text can be registered across different places.

At one point in the discussion about *Small Island* a reader from the Port of Spain reading group questions our project's interest in Caribbean reading groups. He begins by saying:

> I find it interesting that we've been asked to do these to review these these books it's obvious that someone is thinking are they hitting the mark?

He ironically articulates the supposed identities of the group as they might be construed by the UK-based academics: "the purpose of this exercise is to determine what we home colonials think of writing you know that's meant to be post-colonial" noting that this idea is "off-putting". Another speaker goes on to note that the reading list "was constructed" and the books "assigned" to them, reinforcing the idea that to argue that books such as *Small Island* represent some kind of authentic, located Caribbean experience is a particular kind of theoretical and imposed construct and an argument in which he is not invested.

This first reader goes on to describe the project's interest in Caribbean readers as "patronising", saying about his Caribbean identity: "That may be very well where I come from but that's not how I read". This explicit prioritisation of reading practices is intriguing if, like us, you are not sure that these practices are straightforward indices of other kinds of identities, or explained by these other kinds of identities. This latter kind of analysis powers Elizabeth Long's research in *Book Clubs*, in which the power of reading is viewed as part of a process of self-recognition and social change. Long, of course, is interested in how readers report the impact of reading groups on their reading habits (110), but as her subtitle suggests, a concern for "the uses of reading in everyday life" is necessarily searching for the myriad social meanings of reading. What this means for her analysis is that her concerns often quickly move on from discussing what it might mean to be a reader to a discussion of how being a member of a book group has particular social meanings, how ideally it offers its members "a potentially transformative way of being in the world" (113). Central to Long's thesis is that "the 'doing' of culture appears more integrally implicated in the 'doing' of gender, class, race, and social development in general than theorists generally assume" (17) What this resistant Port of Spain reader suggests is that how we read should not be important only for (or reducible to) its ability to help describe or transform other sorts of identity: in asserting his practice ("how I read") he encourages us to consider him as a reader, rather than as anything else. If this sense of the "doing" of culture-through-reading seems to allow a return to the dominant reception model of the "solitary reader" (a model that Long works against in her study (2–17)), it is in order to see this model in a new context, and to track what we perhaps need to relearn: that the doing of reading can be understood as a distinctive set of practices that are carried out individually, collectively and discursively.

The reader's task, argues Alberto Manguel, is "to take whatever book seems appealing, strip it of its colour-coded covers and place it among those volumes which chance and experience have put upon her bedside shelf" (1997, 235). This model of how to build a personal library outlines some of the norms of reading—in contexts that are both external (the "colour-coded covers" of the publisher and author) and internal ("chance and experience")—that a reader might confront. In this respect a bedside shelf presents the basis for an identity, a micro-located reading identity, and this appeal to other forms of location might be one contextualisation of the reader's assertion that knowing he is from the Caribbean will not tell you about "how I read". A refusal to adopt a Caribbean reading identity flies in the face of a cultural-nationalist and postcolonial logic which argues postcolonial locations require a literature, and a readership, of their own. This reader wants to reject "postcolonial" and "post-postcolonial literature" as his own literature, and himself as its ideal reader. He says, "If you want to get my opinion on literature full stop, I'm there." He rejects the idea that interpretation is determined by a spatial identity, but location still has a key operation in his formulation of the value of his reading practices. His willingness to be "there" for the discussion of "literature full stop" suggests that even as he asserts his autonomy as an individual reader he is also pointing to an interpretive (even real) space in which his practice will be respected.

Listening to reading groups, we have noted how the privileging of certain kinds of readers through their spatial and social identities prevents us from seeing clearly the multiple ways that location informs reading identities. Manguel argues:

> setting aside a group of books or a genre for a specific group of readers (whether Greek novels or the pink-covered novels of my childhood) not only creates an enclosed literary space which those readers are encouraged to explore; it also, quite often, makes that space off limits for others. (1997, 228)

This formulation of how reading can take place "within walls" can be extended by considering the complexities of the group reading discussions. In the Kano group the readers challenge themselves to understand why

Achebe's novel seems to resist being enclosed "within walls". Worries about how literary spaces become enclosed animate the Port of Spain reading group. The enclosures the Port of Spain group anticipates relate not only to their enclosure as Caribbean readers reading Caribbean texts, but as we've seen, other readers' enclosure within an overly narrow literary space that defines the Caribbean and Caribbean literature. In the case of *Small Island* some worry that the novel will define the emigrant "Windrush" generation outside the Caribbean; some worry that it will displace older work by Caribbean writers such as Selvon and Lamming; some worry that it promotes what they call "writing by box-checking"; some mobilise their knowledge of Caribbean texts to defend and attack Levy's novel.

Thinking about how readers resist or work within the walls of an "enclosed literary space" provides a useful way to contextualise how we make sense of location in relation to reading identities. One reader in the Port of Spain group says in response "having just read *Small Island* I personally would be interested to hear what Jamaican readers make of this". This view is then hedged and qualified, perhaps suggestive of his awareness of the difficulty and ambiguous appeal of these assumptions about "legitimate" identity positions that accompany acts of reading: "because I think that they I mean quite apart from sure any reader anywhere in the world will have something interesting and valid to say about this and I you know I completely agree with you but there's also because of the subject matter I think that there's a particular interest in hearing what someone who supposedly comes from the world that's been described here what they think of it you know what what insights they can give to it". The request need not be motivated by a turn to Jamaican readers for an authentic reader response (although there may be an implied criticism of our apparent interest in "Caribbean" responses by a reading group from Trinidad reading a novel by a British writer of Jamaican parentage). This request for located readers might instead be seen as part of an attempt to come to some provisional reckoning of the complexity of location and, we would add, the complexity of the practices of reading. To account for the enduring appeal of locating readers, readings and reception, we must allow for contestation about, just as much as confirmation of, the meaning and value of "the literary space" of books and their readerships.

Notes

1.   'Devolving Diasporas' was an AHRC-funded project running between 2007 and 2010: http://www.devolvingdiasporas.com/. "Devolving" here registers the project's interest in moving beyond certain commonsense locations of meaning, including the "text" itself as the taken-for-granted centre of meaning, or the metropolitan centre as a privileged site of consumption that eclipses other sites of meaning-making. The reception data considered here is taken from a larger corpus of transcribed digital audio-visual recordings of thirty book groups, and

amounting to 3,400 pages of transcription. Involving public libraries, the British Council, mass read events and home-based book groups, our readers met monthly, typically for a period of six months. To respect the privacy of the book group members, we have anonymised all names.

2. Ethnomethodology is the study of the ways in which people display their understandings of the world around them to others, negotiating those understandings with one another and in this way producing social order.

3. The New Delhi, India group read Hari Kunzru's *Transmission* (2004); the Kano, Nigeria groups read Chinua Achebe's *Things Fall Apart* (1958); the Glasgow and Edinburgh groups read Suhayl Saadi's short story *"Extra Time in Paradise"* (2003); the Kingston, Ontario (Canada) group read Dionne Brand's *What We All Long For* (2005) and the Port of Spain, Trinidad and Kingston, Jamaica groups read Junot Diaz's *The Brief and Wondrous Life of Oscar Wao* (2007).

4. For an elaborated account of the "morally accountable" status of reading see Benwell, Procter and Robinson 2011.

5. The novel has been translated into over twenty languages, and garnered the Whitbread Prize and the Commonwealth Writers' prize, the Orange Prize for Fiction (and Orange's 10-year fiction award). It was also chosen in the UK as part of a national drive to coincide with the bicentenary commemorations of the end of the British Slave Trade in 2007. The adaptation of the novel won an International Emmy in the US for best TV movie/mini series in 2010 as well as a UK Broadcast Award for the Best Single TV Drama. The Orange Prize for Fiction official website notes that "The bestselling Orange Prize winner is Andrea Ley's *Small Island* (Headline Review) with sales of 834, 958".

References

Achebe, Chinua. 1958. *Things Fall Apart*. London: Heinemann.

———. 1988. "Colonialist Criticism." In *Hopes and Impediments*, 46–61. London: Heinemann.

"Andrea Levy." Andrea Levy. http://www.andrealevy.co.uk/.

Benwell, Bethan. 2009. "'A Pathetic and Racist and Awful Character': Ethnomethodological Approaches to the Reception of Diasporic Fiction." *Language and Literature* 18(3): 300–315.

Benwell, Bethan, James Procter and Gemma Robinson. 2008. "'That May Be Where I Come from but That's Not How I Read': Diaspora, Location and the Limits of Reading Group Data." Paper presented at *Evidence of Reading, Reading the Evidence* Conference, the Institute of English Studies, University of London, July 22.

———. 2011. "Not Reading *Brick Lane*." *Reading after Empire: Special Issue of New Formations* 73: 90–116.

Brand, Dionne. 2005. *What We All Long For*. Toronto: Vintage Canada.

Casanova, Pascale. 2004. *The World Republic of Letters*. Cambridge: Harvard University Press.

Diaz, Junot. 2007. *The Brief and Wondrous Life of Oscar Wao*. New York: Riverhead.

Frow, John. 1995. *Cultural Studies and Cultural Value*. Oxford: Clarendon Press.

Harindranath, Ramaswami. 2005. "Ethnicity and Cultural Difference: Some Thematic and Political Issues on Global Audience Research." *Participations* 2: 1–17.

Hooker, Ginny. 2011. "Best Holiday Reads." *The Guardian*, June 17. http://www.guardian.co.uk/books/2011/jun/17/best-holiday-reads.

Innes, C. L. 2007. *The Cambridge Introduction to Postcolonial Literatures in English*. Cambridge: Cambridge University Press.

Jauss, Hans Robert. 1982. *Toward an Aesthetic of Reception*. Translated by Timothy Bahti. Minneapolis: University of Minnesota Press.

Kay, Jackie. 1991. *The Adoption Papers*. Newcastle upon Tyne: Bloodaxe.

Kunzru, Hari. 2004. *Transmission*. New York: Dutton.

Lamming, George. 1954. *The Emigrants*. London: Michael Joseph.

Levy, Andrea. 2004. *Small Island*. London: Headline.

Long, Elizabeth. 2003. *Book Clubs: Women and the Uses of Reading in Everyday Life*. Chicago: Chicago University Press.

Manguel, Alberto. (1996) 1997. *A History of Reading*. London: Penguin.

"Orange Prize FAQs." Orange Prize for Fiction. http://www.orangeprize.co.uk/about_faqs.html

Procter, James. 2009. "Reading, Taste and Postcolonial Studies: Professional and Lay Readers of *Things Fall Apart*." *Interventions: International Journal of Postcolonial Studies* 11(2): 180–98.

———. 2010. "Diasporic Readers and the Location of Reception." In *Diasporas: Concepts, Intersections, Identities*, edited by Kim Knott and Sean McLoughlin, 256–62. London: Zed Books.

Saadi, Suhayl. 2007. "Extra Time in Paradise." Devolving Diasporas. www.devolvingdiasporas.com.

Selvon, Samuel. 1956. *The Lonely Londoners*. London: Allan Wingate.

Smith, Zadie. 2000. *White Teeth*. London: Penguin Books.

3 "Bollywood" Adolescents
Young Viewers Discuss Class, Representation and Hindi Films

Shakuntala Banaji

Ideological Change: From an Ethics of Poverty to an Aesthetics of Wealth

Historically the issue of class has been seen to be of overt significance in structuring narratives and representations of young people in the Romantic genre in Hindi cinema, and in the last few decades representations of class have altered almost beyond recognition. In the 1970s, young heroes or heroines tended to be poor, from single-parent families or impoverished areas.[1] Malhotra and Alagh argue that depictions of class in these films are tied to an ethics-driven postcolonial vision: "wealth was linked directly to the corrupt, exploitative and dissolute world of old money or the landowning classes who aligned themselves with the colonial masters" (2004, 25). The 1990s saw a superficially comical shift. Released in 1994, after the dramatic liberalisation of the Indian economy (Fernandes 2000a and 2000b), *Hum Aapke Hain Koun* (HAHK: *Who am I to you?* dir. Sooraj Barjatya) is set in an elite India of fast cars and brand-names, while its heroines possess the traits of docile, traditional Indian daughters-in-law. It depicts as commonplace the everyday reality of a miniscule elite (Saldanha 2002, 341). Subsequent family melodramas placed commercial culture centre-stage, with teenage heroes driving convertibles, wearing branded clothing and jetting off in private helicopters to million-dollar apartments.[2] A viewer in Rao's ethnography (2007, 64) comments: "If someone makes a film where the hero is not rich then they call it an *alternative* film. Why is a film about a poor man alternative in India? Majority of Indians are poor!" Saliently, noting the films' resonance with political propaganda of neoliberal and far-right religious-political elites, textual accounts of this era of Hindi cinema deplore commercial films as depoliticising, capitalist fantasies (Bharucha 1995; Juluri 1999).

Locating the Audience

Concern with the "effects" of Hindi films is not new: in fact it is the primary theme of much writing on the subject (Mathur 2002; Chatterji 2003; Shukla

2005). Fareed Kazmi's Gramscian conclusions sum up a number of anxieties about the "dangers" of Hindi films:

> Conventional films do not simply reflect the social world, but actually construct a coherent version of social reality within which ideological tensions can be contained and resolved . . . [i]n other words, through highly complex and devious means, it privileges "preferred" meanings over "excluded" meanings, thereby reinforcing the "given" of the system, and absorbing or referencing out all potentially oppositional connotations. (Kazmi 1999, 215–16)

There are numerous reasons why theorisations of Hindi films as closed and coherent systems remain prevalent. In particular, unease about xenophobic nationalism in India (Mankekar 2000; Bhatt 2001) and the erasure of working-class characters (Bharucha 1998; Kazmi 1999) from blockbusters appears to emphasise the need for an understanding of links between social behaviours and spectatorship. This is all the more the case as, in the opinion of numerous textual critics (Barnouw and Krishnaswami 1980, 281; Valicha 1988, 48–60), audiences uncritically watch films that seem at best to ignore and at worst to encourage authoritarian, non-egalitarian beliefs and circumstances.

While each of these accounts of Hindi films appears to describe aspects of the *texts* accurately, the nature of commentators' assumptions about *audiences* raises problematic questions. Are all the romance, music, costumes, dialogues and settings of contemporary Hindi films equally ideologically "suspect"? Of course, some theorists (Nandy 1998, 3–14; Thomas 1985, 126–28) have summarised their assumptions about Hindi film audiences in relation to the *pleasures* of spectacle and emotional excess, an avowed "need" for tradition in a threateningly modern world. But are these pleasures politically dubious by virtue of their connection to an Indianised neoliberal ideology which mixes elite economic globalisation with superficial pop-cultural modernity and oppressive social traditions as Vishwanath (2002) suggests? Surely, while pertinently connecting films to socio-cultural contexts, this framework too homogenises audiences dangerously? To find out, for instance, how and *why* particular viewers interpret and use Hindi films, it proves necessary to allow them opportunities to "talk back",[3] to explain what, and in which conditions, they interpret and act on discourses of social class, gender, youth and sexuality in films.

Hodge and Tripp argue that "ideological effects cannot simply be read off from ideological forms analysed in isolation from the cognitive and social processes that constitute them" (1986, 99). The expansion of media ethnography and cultural studies in recent years as tools for recording and understanding audience responses has ensured that the question of how different audiences "read" film narratives is to some extent addressed (Derne 2000; Mankekar 2000; Dudrah 2002; Banaji 2006; Rao 2007). Derne's examination of the ways in which "mainstream" male viewers interpret Hindi film messages leads him to analyse their responses in the light of studies which have tended to support the belief that many viewers read "against the grain" of texts (Walters 1995, 77, in Derne 2000). In this respect, Derne acknowledges that there are aspects of his interviewees' responses which support Stuart Hall's notion of oppositional readings of cinema messages; however, he also cautions that whether filmgoers will be sceptical of or adopt cultural messages present in films cannot be taken for granted or known *a priori* (ibid., 11). Arguably then, different individuals and different groups of viewers could position themselves very differently in relation to film discourses. However, this interpretive binary of resistance/acceptance of "film messages" continues to sit uneasily alongside the myriad and contradictory things individual viewers testify to feeling and doing in relation to films. Therefore, with a view to theorising meaning-making which does not fit within that arguably reductive framework, this chapter explores the ways in which young urban Indian audiences reflect on representations of class and family life. It argues that while they are both aware and critical of the absence of representations of working- and lower-middle-class characters in most Hindi films they use existing representations in both pleasurable and critical ways to engage with their own actual and potential contexts and experiences.

Methods

Out of over one hundred young people interviewed in-depth about Hindi films, wider media use and their beliefs, behaviours and attitudes since 2000, this chapter draws particularly on a series of semi-structured pair interviews conducted between December 2007 and September 2009 in Bombay and Delhi. Interviews lasted between one and four hours and were analysed thematically in the light of forms of discourse analysis stemming from social psychology (Potter and Wetherell 1987; Hollway 1989) and in a tradition of audience research that foregrounds individual viewers as parts of a knowing, experienced interpretive community (Barker and Brooks 1998). Thus, although aspects of viewer identity such as class, gender and religion are seen as being significant in inflecting experiences of life and film, interviewees' accounts are presented as part of a snapshot[4] of Hindi film viewing and use rather than as representative of entire communities' viewing positions. Responses were first coded in relation to topics of central significance in textual studies: nation, class, sexuality, sex, gender, religion and education, with further attention paid to aspiration, media and consumption, and moral perspectives about happiness and life. As with all truncated accounts of data generated through interviews, summaries of factual information about interviewees emphasise aspects of their experiences that seemed significant in relation to topics discussed but are not meant to frame all their comments with some extra-textual explanatory power.

Following Miller and Glassner (1997, 101), the language of interviewing cannot be seen as a straightforward reflection of an unproblematic reality. The interview questions and the categorisation in this account, as noted in the conclusion, have resulted in the "fracturing of stories", the telling of parts and not others. Further, despite efforts to reduce the power differential between myself and interviewees by giving them access to details about my life, spending extended periods of time with them viewing films before the interviews, it must nevertheless be noted that interview questions and interventions were sometimes interpreted as inviting very particular responses in light of my position as an adult and an educator. Given tensions over issues relating to sexuality, independence, leisure, relationships and consumption between many young people and their parents in India, permission to discuss these matters was obtained from the parents of the under-fifteen-year-olds, and those interviews were conducted in home settings but with parents in another room. Older young people were interviewed in settings where they did not have to worry about upsetting or offending parents whom they respected but did not necessarily agree with. Trust and confidentiality were maintained throughout (names and details have been altered to maintain anonymity). I was also sensitive to the ways in which some of the issues were felt to be embarrassing in the interview situation: discussing class in any setting can be emotionally fraught. Saliently, following insights suggested by Jay Ruby (1991) in relation to documentaries but equally applicable to other kinds of qualitative fieldwork, I informed each of the young people (excepting one, who had by the time migrated to another city) how I was interpreting and using what they had told me. In one case I accepted corrections to a transcript; in another I agreed that I would include my interpretation alongside an interviewee's critique of that interpretation.

Meaning, Class and Contemporary Hindi Films: Six Viewer Accounts

Jacob (18), a Catholic, and Munni (17), a Hindu, are boyfriend and girlfriend. Both are middle-class. Their fathers are restaurant managers; their mothers housewives. They have been educated at a government-aided school. There are, of course, vast differences between economic power and social positions even within the middle classes of an urban metropolis (Fernandes 2000a; Srinivas 2002) which entail differential experiences of jobs and life choices. Among other affective engagements, anxieties about the ways in which marriages are frequently tied to financial gain for middle-class Indian families emerge as central to their film commentaries:

Munni (glancing at J): I like to laugh. I get upset watching serious films. Always something is going wrong. Usually the girls' or the boys' parents are not accepting something because there is *not enough money* or the religion is wrong . . . But some pictures are nice . . . Did you see *What's Your Raashi*? (*What's Your Star Sign?* 2009, dir. Ashutosh Gowarikar)

Jacob: [sotto voce]: Bekaar (Rubbish) picture . . .

Interviewer: Yes?

Munni: Hmm, everything in that picture is on romance and family and money. You marry someone for money to save your family [. . .]

Jacob: But if you notice carefully, the boy always has an expensive car and stylish jeans and shoes . . . He marries a very rich NRI (non-resident Indian)[5] girl and his grandfather who is a multimillionaire gives him lakhs like it means nothing to them.

Interviewer: But it was a happy ending—you don't approve?

Jacob: It doesn't matter if we approve or not. People will always go to the pictures because where else is there to go? . . . I was disgusted by the emptiness of the story, the lack in ideas other than the initial concept [a man dates women from twelve different star signs after being told he has to choose a wife in six days or lose his inheritance]. The characters have no sense to do anything except escape from their families, or have a wedding and make money. [Pause]. He could have chosen (to marry) the Doctor girl who wants to make a difference in India's villages, but it is clear that though he likes her and she likes him, her proposal that he gives up his expensive job in the US to follow her is unacceptable. It's not just unacceptable to the character of the boy, don't mistake me [. . .] it is unacceptable to the audience of mamas and papas—even to most of the boys and girls in the audience. The whole Himalayas would come falling on his head if a man gives up career to follow his wife, or if we choose a life of social work over a life of successful business . . . And the girl he does marry—she was independent at the beginning, she had chosen to marry a man who is half African. He is caught cheating on her.

Munni: It was just to watch. Eye-candy. I enjoyed it, but it didn't teach me. In our situation (shyly) we have to think how would we live without too much of money, just on our two jobs if our parents do not accept.

Interviewer: But there are films that do "teach you"?

Jacob: I don't watch Hindi films to learn.

This excerpt reveals tensions felt around family and personal choice as well as the ways in which this inflects readings of and feelings towards specific film narratives. Munni's wish to learn from Hindi films ("it didn't teach me") which might support her immediate circumstances—she is dating a young man from a different religion—is offset by her emphasis on forgetting the seriousness of her situation, laughing, being entertained. She names a recent light romance, *What's your Raashi?*, as fun to watch. She suggests with irony that the ethics of the film are dubious: "you marry someone for money to save your family", clearly acknowledging that this is *not* what she hopes to do.

Jacob too uses the film subtexts to voice discomfort with his own life circumstances and with wider social practices he has observed. The film's inability to endorse non-mainstream (feminist, culturally challenging or non-monetary) life-courses for a young Indian middle-class man and his dissatisfaction with the stereotyped imaginaries offered—"the boy always has an expensive car and stylish jeans and shoes"; "she was independent at the beginning, she had chosen to marry a man who is half African. He is caught cheating on her"—segue with discussions of his parents' world-view and beliefs not quoted (including the fact that he was studying commerce at their behest, rather than arts and literature, his "passion"). All of this suggests how broader non-fiction rhetorics about modern India's economic success since the 1990s (epitomised by the politically motivated "India Shining" campaign of the Hindu Right BJP in 2004[6]) permeate contemporary film representation; and how personal life experiences inflect interpretations for viewers.

Other young people from lower-middle-class families evince distaste for films celebrating wealth and consumption and are priced out of cinema-halls by the tickets. Kadam (13) and Zulaiya (18) are brother and sister. Their mother is a housewife raised in a village. Their father works as an employee for a company. Zulaiya mentions that they are in need of money. Kadam has a hearing impairment. By urging him to excel at sport, his family feel they are protecting him from jibes about disability that are common. Sport features in these young people's accounts as an inspiring life-course:

Kadam: I love cricket. I've watched *Lagaan* over twenty times—on vcd—theatres are too much expensive these days . . . and I like to use the subtitle function to support, you know, if I make mistakes. She's watched *Chak de, India* every time it comes on.

Zulaiya: We watch any movie about sport, even English pictures. We are sport mad in our family. I played cricket too and also hockey . . .

Interviewer: What do you like about films that have sport in them? Why don't you just watch sport on TV?

[. . .]

Kadam: I like to see all the inside stuff like how did they train to become successful, what was their mental picture, mental strength. It takes so much of courage to pursue your dream if your parents and friends are calling you to study all the time–

Zulaiya: *Lagaan, Chak de, India*—it doesn't matter if you are poor or rich. You can be the best. You can beat the opposition. It shows teamwork. You can respect your religion and God will support you to win the game, win the prize. Nowadays in the dirty pictures that are coming all about [lowers voice] "sex" and corruption they are forgetting traditions and forgetting religion to get what they want or they are showing gangs and terrorism, which is against our religion [. . .] K3G was also nice, very good songs, lovely costumes. But they have to make troubles for themselves, because they have so much money, so many cars, in fact helicopters, boats, whatever their heart wishes. That is why the stories are all on families fighting. In fact I know some of the people in this neighbourhood are like this.

The films they choose to comment on extensively construct a sporting team in the image of a united Indian nation with critical forays aimed at regional, caste, class and religious discrimination. For these Muslim teenagers who have grown up in a newly neoliberal India in the wake of two documented anti-Muslim pogroms (Bombay in 1992–1993 and Gujarat in 2002), with religious teachings, paternal expectations and financial scarcity placing conflicting demands on their identities, sport-centred Hindi films could be seen to provide a promise of equality and civic agency. The idea of a benign collective endeavour as opposed to one which overtly centres on a nationalist project which is frequently anti-Muslim (Vasudevan 2001; Chatterji 2003), fortified by hard physical labour (training), self-discipline and competitive drive, which results in ultimate success and in which gender, class, caste and religion are irrelevant but nationalism is rewarded can be seen in both their accounts to prove irresistibly enjoyable. When I discussed my interpretation with Zulaiya, she was at first disconcerted that I should think her religion—in its sociological incarnation, rather than as a faith-based identity—had so much to do with her enjoyment. Her discomfort provoked me to place her filmic preferences in the context of enthusiastic statements about the pleasures of film songs and costumes and more normative and gossipy ones about the idle, dissatisfied rich in her locality, lessening the importance of religion as an interpretive category. However, it is possible to understand her self-positioning in relation to film discourses as both "structural"—linked to her social position in a post-9/11 India— "they are showing gangs and terrorism, which is against our religion"—and initiated by more personal tastes or circumstances. Saliently in this regard, Kadam's description of the interface between sports films and his life treats the films as reflections of a psychological "reality" to which simply watching sport on television does not provide access. This overt acknowledgement of Kadam's use of the films as mentoring devices and pedagogic tools is in marked contrast to Jacob's more sophisticated or more cynical view—"I don't watch Hindi films to learn".

Kaveri (11) and Nimmi (12), cousins, speak of class and consumption interlinked with gender and community. Kaveri's parents work as shop assistants in a small family-run business. They are interested in spirituality and "social improvement" and have taught their daughter not to think about material goods. Nimmi's parents have aspirations, servants and investments, which are paying high dividends.

Interviewer: You were telling me about that film *Fashion* [dir. Madhur Bhandarkar, 2008]. I'm surprised you were allowed to watch that.

[. . .]

Kaveri: [smiling] I think my mamma took us to that picture because she wanted us to think about how you can spoil your life running after material things, running after more. But [shyly] Nimmi was very excited to see all the costumes.

Nimmi [confident]: Why was everything so beautiful and shown again and again by the camera if we weren't supposed to like it? It was like an advert. [Pause]. I would have a balance in my life, not like those models who take cigarettes all the time and drink Pepsi for breakfast. But I want to look good [whispers, English], *sexy*. Some costumes are so beautiful—girls should be able to choose how they dress.

Kaveri: Yes, I agree with her that on one side the films make bad and dirty things very beautiful to watch and then on the other side we are told don't do this, this is not good. So it is hard to know which one to believe. But that is why we have to follow our own upbringing. I know what is right, what is wrong. Designer clothes and high grades in class and lots of money do not make someone a good human being. We should make our philosophy like *Three Idiots* (Rajkumar Hirani, 2009). Do something because it is a good thing to do . . . That way even if you become lame or encounter difficulty or lost your family you still know which path to follow. [Laughing] But most people in our family agree with Nimmi, not with me and my parents.

Interconnected discourses drawn from strands of Gandhian, humanist, feminist and post-feminist thought surface during this exchange. Kaveri's moral imperative is to reject commercial youth culture as well as film representations of feminine perfection and economic achievement. She interprets the outing to see *Fashion*, a film about the glamorous, sleazy life of supermodels, as an attempt at moral education, which, ironically, has failed to work on her cousin. Nimmi, whose parents would be disturbed at the notion of her wanting to appear "sexy" and yet who gratify her every request when it comes to clothing and make-up, acknowledges the visual pleasures of clothing and beautiful women on-screen; she uses Hindi film displays of fashion as a way of inspiring new outfits for herself. In line with her parents' beliefs, Kaveri points out that brands are exclusive in terms of class, and inscribed with problematic versions of femininity. Nimmi too chooses to reinterpret "fashion" through a feminist discourse of autonomy; however, this supports her choice to clothe herself trendily but also in ways that might seem risqué or even completely unacceptable—for a chaste young girl—to conservative members of her family and community ("girls should be able to choose how they dress"). She also raises a perennial question for media literacy about the double-edged openness of interpretation in the depiction of situations and events which are, apparently, being represented disapprovingly: "Why was everything so beautiful and shown again and again by the camera *if we weren't supposed to like it?*" Kaveri sidesteps her cousin's critique of constraints arising from ideological conditioning and contemporary community discourses.

Saliently, critiquing *Fashion*, Nimmi and Kaveri comment on the camera's tendency to linger on shots of what is deemed desirable but to overlay this with overt moralistic dialogues. Referring to such sequences, Leela Fernandes has argued that "tensions stemming from the possibility that globalising forces may overwhelm the Indian nation are displaced onto the terrain of a gendered politics" (2000b, 625) resulting in a "politics of purity". Although this critique might not be specifically applicable to the discursive world of *Fashion*, whose director has a history of challenging gender violence and patriarchy as much as he might decry aspects of global industries, there is clearly truth in the notion that the management of problematic aspects of globalised culture in contemporary India tend to be played out disproportionately, given the underrepresentation of working-class characters, in middle-class women's lives on-screen.

What's at Stake in Discussions of Class, Youth and Film Interpretation in India?

Actual discussions with young people are instructive for textual, audience- and producer-centred accounts of film. A clearly defined range of discourses on sexuality, gender, family, nation and class is in evidence in this chapter, which both replicate and challenge the assumption that coherent changes in textual representations reflect and affect the consciousness of young audiences in some straightforward manner. Notably, here as in my more extended study (2006), critique and enjoyment may be present in the same accounts, as is the case for viewers like Munni, Kaveri and Zulaiya, while contradictions between beliefs expressed about on-screen behaviours or beliefs and viewers' off-screen value systems are a consistent feature of film-related talk. The lower-middle-class young people interviewed for this study evince both enjoyment of the wealthy lifestyles represented through material goods, clothing and holiday destinations in mainstream Hindi films *and* irritation at snobbery, exclusiveness, hypocrisy or didactic morality. However, it is also obvious that critique is far more likely in cases where the young people or children already hold worldviews at odds with particular screen representations, as is the case with Jacob, Kaveri and Zulaiya, who, albeit for very different reasons, are frustrated by many mainstream depictions of gender, sex and class lifestyles.

Additionally, as suggested in discussions with young audiences referenced here and elsewhere (Banaji 2006, 2008), themes like wealth, globalisation and social class are not generally introduced by directors and experienced or used by audiences in isolation from themes such as gender, family, nationalism and sexuality. Several interviewees reference their use of films as potential pedagogic resources or their disappointed expectations when films turn out to offer no new vision. And these "visions" when offered are far from uncomplicated in political terms. The films Kadam feels he learns from are *Lagaan* and *Chak De, India*, both about the building of teams and team spirit, in a profoundly divided society. Both films revert to a now less commonly utilised Hindi film narrative of Indian underdogs against "outsiders": in the first instance the outsiders are the British colonisers, as *Lagaan* is set in the past; in the second they are other national sporting sides, each epitomised in a series of easily recognisable and xenophobic stereotypes. The film Kaveri chooses as epitomising her philosophy and that of her parents is *Three Idiots*, where a working-class college student inspires his two friends to challenge the crushingly conformist educational system and upset class expectations by pursuing their dreams rather than their parents' wishes. Although the last sequence of *Three Idiots* reaffirms financial success and able-bodiedness, other young viewers too maintained that this film was a critique of the "wealth culture" and "exam-culture" which dominates in middle-class, urban India and in contemporary "Bollywood"; several commented ironically that their parents were not willing to "act on this message". A disproportionate tendency on the part of textual commentators on Hindi cinema to read film meanings—and ideological messages—primarily in light of final sequences, or in light of a single, linear viewing, can thus be confirmed as problematic. In fact, audience research in this chapter has emphasised that it is important to approach Hindi films as internally fractured, with contradictory discourses expressed visually and verbally or by songs and narrative moments or different narrative sequences within a single three-hour narrative. Films, like other cultural texts, refer both to *other texts* and to *social worlds beyond themselves*.

I have argued here that both distinctive experiences and shared social formations upon which children and young viewers call in their interpretation of film narratives are acutely relevant to the uses to which they put aspects of film discourse. As Janet Staiger has suggested (2000, 44–54), spectatorial identities may be shaped by intersecting and contingent aspects of history and experience. Evidence in this chapter and my other studies suggests that the appropriation of films in the construction of alternative, pedagogic and/

or pleasurable imaginaries is one of their most widespread uses. Problematically, however, like much research, this chapter presents only a partial snapshot of a far more complicated whole. Space constrains even discussions of class and alternative interpretations of viewers' assertions, rendering far too determinist a picture, and giving little leeway to discussions of exclusions and absences, to what was *not said*, and perhaps to the reasons why some issues do not figure in discussions with these particular young people. Indeed, if one draws on the perspectives of working-class young people and children in both urban and rural areas as I have done elsewhere (Banaji 2006, 2010a and 2010b) then an interesting pattern emerges, with debates over social injustice and political violence occupying proportionately greater percentages of interview space compared to those relating to choice, sexuality and romance. While these are merely heuristic observations emerging from qualitative research, they suggest avenues for future research. A significant minority of the films watched and screened in the past two decades, particularly in the gangster genre, deal either centrally or tangentially with working-class lives; here stereotypes abound and are challenged by working-class young people (Banaji 2006 and 2010b). The consistent stereotyping and/or erasure of the everyday lives of the poor, the working class, regional and minority religious groups from most big-budget films speak both of middle-class arrogance and of fear on the part of producers; this issue was foregrounded in mediated debates around Danny Boyle's *Slumdog Millionnaire* (Banaji 2010b). Textually, this lack of interest in the visual and emotional depiction of the milieu in which a majority of Indian audiences live also signals a distinct break from the overall integrationist postcolonial vision of numerous Hindi films in the post-independence decades and a sense in which capital—in its broadest sense—rather than labour (and "the people") is now constructed as India's strength in the global arena by those who produce much of this fictional representation. However, as is evidenced by my interviewees' responses, the popularity of the films categorically does not stem merely from an endorsement of this new upper-middle-class vision among all sections of the audience.

Notes

1. In a series of films—*Roti Kapda aur Makaan* (*Bread, Clothing and a House*, 1974, dir. Manoj Kumar), *Trishul* (*Trishul*: Three Pronged Weapon, 1978, dir. Yash Chopra) and *Deewar* (*The Wall*, 1975, dir. Yash Chopra)—directors showcased the emptiness of economic achievement if unaccompanied by loyalty, integrity, maternal love or national pride.
2. E.g., (*Yaadein* (*Memories*), dir. Subhash Ghai, 2001; *Kabhi Kushi Kabhi Gham* (*Sometimes Happiness, Sometimes Sorrow*), dir. Karan Johar, 2003)
3. A term used by bell hooks to describe her experience of challenging an adult authority figure (http://writingcollaboration.wordpress.com/1-introduction/1a-bell-hooks/).

68   *Shakuntala Banaji*

4. Used here to mean a moment in cultural time and space that has absorbed and thus reflects key meanings, values and discourses from its surrounding sites of culture.
5. NRIs live and work in Europe or the US and have featured increasingly in post 1980s blockbusters.
6. http://www.indiatogether.org/2004/mar/edu-heads.htm; http://news.bbc.co.uk/1/hi/world/south_asia/3756387.stm

References

Banaji, Shakuntala. 2006. *Reading "Bollywood": The Young Audience and Hindi Film.* Basingstoke: Palgrave-Macmillan.
———. 2008. "Fascist Imaginaries and Clandestine Critiques: Young Hindi Film Viewers Respond to Violence, Xenophobia and Love in Cross-Border Romances." In *Filming the Line of Control: The Indo–Pak Relationship through the Cinematic Lens,* edited by Meenakshi Bharat and Nirmal Kumar, 157–78. Oxford: Routledge.
———. 2010a. "'Adverts Make Me Want to Break the Television': Children's Responses to the Audiovisual Media Environment in India." In *South Asian Media Cultures: Representations, Contexts and Audiences,* edited by Shakuntala Banaji, 51–72. London: Anthem Press.
———. 2010b. "'Seduced Outsiders' Versus 'Sceptical Insiders?': Approaching Slumdog Millionaire through Its Re/Viewers." *Participations: Journal of Audience and Reception Studies* 7 (1): n.p. http://www.participations.org/Volume%207/Issue%201/banaji.htm.
Barker, Martin, and Kate Brooks. 1998. Knowing *Audiences: Judge Dredd, Its Fans, Friends and Foes.* Luton: University of Luton Press.
Barnouw, Erik, and S. Krishnaswamy. 1980. *Indian Film.* New York: OUP.
Bharucha, Rustom. 1995. "Utopia in Bollywood: *Hum Aapke Hain Koun . . . !*" *Economic and Political Weekly* 30(15): 801–4.
Bharucha, Rustom. 1998. In the name of the secular: contemporary cultural activism in India. Oxford and New Delhi: OUP.
Bhatt, Chetan. 2001. *Hindu Nationalism: Origins, Ideologies, and Modern Myths.* Oxford: Berg.
Chak de, India! (Go For It, India!). 2007. Shimit Amin, dir. Distributor: Yash Raj Films.
Chatterji, Saibal. 2003. "War Films Are Right Up the Parivar's Street." *The Hindustan Times,* November 20.
Deewar (The Wall). 1975. Yash Chopra, dir. Distributor: Trimurti Films Pvt. Ltd
Derne, Steve. 2000. *Movies, Masculinity and Modernity: An Ethnography of Men's Film-Going in India.* Westport, CT: Greenwood Press.
Dudrah, Rajinder. 2002. "Vilayati Bollywood: Popular Hindi Cinemagoing and Diasporic South Asian Identity in Birmingham." *The Public* 9(1): 19–36.
Dwyer, Rachel. 2000. *All You Want Is Money, All You Need Is Love.* London: Cassel.
Fernandes, Leela. 2000a. "Restructuring the New Middle Class in Liberalizing India." *Comparative Studies of South Asia, Africa and the Middle East* 20(1–2): 88–104.
———. 2000b. "Nationalising 'The Global': Media Images, Cultural Politics and the Middle Class in India." *Media, Culture & Society* 22(5): 611–28.
Hodge, Bob, and David Tripp. 1986. *Children and Television.* Cambridge: Polity Press.
Hollway, Wendy. 1989. *Subjectivity and Method in Psychology: Gender, Meaning and Science.* London: Sage.
Juluri, Vamsee. 1999. "Global Weds Local: The Reception of *Hum Aapke Hain Kaun . . . !*" *European Journal of Cultural Studies* 2(2): 231–48.

Kazmi, Fareed. 1999. *The Politics of India's Commercial Cinema: Imaging a Universe, Subverting a Multiverse.* New Delhi: Sage.

Lagaan (Tax). 2001. Ashutosh Gowarikar, dir. Distributor: Sony Pictures Classics.

Maine Pyar Kiya, I've Fallen in Love. 1989. Sooraj Barjatya, dir. Distributor: Rajshree Productions.

Malhotra, Sheena, and Tavishi Alagh. 2004. "Dreaming the Nation: Domestic Dramas in Hindi Films Post-1990." *South Asian Popular Culture* 2(1): 19–37.

Mankekar, Purnima. 2000. *Screening Culture, Viewing Politics: Television, Womanhood and Nation in Modern India.* New Delhi: OUP.

Mathur, Vrinda. 2002. "Women in Indian Cinema: Fictional Constructs." In *Films and Feminism: Essays in Indian Cinema*, edited by Jasbir Jain and Sudha Rai, 65–72. Jaipur: Rawat.

Miller, J., and B. Glassner. 1997. "'The Inside and the Outside': Finding Realities in Interviews." In *Qualitative Research: Theory, Method and Practice*, edited by David Silverman, 99–112. London: Sage.

Nair, Bindu. 2002. "Female Bodies and the Male Gaze: Laura Mulvey and Hindi Cinema." In *Films and Feminism: Essays in Indian Cinema*, edited by Jasbir Jain and Sudha Rai, 52–58. Jaipur: Rawat.

Nandy, Ashis. 1998. Introduction to *The Secret Politics of Our Desires: Innocence, Culpability and Indian Popular Cinema*, edited by Ashis Nandy, 1–18. New Delhi: OUP.

Potter, Jonathan, and Margaret Wetherell. 1987. *Discourse and Social Psychology: Beyond Attitudes and Behaviour.* London: Sage.

Rao, Shakuntala. 2007. "The Globalization of Bollywood: An Ethnography of Non-Elite Audiences in India." *The Communication Review* 10(1): 57–76.

Roti Kapda aur Makaan (Bread, Clothing and a House). 1974. Manoj Kumar, dir. Distributor: Digital Entertainment Inc.

Ruby, Jay. 1991. "Speaking For, Speaking About, Speaking With, or Speaking Alongside–An Anthropological and Documentary Dilemma." *Visual Anthropology Review* 7(2): 50–67.

Saldanha, Arun. 2002. "Music Space and Identity: Geographies of Youth Culture in Bangalore." *Cultural Studies* 16(3): 337–50.

Shukla, Arti. 2005. "Pakistan through the Window: Identity Construction in Hindi Cinema." Culture Wars. http://culturewars.org.uk/2005–01/indopak.htm.

Srinivas, Lakshmi. 2002. "The Active Audience: Spectatorship, Social Relations and the Experience of Cinema in India." *Media Culture Society* 24: 155–73.

Staiger, Janet. 2000. *Perverse Spectators: The Practices of Film Reception.* New York: New York University Press.

Thomas, Rosie. 1985. "Indian Cinema: Pleasures and Popularity." *Screen* 26(3–4): 116–31.

Three Idiots. 2009. Rajkumar Hirani, dir. Distributor: Reliance BIG Entertainment.

Trishul (Three-Pronged Weapon). 1978. Yash Chopra, dir. Distributor: Yash Raj Films and Trimurti Films.

Valicha, Kishore. 1988. *The Moving Image.* Bombay: Orient Longman.

Vasudevan, Ravi. 2001. "Bombay and Its Public." In *Pleasure and the Nation*, edited by Rachel Dwyer and Christopher Pinney, 186–211. New Delhi: Oxford University Press.

Vishwanath, Gita. 2002. "Saffronizing the Silver Screen: The Right-Winged Nineties Film." In *Films and Feminism: Essays in Indian Cinema*, edited by Jasbir Jain and Sudha Rai, 39–51. Jaipur: Rawat.

What's Your Raashi? (What's Your Star Sign?). 2009. Ashutosh Gowarikar, dir. Distributors: UTV (India); IG Interactive Entertainment (UK) and Video Palace House of Distribution (Canada).

Part II
Readers and Publishers

4 Does the North Read the South?
The International Reception of South African Scholarly Texts

Elizabeth le Roux

Introduction

Questions of who reads whom and who reads what are closely linked to global power relations. Books are not read in isolation; rather, as Isabel Hofmeyr argues, their readerships and circulation are embedded in transnational networks and structures (2005). Because of this, issues of reading should not be divorced from their material context, including the wider publishing context. The structure of publishing as an industry reflects the unequal power relations at play in so many other contexts (political, economic, social): a small number of powerful multinational companies work in the powerful centres of publishing, and a host of smaller publishing houses operate within local and niche networks. Moreover, the international structure of book distribution equally reflects these market dynamics, affecting which books are sent where in the world, and determining (to some extent, at least) who reads what.

When the question of access and the ethics of access to knowledge arises, the problem tends to be defined in terms of an information divide between centre and periphery, "North" and "South", or "developed" and "developing" nations. During the colonial period, raw materials flowed to the centre, and finished goods, including cultural products such as books, to the periphery. Only rarely was this traffic able to flow in the other direction: "in terms of cultural production, the relationship is emphatically one of dependence" (Van der Vlies 2006, 2). Since decolonisation, this picture has been disrupted, and the model of centre and periphery itself has been called into question, as Hofmeyr (2005), among others, points out, but the most significant flow of cultural products remains from North to South. This flow, moreover, as analysed by a number of commentators over the years, has not solved the "book hunger" (Barker and Escarpit 1973) of so many still-developing countries. The solution usually proposed for this apparent predicament tends to be couched in the language of assistance or altruism, and funded by donors: to send books *to* the countries of the global South, to set up channels for ensuring that the literature (often conceived as fiction, not non-fiction, except for textbooks) of the North is available in the emerging economies and developing countries—with initiatives such as Book Aid and subsidised journal supply programmes. A complementary effort to send books from the South to the North has been attempted only on a small scale. As Britz and Lor point out, "[t]he South-North flow of information from the developing countries to the developed receives less attention" (2003, 161). This issue is closely linked to the ethics of reading, and the degree to which writers and researchers in the developed nations have access to material produced and published in developing areas, and, of course, vice versa.

Theorists have suggested that the complex nature of circulation and interplay in both the colonial and postcolonial periods has meant that a simple model of centre and periphery is not sufficient when considering how books circulate (Hofmeyr 2005). For instance, they point to a trend that has been discernible for some time now, of the so-called margins "talking back" to and in turn influencing the imperial centre; South African writers such as Nadine Gordimer, J. M. Coetzee and, more recently, Zoë Wicomb have all engaged in "writing back" to the centre and debated their place on the "margins" (Parker 1994). Furthermore, it has been suggested that such writers are specifically writing with an international, "cross-border" reader in mind (Nkosi 1994). Later studies by Andrew Van der Vlies (2006) and Clive Barnett (1999) analyse the reception of certain South African texts in the transnational economy, and Hofmeyr and Kriel seek to show "how, through this movement of symbolic capital, a particular idea of 'South Africa' is created in a global arena" (2006, 17).[1] These currents and cross-currents of book circulation destabilise the pattern of a North-South polarity.

Nevertheless, when considering whether locally published books find an international readership—or become "small texts on a world-wide stage" (Boehmer 2004, 257)—we often encounter the perception that the "mainstream markets in the dominant global knowledge economies are not receptive to publications from developing countries on the margins of the . . . publishing world" (Van der Vlies 2006, 2). Ripken (1991, 289) points out, bluntly, that "books published in Africa are hardly being noticed in Europe"; Nyamnjoh (2004) and Zeleza (2002), among others, argue eloquently that the playing field is not level for African publishers *or* authors, and that a politics of cultural exclusion is at work. Ripken, again, is blunt: "[w]hen it comes to the problem of whether African literature is being seen as part of world literature, I am tempted to use strong words: it is not only quantitatively marginal, it is also qualitatively marginalized" (1991, 290). The "most charitable explanation for this may be that the African journals [and books] are perceived as being difficult to access in Europe or North America. A less charitable explanation is that work published in African journals is simply dismissed a priori when a literature search is undertaken" (Britz and Lor 2003, 163).

One of the key sites of interaction for a transnational audience is that of knowledge production, and more specifically scholarly knowledge production. But there is a significant gap in research: the majority of studies of

African publishing and its distribution focus on the reception of literature or literary fiction (including most, if not all, of the studies mentioned earlier), and there is little analysis available of the situation with regard to non-fiction or academic publishing and reading—an important element of the global knowledge economy. A case study of scholarly publishing provides interesting insights into the global circulation of texts, precisely because scholarship itself is increasingly being conceptualised as global, as transnational and as based on the sharing of (usually published) knowledge, often in a global language such as English.

In this chapter, an examination of texts, their material contexts, and specifically their circulation and reception (their "socialisations", to use Jerome McGann's (2002) term) reveals how scholarly texts are received, circulated and evaluated in international knowledge economies. In the context of a potentially global market and audience for literature and knowledge, wherever it may be produced, this chapter interrogates aspects of the international circulation and consumption of South African scholarly publishing. Given the globalised nature of publishing as an industry, and of academia as a profession, the question is asked: in today's digital and interlocking environment, is it important where a text is published?

Strategies of Circulation

What is a "locally" published text? It is true that there are complications when it comes to defining a "local" publisher, in a context where some of the best and most innovative "local" publishing is carried out by the South African branches of multinational publishers, such as Oxford University Press, Random House and Penguin. As a result, "[i]n Africa, concerns loom large about how local books are to be published in an environment in which the economic and political interests of multinational firms dominate" (Altbach and Teferra 1998). These firms often have large marketing departments, which are able to market the texts they publish in a number of territories. They also have better access to and even vertical integration with bookselling networks—an exclusive and exclusionary network of power. Smaller publishers are immediately placed at a disadvantage.

Marketing and the creation of awareness are key to the question of whether a text is widely circulated and read. It has been suggested that "African writers do not get on the world stage via African publishers except through activities like Africa's 100 best books prepared and promoted by ZIBF [Zimbabwean International Book Fair], ABC [African Books Collective] and others, and some activities of NGOs (Reading Africa, African Book Trail) working with library and book group promotions" (Smith 2005, 2). In other words, highly focused and specialised marketing efforts are usually required to overcome the broader obstacles of disseminating African publishing. Yet Hans Zell (2003, 6) notes (and Chakava 1997 concurs) that "promotion and marketing remains an area that is weak at home and abroad, and vis-à-vis the overseas markets, there is the dismal failure of many African publishers to bring their books to the attention of a world-wide buying public".

It is easy to see what Zell means when he refers to the lack of marketing and awareness-creation strategies among African publishers. Try to locate the websites of a host of such publishers, and you will find either nothing or a very meagre offering. This low visibility means that Smith's findings still stand and many African publishers are not on the "Internet world map" (Smith 2005, 3). In the age of Google and Amazon, and with growing evidence that the "long tail" of backlist titles may create ongoing revenues over the Internet, this could be seen as a fairly simple strategy for publishers to create a presence and to register on the radar of their potential readers. Moreover, "[t]o a certain extent, on the Internet, no one cares where those publishers are in the physical 'world map'. So a book from Nigeria can occupy this space as legitimately as one from Norway, New Zealand or Nicaragua" (Smith 2005, 4). But what this simplified vision of publishing's distribution system does not take into account is that even an online presence demands an active and committed reader, who is willing to seek out publications and publishers of interest, and to order them directly (and to trust that they will arrive, undamaged and in good time).

Once an awareness has been created that a book is "out there", the next, and linked, step is to ensure that the texts are physically available and accessible to readers around the globe. This, too, is easier said than done. While initiatives such as Book Aid aim to make books from the North available in the South, there are only a few that concentrate on information flows from South to North. A notable example was Reading Africa, which "began as a project to support the publicising of the list of Africa's 100 Best Books" and which had the main aim of contributing "to raising awareness of, and interest in, African writing and publishing and to encourage reading of African books in the UK" (SABDET, 2008). The aims of Reading Africa were:

1. To publicise the list of 'Africa's 100 Best Books of the 20th Century';
2. To raise awareness of the potential of the list for reading promotion, learning about Africa and African writing and publishing, and encouraging the wider dissemination of African-authored books;
3. To bring together key players in achieving the dissemination and promotion of African-authored books, including publishers, writers, booksellers and distributors, librarians, book and reading promotion organisations, educators and African-interest groups;
4. To facilitate and encourage networking and the emergence of practical marketing, promotional and educational initiatives.

However, with a loss of donor funding, the Southern African Book Development Trust that ran Reading Africa was closed down in 2008. At the same time, the list of Africa's 100 best books appears to have been a one-off marketing initiative, perhaps linked to the decline of the Zimbabwe International Book Fair and its specific aims and agenda. (The decline of ZIBF may be partly attributed to the political situation in that country, but the ongoing difficulties surrounding the Cape Town International Book Fair reveal that the North-South dynamics of the publishing industry are also at play. Supported by the pre-eminent symbol of Northern book circulation, the Frankfurt Book Fair, the CTBF nonetheless received little participation or interest from metropolitan publishers.)

The African Books Collective (ABC) was specifically created in an attempt to resolve the twin issues of awareness and distribution, "to improve the free flow of communications through published material from Africa to the North" (Ljungman and Singh 2006, 3), by acting as a distributor for African publishers in the UK and US. It, too, has struggled with sustainability after the withdrawal of Scandinavian donor funding, which points to the concern that the global publishing industry is so skewed in favour of the North that African publishers can, potentially, be assisted only through the intervention of donors. And what happens when this funding is withdrawn, or when priorities change? This is a perennial problem of dependence on donor funding, and ABC's response to this was to establish a more sustainable business model based on print-on-demand. Yet, while it has shown some success in creating revenue flows for its 124 African publisher members through more widespread distribution and improved revenue flows, it is difficult to assess whether it has really had much impact. Sales figures have certainly grown, but a 2006 report revealed annual remittances to the entire group of member publishers as being in the region of £184,000 (Ljungman and Singh 2006, 20). This does not indicate a significant flow of books from South to North.

A further strategy used to achieve inclusion in wider, more mainstream distribution networks is that of co-publishing: a strategy that complicates questions about the localities of book publishing. A good example of "engaged" co-publishing is that of James Currey. Their specific publishing strategy—as a UK-based publisher of work on and by Africans—has been to co-publish with a network of publishers in Africa:

> We set up our firm to publish the large amount of excellent work by academics, both in Africa and universities across the world, which was emerging in the sixties and seventies. We hoped that we had a good chance of surviving as a "niche" publisher of academic studies in clothbound editions at high prices supplying the library shelves of the rich world with worthwhile but inaccessible academic studies of Africa. (Currey 2002, 6)

Specifically focusing on scholarly publications, James Currey has enabled a variety of publishers in African countries to reach a wider audience—and at the same time to maintain accessible pricing levels in their national markets. The use of a joint imprint creates exposure in the direction of both markets, or even multiple markets when territorial rights are sold to a larger group of participating publishers. This collaboration has been beneficial for South African scholarly publishers, among others, who strive to reach a "niche" audience, which is also potentially a highly dispersed and globalised community of scholars.

Distributing South African Scholarship

The question of the cross-border readership of South African scholarly publishing can be examined through three main axes: their distribution channels, outside of South Africa; their key marketing strategies to the "outside"; and the reception or impact of their texts, as measured through the existence of book reviews. Although at times it is difficult to obtain definite figures, some indicative trends emerge concerning the locations of distribution networks, publishers' strategies for improving global awareness and audience reception. For the publishers in question—Wits University Press (WUP), University of KwaZulu-Natal Press (UKZN Press), Unisa Press, University of Cape Town (UCT) Press and HSRC Press—the policy (and politics) of publishing in a global language, such as English (which automatically inserts the text into a "supra-national" system of publishing), is central to understanding the strategies for making texts accessible to a world-wide audience.

These issues—complicated in themselves—are further complicated by the asymmetrical power relations among nations and corporations, and by (often negative) perceptions of publications from an unfamiliar or even unknown area. For example, after years of unsuccessful attempts to develop a relationship with a mainstream distributor in Europe, a group of South African scholarly publishers was finally able to sign an agreement with a large academic distribution agency, Eurospan, after forming a consortium (this informal association is known as CAIPSA, the Consortium of Academic and Independent Publishers of South Africa). Distribution agreements with US distributors have, perhaps because of the size of the market, been much easier to sign on an individual basis. The use of mainstream international distributors has, according to the Directors of UKZN (who distribute through International Specialized Book Services), WUP (Transaction Publishers) and HSRC Press (IPG) when interviewed, become more lucrative and successful in recent years—but it was stressed that the first few years with a distributor usually bring in very low revenues.

In spite of such efforts to reach agreement with international distributors, a perception, which has prevented a number of academics from publishing with the South Africa university presses, is that their reach is very limited.

This perception recurs regularly in meetings, workshops and publications on scholarly publishing (see e.g., Ngobeni 2010). For instance, in the early 1980s WUP authors were regularly complaining that "WUP does not sell enough books" (Wilson 1983, 2). Yet the reality is that these presses have been concerned with distribution from their inception. In 1922, when WUP published the first title under its imprint, it already used Longmans, Green & Co in the UK as distribution agents because of an awareness of the importance of widespread dissemination of research work. Correspondence regarding distribution can be found throughout the archives of the university presses. For instance, there is ongoing correspondence between WUP and Oxford, concerning possible distribution in the UK, as well as with a range of other booksellers and distributors, including Simpkin Marshall and Kegan Paul. The Wits point of view is put across clearly in a letter written to OUP in 1941: "We feel that publishing in this country, while it is satisfactory as far as the Union [of South Africa] is concerned, will not give adequate publicity to what we consider to be useful material" (Raikes and Milford 1941).

Distribution in the US was not as successful as in the UK, based on WUP sales figures, but efforts were also made in the direction of the largest English-language market for books. In 1948, WUP actually declined representation in New York, writing that "We have so few publications of interest to the American people" (Freer and Hoffman 1948). This feeling was to change. In the mid-1950s, Dr C. Kenneth Snyder, the US Cultural Affairs Officer, gave WUP advice on the matter, and as a result an approach was made to several US university presses to act as agents for WUP books. There was no success from these approaches, but efforts continued, and today WUP enjoys a close working arrangement with Transaction Publishers to distribute their work in the US.

These distribution strategies tend to focus on the key audiences located in the North, especially in the major English-language markets of the UK and US. UCT Press (although owned by a commercial textbook publisher, Juta) has pursued co-publishing contracts with international publishers, such as Lynne Rienner Publishers in the US and Zed Books in the UK, and sees this as a specific strategy to make books cost-effective through economies of scale. While there is some rhetorical adherence to the notion of promoting South-South ties through the sharing and dissemination of ideas, in practice such connections have been made only very seldom, and then on an ad hoc basis. For instance, Unisa Press has signed a (ground-breaking) co-publishing arrangement with Penguin Books India for the distribution of a single, selected title from a series (*Eyes Across the Water: Navigating the Indian Ocean*, edited by Pamila Gupta, Isabel Hofmeyr and Michael Pearson). Ties with Africa—in spite of rhetorical flourishes (such as Unisa Press (2006) claiming to be "a growing voice on the African continent" in its marketing material and WUP (2008) claiming on its website that it is "strategically placed at the crossroads of African and global knowledge production and dissemination")—tend to be weak, and distribution poor. Of course, it could be argued that South Africa is a centre as far as African knowledge production and publishing are concerned, and the rest of Africa diverse sites of margins. But this centre has, on the whole, failed to engage with or penetrate these margins in any significant way. The circulation of knowledge thus continues to flow along the lines established during empire.

Two other distribution strategies have created a slightly different picture. One is the sub-licensing of subsidiary rights, and specifically foreign language rights in other territories. While none of the South African scholarly publishers has been proactive in selling rights, until quite recently, all have sold translation rights from time to time, largely as a result of ad hoc requests. In 1957, for instance, WUP sold their first translation rights, for Martienssen's *The Idea of Space in Greek Architecture with Special Reference to the Doric Temple and Its Setting* into Spanish (first published in 1956, the Spanish edition was published in 1958 by Editoral Nieva Visión of Buenos Aires). This title also saw a US edition, with territorial rights being sold. It is interesting to note that this example reveals South-South interaction, and indeed Spanish-language rights for South African titles tend to be sought by South American publishers. If such a linkage could be pursued as a coherent strategy, it would complicate the North-South binary in interesting ways, introducing a cross-border readership in other areas of the South as well as across linguistic divides.

The second distribution strategy that is successfully reaching a wider audience globally is the increased use of technology in the sense of selling books online (through www.kalahari.net, the local version of Amazon) or through a publisher's own e-commerce site. The Human Sciences Research Council (HSRC) Press has gone further in using technology than any other South African publisher: all of their titles are available in open access form on their website, as well as being available for purchase in print editions. The HSRC Press reveals an increase in sales of up to 247 percent on some titles, thanks to this strategy, as well as widespread readership, often in quite unexpected places (Bruns 2008). Former director Garry Rosenberg (2008, 7) notes that the HSRC Press "distributes books in three regions comprising about 11 countries, but has online readers from 184 countries". Thus, it appears that the physical distribution of printed books limits the possibility for transnational circulation, while at the same time the use of technology (open access, print on demand) could destabilise this binary into a picture of multiple, intersecting sites of circulation and readership.

A related strategy that is being developed is that of engaging directly with communities of readers, especially through social networking sites, although this requires a great deal of market and other research on the part of the publisher. Readers gain agency through such a strategy, and emerge not just as passive consumers, but as engaged in active dialogue with the publishers. Interestingly, this strategy was highly effective during the apartheid period, as resistance activism created a "ready-made" audience for many oppositional titles—an instance of an ethical force outweighing the usual market forces. As Peter D. McDonald (2009) has shown, the repressive effects of apartheid on the publishing industry also forced many authors to publish abroad, usually in the North, which in turn guaranteed a wider transnational audience. This large, international and highly engaged audience has all but disappeared with the ending of apartheid. As David Philip (2000: 48), himself a respected publisher of scholarly work in South Africa, pointed out at the end of the apartheid period, "South African publishers are already welcome back into the world. They should expect to find themselves of less absorbing interest to it", leaving publishers with the unenviable task of seeking out new readerships with an interest in South Africa and its knowledge production.

Creating Awareness Across Borders

In contrast to distribution, marketing efforts appear not to have featured strongly on the agendas of the local scholarly publishers. In 1948 (a full twenty-six years after their establishment), WUP produced their first list of books published—a precursor to later catalogues. They also began to advertise sporadically in journals, around 1947. Their first international exhibition was in Chicago in 1957, and from 1964 WUP began to exhibit at the Frankfurt Book Fair (where they are still regular visitors) and other exhibitions in London, Paris and Hong Kong. The first proper publications list at Unisa was produced in 1972/1973, sixteen years after establishment. Marketing and awareness creation efforts have, however, improved in recent years. The scholarly publishers all have active websites, with catalogues, information for authors and blog-style news. Direct marketing to libraries and academics is carried out, and exhibitions at conferences, such as the American African Studies Association meetings, provide much-needed international exposure. Attractive and useful print catalogues are produced, and book fairs are attended—although generally in the metropolitan centres of Frankfurt and London, as well as the local Cape Town Book Fair, but emphatically not in the global South. Once again, a pattern emerges of an engagement and interaction between centre and periphery, but not among the margins. At the level of marketing, then, the potential for diversification of markets, opening up readerships in multiple sites, has not yet been realised.

Another means of identifying a global pattern of circulation is to examine the international reviews published of South African scholarly texts. While reviews cannot stand entirely as a proxy for readership, they do provide evidence of global reach, and of insertion into the key metropolitan processes of reception and criticism. One trend that can be identified is that particularly the books published by WUP and Natal appear to have been widely reviewed, world-wide, and received with some respect well into the 1960s, before a decline in the 1970s and 1980s. This shows a global pattern of circulation, and of interest in South African books before the high point of apartheid repression and the academic boycott. For example, as early as 1942, Dr Kurt Colsen's *Fractures and Fracture Treatment in Practice* was being hailed by the *BMJ* as "a South African product which should export well" (*BMJ* 1943, 169) and a US edition of the textbook was produced by Gruno and Stratton in New York in 1945. Moreover, as this was a work highly sought after by military surgeons, WUP had no difficulty in obtaining permission to print from the Controller of Paper, and in sourcing sufficient paper supplies despite restrictions. The textbook was prescribed in South Africa for twenty years (Hutchings 1969, 44).

A 1950 review of Hilda Kuper's "depressing" study of interracial relationships in Swaziland, *The Uniform of Colour* (WUP 1947), reveals an awareness of the situation in South Africa, and accepts the work of the author on its own merits: "Despite the gruesome quality of the tale, the author has obviously pulled her punches in what must have been the vain hope of avoiding offense in South Africa" (Goldschmidt 1950, 101). Reviews of celebrated academics such as the Bantu linguists Clement Doke and Desmond Cole acknowledge their contribution to the field, internationally, usually without even remarking on their location or place of publication in far-off South Africa. For instance, a US review refers to their work as "widely influential" and as laying "indispensable groundwork" in the field (Greenberg 1963, 1194). Similarly, the reports published in the Natal Regional Survey by Natal University Press (now UKZN) were very favourably reviewed in journals such as *The Annals of the American Academy of Political and Social Science* (Munger 1954, 200–201).

While only a few selected reviews have been quoted, the pattern that emerges is one of local published works receiving regular reviews in academic journals—in the metropoles of the UK and US—when there is international agreement about the importance of the scholarship, or at times when South Africa is prominent in the global media. Research has shown that in recent years up to 20 percent of South African scholarly books are reviewed internationally, almost entirely in the English-speaking markets of the UK and US (CREST research quoted in ASSAf 2009, 123). Although this might be regarded as a small scale, this penetration is in contrast to the perception that local publishing is not being received well in the metropolitan centres.

Conclusion

An examination of the circulation (marketing and dissemination practices) of South African scholarly publishers in part subverts the received wisdom that African publishers are always consumers, rather than producers, of knowledge. No assumed one-way movement from North to South can be sustained. Nonetheless, an examination of the circulation of academic texts shows that the dominant relationship is still one of a centre/periphery binary rather than of a transnational network.

What this study also shows is that the location of a publisher still does influence the reception of its texts, even in a globalised context—there are still borders to be crossed, even in a so-called borderless world. The physical distribution of books still takes place along the lines of power and authority established in the colonial and early postcolonial period. Moreover, the distribution of books remains expensive, bureaucratic and subject to prejudice and bias from potential buyers. Local publishers have thus turned to a number of strategies, the key ones being the use of international distributors and co-publishing with international publishers. A secondary, but growing, strategy is the use of technology to reach across borders, especially by means of print on demand, online publishing and e-commerce. The intention, explicitly, is to reach a cross-border readership in both local and international markets and to disrupt the North-South binary in favour of a more dispersed network model of circulation. Ironically, it appears that there was more widespread distribution of and interest internationally in South African publishing during the apartheid era, when there was global support for the anti-apartheid movement—an early instance of the communities of interest that contemporary marketing strategies seek to promote.

While this chapter has focused on the international market for South African scholarly work, some have suggested that the local market for South African university press books has disappeared altogether: "While the essential mission of a university press is to publish works for and by academics, and to keep alive scholarly debate in the community, this has become increasingly problematic in the absence of real markets for university press books [in South Africa]" (Gray 2000, 178). This leads to a related perception that university presses are vulnerable: "Scholarly publishing is in decline due to the drop in the levels of funding of universities, libraries and research institutes" (Ngobeni 2010, 80). However, I hold that this is not borne out by current efforts at improving marketing and distribution. Yet, the problem of operating within a transnational context remains. One conclusion that could be drawn is that South African publishers do not really see themselves as global players. The HSRC Press, for instance, argues that "Some of our works are . . . of very particular interest and not appropriate for international publication" (HSRC, 2008). This occurs in a context where an international publisher takes the opposite strategy: Cambridge University Press labels its local, African branch "proudly South African"—a brand recognising significant local investment—and yet continues to have a vision of becoming "the world's most respected publisher" (according to one of its 2008 catalogues). This balancing act, of straddling both the local and the global, has not yet been mastered by the publishers of the South.

84   *Elizabeth le Roux*

Notes

1. Several papers on similar lines were also presented at the Reading after Empire conference in Stirling in September 2008.

References

Altbach, Philip G., and Damtew Teferra. 1998. "Preparing for Multinationals in African Publishing: The Inevitable Impact." *Bellagio Publishing Newsletter* 22. http://www.bc.edu/bellagio.

ASSAf. 2009. *Scholarly Books: Their Production, Use and Evaluation in South Africa Today.* Pretoria: Academy of Science of South Africa.

Barker, Ronald, and Robert Escarpit. 1973. *The Book Hunger.* Paris: Unesco.

Barnett, Clive. 1999. "Constructions of Apartheid in the International Reception of the Novels of J. M. Coetzee." *Journal of Southern African Studies* 25: 287–301.

BMJ. 1943. Review of *Fractures and Fracture Treatment in Practice*, by Kurt Colsen. *BMJ* 7(August): 169–70.

Boehmer, Elleke. 2004. *Colonial and Postcolonial Literature.* Oxford: OUP.

Britz, Johannes J., and Peter J. Lor. 2003. "A Moral Reflection on the Information Flow from South to North: An African Perspective." *Libri* 53: 160–73.

Bruns, Karen. 2008. "Open Access: Why the Fuss?" *Mail & Guardian* March 4, 4.

Chakava, Henry. 1997. "Book Marketing and Distribution: The Achilles Heel of African Publishing." *Development Dialogue* 1997(1–2): 39–60.

Currey, James. 2002. "James Currey Publishers." *BookLinks* (Book Aid International newsletter) 1: 6.

Freer, P., and L. Hoffman. 1948. Correspondence. Wits archival files (uncatalogued), Johannesburg: University of the Witwatersrand.

Goldschmidt, Walter. 1950. "Review: *The Uniform of Colour* by Hilda Kuper", *American Anthropologist*, 52 (1), January–March: 101–102.

Gray, Eve. 2000. "Academic Publishing in South Africa." In *The Politics of Publishing in South Africa*, edited by Nicholas Evans and Monica Seeber, 163–88. Scotsville: University of Natal Press.

Gray, Eve H., F. Van Schalkwyk and Karen Bruns. 2004. "Digital Publishing and Open Access for Social Science Research Dissemination." Paper presented at Codesria conference on Electronic Scholarly Publishing, Dakar, Senegal, September 1–2.

Greenberg, Joseph H. 1963. Review of *Contributions to the History of Bantu Linguistics*, by C. M. Doke and D. T. Cole. *American Anthropologist* 65(5): 1193–94.

Hofmeyr, Isabel. 2005. "The Globe in the Text: Towards a Transnational History of the Book." *African Studies* 64(1): 87–103.

Hofmeyr, Isabel, and Lize Kriel. 2006. "Book History in Southern Africa." *South African Historical Journal* 55: 1–19.

HSRC Press. 2008. "About us." http://www.hsrcpress.ac.za.

Hutchings, M.A. 1969. "Witwatersrand University Press 1922–1969." Unpublished report. Johannesburg: University of the Witwatersrand.

Ljungman, C. M., and T. Singh. 2006. *The African Books Collective: SIDA Evaluation 00/06.* Stockholm: SIDA.

McDonald, Peter. 2009. *The Literature Police.* Oxford: OUP.

McGann, Jerome. 2002. "The Socialization of Texts." In *The Book History Reader*, edited by David Finkelstein and Alistair McCleery. London: Routledge: 39–46.

Munger, Edwin S. 1954. Review of Natal Regional Survey additional report no. 3 and no. 4. *Annals of the American Academy of Political and Social Science* 292: 200–201.

Ngobeni, Solani. 2010. "Scholarly Publishing in South Africa." In *Scholarly Publishing in Africa: Opportunities and Impediments*, edited by Solani Ngobeni. Pretoria: Africa Institute of South Africa: 69–82.

Nkosi, Lewis. 1994. "Constructing the 'Cross-Border' Reader." In *Altered State? Writing and South Africa*, edited by Elleke Boehmer, Laura Chrisman and Kenneth Parker, 37–50. Sydney: Dangaroo.

Nyamnjoh, Francis. 2004. "From Publish or Perish to Publish and Perish: What 'Africa's 100 Best Books' Tells Us About Publishing Africa." *Journal of Asian and African Studies* 39(5): 331–55.

Parker, Kenneth. 1994. "In the 'New South Africa': W(h)ither Literature?" *Wasafiri* 9(19): 3–7.

Philip, D. 2000. 'Oppositional Publishing in South Africa from 1945 to 2000', *Logos*, 2(1): 41–48.

Raikes, H. R., and Humphrey Milford. 1941. Correspondence. Wits archival files (uncatalogued). Johannesburg: University of the Witwatersrand.

Ripken, Peter. 1991. "African Literature in the Literary Market Place Outside Africa." *African Book Publishing Record* 4(17): 289–91.

Rosenberg, Garry. 2008. "Broadening the Exchange of Knowledge." *Mail & Guardian*, June 13, 7.

SABDET (Southern African Book Development Education Trust). 2008. Archive. http://www.europublishing.info/sabdetarchive/index.htm.

Smith, Kelvin. 2005. "African Publishers and Writers in British and International Markets." Paper presented at African Publishing and Writing conference, London, October 17.

Unisa Press. 2006. *Catalogue 2006*. Pretoria: Unisa Press.

Van der Vlies, Andrew. 2006. "'Local' Writing, 'Global' Reading, and the Demands of the 'Canon': The Case of Alan Paton's *Cry, the Beloved Country*." *South African Historical Journal* 55: 20–32.

Wilson, N. H. 1983. "Witwatersrand University Press and Authors." Memorandum to Publications Committee, July 26.

WUP. 2008. "About us". University of the Witwatersrand. http://www.wup.ac.za.

Zeleza, Paul. 2002. "The Dynamics of Book and Library Development in Anglophone Africa." In *The Book Chain in Anglophone Africa*, edited by Roger Stringer. Oxford: INASP: 3–7.

Zell, Hans. 2003. "The Movement of Books." *African Publishing Review* 12(4–6): 6.

Zimbler, Jarad. 2004. "The South African Publishing Context of J. M. Coetzee's *Foe*." *English Studies in Africa* 47(1): 47–60.

5 William Plomer Reading

The Publisher's Reader at Jonathan Cape

Gail Low

In *The Truth About Publishing*, Stanley Unwin drew attention to the important role played by publishers' readers in the process of publishing and also, ironically, of their relative *invisibility*. Unwin wrote that the number of manuscripts that have been "completely recast or improved out of all knowledge at a reader's suggestion is far greater than it is commonly supposed", and yet, the reading public "knows little or nothing about this" and "few are the authors who are prepared to recognize publicly the benefits they have derived from their friendly suggestions and criticisms" (Unwin 1946, 29). Throughout the late nineteenth century and for a good part of the twentieth century, publishers had at least one advisor in addition to their in-house editorial staff who also read and advised on manuscripts.[1] Where houses had primary readers or where readers had worked for the firm over an extended period of time, individuals could wield significant influence within the firm. Examining the role of publishers' readers can help us better understand the interface between aesthetics and commerce underpinning the business of books and shed light on the processes of manuscript selection, gatekeeping practices, canon formation within publishing lists as well author-publisher relations.

Research in book history has begun to document this relatively unexplored aspect of publishing (Fahnestock 1973; Fritschner 1980; Collin 1991; Nash 2003; MacDonald 2009) but much more needs to be done. In relation to recent debates on the commodification of postcolonial literature (Brennan 1997; Huggan 2001; Brouillette 2007), access to the decision-making process may provide evidence of these processes or, equally, provide information that might counter some of these claims. Access to house reports and editorial correspondence gives rare glimpses into the ethos and mindset of the company and also what kind of audiences they imagine their readers to be. As Andrew Nash writes, research into publishers' readers shows not only "what kind of books the firm was interested in; how it set out its parameters in terms of subject matter, literary quality and commercial incentives" but also how the firm "responded to new trends in literature" and to "perceived values and tastes" (176). My research on the publishing of West African and Caribbean writing by metropolitan writers in the post-war period suggests that, as texts cross national and cultural boundaries, questions of (how to) value dominate the selection processes and generated moments of real anxiety for both publishers and writers. Questions of exoticism, audiences and markets crystallised around exactly who publishers were publishing West African or Caribbean writing for and why (Low 2011).

This chapter is based on reading 530 reports located in the Cape papers at the University of Reading Special Collections and aims to add to a potentially rich seam of research. By focusing on a selection of archived reports for Jonathan Cape between 1961 and 1973 that were written by William Plomer, I offer a preliminary investigation of his reading practices and his distinctively cosmopolitan responses for an English publishing house.[2] Except for a short period of time when he served with the Admiralty during the Second World War, Plomer read for, and was involved in key projects with, Jonathan Cape from 1937 until his death in 1973. As a publisher's reader, he is now best remembered for "discovering" Ian Fleming, and latterly, perhaps also for advocating the publication of writers as diverse as Derek Walcott, Ted Walker, John Fowles, Ted Hughes and Arthur Koestler. Yet Plomer was a formidable and established literary persona in England in his own right, particularly in the late fifties and sixties; he was not only a respected writer and librettist but a well-known and well-connected critic who served on the Arts Council, and sat on judging panels of literary prizes. Plomer's broad international outlook and range of interests are reflected in the manuscripts he read; these ranged from thrillers to social and political histories on Africa, China, Tibet or American international relations, in addition to fiction, poetry and drama from the Anglophone and from Europe. He was also asked to read submissions in translation from European languages and in French. In most, if not all, of his detailed reports, he would often write his summary judgements: "Decline", "Very doubtful", "Doubtful", "Well—no", "No enthusiasm from me". "Unusual, but—" and also "For consideration", "Worth Further Consideration", "A possibility", "Recommended", "Highly Recommended" or "Publishable".

Plomer was born to English parents in South Africa. As a boy and young man, Plomer shuttled between South Africa and England. His biographer, Peter Alexander, has argued such a peripatetic youth and his discovery of his homosexuality fostered feelings of being an outsider (1989). He was also secretive about his private life; his sexuality or his love affairs are, for example, glossed over or not discussed in his autobiography (245–46, 298). Plomer did not identify as South African; Alexander records that Plomer would "bristle" if described as a South African (292). Andrew Van der Vlies remarks that Plomer's relationship with the land of his birth was "always ambivalent", at once railing against its colonial "bourgeois philistinism", dissociating himself from the country for most of his career but mellowing in his later years (48). Plomer's father's role as a district officer in the Department of Native Affairs and, later, as a trader and storekeeper in Natal provides a context for Plomer's attitudes towards Africans and towards British colonialism. Thought a "negrophile" (Alexander, 16), Charles Plomer's relations with black Africans were a product of an imperial mindset but such cross-cultural contact brought his son out of an exclusively white, complacent and insular colonial childhood. Plomer's youthful association with Edward Wolfe also influenced his rebellion against a deeply entrenched, racialised colonial culture (Alexander, 43–44). Originally published as *Double Lives*, the first section of *The Autobiography of William Plomer* repeatedly rails against accepted codes of behaviour—"The Thing" one was expected to do (129, 144)—and "the Berlin Wall of racial and social segregation" (166). Wolfe, who painted black Africans, also lent his name and persona to Plomer's first novel of a European painter who runs a store in Lembuland. *Turbott Wolfe*, published by the Hogarth Press in 1926, deals with racism and miscegenation; its publication provoked much hostility in South Africa (Alexander, 97; Van der Post 1985, 10–20). Disowned and banned for a time but then hailed as an early exemplar of literary modernism in South Africa, *Turbott Wolfe* has a significant place in the South African literary canon (Van der Vlies 2007, 48). Plomer also helped found *Voorslag* with Roy Campbell and Laurens van der Post in 1926. The South African literary little magazine, translated as "whiplash", was openly hostile to and deliberately mocking and satirical of the parochial and racist world of South African culture and letters (Alexander, 100). When all three resigned *Voorslag* in some controversy, Plomer travelled with van der Post to Japan, where he lived for three years. Titling his Japanese interlude in his autobiography as "Gone Native", he described Japan as helping him to "understand that Europe was not everything, and to see Europe from a distance through Asian eyes" (205). Finally, Plomer left for England because staying would only mean "the double life of the exile" (219). Plomer adopted a questioning and self-reflexive attitude to questions of identity and culture; he approached England, as he writes in his autobiography, as "a foreigner" without "the comfortable backing of a settled political and social background, a substantive capital, and secure prospects" (236).

Plomer describes his relocation to England in 1929, and his subsequent adaptation, as a period of "re-occidentation" (264). England was not an entirely alien country in so far as he had spent substantive periods of his childhood and youth there. What writing and his cultural and intellectual endeavours offered him was access to a charmed circle of friends and mentors. He made contact with the Woolfs, who had published not only *Turbott Wolfe* but also two volumes of his short stories and a book of poems. He was taken up by the Bloomsbury crowd and soon after his arrival, the Hogarth Press published his second book of poems. Very quickly, he was writing and reviewing regularly, contributing poems to the *New Statesman*, the *Nation*, *Criterion*, *Life & Letters*, book reviews to the *Listener* and *New Writing* among other journals and, later in the fifties, to the *London Magazine*. Plomer also worked as a broadcaster and made regular broadcasts for the BBC. Van der Vlies's assessment of Plomer's career from *Turbott Wolfe* to *The Child of Queen Victoria* is a story of quick transformations and changing cultural orientations: from a writer in South Africa to "serious *English* man of letters" (60–66). By 1937, he had joined Jonathan Cape as a salaried publisher's reader and to take up Edward Garnett's position as Cape's main reader.

According to Plomer, Cape's reputation at this time was "distinguished and respectable" and a little "safe, genteel and a bit dull" (Howard 1971, 170–71); it was also, in the main, unreceptive to and unenthusiastic about poetry. Cape arrived in the publishing world in 1921 with Charles Doughty's *Travels in Arabia Deserta*; over the course of the next two decades, its stable of writers included H. G. Wells, James Joyce, Radclyffe Hall, Mary Webb, T. E. Lawrence and also American writers such as Ernest Hemmingway (Howard, 170, 172). Cape employed a serial succession of primary readers such as Edward Garnett, Plomer and David George (Bunting); the latter two worked together for a spell. Under Jonathan Cape, Plomer's reading duties were to report to Cape's offices one day a week to attend the directors' meeting presided over by Jonathan Cape, where manuscripts accepted or rejected would be discussed. He would submit his written reports and leaf through the slush pile and pick up new manuscripts to take home with him. Later, when Tom Maschler and Grahame C. Greene took over the reins of the company in the early sixties, and reports were kept more systematically, a slightly different picture emerges. A small circle of readers were now in post; manuscripts seemed to be read serially by two readers, and in cases that needed second opinions, manuscripts and reports were passed from one reader to another; often divergences or convergences between the two or three readers were alluded to in their reports and a conversation about the book sometimes ensued. Manuscripts were, of course, also passed to Greene, Maschler and Michael Howard (director and son of one of Cape's original founding partners) to read.

Plomer's own overview of his long stint with Cape is revealing. He wrote of the sheer "drudgery" of the task: the reader had to sit in "his study knee-deep among the empty shells of disappointed expectation" to gain the treasures within. Manuscripts that were rejected were represented as the "kind of writing which titillated the least exacting kinds of reader by appealing to the cheaper and shallower emotions—easy lust, sentimentality, or excitability—and by flattering uncultivated understandings, ignorance, prejudice, self-complacency, and accepted ideas" (Plomer 1975, 357, 355). Reading was thus like diving for pearls. Yet Plomer's metaphor belied the editorial work and suggestions that he and others sometimes contributed to the shaping of manuscripts that were accepted; as he himself adds, the public are "unaware of the great obligations not only of would-be authors, but of accepted and admired authors, to the careful thought, the patient coaching, and the laborious revisions" that make up his tasks (361).

As a publisher's reader, Plomer was obliged to see both the manuscript and its writer as an aesthetic *and* commercial investment. Given both his own literary credentials and preferences, it might be somewhat surprising to learn that "literary" merit was not Plomer's *primary* consideration as a reader even when it constituted a very important one. Reflecting on what he was "likely to commend", he drew up a hierarchy of value:

1. books with literary merit of *some kind* and with good and immediate commercial prospects;
2. books with literary merit and possible long-term commercial prospects;
3. books with literary merit and no prospects of sales;
4. books of topical interest or importance;
5. books that might have prospects if they were improved, reduced, or expanded.

(my italics, 358)

Plomer felt that one had to be as mindful of the firm's reputation, the book's financial success, as much as its "literary merit" or "topical interest". Manuscripts were likely to be rejected if they were "hopelessly obscene or libellous", "out of keeping with his list" or if they were "cheap, pretentious, dim, flashy, or mushy" (358). As literary "barometers", readers were to judge the "timeliness" of the offering, "discern[ing]" the "saturation point" of any particular genre or text. Readers had to be "*au courant* with changes in habits, taste and education, and with the effects upon them of economic change and pressure" (362).

The ideal publisher's reader was one who was knowledgeable of changes in taste and habits as well new literary innovations. To this end, he must be at home in the society that he read for. Plomer's own position as an insider within the literary establishment is evinced by the roles he occupied as writer, reviewer, critic and award judge, and, later, in the CBE conferred on him. For Plomer himself, this occasioned gradual embedding, a "re-occidentation" without losing sensitivity to those marginalised, for example, by racism in a Britain that was coming to terms with the end of empire or to the suppression of homosexuality. In his autobiography, Plomer's invention of an imaginary migrant, Dr Gruber, allowed him to play out this contrapuntal motif of estrangement and dislocation to the narrative's main theme of settlement. The figure of Dr Gruber allows Plomer's narrative voice to signal other versions of himself—"disorders of, a discarded, earlier self" (381)—or other identities that he might have developed. Significantly, the chapter title for this section of *At Home* reads 'If I were Doctor Gruber' (415). Gruber is "a humane and tolerant man with . . . psychological curiosity and powers of observation, and a readiness for varied experience" (415); a Jewish medical doctor whom Plomer imagines as domiciled in England, Gruber is nevertheless still cast as an exile, called "foreigner" in a much similar manner as "words 'nig-ger', 'Kaffir' or 'Jew' are used in various parts of the world" (418). Gruber's residence in England would have caused him to reflect a little upon the rise and decline of the British Empire. In creating a figure who "though natural-ized, as an exile" cannot consider himself at home (421), Plomer is sensitive to what might *not* have been, or how easily one could turn into an outsider. If Plomer's pleasure at being "at home" is where his autobiographical nar-rative finally settles, it is a commitment to an ideal of Englishness that was notably anti-imperialistic, expansive, encompassed change, adaptation, an inclusiveness that was significantly still "part of the strength and wisdom of the English tradition" (395).

At home in England but, equally, aware of others who might not be and of how easily his own set of circumstances might have been different—how does this ambivalence affect Plomer's fulfilment of his role as publisher's reader, and of his sense of who his audience might be? Both Plomer's reports and what he was asked to read indicate that he was not narrowly parochial. While his duties might have been undertaken during a time when publishers' read-ers were expected to read a range of material and not merely in their narrow area of expertise, Plomer's intellectual curiosity, his self-consciousness and anti-colonialism, and his readiness to engage with other cultures indicate the measure of his interest in the wider world, and the political and topical issues of the day; it made him very willing to look at manuscripts relating to politics and history as well literary and cultural affairs. Plomer read manuscripts on American foreign policy, black power and race relations in the US and in South Africa, the United Nations in the Congo, British military history, liter-ary biographies, political autobiographies, travel writing on China and India, literary criticism—even some popular science (albeit with some wariness). He also read literary manuscripts by novelists and poets from Europe and the wider world, including Mexico, Europe, America, China and Tibet, and the Caribbean. While the English-language book market still revolved around an Anglo-American axis, concerns about decolonisation, expanding readerships and markets, and the beginnings of globalisation come through these reports through a desire to know about the wider world, even when possible domestic sales do not always recommend the publication of the manuscript.[3]

Plomer's reports seem to indicate that a writer's background, location and subject matter would not necessarily hinder him or her for commendation for an English publishing house especially if the quality of the submission was high; yet Plomer's reports sometimes make fine distinctions between differ-ent Anglophone markets and seem to return to the question of what would be of interest or would sell to (specifically) English audiences. This seems to be especially true for books that were about to be—or were already—pub-lished in North America. Cape, of course, had a reputation for publishing American writers, initiated firstly by Jonathan Cape and then, later, by Tom Maschler, who continued the Cape tradition of American visits, publishing writers such as Joseph Heller and Phillip Roth. Given the boom in American literature, publishing literary writing from across the Atlantic gave the English publishing house more of an international reputation. Yet in the decade that this chapter is concerned with, Plomer's reports were noticeably careful to make a distinction between English and American audiences, and to query the easy transfer from one English-speaking culture to another. Here one has glimpses of how Plomer's commitment to Englishness might affect how he viewed audiences and texts. In terms of political and historical subjects, the question of topicality and relevance for English audiences was one important consideration, and a manuscript might be dismissed because the writer was "addressing himself to American readers" or the subject was too "American" to be of much interest to English readers.[4] Lawrence Thompson's second volume of Robert Frost's biography, *Robert Frost: The Years of Triumph 1915–1938*, comes in for a sharp response: "Frost wasn't Shakespeare, and we aren't American".[5] Plomer's consideration of Canadian texts seems to signal the limits of that North American world; the label "Canadian" was used as shorthand to indicate the limitations of its appeal in terms of its subject and the provincial nature of its concerns. For example, included in Plomer's recommendations, often written as an epithet or final judgement, is one that reads "lively but Canadian".[6] Although more archival work needs to be done, Plomer's attempts to distinguish between English and North American texts and audiences, sometimes to the detriment of the latter and in keeping with the creation of his own persona, are perhaps a renewed recuperation or a restatement of his Englishness that could be urbane, cosmopolitan and crucially, and interestingly perhaps also anti-colonial or postcolonial, given especially anxieties about the rise of the US as a post-war superpower.

After he left for Japan, Plomer made the journey back to South Africa only once when he was invited by the University of Witwatersrand to deliver a lecture in 1956; the trip led to a renewed interest in South African writing, a direct manifestation appearing in his editorial contributions to the *London Magazine* special South African number, and some of the poetry written soon after. Plomer's archive of papers also indicates that he did keep up a close personal correspondence with writers such as Nadine Gordimer, Jack Cope and Guy Butler, and others whom he met in Witwatersrand; many of these sent remarkably detailed and discerning commentaries on South Africa under apartheid. That these letters were part of an exchange on South African literary culture and politics suggests that he did maintain an interest in and connection with the region. Furthermore, in collaboration with Cope, Plomer helped translate, edit and collate a posthumous volume of Ingrid Jonker's poems published by Cape in 1968. Plomer's own reputation as "anti-imperialist" writer was a clear feature of his public persona (Van der Vlies, 63). Yet as a Cape reader, a frequent theme in his reports throughout the sixties is an expressed reservation about the explicitly politicised material that emerged from the region and whether audiences for such books had not reached their limits. There were, of course, positive reports. Russell Palmer's study of the South African treason trials earned the comment that the author was able to "write directly and factually and to hold the reader's attention"; the "durability" of its subject which would "interest a good many and various readers for sometime" and the book would also appeal to an export market. Ronald Segal's autobiography, *Into Exile*, was commended for "his passionate concern with South African racial and political affairs and his fluency", making it a "decidedly interesting book"; yet in spite of the praise, Plomer also noted, "must one not allow for a certain resistance on the part of a good many intelligent readers to more about S African politics?" John Peter's Doubleday Canadian Prize–winning novel, *Along the Coast*, was judged to be "literate, readable and interesting", but Plomer was ambivalent because "one doesn't warm much nowadays at sight of a novel about South Africa". Douglas Livingstone's poetry was dismissed curtly with the sentence, "half-a-dozen half-baked poems from Natal, showing neither performance nor promise." *The Silent Conspiracy*, by Johannes Meintjes, later published by Michael Joseph, was turned down with the remark that it offered a "highly romantic, sensuous, and in some ways overdrawn picture of South African life" and, crucially, little prospect of a domestic audience for the book.[7] While putting forward Nadine Gordimer's novel, *A Guest of Honour*, "For consideration", Plomer's commendation was distinctly luke-warm about its mixture of politics and literature. Gordimer's intentions to write an "important political novel"–"the Great African Novel"–was found lacking, "inordinately long and devoid of suspense", "misconceived, far too ambitious, and artistically a failure". Plomer complained of the "boredom of the political events, intrigues, and endless sociological instructiveness" and argued that it had little commercial prospect.[8] Gordimer's novel was never-theless published by Cape to critical acclaim, winning the James Tait Black Memorial Prize. In contrast, Alan Paton's memoir, *Kontakion*, which was writ-ten as a part celebration of his recently deceased wife, had for Plomer the "dual appeal of personal (or "private") emotion and political interest." Paton was also a writer of both international stature with bestseller status. Plomer recommended publication, stressing that Paton managed to combine the "professional and political".[9]

Plomer's somewhat contradictory attitude towards South African writing can perhaps be located in the more traditional view of literature as repre-senting more *universalist* concerns rather than what he saw as *narrower politi-cal* ones. This is certainly consistent with Peter D. McDonald's remarks on Cape's framing of Gordimer's work, for global transnational audiences in literary as opposed to sociological or documentary value so as "not [to be] constrained by its [specific] South African setting and concerns" (McDon-ald, 221). But Plomer's wariness about the dominance of the political and abeyance of literary and aesthetic concerns in writing from such conflicted zones, was personal—or was represented as personal. The insistence that literature ought to be "political" was a demand that was of course felt keenly by South African writers; yet Plomer, a product also of the modernist movement, wrote in his autobiography that the demand to be political did not have any "novelty" value for him because he "had to live from an early age among the tensions created by 'problems'" (423). Van der Vlies has recently corrected the erroneous impression that Plomer's reader's report on *Cry the Beloved Country* was overwhelmingly enthusiastic. He reports that Plomer had reservations about Paton's ability to enter into the mindset of black Africans and felt that despite its "considerable merits" as a piece of "social commentary", it was "essentially a propagandist novel" (76). Plomer's judgements seem to indicate that he saw his own preoccupations as a reader in terms of a wider moral and aesthetic concern rather than what for him would be a more restrictive and overtly political one, and this inclination swayed some of his reports on literature despite his recommendations of more straightforwardly political and historical texts to Cape publishers. As MacDonald's research indicates, the vexed and thorny problem of how the literary interfaces with the political, and their relative autonomy or distinctiveness is perhaps more acutely felt in South African textual cultures and its audiences than almost anywhere else.

In contrast with his reports on fiction and non-fiction in this period, Plomer's judgements on poetry are altogether more assured, confident and less likely to request a second opinion. Poetry manuscripts that were accepted were praised for their craft above all else, and established poets who fell short were only very grudgingly admitted through the gates. With poetry, Plomer seems to have felt less pressure to consider commercial considerations; few reports make mention of sales, and where they do, sales are almost always in relation to other verse collections published by the same writer as a Cape book. Plomer's strongly worded and (by his standards) lengthy recommendation of Derek Walcott's *In a Green Night* is a case in point. Plomer's report makes mention of Walcott's "fine technique"; unlike others, Walcott's work was not "obscure" but bore witness to his "clear intelligence, sensibility, powers of observation and a good ear". As I've indicated elsewhere, Walcott's French and English literary influences (these were perhaps important to establish Walcott's literary pedigree) and his ability to work different forms of poetry and mood—elegiac, satirical, love poems, etc.—recast value in terms of aesthetics and prestige that publishing Walcott would confer on Cape (Low, 111). In publishing Walcott, Cape would have much to gain; literary worth would offset the relative poverty of sales. Plomer reminded Maschler that other publishers would bring Walcott out in print if Cape did not:

> I need not draw attention to the doubtful returns to be expected from publishing a book of verse by a new poet. But when the poet has exceptional talent and accomplishment there is a good chance of some immediate recognition and a possibility of long-term advantages.

I have already seen some of this author's work, have thought it quite outstanding, and have found it very well thought of by a number of other poets, and not merely at the London Magazine, which has printed some of Walcott's work. Walcott is 30, and so far as I can see, the best poet in English of his generation. . . . I have no idea how he will develop, or whether he intends only to write poetry. But I have no doubt that he would have no difficulty in finding a good publisher here, and I should like to see Cape's [sic] as his publisher. I think his work, even if it doesn't at once "pay", would give prestige to Cape's list—in which poetry is I believe at present only represented by the dead and the middle aged.[10]

Plomer's recommendation of Walcott's follow-up volume, *The Castaway*, again stressed craftsmanship and feeling for form, showing Walcott's "development of technique and extension of range" marrying what was local and immediate to the Caribbean with "an instinctive, traditional command of idiomatic English and literary instinct".[11] In all his reports, Plomer also emphasised Walcott's alignment with a cosmopolitan and literary Englishness; advance notices for *The Castaway* drew again on Plomer's report, describing the poet as "the bearer of an older culture and the first craftsman of the New World".[12]

In his treatment of Walcott, to use Linda Marie Fritschner's distinctions between late Victorian publishers' readers (1980), one can also see clearly how Plomer behaved more as an "advocate" than as a "gatekeeper". In addition to his overwhelmingly enthusiastic reception of Walcott, Plomer wrote the advance publicity notices for the first three of Walcott's collections of verse. Plomer put forward Walcott's name as one of the poets invited to write for the Shakespeare Quartercentenary, and Walcott's 'Goats and Monkeys' was duly submitted. Plomer also sat on the judging panels for both the Guinness Prize for Poetry and also the Cholmondeley Award. The latter was awarded to poets of talent and merit but also included other criteria such as financial support or long-standing services to poetry.[13] Plomer was very keen to see *In a Green Night* honoured, and his admiration won Walcott other admirers too and Walcott won both awards. He also wrote to Lady Chomondeley before the publication of *Another Life* to commend the long poem with an eye to the 1973 award.[14] Plomer's support of Walcott's work also extended to other areas and a mentoring and nurturing role. When an early version of *Another Life* was submitted to Cape in 1968, Plomer judged the "long elegiac poem" as "characteristically Walcott" with an "acute sense of the 'tristes tropiques' . . . [which] could only have been written by somebody brought up in the tropics." The merits of the poem were evident in its "atmosphere and visual detail", with its "nostalgic, melancholy imagery, and broodings over the evanescence of ambition and hope and love, and the certainty of death". Yet, Plomer had reservations about its structure and pace which he felt was "slow, ambling", "rather on one note" and "less taut and vigorous than previous work". However, these worries and also difficulties in the reading of the poem were mitigated by the "cumulative effect" of its "good lines", and Plomer's sense that the poem represented the most ambitious and "best long poem so far from a Caribbean author". Crucially, Walcott's growing stature as a poet merited support despite Plomer's reservations. Yet Plomer's concerns about the reader's ability to follow the poem were serious enough to warrant a request that Walcott provide a blurb for the poem so as to avoid "misrepresentation", and to "ask him if he would be a little explicit about the region and persons in the poem.[15]

However, two days later Plomer wrote to Maschler after having spoken with Alan Ross of the *London Magazine*, who was instrumental in showing Walcott's first collection to Cape. Plomer, who initially expressed diffidence about asking Walcott for revisions, now seemed more certain of his judgements having heard of both Margaret Walcott and Ross's doubts. He advised Cape against a rushed publication of this early version of *Another Life*, which he felt "rather lax [and] which would get bad reviews and do nothing to strengthen Walcott's reputation".[16] Yet, such was Maschler's enthusiasm for Walcott's work that Cape would have published if Walcott desired it; however, Maschler did inform the poet that Plomer's advice contained sound recommendations.[17] Plomer's letter to Walcott with his recommendations for revision is lost, but Walcott wrote to Plomer conceding some of Plomer's reservations. Given that the prize money from the Chomondeley Award was in hand, *Another Life* was taken back and reworked before final publication in 1973.

To sum then, what was the impact of Plomer's work with Cape? Plomer's influence over the poetry list is perhaps far greater than over the fiction and non-fiction submissions. Plomer is credited by both Howard and Maschler in their history of the firm and their memoirs for reviving poetry's fortunes in Cape. He had greatest influence on the poetry list especially after the appointment of Tom Maschler, and wrote positive reports for the first new poets who appeared in the sixties. Cape's attitude towards poetry had changed from indifference or lukewarm support to a positive investment in poetry (Howard, 316). Edward Baugh and Colbert Nepaulsingh have called Plomer "clearly one of Walcott's most sensitive readers" (2004, 15), and Plomer's reports on Walcott are written with a seriousness and attentiveness to craft that comes from a fellow poet. The legacy of Plomer's "reoccidentation", his commitment to and inhabitation of the position of an Englishman of letters, is evidenced in his desire to distinguish between English and North American audiences for his writing, and in his support for a fellow literary cosmopolitan such as Walcott, with his feeling for English poetry. Plomer's modernist allegiances and his wish to hold onto the distinctiveness of literature might also have made him wary of certain types of South African writing. If Plomer did not possess a "substantial power in shaping policy" which Fahnestock has claimed for Edward Garnett in an earlier period with Cape, Plomer's range of interests, his peculiar combination of Englishness and cosmopolitanism, and his enthusiasms which embrace both the avant-garde and popular thrillers, in many ways, still chimed with and spoke to the catholicity and `internationalized' nature of Cape's list in a postwar publishing world that emerged from the end of Empire.

Acknowledgements

I am grateful to Random House and Duff Hart Davis for permission to quote from William Plomer's reports and letters. Thanks also go to Jean Rose of the Random House Archive and Library, Nancy Fulford and Guy Baxter of the University of Reading Special Collections, and Andrew Gray of the University of Durham Special Collections for facilitating archival access.

Notes

1. This contrasts with today's publishing houses who are likely to use the firm's own editors, or rely on literary agents who have already vetted and edited manuscripts they front.
2. Archived reports were kept systematically only from 1961.
3. See, for example, the reader's report on 'Tom Kaye (Barrington Kaye)', 15/3/61, RR 1961; Report on T. Y. Pemba, 'Idols on the Path', 25/8/65, second report on Han Suyin, 'The Crippled Trees', 12/2/65; RR 1965. Unless otherwise indicated, all reader's reports are drawn from the Jonathan Cape Archives, University of Reading Publishing Archives.
4. See the reader's report on Frank Tannenbaum, 'Mexico: The Struggle for Peace and Bread', 18/12/63; RR 1963, on Charles Silberman, 'Crisis in Black and White', 9/9/64; RR 1964, or Plomer's exasperation with a pile of manuscripts on Robert Frost.
5. Report on Lawrence Thompson, 'The Years of Triumph', 11/2/70: RR 1970.
6. Report on Robert Troop, 'The Sound of Vinegar', 7/3/62; RR 1962.
7. Second report on Russell Palmer, 'The Rivonia Trial' 19/8/64, RR 1964; first report is attached to second report. First report on Ronald Segal's *Into Exile*, 'Reorientations' 9/5/62, RR 1962; see also second report 26/9/62; report on John Peter, 'Along the Coast' 1/7/64, RR 1964; report on Douglas Livingstone, 'Verses', 2/12/64, RR 1964. Report on Johannes Meintjes, 'The Silent Conspiracy' 12/2/64, RR 1964.
8. Report on Nadine Gordimer, 'A Guest of Honour' 25/3/70, RR 1970.
9. Report on Alan Paton, 'Kontakion' 11 /12/68, RR 1968.
10. Report on Derek Walcott, 'In a Green Night: Poems 1948–1960' 31/5/61, RR 1961.
11. Report on Derek Walcott, 'The Castaway' 20/1/1965, RR 1965.
12. 'The Castaway by Derek Walcott', Cape Book File JC56/6 1080606.
13. See, for example, William Plomer to Lady Sybil Chomondeley, 5/6/71 (PLO 24711/1–4), 11/5/71 (PLO 247/10/1–2 or 6/4/73 (PLO 247/16/1–2; William Plomer Papers; Durham University Library Special Collections.
14. William Plomer to Lady Sybil Chomondeley, 2/9/72; PLO 24714/1; William Plomer Papers; Durham University Library Special Collections.

15. Report on Derek Walcott, 'Another Life', 22/5/68; Photocopy of reader's report in the possession of Corbett Nepaulsingh. For a full discussion on the evolution of the poem, see Baugh and Nepaulsingh (2004).
16. William Plomer to Tom Maschler, 24 May 1968; JC121/4 1108886, Cape Book file: *The Gulf*, Jonathan Cape Archives, University of Reading publishing archives.
17. Tom Maschler to Derek Walcott, 30 May 1968; JC121/4 1108886, Cape Book file: *The Gulf*, Jonathan Cape Archives, University of Reading publishing archives.

References

Alexander, Peter. 1989. *William Plomer: A Biography*. Oxford: Oxford University Press. Baugh, Edward, and Colbert Nepaulsingh. 2004. "Reading *Another Life: A Critical Essay*." In *Another Life: Fully Annotated*, by Derek Walcott, edited by Edward Baugh and Colbert Nepaulsingh. London: Lynne Rienner. 153–217.

Brennan, Timothy. 1997. *At Home in the World: Cosmopolitan Now*. Cambridge, Massachuetts and London: Harvard University Press.

Brouillette, Sarah. 2007. *Postcolonial Writers in the Global Literary Marketplace*. Basingstoke and New York.

Collin, Dorothy W. 1991. "Edward Garnett, Publisher's Reader and Samuel Rutherford Crockett, Writer of Books." *Publishing History* 30: 89–121.

Fahnestock, Jeanne Rosenmayer. 1973. "Geraldine Jewsbury: The Power of the Publisher's Reader." *Nineteenth-Century Fiction* 28(3): 253–72.

Fritschner, Linda Marie. 1980. "Publishers' Readers, Publishers, and Their Authors." *Publishing History* 7: 45–99.

Howard, Michael, S. 1971. *Jonathan Cape, Publisher*. London: Jonathan Cape.

Huggan, Graham. 2001. *The Postcolonial Exotic*. London and New York.

Low, Gail. 2011. *Publishing the Postcolonial*. London and New York.

MacDonald, Peter D. 2009. *The Literature Police*. Oxford: Oxford University Press.

Mumby, Frank Arthur. 1954. *Publishing and Bookselling*. London: Jonathan Cape and R. R. Bowker.

Nash, Andrew. 2003. "A Publisher's Reader on the Verge of Modernity: The Case of Frank Swinnerton." *Book History* 6: 175–95.

Plomer, William. 1975. *The Autobiography of William Plomer*. London: Jonathan Cape.

Unwin, Stanley. 1946. *The Truth about Publishing*. London: George Allen and Unwin.

Van der Post, Laurens. 1985. "Introduction: The `Turbott Wolfe' Affair", *Turbott Wolfe*, by William Plomer. 9–55.Oxford: Oxford University Press.

Van Der Vlies, Andrew. 2007. *South African Textual Cultures*. Manchester: Manchester University Press.

6 Too Much Rushdie, Not Enough Romance?

The UK Publishing Industry and BME (Black Minority Ethnic) Readership

Claire Squires

The UK publishing industry in the twenty-first century is one populated by high-profile, multicultural authors. Monica Ali, Hari Kunzru, Andrea Levy and Zadie Smith have enjoyed critical and commercial success, building on the literary and marketplace achievements of postcolonial writers such as Salman Rushdie, Ben Okri and Arundhati Roy. Postcolonial and multicultural writers, and novels with multicultural characters and with postcolonial themes, have been foregrounded by the mechanisms of the industry: its marketing activities; its literary awards; and by the literary media. Yet how does the British publishing industry cater for multicultural consumers, or, in the acronym predominantly used in official UK discourse, a BME (Black Minority Ethnic) readership?[1] Using industry data and surveys, this chapter explores this question with regards to content, genre and access to reading material, and analyses how the operation of the book trade, and demographics of industry workers, might affect readership. It also considers whether the visibility of multicultural literary authors has inflected the production and consumption of works towards an exoticising mode which, it is argued, does not encompass diversity of writing and reading practices, including in terms of genre.

The framework adopted in this chapter draws on Robert Darnton's book communications circuit, with its organising principles of agents within that circuit (including authors, publishers, printers, booksellers and readers), and the impact of the "economic and social conjuncture" in which the circuit is embedded (Darnton 1990). It also draws on revisions to his "model circuit" by those who have sought to politicise and foreground the gatekeeping role of publishers, such as Simone Murray's call for a "rewiring" of the communications circuit in *Mixed Media: Feminist Presses and Publishing Politics* (2004, 13).

In the communications circuit of the contemporary British literary marketplace, BME authors have been highly visible, as well as commercially and critically successful. Zadie Smith's *White Teeth* (2000) is a case in point: with a black Jamaican mother and a white English father, a childhood spent in multicultural northwest London, and a very recently completed degree in English literature from Cambridge, Smith was a highly promotable author, endorsed by Rushdie himself (Squires 2002; Smith 2000, front cover).

Journalists self-reflexively referred to her marketability, with the *Daily Telegraph* describing her as "the perfect package for a literary marketing exercise", and the *Guardian* commenting, with some knowingness, that "she ha[s] the fortune, or misfortune, to be the perfect demographic" (Wallace 2000, 18; Hattenstone 2000, 7). The novel's success built on Smith as a promotable young author, and the themes and content of the book itself, but also upon external factors. Not the least of these was the visibility of postcolonial novelists as both shortlistees and winners of the Booker Prize, and the consequent market focus the UK's highest-profile literary award has brought to postcolonial and multicultural writers and their works.

Narratives surrounding the Booker Prize, produced by those connected to the award and the broader commentary of literary journalists and critics, have emphasised Booker's role in foregrounding, promoting and celebrating diasporic writers, including Rushdie, Ben Okri and Arundhati Roy (winners in 1981, 1991 and 1997). There is an aspect of mutual celebration in these narratives, in which the prestige bestowed on writers reflects back to the Booker, which then represents itself as progressive in its consecration of non-white and/or postcolonial writers (white writers from postcolonial nations, including Margaret Atwood, Peter Carey and J. M. Coetzee are also brought into these narratives) (Todd 1996; Niven 1998; Huggan 2001; Squires 2004; English 2005; Ponzanesi 2006). These Booker Prize–winners, and subsequent celebrated writers of the 2000s, including Smith, Ali, Kunzru and Levy, might well be thought to denote a publishing industry receptive to and appreciative of writers of colour and works featuring multicultural characters and themes. However, while representing a diversity of author biography and novelistic theme, these writers broadly fall into one particular category in the publishing marketplace: that of literary fiction.

Defining "literary fiction" is a complex process, although a convenient shorthand can be found. Industrially, literary fiction can be defined in two ways: by a process of negation; and contextually. The former process, explained by Steven Connor, would suggest that literary fiction is "not formula fiction or genre fiction, not mass-market or bestselling fiction—and, by subtraction, it is what is left once most of the conditions that obtain in contemporary publishing are removed" (1996, 19). In *Marketing Literature* (2007a), I argue that market conditions apply to literary as well as mass-market fiction. Connor's formal definition is still useful, though, and the generic divisions to which it refers are used in the contextual definitions of the publishing industry. Literary fiction is that published by literary imprints and companies (e.g., Jonathan Cape, Faber and Faber, Picador and Sceptre), packaged and formatted in certain ways to look "literary", and entered for the more "literary" of book awards, such as Booker. Such a definition is circular, and it does not fully explain how agents within and surrounding the communications circuit (e.g., publishers, literary agents, the media, academics) construct the categories by which fiction is classified, and how this is a dynamic, negotiated process.

Nonetheless, it offers a broad view of the processes by which marketplace categories are constructed. For the purposes of this chapter, it is sufficient to acknowledge that constructions of literary genre pertain strongly within the publishing industry, and are actively used in the marketing of books.

The question of genre and definitions of literary/other types of fiction is relevant to an analysis of BME readership. Literary fiction by multicultural writers, and with multicultural themes and characters, has undoubtedly been critically and commercially successful at the turn of the twentieth and twenty-first centuries in the UK and in the broader English-language speaking markets to which the British industry exports. But is such success appreciated by a British BME readership? Does it necessarily cater to its tastes, as far as these "tastes" can be discerned or grouped? And—from a commercial perspective—is it the most effective form of publishing to reach the pockets of a BME readership? Or, as the title of this chapter asks, is this a case of too much Rushdie and not enough romance; an over-emphasis on the literary novel and an undervaluation of mass-market fiction?

Two surveys of multicultural readers conducted at the end of the first decade of the twenty-first century refer in some detail to questions of genre. The first, *Getting Closer to the BME Bookmarket* (a collaboration between the publisher HarperCollins, The Reading Agency (TRA), an independent charity which promotes reading in the UK, and *The Bookseller*), was published in 2008; the second, from 2010, was conducted on behalf of the DSC South Asian Literary Festival (SALF), also in association with *The Bookseller*. Both surveys operated a consumer survey methodology with substantial sample sizes in order to examine reading, book buying and borrowing behaviour and attitudes, using ethnic demographic categories, premised on the hypothesis that the publishing industry could cater more effectively for a diverse readership. *Getting Closer* compared a self-designated BME reader sample to a separate, general reader (i.e., an overall population with no ethnic breakdown) sample. The SALF survey focused on readers who designated themselves as Asian/British Asian, in the context of an overall population, other ethnic designations, and (for the purposes of the headline report) a White: British sample.

Getting Closer, while asserting that no simplistic link exists between BME authorship, content and readership (identifying that the "most frequent reading choices for BME readers are the bestsellers that are popular across the board" (Hicks and Hunt 2008, 38)), suggested that publishers were failing to provide adequately for, or understand, BME readers in the UK. This failure derives in part from the marketplace successes of literary BME authors (a genre which has a strong appeal to non-BME readers), and neglecting other market sectors including some types of mass-market fiction and memoirs (Hicks and Hunt 2008, 38). With regards to fiction, although the BME and general population both demonstrated the highest preference for crime and thrillers, compared to the general population, BME readers showed a greater liking for romance, whereas literary fiction was less widely read. However, romance and literary fiction were equally popular among BME respondents, each being read by 26 percent (Hicks and Hunt 2008, 12). The point, therefore, is the difference between the BME and general panel, not that BME readers prefer romance to literary fiction.

With non-fiction, a high proportion of respondents (39 percent) had read "true life stories", which the report glosses as "inspirational memoirs" (Hicks and Hunt 2008, 12). When all respondents were asked to name the title they had most recently read, the general panel's list showed a preference for literary authors (Levy, Smith, Ali, Chimamanda Ngozi Adichie). The BME list accentuated "stories that reflect real life set in the UK", including Constance Briscoe's memoir *Ugly* (2006), which documents an abusive childhood before her rise as a black female barrister and judge (Hicks and Hunt 2008, 24). This book was mentioned seven times by BME readers, but not at all by the general panel.

The SALF report had some analogous findings. The survey asked its respondents about genres that they liked to read (with respondents being able to cite as many genres as they wanted), rather than ones they had actually read. A range of demographic data (including age and gender as well as ethnicity) was recorded, but the report focused on a comparison between the South Asian and White: British population (indicating an assumption that the UK publishing industry is structured around the reading patterns of white readers; for the purposes of this discussion, the total sample responses have also been included). There were distinct differences between the South Asian, White: British and total population respondents in terms of the preference for fiction genres: crime/thriller (33/75/69 percent respectively); classic "i.e. pre-C20th" (50/64/63 percent); historical (39/56/54 percent); science fiction/fantasy (24/36/35 percent); and poetry/plays (29/22/24 percent), with the latter being the only genre that the South Asian readership liked more than the White: British and total readership. Figures for literary (56/62/63 percent) and romance/love stories (31/32/31 percent) were more similar. Overall, the fiction genres had (apart from the poetry/plays category) higher preference among the White: British and overall respondents than the South Asians (*DSC South Asian Literature Festival UK Readers' Survey* 2010, Volume 1, 8). Further figures from the SALF survey reveal striking differences in terms of the non-fiction genres: auto/biography/memoir, travel and humour had similar figures, but a disparity arises between South Asians, White: British and the total population with self-help/motivational (43/13/18 percent respectively); religious/spiritual (52/12/17 percent); and politics (29/12/15 percent). South Asian readers, as the authors of the report commented, generally expressed a much greater liking for, and readership of, non-fiction than the White: British group (*DSC South Asian Literature Festival UK Readers Survey* 2010, Volume 1, 7–8).

The SALF survey went on to investigate attitudes towards books with "South Asian influences, characters, subjects or settings, and which are written in or translated into English" (2010, Volume 1 Summary Report 2). These questions produced a shift in preferred genres for the overall population, with crime/thriller dropping from the top spot to sixth, behind (in order of preference) literary fiction, historical fiction, classic fiction, travel and history. Moreover, when the South Asian respondents were asked whether they would read more books with a "South Asian influence" if they were available, responses showed that there would be preferences for the categories of literary fiction, religious/spiritual, historical and auto/biography. As the report comments, "only 2% of relevant [i.e., South Asian] respondents felt there were sufficient books already" with a "South Asian influence" (*DSC South Asian Literature Festival UK Readers' Survey* 2010, Volume 1, 14–16). The survey also probed attitudes towards the children's book sector, with respondents voicing a clear demand for children's books with a South Asian influence: 46 percent of the total wanting more, 38 percent of White: British, and 89 percent of South Asians (*DSC South Asian Literature Festival UK Readers' Survey* 2010, Volume 1, 17).

Both these industry reports, and discussion at events such as the 'Discovering Britain's Biggest Untapped Market–Muslim Focus' seminar at the 2010 London Book Fair (which included a discussion of genres seemingly less favoured by Muslim writers but wanted by Muslim readers, including children's books and mass-market fiction), demonstrate a mismatch between the production of books (be it by authors or publishers), and the desires of consumers. The data from the two surveys demonstrates key discrepancies (the difference between the strong BME liking for crime fiction in the 2008 survey, for example, compared to its lesser appeal to the more narrowly defined segment of South Asians in 2010). The evidence they provide, therefore, only begins to hint at a full understanding of the nuances of demographics with relation to BME readership (with those demographics broadening to include gender, age, social class, educational level). Claire Chambers, one of the speakers at the 2010 London Book Fair seminar, discusses in her article "Multi-Culti Nancy Mitfords and Halal Novelists: The Politics of Marketing Muslim Writers in the UK" (2010) the addition of the category of faith (particularly in terms of Islam) into the demographic discussions of writing, publishing and reading. A discussion of a unified BME "segment" is in itself, therefore, a misapprehension of the diversity of groupings of non-white readers, and both surveys make normative assumptions about reader behaviour: both of BME groupings and sub-groupings, and the "general" and/or "White: British" population to which they are compared. However, while normative assumptions should be questioned, not least if it is assumed that the "White: British" population is the norm, such groupings are central to the methods of action research, are the foundation of marketing, and also underpin the attempt to analyse the political role of gatekeeping on the publishing industry.

Analysing the relationship between writers, content and readers is a highly complex process, which is still rarely done in trade publishing, although it is crucial to an informed consideration of segmentation strategies (Squires 2007b). Moreover, as *Getting Closer* itself states, "What will not work is to simplistically assume that the BME tag will connect the BME book up to the BME reader" (Hicks and Hunt 2008, 38). Nonetheless, an accompanying *Bookseller* article to the SALF survey, which begins with a brief overview of the successes of South Asian writers, not least in terms of book awards, attempts to draw some conclusions about South Asian readers. Asking whether the UK publishing industry is "reaching out to this growing demographic", Tom Tivnan concluded that, based on the evidence in the survey, "The answer may be that the industry is not doing enough to attract South Asian readers and that there is a need to have more books geared towards the South Asian community. Perhaps publishers are missing out on an untapped market?" (Tivnan 2010).

The challenge of the "untapped market" is a commercial one, configured in the language of market segmentation and expansion: the managing director of Waterstone's (the UK's biggest high-street bookseller) demonstrated his eagerness to see the detailed survey results (Denny 2010). The SALF survey additionally asked its respondents about barriers to buying or reading more books with a South Asian influence. Eighty-nine percent of the Asian/British Asian sample surveyed said there were barriers compared to only 23/13 percent of the total and White: British sample (such books being "not easy to find in bookshops, even where they are available"; "bookshops don't stock them"; they are "not readily available in libraries" or "schools"; and potential readers "cannot find them easily on the internet") (*DSC South Asian Literature Festival UK Readers' Survey* 2010, Volume 1, 19). Other questions in both surveys probed habits and attitudes with regards to bookshops, touching on the question of where and how books with BME and/or South Asian influence should be shelved and promoted, offering some specific channels of investigation for booksellers stocking books for the "untapped market".

The motivation behind both surveys, however, went beyond commercial expansion of the market, incorporating an interest in how reading habits could be inculcated and enhanced. *Getting Closer* provided recommendations to the public library system about support for BME readers, and the promotion of books by BME writers and/or with BME content. These recommendations were coupled with previous research conducted by The Reading Agency, in which Public Lending Right (PLR) figures demonstrated the key role libraries have in "growing the market for BME writing" (Hicks and Hunt 2008, 40). TRA is an advocate for the role of libraries in promoting areas of "specialist interest" (which is, according to its own evidence, underrepresented in mainstream publishing and/or less commercially viable) and in reader development (which has alternate drivers to those of the commercial publishing industry). Yet TRA worked in cooperation with one of the conglomerate publishers for its survey, showing that different drivers in the promotion of BME books and support for BME readers can work in effective partnership. However, the public library system and the non-commercial promotion of books, reading and literacy have a particular role to play, which, in working for and with groups often less effectively catered for by the mainstream commercial publishers, is ideologically motivated. The announcement of swathing funding cuts to public libraries and reader development agencies such as Booktrust and the National Literacy Trust (NLT) under the UK government's Comprehensive Spending Review and via local councils at the end of 2010 and beginning of 2011 caused outcry, not least because they threatened the balance between private and public partnerships in the world of books and reading. The impact of such cuts is that one of the key modes of transmission of information, education and culture risks being left predominantly to commercial organisations, which, in addition to privileging the mainstream, are by their nature subject to "market censorship", in André Schiffrin's terminology from *The Business of Books* (2000, 103–28). Schiffrin's subsequent book *Words and Money* (2010) makes an impassioned plea for the role of public money in cultural production and consumption. His broader argument about state and philanthropic intervention can be applied to the BME book market.

The active promotion of reading, with an underpinning ideology of combating social exclusion, was a key strand of UK government policy in the 1990s and 2000s, frequently operating via private and public partnership funding models. Campaigns such as the NLT's Reading Champions and Reading the Game enlisted the aid of "Premier League Reading Stars" for school visits, and produced a variety of promotional materials, such as a 2009 poster campaign featuring footballers Rio Ferdinand, Ashley Cole, David James and Alan Smith. The primary demographic target for these NLT campaigns was boys generally, but using sports stars enabled a high proportion of BME reading advocates—three out of four of the 2009 poster stars, for example. Diversity of genre was emphasised in the "Reading the Game Movie" (a promotional video in sports programme style) in which footballers talked about their reading habits: their favourite childhood story books, but also their current reading habits of newspapers, magazines and in particular auto/biographies ("Reading Champions"; "Reading the Game"; "Champions Read"; "RTG"). Genre diversity and a concern to find the right reading materials for individuals and communities link to NLT research in which young people's self-perceptions as readers found its respondents had seemingly internalised perceived literary hierarchies, so that the term "reader" was closely associated with reading fiction or poetry. Unless they regularly read these genres, many of the young people surveyed did not designate themselves as "readers", even if they regularly read newspapers and magazines (Clark, Osborne and Akerman 2008; cited in Squires 2009). This survey did not explore BME demographics, but its findings around the perceived valorisation of some genres (here by gatekeeping teachers and librarians) over others connect to the issues surrounding genre in the BME market.

This survey evidence hints at the ways in which genre hierarchies are produced, mediated by a variety of gatekeepers and (with degrees of resistance or acceptance) received in the contemporary communications circuit. All agents in the circuit begin as readers, but their varying positions—as commissioning editors, literary reviewers, teachers, librarians—combine to effectuate patterns of literary and demographic stereotyping. Such stereotyping forms the basis of market segmentation, but this can be altered by commercial, sociological, cultural and, as Chambers (2010) describes, political perspectives. Chambers draws on the work of John K. Young, who makes the argument in *Black Writers, White Publishers: Marketplace Politics in Twentieth-Century African American Literature* (2006) that "an editorial emphasis on race raises important questions about who editors are. It hardly seems coincidental that a field that has been populated primarily by white men has focused its energies primarily on white, male authors" (32). His argument holds true in an interrogation of the twenty-first-century British market, in which various initiatives have demonstrated, and attempted to act upon, the gatekeeping role of the publisher: a "rewiring" of the communications circuit, in Murray's terminology.

Chambers traces this contestation of "editorial emphasis" through the Arts Council England (ACE)'s decibel programme, which began with a survey of diversity in the publishing workforce. 'In Full Colour: Cultural Diversity in Book Publishing Today' noted that only 13 percent of its respondents from the UK publishing industry were from black or Asian backgrounds (Kean 2004a). This statistic was greater than the UK population as a whole (cited from census data as 8 percent), but—given that publishing is principally based in London (where almost 80 percent of respondents were based)—it did not match the BME population of London (almost 30 percent). Moreover, the industry respondents themselves perceived that publishing had a homogenised white, middle-class and even Oxbridge-dominated workforce, one in which BME workers had "experiences of institutionalised racism, tokenism and insensitivity" (Kean 2004a; 2004b; 2005, 36). The specific warning made by the report was that this homogenous workforce meant that publishing was not allowing itself access to a "share of the £32bn spending power of Britain's minority ethnic communities" (Kean 2004b, 5). By not admitting enough individuals from BME backgrounds into gatekeeping positions in the communications circuit, the report argues, the industry was not creating sufficient expertise to capitalise on all potential demographic market segments.

Following 'In Full Colour', various initiatives were set up to diversify the gatekeeping role. DipNet (the Diversity in Publishing Network) was established in 2005 to provide a support network for BMEs already in, or wishing to enter, the publishing industry. ACE sponsored bursaries for BME interns at a number of publishing companies; workshops were held where unpublished BME writers could meet with publishers (Kean 2005). A draft 'UK Publishing Equalities Charter', a collaboration between ACE, DipNet, the

Independent Publishers Guild (IPG), the Publishers Association (PA), Skillset and the Society of Young Publishers (SYP), was launched in 2010 with the aim of helping "promote equality and diversity across UK publishing and bookselling, by driving forward change and increasing access to opportunities within the industry" (UK Publishing Equalities Charter Supplementary Information Q&A Consultation Phase II 2010).

Chambers traces this history of the publishing workforce in specific relation to the publishing, marketing and reception of British Muslim writers. Despite seeing a largely positive trend for increasing access to non-white industry workers and openness to non-white authors, Chambers identifies (pace Graham Huggan's argument in *The Postcolonial Exotic* (2001) that the marketing activities of metropolitan publishing industries exoticise non-white authors and their books) an anthropologically stereotyped commodification of British Muslim writers in the twenty-first century, one which, moreover, tends to focus on literary fiction rather than other genres. The article 'Still Not in Full Colour', written by Kean four years after 'In Full Colour', and in response to 2008's *Getting Closer* report, substantiates Chambers's claim about genre and anthropological commodification. At the seminar launching *Getting Closer*, HarperCollins's managing director apparently commented that "Publishers must act like cultural tourists to find mass appeal products and look beyond the literary genre [. . .] We need to source and encourage new voices" (Barnicoat 2007, 6). While not contesting the comment about literary genre, Kean responded that, "'tourism' is the wrong simile: a 'tourist' is not the same as someone with roots in a market. Tourist publishers trying to 'get down with the locals' risk being the publishing equivalent of Ali G: fake, laughable, patronising and ultimately mistaken in their assessment of what a market wants" (Kean 2008). Kean is also sensitive to tokenism in bringing in BME commissioning editors and other book-trade gatekeepers as native informants on their cultures or readership communities, particularly in order to commercialise opportunities relating to them. Her article 'A Year in Diversity' featured several BME writers and publishers commenting on white publishers enforcing—knowingly or otherwise—a narrow "spectrum of writing": white publishers still tied up in a "colonial attitude"; as "reluctant to consider books by black authors that deal with anything other than race as a central theme"; with a "preference for books that highlight the white experience of minority ethnic culture"; and as "looking for a certain type of writing and if your writing doesn't hit that market they are not interested" (Kean 2005, 36–37).

Publishing initiatives from within the BME community have sought to respond to and overcome this lack of representation, tokenism and the role of the native informant. Just as Virago and other feminist book trade organisations of the 1970s and 1980s strove to increase access at every point in the book communications circuit (women as writers, publishers, booksellers and readers, and as subject matter) (Murray 2004), so a variety of companies have sought to open the British book market to BME participation and content. In 'Material Factors Affecting the Publication of Black British Fiction' (2010), Philippa Ireland traces this post-war history, referring both to established companies (such as Allan Wingate, Chatto & Windus, Jonathan Cape and Faber & Faber) publishing black British writers, and the foundation of "pioneering black publishers" in the late 1960s (New Beacon Books and Bogle L'Ouverture) and, with the establishment of the X Press in 1992, a more mass-market, even "sensationalist" approach to the fiction market (2010) (142, 159, 162). In the children's market, Tamarind began to produce multicultural books for children and schools in 1987, following founder Verna Wilkins's experience of seeing her black son depict himself, for the cover of a booklet he was making at school, with a "bright pink face". Her impetus to become a writer and publisher developed from that of the parent and reader, with the purpose of "redress[ing] the balance in publishing", focusing on the children's market (Wilkins 2008). Initiatives aimed at promoting diversity in the twenty-first century also include book prizes: the Diverse Voices Award, and the Commonword Children's Diversity Writing Prize ("Frances Lincoln" 2011; "Press Release" 2010). Urbantopia, another children's publisher, was established in 2010 in specific response to *Getting Closer*'s call to "address the lack of diversity and representation" and to "source and encourage new voices" ("Birth").

Such initiatives developing BME writing, publishing and reading demonstrate awareness of, and positive action to change, the relationship between various agents in the communications field, including the gatekeeping role of the publisher and others such as literary prize judges. However, the UK book publishing industry has some distance to go before it can claim to be catering effectively for a BME readership, whether in commercial, cultural or political terms. There is still much to be done to establish professionalised readers within the book communications circuit– in other words, BME industry workers. There is not a simple correlation, however, between having BME agents in significant positions in the publishing industry, and the encouragement of, and effective provision for, multiple BME readerships, without falling into the traps of tokenism, exoticisation and normative assumptions. And yet, if BME readers are to be effectively catered for—commercially, culturally or politically—it is clear that the industry needs to consider carefully, and act on, issues of diversity in its workforce. It must also have a diversified approach to the provision of reading matter, and seek to redefine attitudes to genre.

An examination of issues relating to BME readerships demonstrates how the critical and commercial successes of postcolonial literary writers has operated alongside—even perhaps inflected—the publishing of non-white writers away from other genres, some of which have been shown to be of particular appeal to BME readers. The relationship between readers, writers and publishers (and other book-trade gatekeepers such as literary agents, booksellers, librarians and literary prize judges) structures the production and reception of the publishing industry. An interrogation of aspects of this relationship would seem to suggest that, although positive action is underway in a variety of initiatives, positions of power in the communications circuit are still having a negative impact on BME readers. Analysis of BME readership and literary consumption, as well as the demographics of publishers, writers and the contents of their books, leads therefore to a set of key questions about literary production. Only by asking these questions, and acting upon the answers, will a properly diversified publishing industry be enabled.

Notes

1. Precise definitions and derivations of BME vary and exist only in draft form for the OED ("of or designating members of black and ethnic minority (esp. South Asian) communities in the United Kingdom"). The UK Census has collected data on ethnicity since 1991, with categorisation self-assigned by respondents. Oxford English Dictionary, "Draft Additions September 2008", http://www. oed.com.ezproxy.stir.ac.uk/view/Entry/14168?redirectedFrom=bme#eid12804 2566, accessed June 26, 2011.

References

Barnicoat, Laura. 2007. "BME Readers Demand Diversity." *The Bookseller*, November 30, 6(5309). "The Birth of Urbantopia." n.d. Urbantopia. http://www.urbantopia. co.uk/about-us.html.

Briscoe, Constance. 2006. *Ugly*. London: Hodder & Stoughton.

Chambers, Claire. 2010. "Multi-Culti Nancy Mitfords and Halal Novelists: The Politics of Marketing Muslim Writers in the UK." *Textus* 23: 389–404.

"Champions Read." n.d. National Literacy Trust. http://www.literacytrust.org.uk/ assets/0000/2969/footieposters.pdf.

Clark, Christina, Sarah Osborne and Rodie Akerman. 2008. *Young People's Self-Perceptions as Readers: An Investigation Including Family, Peer and School Influences*. National Literacy Trust, January. London (or url http://www.literacytrust.org.uk/ assets/0000/0558/Self-perceptions_as_readers_2008.pdf)

Connor, Steven. 1996. *The English Novel in History 1950–1995*. London: Routledge.

Darnton, Robert. 1990. "What Is the History of Books?" In *The Kiss of Lamourette: Reflections in Cultural History*. London: Faber and Faber. First published in *Daedalus* 11(3): 65–83.

Denny, Neill. 2010. "South Asians Less Likely to Use Chains." *The Bookseller*, November 26. http://www.thebookseller.com/news/136094-south-asians-less-likely-to-use-chains.html.

DSC South Asian Literature Festival, in association with *The Bookseller*. 2010. *DSC South Asian Literature Festival UK Readers' Survey*. London: BML.

English, James. 2005. *The Economy of Prestige: Prizes, Awards, and the Circulation of Cultural Value*. Cambridge: Harvard University Press.

"The Frances Lincoln Diverse Writers Award 2011." 2011. Seven Stories. http://www. sevenstories.org.uk/learning/projects/the-frances-lincoln-diverse-voices-award-2011-p327.

Hattenstone, Simon. 2000. "White Knuckle Ride." *Guardian*, December 11, G2 section, 6–7.

Headley, Victor. 1992. *Yardie*. London: X Press.

Hicks, Debbie, and Catherine Hunt. 2008. *Getting Closer to the BME Bookmarket: Detailed Research Findings*. HarperCollins and The Reading Agency.

Huggan, Graham. 2001. *The Postcolonial Exotic: Marketing the Margins*. London: Routledge.

Ireland, Philippa. 2010. "Material Factors Affecting the Publication of Black British Fiction." PhD diss., The Open University.

Kean, Danuta. 2004a. "In Full Colour: Cultural Diversity in Book Publishing Today." London: Bookseller Publications.

———. 2004b. "Diversify or Die, Warns Report." *The Bookseller*, March 12, 5.

———. 2005. "A Year in Diversity." *The Bookseller*, March 11, 36–37.

———. 2008. "Still Not in Full Colour." Danuta Kean. http://www.danutakean.com/blog/?p=305 (first published in *The Author*, Spring 2008).

Murray, Simone. 2004. *Mixed Media: Feminist Presses and Publishing Politics*. London: Pluto Press.

Niven, Alistair. 1998. "A Common Wealth of Talent." In *Booker 30. A Celebration of the Booker Prize for Fiction. 1969–1998*, 40–42. London: Booker.

Ponzanesi, Sandra. 2006. "Boutique Postcolonialism: Literary Awards, Cultural Value and the Canon." In *Fiction and Literary Prizes in Great Britain*, edited by Wolfgang Görtschacher and Holger Klein in association with Claire Squires, 110–37. Vienna: Praesens Verlag.

"Press Release: Partnership and Prize to Encourage Diversity in Children's Fiction." 2010. Commonword. http://www.cultureword.org.uk/wp-content/uploads/2011/01/Commonword-Childrens-Diversity-Prize.pdf.

"Reading Champions." n.d. National Literacy Trust. http://www.literacytrust.org.uk/reading_champions.

"Reading the Game." n.d. National Literacy Trust. http://www.literacytrust.org.uk/reading_the_game.

"RTG The Movie." n.d. National Literacy Trust. http://www.veoh.com/browse/videos/category/sports/watch/v181058412ydRwh7c.

Schiffrin, André. 2000. *The Business of Books: How International Conglomerates Took Over Publishing and Changed the Way We Read*. London: Verso.

———. 2010. *Words and Money*. London: Verso.

Smith, Zadie. 2000. *White Teeth*. London: Hamish Hamilton.

Squires, Claire. 2002. *Zadie Smith's* White Teeth: *A Reader's Guide*. London: Continuum.

———. 2004. "A Common Ground? Book Prize Culture in Europe." *Javnost The Public* 11(4): 37–47.

———. 2007a. *Marketing Literature: The Making of Contemporary Writing in Britain*. Basingstoke: Palgrave Macmillan.

———. 2007b. "The Global Market 1970–2000: Consumers." In *A Companion to the History of the Book*, edited by Simon Eliot and Jonathan Rose, 406–18. Oxford: Blackwell Publishing.

———. 2009. "Marketing at the Millennium." In *Children's Literature: Approaches and Territories*, edited by Janet Maybin and Nicola J. Watson, 183–98. Basingstoke: Palgrave Macmillan.

Tivnan, Tom. 2010. "An Untapped Market." *The Bookseller*, November 26. http://www.thebookseller.com/in-depth/feature/136096-an-untapped-market.html.

Todd, Richard. 1996. *Consuming Fictions: The Booker Prize and Fiction in Britain Today*. London: Bloomsbury.

UK Publishing Equalities Charter Supplementary Information Q&A Consultation Phase II. 2010. http://www.dipnet.org.uk/

Wallace, Sam. 2000. "Cutting Her Teeth with a Book Deal." *Daily Telegraph*, January 15, 18.

Wilkins, Verna. 2008. "The Right to Be Seen." Tamarind Books. http://www.tamarindbooks.co.uk/downloads/tamarind_righttobeseen.pdf.

Young, John K. 2006. *Black Writers, White Publishers: Marketplace Politics in Twentieth-Century African American Literature.* Jackson: University Press of Mississippi.

Part III

Reading in Representation

7   Rushdie's Hero as Audience
Interpreting India through Indian Popular Cinema

Florian Stadtler

In his essay 'In Good Faith' in defence of *The Satanic Verses* (1988) Rushdie states: "the liveliness of literature lies in its exceptionality, in being the individual, idiosyncratic vision of one human being, in which, to our delight and great surprise, we may find our own image reflected. A book is a version of the world" (Rushdie 1992, 412). Ever since Rushdie had his literary breakthrough with the Booker Prize–winning *Midnight's Children* (1981) and after the controversies around the publication of *The Satanic Verses* in 1988–89, his position on the international literary scene, the global reception of his books and that idiosyncratic vision and version of the world have been the cause for debate. This chapter concentrates on how concerns with reception and audience are articulated within his fiction. It will highlight how the consumption of popular culture influences Rushdie's narratives by focusing in particular on the narrator-protagonists' viewing practice of Indian popular cinema. I argue that their viewership of these popular cultural productions plays an important role in allowing the narrators to sustain an ironic commentary on the politics of post-independence India and a fast integrating world.

Rushdie's Reception and His Global Audiences

In *Midnight's Children* and *The Moor's Last Sigh* (1995) the first-person narrators Saleem and Moraes are constantly reflecting on the reception of their story by their audiences within the novel, Padma and Vasco Miranda. The value judgements of these auditors/readers lead the narrators to concerted aesthetic choices that reflect on Rushdie's own concerns with the multiple audiences for his work across the world. As Rushdie has commented in a 1983 lecture, "many people, especially in the West, who read *Midnight's Children*, talked about it as a fantasy novel. By and large, nobody in India talks about it as a fantasy novel; they talk about it as a novel of history and politics" (Rushdie 1985, 15). The different audience responses to the novel in India and the West illuminate how readers connect with differing elements of the narrative and fit these into their localised interpretative frames of reference. This complicates the analysis of Rushdie's reception among global audiences, as his own experience as a migrant enables him to modulate with ease sub-continental, British and American popular cultural references to articulate his "version of the world". Bombay-born, Rushdie comes from an urban, Muslim middle-class background. Privately educated at Rugby School in England, he studied history at King's College, Cambridge. After completing his degree, he briefly relocated to Pakistan, where his family had moved. He soon returned to London, embarking on a career as an advertising copywriter, before turning to writing full-time. He settled in New York in 2001.

Rushdie's biography shows him as a global itinerant, and, as Timothy Brennan has remarked, "Rushdie's story had as much to do with England as with India and Pakistan. Thus, the 'in-betweenness' of the cosmopolitan—a creature, as Rushdie puts it, of 'translation'—was not only essentially there in his person but theoretically accounted for on every page of his work" (Brennan 1989, x). Rushdie has further commented on this, describing his own positionality as living in the comma between "East, West" (see Reder 2000, 163). This pertinent observation on his "in-between" status, bridging different worlds as a hybrid, translated man, has been an important marketing tool for his novels in an increasingly interlinked world and a globalising publishing industry. It positioned Rushdie as a writer with world-wide appeal, precisely because, as Brennan argues, a "cosmopolitan" writer like Rushdie presents his local, Indian identity to his audiences "as a mark of distinction in a world supposedly exempt from national belonging" (Brennan 1989, 32). This distinction on the one hand and the global circulation of his books, as well as media constructions of Rushdie as "celebrity" writer, on the other, trading on the familiar and unfamiliar, are harnessed by the publishing industry to position Rushdie as a world writer within a global public sphere.

As Graham Huggan explains, "the success of writers like Rushdie [. . .] owes to the skill with which they manipulate commercially viable metropolitan codes" (Huggan 2001, 81). Rushdie articulates these codes through recognisable cultural referents, such as European auteur cinema (Fellini, Goddard, Bunuel), pop music, or literary influences, like Dickens, Forster or Kipling. Yet Huggan's point requires complication, considering the wider global readership of Rushdie. Rushdie uses similarly recognisable South Asian codes– for example, through references to Indian popular cinema. By interlinking these codes, then, Rushdie creates for the postcolonial writer an intermediary's interpretative role between different public spheres. Rushdie's own position as a postcolonial global itinerant has made him an intellectual called upon by the media to comment on varied issues ranging from religious fundamentalism to freedom of expression, global terrorism or the latest outbreaks of sectarian violence. In his fiction, first-person narrators such as Saleem Sinai and Moraes Zogoiby, or the self-consciously interventionist authorial voice in *Shame* (1983) fulfil similar functions. As Sara Suleri argues in relation to the latter novel, "the price a post-colonial writer pays for political discourse is linked in a most literal fashion to the economy of audience:

the more such a text as *Shame* represses and censors its own ambivalence towards the location of its audience, the more likely it will be to seclude itself in a nervous advertisement of self-conscious ideological rectitude" (Suleri 2005, 174–75). For instance, the narrator of *Shame* asks, "is history to be considered the property of the participants solely?" (Rushdie 1995b, 28). He explains further: "My story, my fictional country exists, like myself, at a slight angle to reality. I have found this off-centring to be necessary; but its value is, of course, open to debate" (Rushdie 1995b, 29). Suleri implies that the narrative, having undergone a form of explicitly articulated authorial censorship, has made it accessible to his English-speaking metropolitan audience by offering up a version of "Third World" history that conforms to the image of such countries as it is perpetuated in daily news reportage. Thus while the text seemingly challenges these stereotypes, it perpetuates them at the same time.

The reception of Rushdie as "celebrity" author, his fiction and non-fiction among his audience constituencies across the world is more complex. It is reductive to consider Rushdie's readership only in a metropolitan context. As Huggan highlights, *Midnight's Children* "enjoyed, as indeed his other novels have enjoyed, a large readership in India, nor should it be imagined that responses to his novels are culturally and/or geographically determined in any simple way" (Huggan 2001, 72). Tracking Rushdie's readership and sales figures is difficult. Official data remains a closely guarded secret by his publishers. However, the information available on *Midnight's Children* offers an interesting snapshot. As Liz Calder, his former editor at publisher Jonathan Cape notes, in 1981, "a big fat novel about India wasn't regarded as a very wonderful bet [. . .] at that time it was thought that books about India didn't sell!" (Weatherby 1990, 42). According to Calder, the novel's first printing consisted of 1,750 copies, but boosted by its Booker Prize win it sold over 40,000 copies in the UK in hardback alone (Weatherby 1990, 42). His then American agent Elaine Markson notes that *Midnight's Children* sold a more modest eight to nine thousand hardcover copies in the US (Weatherby 1990, 65). Norbert Schürer cites sales of one hundred thousand hardback copies by 1990 and even larger numbers in paperback, though he does not reveal precise figures (Schürer 2004, 83).

The reception of *Midnight's Children* in India proved controversial. Particularly the novel's representation of Indian history and the portrayal of Indira Gandhi were contentious. The then prime minister of India famously sued Rushdie and his publisher over a short passage in the novel which suggested that her son Sanjay blamed her for the death of her husband at an early age through neglect (Rushdie 1981, 406). Rushdie and his publisher were forced to issue a public apology and remove the libellous passage from subsequent editions of the book (Rushdie 1995a, 421).

In his annual review of publishing in India for the *Journal of Commonwealth Literature*, Shyamala A. Narayan traces the success and impact of *Midnight's*

Children among Indian audiences. He notes that in 1982 the novel "had amazing sales in India even in hardback; now two different paperbacks are available, and his earlier *Grimus* too has been reprinted" (Narayan 1983, 96). After his Booker win, a popular poll for *Gentleman* magazine voted Rushdie "man of the year" (Narayan 1984, 79). His talks across India also drew large audiences. Narayan cites publishers' claims of sales of 4,000 hardback and 45,000 paperback copies, unprecedented for an Indian novelist writing in English (Narayan 1984, 79). These figures are in addition to any pirated copies sold and indicate the demand for the book among Indian readers. According to Weatherby, a Pakistani pirated edition was widely circulated (no affordable English-language Indian edition of *Midnight's Children* has been released), and producers of this cheap, illegal copy audaciously sent Rushdie a "thank you" card on the occasion of the Eid festival (Weatherby 1990, 79). An Indian pirated copy was also widely available from book-stalls across the country and sold at half the official price. The sale of these pirated editions caused controversy during Rushdie's 1983 Indian tour when he refused to sign them.

On the fiftieth anniversary of Indian independence, a Hindi translation of the novel was published.[1] Though the hardback edition of 1,100 copies sold out within a year of publication, Harish Trivedi argues that Rushdie has made little impact in Hindi: "He may be the hottest literary property in the Western world, with translators falling over themselves to lay their hands on his works [. . .]. But translation into Hindi evidently is not a felt need and when attempted serves only to de-mystify and reduce him" (Trivedi 2003, 81). However, the influence and success of *Midnight's Children* in English remain undisputed. Although Rushdie claims that he does not write with a specific reader in mind, "in the case of *Midnight's Children*, I certainly felt that if its subcontinental readers had rejected the work, I should have thought it a failure [. . .] I write 'for' people who feel part of the things I write 'about'" (Rushdie 1992, 19–20).

In an interview with Alfred Arteaga, Gayatri Chakravorty Spivak expands further on who this audience may be in relation to *The Satanic Verses*:

> If you read it from the point of view of a "secular Muslim," he is trying to establish a postcolonial readership—already in existence—who will in fact share a lot of the echoes that are in the book which you and I might miss. I, for example, get the echoes from Hindi films. [. . .] It seems to me, then, that the implied reader of *The Satanic Verses* is this international, global, postcolonial migrant person. This is not the Christian En-lightenment person for whom British literature is written; nor the jaded European of *The Waste Land*. (Landry and MacLean 1996, 22)

Spivak describes the complex multiple audiences which Rushdie addresses and his texts' diverse experiential reference points for his readership in India and its global diasporic community. Indeed she highlights Huggan's point that Rushdie's audiences are not "culturally and/or geographically determined in any simple way" (Huggan 2001, 72). Spivak sees herself as part of Rushdie's intended South Asian diasporic readership whom he wishes to address. The multiple narrative strands in the novel that address racism in 1980s London, a deep questioning of religious faith and issues of living in-between two cultures suggest this global, South Asian postcolonial migrant as its "implied" audience. Yet the novel also engages with the transformations of London from the capital of empire to postcolonial, postmodern metropolis, re-written from Dickens's nineteenth-century realist representation, immediately recognisable to his western readership. In this respect, it seems the novel looked towards different audience constituencies, positioning itself in the comma between "East, West", which created a tension between the novel's different narrative elements and impacted significantly on the reception of the novel among these differing readerships. Thus the novel's "implied" audience and the "actual" audience it reached and violent reactions it provoked stand in stark opposition to each other. As Aamir Mufti explains, the publication of *The Satanic Verses* and the controversy raised wider questions about the conditions of reception of Rushdie's texts; how it "becomes consumed within already existing cultural and political discourses, and becomes an object of debate, dispute, and discussion within different but often overlapping public spheres" (Mufti 1991, 112). This question preoccupies Rushdie in his 1995 novel, *The Moor's Last Sigh*, and its engagement with the rise of Hindu fundamentalism in India paralleled with the decline of fifteenth-century Moorish Spain. As the following section will show, these concerns link further with the narrative importance the text attributes to Indian popular cinema.

Rushdie's Characters as Hindi Cinema's Local, Global and Diasporic Audiences

The global reach of Rushdie's work and his role as a celebrity author have generated varied reactions to his work. For example, *Midnight's Children* was adjudicated the "Best of Booker" by a public audience vote to mark the fortieth anniversary of the Booker Prize in 2008. The novel previously won the Booker (1981) and Booker of Bookers (1993). In 2003, the novel entered the BBC's list of 100 Great Reads at 71, only one of seven modern literary novels on the list. The controversy surrounding the publication of the *Satanic Verses*, while leading to bans in several countries, including Bangladesh, Egypt, India, Indonesia, Iran, Malaysia, Pakistan, Qatar, Saudi Arabia, Somalia, South Africa and Sudan, also turned the novel into a bestseller. The hardback edition remained on the UK bestseller list even one year after publication; in the US, after its initial print run of 50,000, the second printing of 400,000 copies quickly sold out and by May 1989, some 750,000 copies had been sold in the US alone (Pipes 1990, 201). The book also did well elsewhere. In Italy, it sold 350,000 copies within the first five months of publication (Pipes 1990, 201). The global influence of his work is also reflected by the numerous awards and honours he has received, including from Austria, Britain, the European Union, France, Germany, Ireland, India, Italy, Sweden, Switzerland and the US. According to his official website, his novels have been translated into over forty languages.

His position as a writer has been shaped by a new form of aggressive business model developed by the Wylie Agency. Its global representation of Rushdie allowed for a streamlined and coherent global marketing model for his fiction through multinational publishing conglomerates.[2] His forthcoming memoir (2012) will be published by the same publisher, Random House, in the US, Britain, Canada, Australia, New Zealand, India and South Africa, in English. Random House has also secured the non-English rights for the German-language market in Germany, Austria and Switzerland, and Spanish-language rights for Spain, Argentina, Mexico, Colombia, Chile, Venezuela and Uruguay. Rushdie is aware of his positionality and the global marketability of his writing to diverse audiences, a concern which finds a further expression within his fiction. This can be traced from *Midnight's Children* to *Shalimar the Clown* (2005), where characters act not only as narrators, but also as consumers of cultural productions.[3] This is particularly evident in relation to film. For example, Saleem Sinai's narrative method is informed by the Bombay Talkie (see Rushdie 1995a, 346–50); Moraes in *The Moor's Last Sigh* draws on the film *Mother India* (1957) to articulate his version of the syncretic Indian nation and its decline. As the following discussion will show, characters like Moraes use films as pathways to understand contemporary Indian politics and its impact on their own situation. They articulate a wider argument about postcolonial, post-independent India. These interconnections between filmic texts, genres and narratives, filtered and refocused through the narrator as consuming viewer, extend the interpretative framework of the novels for Rushdie's "implied" sub-continental and diasporic readership.

Rushdie's novels are populated by a range of audiences: listeners, readers and viewers. Padma sits at Saleem's feet, listening to his life story in *Midnight's Children*. In the *Moor's Last Sigh*, Vasco Miranda, artist and crazed admirer of Moraes's mother Aurora, imprisons him in his Spanish villa and avidly consumes his tale. Reminiscent of Scheherazade's precarious position as storyteller to King Shahryar in the *Thousand and One Nights*, Moraes remains alive only for as long as he entertains the mad painter. These relationships are often complex and reveal the narrators' wider connection with the fictional worlds they inhabit. Yet references to popular cultural productions are also one way of linking the narrative setting to the wider world outside the respective fictional worlds. In this respect the narrators and their audiences within the novels become important mediators between their story-worlds and the readership of the novel, where the level of engagement with the specific narrative elements depends on the readership's recognition of numerous

popular cultural texts that map across Rushdie's oeuvre a geographical trajectory from India and Bombay to Britain and London to the US and New
York.

Arguably then, we can distinguish between three levels of interaction
with popular-cultural productions. Firstly, Rushdie's first-person narrator,
who also acts as a character in the novel, is a consumer of popular culture,
which allows him to connect these products to his own narrative. Secondly,
the auditor of the story within the novel, who functions as an intermediary
between the narrator and the wider readership of the novel, too, has knowledge of the same popular cultural productions, recognises, interprets and
mediates them for the wider readership in the context of the narrative world,
such as Padma in *Midnight's Children* and Vasco Miranda in *The Moor's Last
Sigh*. Thirdly, the novel's global audience also recognises popular cultural
elements in these stories; however, the level of access depends on region,
class and culture, with references resonating more with one section of Rushdie's audience than others. Thus, Rushdie has to balance and modulate these
references or link them to wider frames, so that audience sections less aware
of one particular popular cultural context understand their relevance to the
story and can connect them with the argument of the novel.

Rushdie begins to develop this in interesting ways in *Midnight's Children*.
The novel's first-person narrator, Saleem Sinai, writes the story of his life in
his ayah's pickle factory and narrates it to Padma, who cares for him in his
state of decay. She acts as a constant judge for his narrative, commenting on
its plausibility and entertainment value. Padma has a set idea, influenced by
Indian storytelling traditions, of how a narrative should be structured and
advises Saleem on its pacing and the plausibility of events (see 1995a, 38). As
Abdulrazak Gurnah has argued, "these interruptions refine the cultural context of the narrative's reception, but they also give Rushdie the opportunity
to describe his method" (Gurnah 2007, 97). In her role as audience within
the novel, she becomes a mediator between Saleem/Salman and his wider
readership. By having a direct audience at his feet, who offers an immediate
value judgement on his activities, Saleem can test out whether his narrative
that defies linearity and accords in idiosyncratic ways retrospective significance to past events is modulated to entertain his audience. This enables him
to bestow the sought-after meaning for his life and the Midnight's Children,
who he works into a powerful symbol of betrayed hope for the newly independent India.

The interrelationship between fiction and Indian popular cinema's audiences plays an increased role in *The Satanic Verses* in the figure of Gibreel
Farishta, who faces a crisis of faith after having impersonated too many gods
in mythological films. The novel explores how the star-figure in Indian popular cinema is offered up for consumption as a screen icon through cinematic
performances and gossip that generate a particular star image. *The Satanic
Verses* highlights this in the context of the South Asian diaspora in Britain–for

example, in the meeting between record store and nightclub owner John Maslama and Gibreel on the train to London. Recognising the famous star, Maslama offers his view on his performances, calling him "a rainbow colla- tion of the celestial" (Rushdie 1998, 192). In this instance Gibreel as global movie superstar realises that any interpretation of the figures he represents is out of his control, as his audiences see their own realities mirrored in the fictional worlds he inhabits. Thus Gibreel comes to realise that "fictions were walking around wherever he went [. . .] fictions masquerading as real human beings" (Rushdie 1998, 192). Rushdie develops this further through the character of Hind. Migrating with her husband and her two daughters to London and now running the Shaandaar Café, Bengali and Hindi mov- ies and magazines like *CineBlitz* provide her with a connection to home. In these instances Gibreel too becomes a projection of her hopes aspirations and dreams, a way of escaping her disappointments in life, now residing among a culture from which she feels thoroughly alienated, a situation that is exacerbated by the sudden disappearance of Farishta, which compounds her frustration and dejection (Rushdie 1998, 251).

These examples show the complex interactions between characters-as-au- dience in Rushdie's fiction, but they gain further significance in the contexts of *The Satanic Verses* affair, considering the novel's deliberations on how an artist may lose ownership over his creative productions, as audiences project their own meanings and interpretations. As Gayatri Spivak has pointed out, "literature is transactional. The point is not necessarily and exclusively the correct description of a book, but the construction of readerships" (Spivak 1990, 50). These complexities around audience reception and multiple read- erships preoccupy Rushdie in his later novel, especially *Fury* (2000).[4] How- ever, they are also particularly relevant to Rushdie's 1995 novel, *The Moor's Last Sigh*, where these considerations are significant for Moraes's narrative construction of his mother Aurora Zogoiby's public persona as an eclectic metropolitan version of "Mother India" tempered by lurid gossip and popu- lar mythology through his own subversive reading of Hindi cinema's classic, *Mother India*.

"Mother India" and Moraes as Audience

In *The Moor's Last Sigh*, Moraes draws parallels between his mother's rise to fame and her fall from grace as an artist, embodying an urban version of the multilayered figure of "Mother India" and Hindi film superstar Nargis's inter- pretation of the role in Mehboob Khan's *Mother India*. By using the film as an interpretative tool, the ideological investments in the figure of "Mother India" mutate into a motif, which Moraes deploys to mythologise his own mother as "Mother India", which compares and contrasts in equal measures with its filmic popular cultural representation (see Stadtler 2007, 175–90; Thiara 2009, 122–57). Furthermore it reinvents "Mother India" for a modernising, urbanising India, rather than the setting of the film in rural India. Having viewed the film as audience, the narrator/character subsequently engages in his own acts of interpretation, using film as a prism through which he deconstructs India's postcolonial reality.

The conceptualisation of "Mother India" as a nation-defining trope is tightly interwoven with the history of India's move towards independence and has particular resonance in the novel. Gayatri Chatterjee notes that "Mother India" was an important tool for nationalism and the freedom movement, reflected in anti-imperial battle cries such as *Bharat-mata ki jai* (May Mother India be victorious) and *vande mataram* (Hail Mother) (Chatterjee 2002, 49). Sumita Chakravarty explains that in the post-independence era, Indian popular cinema reworked these precursors for a new myth of nation that presented India on the one hand as a timeless mythic entity and on the other as a modern secular state under the rule of law (Chakravarty 1993, 132). Indian popular cinema played a crucial part in creating a new sense of belonging in the post-independence era, after the violence of partition, when the state still sought to establish itself as a new source of authority. India's diversity in language, religion, caste and cultures directly challenged the unity of the newly constructed country and necessitated the creation of these new myths for the nation. As Moraes stresses: "Motherness [. . .] is a big idea in India, maybe our biggest: the land as mother, the mother as land, as the firm ground beneath our feet" (Rushdie 1996, 137). *Mother India*, released in the tenth anniversary year of Indian independence, is part of a larger post-independence project to give the young nation a new sense of unity aimed at creating a feeling of allegiance and belonging on the part of its audiences. As Chakravarty notes, *Mother India* presents the powerful nation through its representation of the land as mother and the mother as land as it is enshrined in a discourse of nationhood (Chakravarty 1993, 149). The ideologically constructed figure Mother India, personified in the film by the peasant woman Radha, is celebrated in her role as the long-suffering, stoical mother who through endurance overcomes seemingly insurmountable hardship. She is mythologised as such in the film and consumed by the cinema-going audience and conflated with the actress Nargis.

Nargis was one of the key actresses of 1950s Hindi cinema, and Radha in *Mother India* was the role with which the cinema-going public most closely associated her for the rest of her life, eclipsing her partnership with actor Raj Kapoor. Behroze Gandhy and Rosie Thomas in their essay 'Three Indian Film Stars' outline in interesting ways how the persona of Nargis in the public imagination is constructed on the basis of rumours, especially that of her affair with Raj Kapoor, whose on- and off-screen pairing made them the "golden couple" of Indian cinema. When the affair ended, Nargis was seen by her audience as a fallen woman, but her role in *Mother India* redeemed her in the public imagination. As Gandhy and Thomas point out:

While *Mother India* can be seen to be negotiating a number of contradictory images of womanhood, tying them together through a story
which emphasises the necessary constraint on female sexuality, the gossip stories tie together similar if apparently contradictory facets of modern Indian womanhood: the Muslim courtesan, the passionate goddess
Radha, the "westernised" free lover, the devoted Hindu wife, the ador-
ing mother [. . .] While the diversity of representation of femininity in
traditional Indian mythology has been encompassed within the Nargis
persona, both on and off-screen, a key concern is with woman deified
and idealised as "mother", an image that attributes to her moral and
emotional, as opposed to physical, strength.

(Gledhill 1991, 121)

The complex construction of Nargis in the public imagination, the manner in
which her story is read and interpreted by the public in relation to discourses
on nationhood and femininity provides Moraes with a template for his own
narrative construction of Aurora in relation and in opposition to Nargis and
reveals the complex, multiple interpretative models he uses, always conscious
of the audiences of his tale, most immediately the painter Vasco Miranda.
However, one might also argue that this frame of reference is also obvious
to Rushdie's South Asian audiences, not only familiar with the film, but also
with the background story and gossip surrounding the biography of Nargis.
Thus, for this audience, as Gandhy and Thomas outline, "the persona of Nargis, in all its contradictions provides an (ongoing) forum for working through
difficult questions of a society in change" (Gledhill 1991, 123).

The over-towering status of *Mother India* in the Bollywood canon is confirmed by its enormous box office success. Still screened today, the film regularly attracts capacity audiences. After its 1958 Oscar nomination for best
foreign film, the film was also shown widely in the West. Why is *Mother
India* such a useful text for Moraes? As Rosie Thomas argues, the film "is
most usefully seen as an arena within which a number of discourses around
female chastity, modern nationalism, and, more broadly, morality intersect
and feed on each other, with significant political effect" (Thomas 1989, 13).
Moraes as narrator and film viewer taps into the rich multilayered meanings
of *Mother India* to write his own urbanised, modern version, transforming his
artist mother Aurora's eclecticism into a powerful symbol for the decline of
the postcolonial promise for independent India: socialist, secular, democratic
and pluralistic. Moraes keenly points out many connections and analogies:

The year I was born, Mehboob Productions' all-conquering movie
Mother India—three years in the making, three hundred shooting days,
in the top three all-time mega-grossing Bollywood flicks—hit the nation's
screens. Nobody who saw it ever forgot that glutinous saga of peasant
heroinism, that super-slushy ode to the uncrushability of village India

made by the most cynical urbanites in the world. And as for its leading lady—O Nargis with your shovel over your shoulder and your strand of black hair tumbling forward over your brow!—she became, until Indira Mata supplanted her, the living mother-goddess of us all. Aurora knew her, of course; like every other luminary of the time the actress was drawn towards my mother's blazing flame. But they didn't hit it off, perhaps because Aurora could not refrain from raising the subject—how close to my own heart!—of mother-son relations. (Rushdie 1996, 137)

Moraes highlights here on the one hand the powerful symbolism of *Mother India* in the popular imaginary and on the other the tension between rural and urban imaginations of "Mother India" in a modernising postcolonial India. Moraes then moves on to parallel and contrast the embodiment of "Mother India" in the public personae of Hindi film superstar Nargis, politician Indira Gandhi, who in her slogan "Indira is India, India is Indira" styled herself as Mother India, and Aurora in her role as public artist and his mother. Amid the patriarchal male-dominated discourse and conception of Nation as Motherland, Aurora encapsulates alternative versions of "Mother India", ultimately constructed in competition with the filmic representation of the stoic, nurturing Mother as a stand-in for the long-suffering Nation in *Mother India*, the star persona of Nargis and the political figure Indira Gandhi. Thus Moraes offers competing interpretative models to his various audiences, drawing varyingly accessible analogies between Nargis, Indira and Aurora and the filmic representation of "Mother India".

The Moor's Last Sigh chronicles the decline of the pluralistic ethos of Bombay that culminated in the worst communal riots in Bombay's history in 1992/93 followed by a series of ten bomb blasts in March 1993, triggered by the destruction of the Babri Masjid in Ayodhya. Through the symbolism of the "Mother India" motif, Moraes argues that Indian nationalism has been contaminated by exclusionist, ethnocentric religious politics ever since the Emergency in 1975. *The Moor's Last Sigh* takes on crucial debates surrounding religion, secularism and its relationship to a political and cultural public sphere, and this is developed through the ideological investments in the notion of "Mother India". Thus Moraes's own reading of *Mother India* contains multiple meanings for Rushdie's different audience constituencies. These differing connotations enable Moraes to work the notion of "Mother India" into a continually transfiguring theme becoming, as Rushdie describes, "the intellectual way into the book" (Chauhan 2001, 199). Moraes invites a metaphorical reading of Aurora by offering up these popular cultural analogies immediately recognisable to Rushdie's South Asian audience both at home and in the diaspora, but less obvious for other readers.

As this discussion has shown, the film viewing practice of Rushdie's narrators and their audiences and the manner in which they interpret filmic texts reveal and open up the debates around preconceived notions of nationhood, migration and diaspora. Thus, films are specifically used by the narrators as important, if varyingly accessible, interpretative tools to convey different meanings to the immediate fictional reader/auditor in the novel to whom the narrator addresses himself in the first instance. In this process popular culture and film are transformed into important interpretative instruments with which Rushdie articulates and interrogates in his novels "a version of the world" for his local, global and diasporic audiences.

Notes

1. Rushdie, Salman. 1997. *Aadhi Raat Ki Santaanen.* Translated by Priyadarshan. Delhi: Vani Prakashan.
2. Rushdie's publishers Jonathan Cape (UK), Alfred Knopf (US) and Vintage (UK/US) are all owned by Random House, Inc., which in turn is controlled by the Germany-based multinational Bertelsmann media group. For a discussion in relation to *The Satanic Verses,* see Weatherby (1990, 108–22).
3. Rushdie's 2008 novel, *The Enchantress of Florence,* set in Mughal India and Renaissance Florence, does not fit with this description as the novel develops a different relationship between audience and characters. The novel maintains a sense of detachment between the two. Furthermore, the novel does not feature the same level of consumption of popular cultural productions as Rushdie's novels set in the twentieth and twenty-first centuries, which is the primary concern of this analysis.
4. For a detailed discussion, see Brouillette (2007, 79–111).

References

Brennan, Timothy. 1989. *Salman Rushdie and the Third World: Myths of the Nation.* New York: St Martin's Press.
Brouillete, Sarah. 2007. *Postcolonial Writers in the Global Literary Marketplace.* Basingstoke: Palgrave Macmillan.
Chakravarty, Sumita S. 1993. *National Identity in Indian Popular Cinema, 1947–1987.* Austin: University of Texas Press.
Chatterjee, Gayatri. 2002. *Mother India.* BFI Film Classics. London: British Film Institute.
Chauhan, Pradyumna S., ed. 2001. *Salman Rushdie Interviews: A Sourcebook of His Ideas.* Westport: Greenwood.
Gledhill, Christine, ed. 1991. *Stardom: Industry of Desire.* London: Routledge.
Gurnah, Abdulrazak, ed. 2007. *The Cambridge Companion to Salman Rushdie.* Cambridge: Cambridge University Press.
Huggan, Graham. 2001. *The Postcolonial Exotic: Marketing the Margins.* London: Routledge.
Landry, Donna, and Gerald MacLean, eds. 1996. *The Spivak Reader: Selected Works of Gayatri Chakravorty Spivak.* New York: Routledge.
Mother India. 1957. Mehboob Khan, dir. Mehboob Productions.
Mufti, Aamir. 1991. "Reading the Rushdie Affair: An Essay on Islam and Politics." *Social Text* 29: 95–116.
Narayan, Shyamala A. 1983. "India." *Journal of Commonwealth Literature* 18(2): 92–109.

————. 1984. "India." *Journal of Commonwealth Literature* 19(2): 79–92.

Pipes, Daniel. 1990. *The Rushdie Affair: The Novel, The Ayatollah, and the West.* New York: Birch Lane Press.

Reder, Michael, ed. 2000. *Conversations with Salman Rushdie.* Jackson: University of Mississippi Press.

Rushdie, Salman. 1981. *Midnight's Children.* London: Jonathan Cape.

————. (1981) 1995a. *Midnight's Children.* London: Vintage.

————. (1983) 1995b. *Shame.* London: Vintage.

————. 1985. "*Midnight's Children* and *Shame.*" *Kunapipi* 7(1): 1–19.

————. (1988) 1998. *The Satanic Verses.* London: Vintage.

————. 1992. *Imaginary Homelands: Essays and Criticism 1981–91.* 2nd ed. London: Granta/Penguin.

————. (1995) 1996. *The Moor's Last Sigh.* London: Vintage.

————. 1997. *Aadhi Raat Ki Santaanen.* Translated by Priyadarshan. Delhi: Vani Prakashan.

————. (2001) 2002. *Fury.* London: Vintage.

————. (2005) 2006. *Shalimar the Clown.* London: Vintage.

————. 2008. *The Enchantress of Florence.* London: Jonathan Cape.

"Salman Rushdie." Salman Rushdie. http://www.salman-rushdie.com.

Schürer, Norbert. 2004. *Salman Rushdie's Midnight's Children: A Reader's Guide.* New York: Continuum.

Spivak, Gayatri Chakravorty. 1990. "Reading *The Satanic Verses.*" *Third Text* 11: 41–60.

Stadtler, Florian. 2007. "Nargis and Aurora Zogoiby: Imaging Mother and Nation in Mehboob Khan's *Mother India* and Salman Rushdie's *The Moor's Last Sigh.*" In *Once Upon a Time in Bollywood: The Global Swing in Hindi Cinema*, edited by Gubir Jolly, et al. Toronto: TSAR: 175–90.

Suleri, Sara. 2005. *The Rhetoric of English India.* New Delhi: Penguin Books India.

Thiara, Nicole Weickgenannt. 2009. *Salman Rushdie and Indian Historiography.* Basingstoke: Palgrave Macmillan.

Thomas, Rosie. 1989. "Sanctity and Scandal: The Mythologization of Mother India." *Quarterly Review of Film & Video* 11: 11–30.

Trivedi, Harish. 2003. "Salman the Funtoosh: Magic Bilingualism in *Midnight's Children.*" In *Rushdie's Midnight's Children: A Book of Readings*, edited by Meenakshi Mukherjee, 69–94. Delhi: Pencraft.

Weatherby, W. J. 1990. *Salman Rushdie: Sentenced to Death.* New York: Carroll and Graf.

8   The "New" India and the Politics of Reading in Pankaj Mishra's *Butter Chicken in Ludhiana*

Lucienne Loh

In 1835, Lord Thomas Macaulay infamously declared that "[A] single shelf of a good European library [is] worth the whole native literature of India and Arabia" (Anderson 1983, 91). If Macaulay's patronising dismissal of Indian literature forms part of the colonial legacy that postcolonial Indian writers have inherited and seek to write back against, they do so, if they write in English, with the double consciousness that they are defending the merit and heritage of Indian literature while being judged, by readers of English, within and through literary traditions in English. Writers from the ex-colonies settled in the metropolitan West and writing in English face a global Anglophone readership as well as readers usually making up a small elite in their home country. Such writers hold an, at times, awkward mirror to themselves and the readers within their society while offering its reflection for other societies' scrutinising gaze. Indian writers, as one of the more prolific groups of writers from the ex-colonial world, however, have acknowledged that both these groups may not necessarily possess mutual needs and expectations. Speaking more specifically about Indian writing in English and its largely cosmopolitan global readership, Pankaj Mishra has attacked what he sees as its "slickly exilic version of India", manufactured by a "cosmopolitan Third World elite [. . .] suffused with nostalgia, interwoven with myth, and often weighed down with a kind of intellectual simplicity foreign readers are rarely equipped to notice" (quoted in Dalrymple 2005, 5). The Indo-Caribbean V. S. Naipaul pragmatically accepts the burden of an English-speaking readership: "I live in England and depend on an English audience" (9). He also discusses the difficulties of portraying a foreign country to English readers. "It is an odd, suspicious situation: an Indian writer writing in English for an English audience about non-English characters who talk their own sort of English" (12). The diasporic Indian writer Pico Iyer is more celebratory, proclaiming that "[T]he shelves of English bookstores are becoming as noisy and polyglot and many-hued as the English streets. And the English language is being revolutionised from within. [. . .] Hot spices are entering English, and tropical birds and sorcerers; readers who are increasingly familiar with sushi and samosas are now learning to live with molue buses and manuku hedges" (Iyer 1993, 54–56).

For Mishra, the non-fiction genre of travel writing in English offers a nuanced verisimilitude about India's vast and diverse national landscape without the barriers of its multifarious tongues. Within the genre of travel writing, the category of "within-the-country" travel (Benson and Conolly 1994, 1586–87) necessarily encourages a writer to negotiate his/her position as "native" (Clifford 1997, 23–24) or even as "national" informant, while trying to describe spaces, places and people unknown both to a more localised and globalised audience. This chapter explores the complex dynamics embedded in these relationships in Mishra's travel narrative, *Butter Chicken in Ludhiana: Travels in Small Town India.* Published in 1995 to much critical acclaim, *Butter Chicken* records Mishra's observations and encounters during his journey through many of India's small towns when the country's social attitudes changed irrevocably in response to new forms of cultural populism, following a spate of economic liberalisation policies pursued by the Indian state in the early 1990s. This new India appeared, to Mishra, to be characterised by a self-obsessed culture preoccupied with wealth and status, and his book was lauded by Amitava Kumar as "the first sustained portrait of travels through the new, tawdry world of Indian small towns" (2002, 61). Significantly, these shifting social attitudes were clearly evinced by the reading choices of people Mishra observed from a distance and of others he encountered more intimately during this travels through small-town India.

Peter Hulme and Tim Youngs (2002) consider *Butter Chicken* as an example of a travel narrative which documents "[T]ravels neither from nor to the imperial 'centre'" (10). Nonetheless, Mishra and his text bear a fraught and contradictory relationship to this "imperial centre." Such contradictions are similarly articulated in the range of definitions which might apply to postcolonial travel writing. In her chapter on 'Postcolonial Travel Writing in the Twentieth Century', Barbara Korte argues that while

> the travelogue seems to have been adopted primarily by English-speaking writers who travel and write in modes which developed in Europe over the last centuries [. . .] these modes can be modified or inverted, but on the whole postcolonial travelers and travel writers, just as their colonial predecessors, appear not to stray very far from the established, Western paths". (156)

Korte therefore sees postcolonial travel writing as perpetuating traditional modes of travel writing complicit in the imperial project itself through highlighting discourses of difference for readers, an argument which had been developed through Mary Louise Pratt's influential book *Imperial Eyes* (1992) and later by David Spurr (1993), Steve Clark (1999) and Douglas Ivison (2003). However, an opposite line of argument exists for Justin D. Edwards and Rune Graulund (2010), for whom postcolonial travel writing distinctly

involves "decentring Europe, North America, globalization and other contemporary forms of Empire through representations of travel" (3).

Mishra's text is placed uncomfortably between these debates since it perpetuates colonial ideologies while at the same time resisting deference to a
globalised and American culture. In particular, representations of readers
articulate Mishra's complex relationship to the genre of postcolonial travel
writing. His narrative at times portrays cultural differences refracted through
the assumptions of "a universal order of reality" based on Western modernity
as well as "a narrative that "correspond[s] to teleologies of [. . .] civilizational
progress" (Ghosh 2006, ix), structures that the travel writer Amitav Ghosh
believes are definitively *not* the markers of good travel writing. Drawing on
reader-response theory affords an opportunity to analyse how Mishra communicates with the implied reader through different frames of reference which
exist largely within modes of Eurocentric forms of knowledge and ontology.
But drawing on theories in non-fiction more broadly (Ohmann 1980, 238;
Heyne 2001, 323; Lehman 1997, 23), it is also important to consider that
when an ex-colonial writer, such as Mishra, depicts a postcolony in non-fiction, authorial gestures also create ethically inflected transactional relationships between author, implied reader and the real people represented, all of
which are themselves sites for postcolonial critique and enquiry. These sites
raise questions about the nexus between authenticity and literary aesthetics
and therefore the politics of representation, but they further foreground the
predicament of writing for a global English readership networked through an
educated transnational elite.

I aim, in this chapter, to explore Mishra's representation of readers as a
means of adding to a new kind of postcolonial textual analysis, one which not
only foregrounds the role of the reader within an Anglophone postcolonial
context, but one which similarly considers the specific material and political
conditions which produce the implied readers identifiable in Mishra's book.
Postcolonial theorists, such as Graham Huggan (2001), and more recently
Sarah Brouillette (2007), have recognised the impact of a Western publishing
industry for the marketing of postcolonial literature to a cosmopolitan and
largely metropolitan audience. Yet, readers' response to this literature is premised on the appeal of narratives bounded by fiction's conventions. Within
the concerns of reader-response theory more generally—authors' attitudes
toward their readers, the kinds of readers various texts seem to imply, the
role actual readers play in the determination of literary meaning, the relation of reading conventions to textual interpretation, and the status of the
reader's self (Tompkins 1980, ix)– an emphasis has been placed similarly on
examining the form fiction takes. Yet, the implications for this range of concerns within non-fiction such as travel writing, and postcolonial travel writing, more specifically, have remained largely unexamined. Bringing together
reader-response theory, postcolonial theory and a formalist reading of travel
writing, I want to suggest that postcolonial writers who aim to appeal to

an English readership within a globalised economy operate within implied forms of cultural signifiers which often align them and their readers within a global cosmopolitan elite. In particular, I wish to focus on how Mishra communicates with his readers through degrees of involvement and detachment in *Butter Chicken* and what this intimates in terms of Mishra's own class position and those of his readers.

In Mishra's book, a variety of class signifiers serves as a significant organising principle for the reader. Indeed, one of Mishra's clearly declared aims is to portray a recognisable Indian middle class formed as one of the most significant aspects of Indian culture in the wake of India's post-independence entry into a global economy. Ten years after his book was first published, Mishra reflects in an afterword to the 2006 reissue that *"Butter Chicken* responded to a very significant event in India's recent history—the movement that the middle class began to expand and rise and reveal themselves as just as culturally ambitious and politically conservative as those classes that have emerged in modern Europe and America" (272). He further confesses that the initial inspiration for his book was Thorstein Veblen's *The Theory of the Leisure Class* (1891), a book that

> details with a half-outsider's curiosity and irony, how industrial capitalism in America was creating a new middle class with its own patterns of manners, dress, education, and ambition. Reading Veblen helped me define my own subject more clearly. I felt myself slip easily into his tone of mordant irony, channeling through humour and mockery the unease I had known during my travels (271).

Mishra's own half-outsider's perspective may well stem from his family's history as displaced and dispossessed Hindu Brahmins who left their village near India's Nepalese border and migrated to the city. After university, Mishra moved to a small Himalayan village to continue his education, to read, write and travel among the mountain towns and old colonial outposts (Goodheart 2005). The predominant tone of irony in the text may stem from Mishra's critical distance created through personal travel and rootlessness married to a commitment to intellectual development rather than material gratification.

Invariably, observations about others' reading interests, habits and inclinations become a consistent motif throughout the text for Mishra to position himself as a reader as well as to situate the reader of his book. In *Butter Chicken*, Mishra represents a range of readers alongside other individuals he distinctly casts as non-readers, whom he describes often with barely restrained ironic relish. This is not a technique unique to Mishra. Other diasporic Indian writers, notably Pico Iyer (1989), V. S. Naipaul (1964) and Amitava Kumar (2002), have similarly referenced reading material of Indians they observe as a means of creating levels of detachment and engagement not only with those Indians being observed, but also with the anticipated readers of their work. Conversations about reading in *Butter Chicken* arise in casual chats with family members of households Mishra visits as a guest, as well as in more spontaneous occasions with strangers when Mishra is in guest houses or hotels or in transit during his travels on board various forms of public transport. But pointed observations about the reading choices of people he does not necessarily interact with also constitute a framework through which Mishra asserts his own narrative perspective. More organised and planned situations where discussions around reading and learning are detailed with greater focus include Mishra's appointment and campus visit to the English department of a provincial university, where he initiates a failed attempt to discuss English literature with students. Interspersed with Mishra's depictions of readers are personal opinions about his own reading preferences and his own engagement with literature not only from the sub-continent but also, notably, from a distinctly Anglo-American and European intellectual and literary tradition. As a more comprehensive picture of Mishra himself as a reader emerges over the course of the text, his earnest desire to be considered part of a global intellectual elite becomes increasingly patent.

The contexts in which Mishra encounters readers and the different ways he presents them are varied throughout the text, but his representation of readers are largely mediated by a mixture of reported speech, retrospective considerations and apparently straightforward reportage. Nonetheless, the critical paradigms Mishra uses to judge and interpret individuals remain relatively consistent throughout the text. He primarily assesses people by their reading choices as well as their relative ability to conduct a conversation about literary and intellectual material. Mishra, however, insinuates his disapproval of those who privilege the acquisition of visible signs of material wealth and social mobility rather than the less tangible signs of intellectual capital. Yet Mishra also highlights singular exceptions of readers who resist prevailing middle-class ideologies. These individuals, who seek spiritual fulfilment, intellectual edification and a wider worldview through reading, serve consistently as Mishra's alternative to an increasingly hollow and materialistic India. In any act of judgement, then, Mishra assumes a certain degree of intimacy between him and the reader. He claims, in an interview that "[A]s both reader and writer, I like a degree of familiarity to exist between the reader and the page. A book like *Butter Chicken*, for instance, assumes the reader will recognize its characters and places, and the mixed emotions of its narrator-observer" (quoted in Edwards and Graulund 2010, 175–76).

The book's implied index for judging represented readers depends significantly on Mishra communicating and establishing a perspective with which he hopes to appeal to his ideal reader. One critical aspect of this putatively shared vision is focused quite distinctly on a disaffection for, and disillusionment of, the new post-independence India captured by his observation of the "growing 'anomie' in Indian society" (239). In the prologue of *Butter Chicken*, Mishra re-creates his initial inspiration for the idea to travel around the small towns and cities of India in order to explore a new modern India while en route to a friend's engagement ceremony in Muzaffarnagar, a town in northern Uttar Pradesh. At the wedding, however, Mishra finds himself with other men who personify this new India. He admits having "little to say to the young men wearing silk Hawaiian shirts, diamond rings and pseudo-Italian shoes, who gossiped about the dowries paid and received by this or that personage [. . .]" (xiii). But Mishra also asserts that another aspect of the visit which claimed his attention was his failed search "to find, a single good bookshop or garden or public park worth its name in the entire city. In place of a newspaper, there was a shoddily printed tabloid reporting on outlandish, probably fictitious crimes" (xiv). Not only does Mishra condemn Muzaffarnagar's civic character by the lack of a "good" bookshop, but he singles out the local tabloid as a significant signifier for the dearth of culture and to convey what he deems the town's puerile spirit.

Mishra appears to be addressing a readership familiar with the differences between a tabloid and more respectable news-worthy publications, necessarily implying that his ideal readers are not only already firmly conscious of the different strata of reading materials present in a more developed publishing industry but also, unlike the everyday readers of Muzaffarnagar's tabloids, likely to be of a different social class. Mishra's perspective is further consolidated only a few pages later, when he quotes from V. S. Naipaul's 1977 non-fiction travel account, *India: A Wounded Civilization,* to explain his own prejudices against what he terms "the wealth of the new provincial middle-classes" in Muzaffarnagar.

> "India's modest middle-class," V.S. Naipaul had once sneeringly commented, "as yet with no common traditions or rooted strength, still only with the vulnerability of the middle-classes of all very poor countries. In the poverty of India, their ambition was great, but their expectations were very small" (xvi).

Offering no introduction to Naipaul, Mishra assumes the reader will recognise the reference to this venerated if controversial travel writer of the Indian diaspora known globally, in elite intellectual circles, for conservative, condescending and thinly veiled colonialist attitudes towards third-world cultures. From within the prologue, Mishra attempts to appeal to his ideal reader through the assumptions of a shared cultural heritage forged through access to an elite global and cosmopolitan intellectual circle.

If modern and postcolonial India is largely shunned by Mishra, then he assumes his reader shares with him, among other sensibilities, an aversion towards the homogenising effects of globalisation, particularly that brandished by the US, a reactionary condescension towards the perceived vapidity of populist culture and an unwavering faith in the aesthetic as a force for human good, especially those forms sanctioned by high culture. Mishra's desire to create more intimacy between himself and his imagined reader based on an imagined community of discerning readers is established quite early on in the text when Mishra spends a few days in Pushkar, a tiny town in the state of Rajasthan. Amid downtrodden state-run hotels, haranguing touts and a parade of doleful businesses, Mishra discovers several "well-stocked second-hand bookstores" and he adds "no touts for these, understandably." The additional irony of "understandably" is directed at a sympathetic reader, who, Mishra assumes, shares his view that the pervasive and tacky commercialism and personal entrepreneurship which the touts of small towns embody are merely emblematic of cultural demise and, like the dish-antenna atop the Jaipur palace, an eyesore, rather than an image of efforts to eke out a living. To this observation on touts, Mishra further concludes that the bookstores

> provided a useful indicator of the decline of reading tastes among tourists. The new arrivals were mostly trash: sex, money, glamour, power, *The Secret Life of Jackie O*, *I'll Take Manhattan*, that sort of thing. The good things were to be found among the dusty, tattered-looking rows. There, I found a paperback edition of John Bayley's only novel. On the same shelf was, surprisingly, V.S. Pritchett's *Dead Man Leading*. That these two grand old men of English letters should be represented here spoke in Pushkar's favour, when nothing else did. (59)

To singularly condemn an entire town, save for the random presence of the English writers Pritchett and Bayley in a second-hand book store, seems a rather exaggerated expression of Mishra's fervent desire to separate himself from the new spirit of modern enterprise, reflected, in part, by entrepreneurial efforts to cater and respond to the changing "reading tastes" of the burgeoning tourist industry. Instead Mishra can only identify and condemn these efforts as "a useful indicator of the decline of reading tastes among tourists". Once again, the seemingly throwaway phrase, "that sort of thing", is addressed to the reader whom Mishra assumes would be adept at distinguishing high from low literary culture. Part of Mishra's disgust with low culture is not disconnected to him feeling that the postcolonial state's efforts at liberalising its economy invariably involve pandering to the forces of globalisation dominated and dictated by the US. This is reflected in Mishra's scathing tone as he thinks of the new book arrivals as "mostly trash" and concerned only with such hackneyed clichés as "sex, money, glamour, power". But Mishra's attitude is further signified by the two books he decides to highlight among the bookstore's offerings: *The Secret Life of Jackie O* and *I'll Take Manhattan*. These two books represent the link between American materialism and politics in the figure of Jackie Kennedy and the city of Manhattan. In drawing our attention to these books, Mishra subtly suggests he sees the Indian government selling itself to the shallow materialism of Western, and specifically, American consumer culture.

The full weight of Mishra's own class position and prejudice that he assumes are aligned with his readers' sympathies reveal themselves most evidently in an encounter with a local police officer in Bundi, a small town also in Rajasthan. In this scene, Mishra is reading Iris Murdoch's novel *The Word Child*; a policeman walks up to him and demands to take a look at what he is reading. Mishra observes that the police officer is a "thick-set, middle-aged man in his late forties or early fifties. He could not have been a direct entrant to the police services" (97). The policeman is curious about the book: "'Can I look at your book?' he asks, in English". "Certainly," Mishra responds. The policeman struggles in English with the text at the back of the book. He reads aloud: "Hilary Burde, saved by education from a delinquent childhood, cheated of Oxford by a tragic love tangle [. . .]". Being predominantly a Hindi speaker, he is understandably puzzled by the expression "being cheated of Oxford". "Why not he go to Oxford?" he asks Mishra quizzically in English. "Because he got injured," Mishra replies, lying, and evidently irritated by the policeman's awkward efforts in English. "Why are you reading this book?" the policeman asks Mishra. "For pleasure," Mishra curtly responds. The policeman looks at the book again, very intently, turns it over in his hand, examines the cover, his brow deeply furrowed in thought, and after a long pause asserts in Hindi: "This looks like such a thick and difficult book. What sort of pleasure can you get out of it?" (97) Mishra apparently says nothing else, and no further comments follow his account of this meeting.

This is a complex scene in which the policeman not only serves as a foil to Mishra, but also as Mishra's critique of the brash confidence and showy ignorance of the postcolonial state. Mishra almost immediately deems the policeman his social inferior solely based on the policeman's physical appearance, lowly occupation, an inability to speak fluent English and a philistine attitude to Mishra's novel. Two seemingly mutually incompatible social spheres are revealed over this brief encounter. Yet what Mishra fails to acknowledge is the policeman's efforts in English and the gesture to bridge the class, cultural and apparent educational gaps between them. Mishra assumes that the reader will judge the policeman in a similar manner to himself. A more sympathetic reader might, however, see Mishra as being insensitive to the policeman's defensiveness—a possible sign of the latter's vulnerability in the face of Mishra's class and education. Keener to flaunt his cosmopolitanism, assert his literary credentials and appeal to his reader, Mishra instead fails to represent the policeman with any complexity. The policeman literally judges the book by its cover. Nevertheless, his halting attempts to interpret the paratextual elements of Mishra's novel suggest a readerly curiosity to understand these features as clues about the novel.

The way in which Mishra depicts this scene is, however, more clearly related to Mishra's irritation with a representative of the postcolonial Indian state. Displaying the policeman's attitude to reading is Mishra's covert attempt to personify what he sees as the anti-intellectual, communalist, self-defensive, egotistical stance of the state's many predominantly Hindi-speaking minions. But Mishra's intellectual prejudices so profoundly mar his representation of this new India that almost anyone who is not part of an elite literary culture is caricatured or parodied in some manner. *Butter Chicken*, then, reveals an unconscious self-obsession. Mishra's intellectual vanity may not be preoccupied with material or commercial gains, but is no less deserving of critique. Such class assumptions are only confirmed in Amitava Kumar's non-fiction text, *Bombay London New York* (2002), in which he recounts this incident in *Butter Chicken*. Kumar says that what stuck with him about Mishra's travel accounts was "the philistinism that the writer [Mishra] repeatedly ran up against." Kumar himself feels that the question posed by the policeman in this scene is both "amusing and also irritating" (62–64).

A critique of Mishra can, however, be balanced by encounters with the rare reader through whom he can convey his belief that reading the right kinds of materials could form the basis for a limited form of epistemological resistance against the shallow materialism Mishra believes has infiltrated all forms of conscious life in India and especially among the lives of the newly rich. In a hotel in Meerut, Mishra meets George, a medical representative. While George admits that his work is very demanding and that most of his colleagues are alcoholics,

> [H]e himself staved off boredom through books. He was a reader; and, now as he spoke further, it became quickly clear that he was no ordinary reader, that his taste in literature ran to the most refined works. Borges and Calvino were his favourite authors. He had not read Proust but had read Gide, and possessed all the four volumes of his journals. He had read widely in modern European poetry. Valéry, Celan, Char, Montale, Saba, Cavafy– he knew their work intimately, and could quote accurately from the English translations he had read them in. (153)

This encounter appears to lack the overriding tone of mordant irony in which Mishra couches most of his other encounters with small-towners. Mishra's account of his meeting with George not only expresses the boredom which might accompany the banalities and pressures of working life in the new India, but George serves as a mouthpiece to underscore Mishra's own personal, and distinctly conservative, belief that the morally uplifting and intellectual outlet for the humdrum frustrations of modern life should be literature itself. George is, first and foremost, identified as "a reader," and he is "no ordinary reader" at that. He is further distinguished by his refined, notably European, literary tastes, and Mishra lists the French poets George is familiar with in order to tacitly convey his own familiarity with the French intellectual tradition. Mishra later meets George "in a tiny coffee-shack" in which they begin a discussion about Thomas Mann. Mishra later describes this conversation as one of the happiest moments in his travels across India

(155). Despite their paltry surroundings in the coffee-shack, Mishra's intellectual conversation with George affords an opportunity to transcend the immediate evidence of poverty surrounding them, and it proves to be such a memorable event that in the afterword to the 2006 edition, Mishra recollects the memory with "the greatest pleasure: the rainy afternoon in Kottayam sipping coffee with a reader of Thomas Mann" (273). George is, once again, identified most clearly as a reader of Thomas Mann, whereby Mishra suggests that any reader of Mann would be a worthwhile companion.

In part, Mishra's respect and sympathy for George reiterate that both he and George are members of the interpretive community that Mishra assumes the reader of *Butter Chicken* belongs to as well. Some Indian readers in *Butter Chicken,* such as George, are evidently part of the community that Mishra is speaking to and on behalf of, but this is one that includes not only European readers, but also an Indian intellectual class and, more crucially, genuine aspirants to that class within India who redeem the image of the shallow and relentless pursuit of crass materialism that marks postcolonial India. In listing the European writers who are favoured by George– all of whom George can apparently quote accurately from in English translation– Mishra notably omits any reference to the first names of any of these writers as an attempt to consolidate and reaffirm the imagined community he writes for, one which he would like to assume is also as familiar with a European intellectual tradition as both George and himself. At another point in a crowded restaurant, Mishra seeks out the company of a reader whom he catches "perusing *The Susan Sontag Reader*" among "people [who] were reading either Judith Krantz or Jackie Collins". They later continue to have a conversation about not only Sontag but also "her son, David Rieff, and his friend, Christopher Hitchens" (174). All of these encounters which reveal an eager spirit of openness almost always involve Mishra meeting with a member of a highly literate and literary elite. But these cumulative experiences, recorded over the course of the book, not only demonstrate Mishra's knowledge of the books, writers and thinkers which serve as the topics in any one conversation, but also accrue to create an image of Mishra's own vast and expansive knowledge and intellect, one he hopes he shares, to an extent, with his ideal reader.

Yet, despite his alliance to European letters, Mishra's privileging of European culture and literature remains ambiguous and problematic particularly because he also consistently expresses a desire to critique and resist the persistent hold that colonialism and forms of neo-imperialism possess over countries such as India. Speaking about what he calls "the shoddy practice of poor parasitic nations," Mishra asserts in *Butter Chicken* that

> [i]n India, [there remains] an unpleasant reminder of old colonial hierarchies: whites at the top, Indians somewhere at the bottom, finding their own different levels of degradation. They spoke, at least, in certain

quarters, of the growing damage, after just forty-seven years of independence, to national self-esteem; and they were the unexplored darker side
of globalization. (167)

Evident throughout his text, however, is Mishra's failure to recognise that he
himself contributes to the preservation of these very colonial hierarchies, the
damaging self-degradation he speaks of and the dent to national self-esteem.
Indeed, the lofty heights from which Mishra judges the poor from his own
position as a reader are further accentuated by the less than self-conscious
fact that he admits his experience of indigence and suffering is gleaned from
books. As he travels to Bihar, one of India's poorest states, he tells us he "had
been reading Arvind N. Das's *The Republic of Bihar*" (242). He explains that
"[T]he book purports to investigate the reasons behind Bihar's current state
of disorder. Commentary frequently breaks down; despair takes over; the
pile of adjectives grows; and the language begins to buckle under the strain
of conveying the full horror and viciousness of Bihar" (242–43). Das's book
represents the way in which Mishra, as a member of a privileged global intellectual class, can only ever experience poverty mediated through aesthetic
or the academic discourses.

Despite Mishra's desire to relate the fragile lives led by the powerless in
this new India, his own efforts to secure his authorial and intellectual credibility only exacerbate and enhance the vast divide between himself and
those less fortunate Indians he represents. The luxury of mobility and travel
as a means for leisure, cultural enrichment and philosophical rumination
rather than as a necessity for livelihood ultimately reflects Mishra's position,
and these are similarly luxuries which he assumes his readers, in all likeli-
hood, possess to some degree. The objectivity of the text is eventually undermined from within the writing itself and, in particular, from representations
of his relationships and encounters with other readers.

References

Anderson, Benedict. 1983. *Imagined Communities*. London: Verso.
Benson, Eugene, and L. W. Conolly, eds. 2005. *Encyclopedia of Post-Colonial Literatures in English*. London: Routledge.
Brouillette, Sarah. 2007. *Postcolonial Writers in the Global Literary Marketplace*. Basing-stoke: Palgrave Macmillan.
Chaudhuri, Amit. 2001. *The Picador Book of Modern Indian Literature*. London: Picador.
Clark, Stephen H., ed. 1999. *Travel Writing and Empire: Postcolonial Theory in Transit*. London: Zed Books.
Clifford, James. 1997. *Routes: Travel and Translation in the Late Twentieth Century*, Cambridge: Harvard University Press.
Dalrymple, William. 2005. "The Lost Sub-Continent." *The Observer*, August 13. http://www.guardian.co.uk/books/2005/aug/13/fiction.arundhatiroy.
Edwards, Justin D., and Rune Graulund. 2010. *Postcolonial Travel Writing: Critical Explorations*. Basingstoke: Palgrave Macmillan.

Ghosh, Amitav. 2006. Foreword to *Other Routes: 1500 Years of African and Asian Travel Writing*, edited by Tabish Khair, Martin Leer, Justin D. Edwards and Hanna Ziadeh, ix–xii. Oxford: Signal Books.

Goodheart, Adam. 2005. "'An End to Suffering': Philosopher King." Review of *An End to Suffering: The Buddha in the World*, by Pankaj Mishra. *The New York Times*, February 6. http://www.nytimes.com/2005/02/06/books/review/06GOODHEA.html.

Hardt, Michael, and Antonio Negri. 2001. *Empire*. Harvard: Harvard University Press.

Heyne, Eric. 2001. "Where Fiction Meets Nonfiction: Mapping a Rough Terrain." *Narrative* 9(3): 322–33.

Holland, Patrick, and Graham Huggan. 1998. *Tourists with Typewriters: Critical Reflections on Contemporary Travel Writing*. Ann Arbor: University of Michigan Press.

Huggan, Graham. 2001. *The Post-Colonial Exotic: Marketing the Margins*. London: Routledge.

Hulme, Peter, and Tim Youngs, eds. 2002. *The Cambridge Companion to Travel Writing*. Cambridge: Cambridge University Press.

Ivison, Douglas. 2003. "Travel Writing at the End of Empire: A Pom Names Bruce and the Mad White Giant." *English Studies in Canada* 29(3–4): 200–219.

Iyer, Pico. 1989. *Video Night in Kathmandu: And Other Reports from the Not-So-Far East*, New York: Vintage Books.

———. 1993. "The Empire Writes Back." *Time*, February 8, 54–59.

Korte, Barbara. 2000. *English Travel Writing from Pilgrimages to Postcolonial Explorations*. Basingstoke: Macmillan Press.

Kumar, Amitava. 2002. *Bombay London New York*. London: Routledge.

Lehman, David. 1997. *Matters of Fact: Reading Nonfiction over the Edge*. Columbus: Ohio State University Press.

Mishra, Pankaj. (1995) 2006. *Butter Chicken in Ludhiana: Travels in Small Town India*. Basingstoke: Picador.

Naipaul, V. S. 1964. *An Area of Darkness*. London: Andre Deutsch.

———. 1972. *The Overcrowded Barracoon and Other Articles*. London: Andre Deutsch.

———. 1977. *India: A Wounded Civilization*. London: Andre Deutsch.

Pratt, Mary Louise. 1992. *Imperial Eyes: Travel Writing and Transculturation*. London: Routledge.

Richard, Ohmann. 1980. "Politics and Genre in Nonfiction Prose." *New Literary History* 11(2): 237–44.

Spurr, David. 1993. *The Rhetoric of Empire: Colonial Discourses in Journalism, Travel Writing and Imperial Administration*. Durham: Duke University Press.

Tompkins, Jane P. 1980. "An Introduction to Reader-Response Criticism." In *Reader Response Criticism: From Formalism to Post-Structuralism*, edited by Jane P. Tompkins, ix–xxvi. Baltimore: Johns Hopkins University Press.

Veblen, Thorstein. 1899. *The Theory of the Leisure Class: An Economic Study in the Evolution of Institutions*. New York: Macmillan.

9 Local and Global Reading Communities in Robert Antoni's *My Grandmother's Erotic Folktales*

Lucy Evans

After five or six of those big eden-mangoes, of course, Moyen had reached she limit. Still, she continued slicing off more cheeks. She continue criss-crossing the orange flesh, turning the rosy cheeks inside-out and biting off the cubes of flesh, until she have consumed the entire pile of mangoes. [. . .] All in a sudden Moyen realised she wasn't feeling too good *a-tall*. The poor child's stomach was so full—so bloat-o with all those big lovely mangoes—that Moyen began to fear she belly might burst in truth. [. . .] And poor Moyen continued to vomit and vomit until she had emptied out she stomach of every one of those mangoes she'd just taken such a great pleasure in filling it up! (Antoni 2000, 52–53)

At first glance, this passage resembles the cover image of the US edition of Robert Antoni's *My Grandmother's Erotic Folktales* (2000), which features a semi-clad young woman holding a mango (see Figure 9.1). The cover design incorporates a photograph by Dorit Lombroso, whose work has been used in advertising campaigns for various multinational corporations as well as Tahiti and Mexico tourist boards. According to her website, Lombroso has developed a "signature style suggesting nostalgia and sensuality". Many of her photographs feature mixed-race women in exotic settings, often alongside tropical fruit ("Dorit Lombroso" 2003). Both the style and the dissemination of these images suggest that they contribute to the "branding and marketing of Paradise" which, according to Mimi Sheller, "underwrite[s] performances of touristic hedonism" (Sheller 2004, 170). Like the seductive young woman in the picture, the pubescent girl in the above extract has "rich musala skin" and "long black hair" (47). The word "musala" invites a comparison to massala, a term used in Trinidad to mean "a mixture of spices (cumin, turmeric, parched coriander seeds, etc)" (Alsopp 1996, 375), and therefore emphasises Moyen's status as a consumable. In addition, both Moyen and the figure on the cover are accompanied by a generous "pile of mangoes". On the surface, then, the extract draws upon an exoticist discourse which associates the sexualised bodies of Caribbean women with tropical fruit. However, the textual version of this scene takes us beyond the cover image, unsettling the exoticist reading it incites. Whereas the figure on the cover is delicately poised above uneaten mangoes, Moyen unrestrainedly devours the "entire pile". While the cover girl remains the object of viewers' desire, Moyen assumes an active, even predatory position as she attacks the mangoes' "rosy cheeks" and "cubes of flesh". During the course of the extract, Moyen shifts between the roles of consumable and consumer.

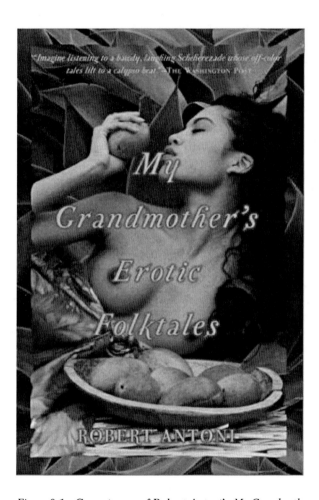

Figure 9.1   Cover image of Robert Antoni's *My Grandmother's Erotic Folktales*. Excerpt and cover image of US edition from *My Grandmother's Erotic Folktales*, copyright© 2000 by Robert Antoni. Cover design by Charles Rue Woods and Marcia Salo. Cover photograph by Dorit Lombroso. Used by permission of Grove/Atlantic, Inc.

Both in its address to readers and in its figuring of fictional consumers, *Folktales* engages in critical debate on the global consumption of postcolonial cultural products. Stating as his subject the "commodification of cultural difference" (Huggan 2001, vii), Graham Huggan asserts the need to interrogate the ways in which postcolonial writing has been made not only "available" but also "palatable" to a "target consumer public" (Huggan 2001, viii). Similarly, Timothy Brennan considers the marketability of the "cosmopolitan" novel to "metropolitan reading publics" (Brennan 1990, 63). In a study which extends beyond literature to popular culture, tourism and the media, Mimi Sheller situates this idea of cultural commodification within the specific social and historical context of the Caribbean and its relations to "The West", considering "the myriad ways in which Western European and North American publics have unceasingly consumed the natural environment, commodities, human bodies, and cultures of the Caribbean over the past five hundred years" (Sheller 2003, 1, 3). While Huggan considers the capacity of postcolonial writers to "contend with *neo*colonial market forces" by subverting exoticist codes from within (Huggan 2001, viii), Sheller proposes that if the language used by writers is "'raw' enough (e.g. 'deep' on the 'creole continuum', vulgar, rough, crude, sexual, violent, harsh on the ear) it will repel any who might potentially 'eat' it" (Sheller 2004, 187).

This chapter explores how through its attention to overlaps between consumed and consumer cultures, and between insider and outsider perspectives, *Folktales* complicates the idea put forward in these studies of a "metropolitan reading public" or a "target consumer public" which is both distinct and distant from a local audience. Moving beyond Eric D. Smith's focus in his analysis of *Folktales* on the text's address to a "Western consumer of Caribbean culture" (Smith 2004, 20–21), I consider how *Folktales* not only opens up a variety of reading positions but also facilitates movement between them, confounding any clear division between "local" and "global" audiences. My reading draws upon more recent studies of the marketing and dissemination of postcolonial literature. Sarah Brouillette challenges homogenising representations of the "global consumer" with her claim that "[a]ttention to the material organization of the current literary marketplace does not reveal a single market, but rather a fragmenting and proliferating set of niche audiences" (Brouillette 2007, 24). In light of these developments in the make-up of global audiences, Robert Fraser makes the following point:

> The last spectre of traditional book history we need to exorcise is the assumption that as objects of possible inquiry readerships stay put, either in the sense of social stability or in the more literal—but here more trenchant—sense of clinging to place. Readerships actually move, and so correspondingly do interpretative communities, reading practices, even varieties of repertoire or text. (Fraser 2008, 186)

With its suggestion that readerships are shifting, unstable, and open to change, Fraser's statement complicates distinctions between "Western" and local audiences of postcolonial writing.[1] My reading of *Folktales* situates both Fraser's concept of mobile reading constituencies and Brouillette's image of a "fragmenting and proliferating set of niche audiences" in the context of a twenty-first-century Caribbean readership which, due to mass migration and the large proportion of Caribbean writing produced in the US, Canada and Europe, is geographically extensive and socially diverse.

Folktales not only highlights its own status as a consumable, but also comments on the global marketing of the Trinidadian calypsos referenced within it. In the final episode, Antoni's narrator announces: "In *my* heart of hearts I am nothing but pure West Indian" (179). She goes on to reveal her fantasy of becoming "the world's first female *Calypsonian*!" (180). With these two statements the narrator balances a belief in cultural authenticity against a desire for international appeal. The friction between the statements reflects the debates around authenticity and audience which Antoni's stories at once give rise to and self-consciously explore. Much of the critical writing on Caribbean popular music addresses the question of authenticity. In a study of the impact of globalisation on Caribbean culture, Jennifer Rahim laments that "at stake" in the international commercial success of calypso is "the integrity of cultural representation" (Rahim 2006, 47). In a discussion of international intellectual property legislation in Trinidad, Robin Balliger expresses similar concerns, asking "how it is possible to foster both a sense of culture as historically shared and as a commodity", and posing the question: "When much of the population becomes excluded from 'their' culture's expressions and profits, what then constitutes community?" (Balliger 2007, 215, 199).

For Gordon Rohlehr and Earl Lovelace, mass migration and the global marketing of calypso have led to a deterioration in Caribbean cultural production. Rohlehr describes how soca, a contemporary form of calypso which is faster paced and less lyric-centred, "has begun to behave like many other popular musics: a kind of fast-food, mass-produced, slickly packaged, and meant for rapid consumption and swift obsolescence" (Rohlehr 1998, 87–88). In his view, contemporary soca music reflects and panders to the demands of a new generation of twenty-first-century listeners, ignorant of the "heritage" of calypso and willing to accept "mediocrity": this "listening public", he reflects, "gets 'the kaiso that it deserves'" (Rohlehr 1998, 95). In this he echoes Lovelace's concern with the lack of critical acuity in contemporary audiences (Lovelace 2003, 133).

In *Folktales*, both the representation of consumers within the stories and the narrator's address to readers beyond the text unsettle the notion of a purely local cultural product or audience, challenging distinctions between insider and outsider positions, and between "authentic" and commercialised culture. Antoni's stories remain culturally specific and politically charged, despite their international marketability. In fact, the stories' underlying politics derive in large part from their critical engagement with the commercial processes in which they are embroiled. With its cover image of the young woman holding a mango, *Folktales* may be, like soca, "slickly packaged", but beneath that appealing outer packaging are undertones of social commentary which hinder "rapid consumption". Readers anticipating an appetising Caribbean consumable do not get "the kaiso that [they deserve]" but something more challenging and thought-provoking.

In *The Middle Passage*, V. S. Naipaul considers the lyrics of Trinidadian calypso as part of a culturally insular "local language". He claims that "the pure calypso, the best calypso, is incomprehensible to the outsider" (Naipaul 2001, 66). Antoni's writing inducts readers unfamiliar with Trinidadian popular culture into an appreciation of calypso, encouraging rather than—as Naipaul does—prohibiting movement between insider and outsider positions. Although at some points in the text references to calypsos are subtle and likely to slip the notice of readers unacquainted with the lyrics, at other moments the references are accompanied by contextual information which would be superfluous for readers conversant with the history of this cultural form. For example, the narrator's enthusiasm over the "Ten-thousand *Yankee* dollars" (77) she has received from the American army echoes almost imperceptibly Lord Invader's refrain of "Working for the Yankee dollar" in his 1943 calypso 'Rum and Coca Cola', which deals with the burgeoning sex trade during the Second World War as a result of the presence of a US naval base in Trinidad. However, should any readers miss this association, it becomes overt on the following page, where there appears an entire verse from the calypso. The narrator glosses it as "the famous calypso that everybody was singing that year" (78), a comment which invites readers to relate the lyrics to the wartime setting of Antoni's stories. Subsequently, readers are in a position to pick up on further mentions of the calypso, as is acknowledged by the narrator with her comment in the final story: "and of course everybody will recognize this one" (185). In this way, Antoni's address to readers blurs the boundaries between local and global audiences.

In rendering Invader's calypso accessible to a foreign readership, Antoni is not simply opening up a formerly insular cultural product to a wider audience. Harvey R. Neptune draws attention to the way in which US soldiers occupying Trinidad in the 1940s supported the calypso tradition both financially and socially, and argues that their endorsement shaped the output of calypsonians, who in their focus on US soldiers' cuckolding of local men, often "created material aimed at satisfying the vainglorious narrative desires and earning the rewards of Americans" (Neptune 2007, 143). At odds with Naipaul's claim that the "best" and "pure" calypso would be "incomprehensible to the outsider", Neptune suggests that Invader's calypso "cannot be fully comprehended minus consideration of the taste of American audiences" (Neptune 2007, 144). Neptune's account of the soldiers' patronage of calypsonians in the 1940s and the wealth of calypsos of that era figuring US soldiers illustrates how the island's calypso tradition has emerged out of inter-actions between locals and foreigners, presenting US audiences as bound within Trinidadian popular culture.

Antoni's concern with reading communities and the reading process is explored in *Folktales* through the dominant theme of consumption; of food, alcohol and female bodies in the stories, and of the stories themselves by listening and reading audiences both within and beyond the text. While Antoni's focus on the global consumption of Caribbean cultural commodi-ties might seem to distance his writing from the region's vernacular culture, it has in fact been prefigured within the Trinidadian calypso tradition. Like *Folktales*, the Mighty Sparrow's 'Congo Man' engages with an exoticist dis-course usually associated with external perceptions of the region. Antoni therefore draws upon a vernacular tradition which already involves an inter-play of inside and outside. 'Congo Man' begins as follows:

> Two white women travelling through Africa
> Chorus: Africa
> Find themselves in the hands of a cannibal witch doctor
> Chorus: Witch doctor
> He cook up one and he eat one raw
> They taste so good he wanted more
> Chorus: more more more
> He wanted more
> I envy the Congo man
> Ah wish it was me I wanna shake 'e han
> He eat until he stomach upset (what about you?)
> And I never eat a white meat yet
> (Sparrow [1965])

Sparrow's subject matter is the exoticist stereotype of black men as "savage" and oversexed, a stereotype structured around the trope of excess, as exces-sive appetite and excessive carnal desire merge in the sexually suggestive image of the Congo man's consumption of white women's bodies. However, his laughter is aimed in more than one direction. He incites laughter at the cannibal figure he impersonates, only to redirect it at back at viewers with the repeated quip: "You never eat a white meat?" and with his aside "What about you?" These questions align his audience, as consumers of an exoticist narrative, with the Congo Man as consumer of human flesh; Sparrow's audi-ence becomes the object of his satire. The focus of laughter in 'Congo Man' is therefore unstable, shifting from the cannibal figure to the audience who laugh at it. In this way, the Congo Man character continually slips between the roles of consumer and consumable.

Antoni's 'The Tale of How Crab-O Lost His Head' further complicates the consumer/consumable power dynamic articulated in Sparrow's calypso.

In this story, Antoni explores racial and sexual stereotypes which continue to have currency not only in external representations of the region, but also within Caribbean popular culture. Dressed "head-to-foot only in white", with "layers upon layers of white frills rippling down she long neck, down over she ripe tot-tots, and down around she smooth, shapely bamsee" (37), the formidable character Blanchisseuse wears a cutlass "tucked beneath the hair" (37). This image of feminine beauty combined with a threat plays into myths of dangerous female sexuality. As such, it draws on the Diablesse figure which has often been the subject of songs by male calypsonians—for example, Lord Invader's 'La Ja Blesse Woman' (1937) and Lord Executor's 'Lajabless Woman' (1938). Rohlehr sees this figure as "the Caribbean version of the most powerfully anti-feminist European myth" (Rohlehr 1990, 171). Like Rohlehr, Antoni traces the European roots of the Diablesse character; the narrator's comment that what the helplessly fixated audience of male "wadjanks" feared "most of all, was nothing more than the cutlass tucked beneath she jackspaniard-nest of hair" calls to mind the Freudian castration complex. However, while Rohlehr is concerned with the translation of European into Caribbean mythology, in Antoni's text the mystification of Blanchisseuse extends into African folklore, since the "wadjanks" also believe her to be "an obeahwoman—or worse still a sukuyant, a lagahoo, or a diabless" (40). The ambivalent figure of Blanchisseuse is therefore a projection of the desires and fears of a culturally diverse collection of viewers.

The range of viewing audiences suggested in Antoni's characterisation of Blanchisseuse is reflected in the narrator's multiple address to groups of readers both depicted within and anticipated by the story. Inside the fictional frame of the narrative is a voyeuristic crowd of village inhabitants, "[a]ll hiding behind the bushes and the boulderstones" (39) to catch a glimpse of Blanchisseuse's daily routine. Beyond this audience is a group of local adolescent boys, "sitting around [the narrator] in a big circle" (35) in order to hear her account of Blanchisseuse. Just as these two fictional audiences are entranced by what they see or hear, readers external to the text are potentially drawn in by the narrator's lyrical descriptions of exotic fecundity—for example, "a tall poui bursting out only in pink" (38), and "trees laden with fruits of every kind that you could ever dream" (48)—images which adopt the conventions of tourist brochure discourse. This alignment of local fictional audiences with an anticipated international audience of readers raises the question, crucial to *Folktales*, of who consumes and who is consumed in the context of twenty-first-century Caribbean societies characterised by a growing trend of migration out of the region as well as a growing population of returnees who contribute to cultural production within the region. Philip W. Scher describes how "Trinidad has been one of the largest contributors to the West Indian migration outflow", but points out that "many wanted to return and did so", either permanently or through temporary visits, so that for many second-generation Trinidadians, trips back "home" are regular events, and exposure to Carnival begins at an early age" (Scher 2007, 86, 88, 90). Like Sparrow's 'Congo Man', Antoni's story problematises the idea of a purely local vernacular tradition, highlighting the centrality of cross-cultural encounter, and of an interchange between inside and outside, to the development of Trinidadian culture. Furthermore, Antoni's figuring of, and appeal to, a varied but overlapping set of audiences in the 'Crab-O' story demonstrates the difficulty of demarcating a Caribbean readership which is becoming increasingly fragmented and dispersed.

Just as the laughter of Sparrow's audience doubles back on itself, in Antoni's story readers ultimately become the target of the narrator's satire. However, there are significant differences between Sparrow's and Antoni's attitudes towards their audiences. In the 'Crab-O' story, the co-presence of watching, listening and reading audiences becomes most pronounced in the scene where Blanchisseuse removes her clothes in order to bathe in the river. The narrator tells us that Blanchisseuse's undressing is "very slow and care-ful, garment by garment by garment" (38), and then goes on to describe the process in a manner which is equally slow and meticulous, beginning with "first the white bodice, one by one unfastening the bright mother-of-pearl buttons following along she spine, before she would unclasp the long frilly skirt" (38) and continuing to the end of the paragraph. Here, the act of narra-tion converges with Blanchisseuse's physical act, so that readers and listeners are invited to follow the process as gradually as the fictional voyeurs.

However, the hypnotic effects of this passage are undercut by the appear-ance of the village inhabitants "assembled like a band of bobolees with they eyes opened wide wide and they long red tongues dripping down" (39). At this point the mesmerising figure of Blanchisseuse is replaced with the comic spectacle of these viewers, shifting our attention from the object to the subjects of desire. Richard Alsopp identifies "bobolee" as a derogatory Trinidadian term for a "gullible person" or a "victim of ridicule". The "band of bobolees" can therefore be compared to readers of Antoni's story taken in by the sensuality of the language and imagery only to become the object of the author's satire (Alsopp 1996, 109). This encounter with Blanchisseuse's fictional audience to an extent encourages readers to reflect critically upon our own reception of the story, and in this way closely resembles Sparrow's persistent inquiry into his listeners' cannibalistic propensities. However, the cartoon-like "band of bobolees" offers us an exaggerated and highly unreal-istic version of ourselves rather than a straightforward reflection. As a result, a full identification on the part of readers with the fictional consumers is impossible, or at least far-fetched. Here and elsewhere in the collection, the viewing and listening audiences fictionalised within *Folktales* facilitate in the minds of readers a simultaneous sense of alignment and disavowal.

Sparrow's dialogue with his audience confronts them with their own exoticist reading practices, exposing their complicity in the perpetuation of the cannibal stereotype. Antoni's appeal to readers in the 'Crab-O' story is similar but not identical. While on one level *Folktales* reveals the dangers of exploitative modes of reading, the satirised consumer figures within the stories also perform another, more affirmative function. Antoni's fictional audiences inhabit positions which actual readers are not obliged to accept as our own. Following Karin Barber's assertion that readers are not "passive recipients of interpellation", since they "have the capacity to say whether they will occupy the position of addressee" (Barber 2007, 174), I suggest that as readers of *Folktales*, we are free to define ourselves against the consumer figures within the text, and moreover that the stories ask us to recognise an asymmetry between ourselves and the caricatured readers. Whereas the visiting US soldiers are *"immobilized"* (31) by the narrator's Venus Flytrap trick, Antoni encourages mobility on the part of readers. There is therefore a discrepancy between the processes of consumption featured within Antoni's text and the kinds of readings it enables.

The embedded tale, 'Gregoria La Rosa's Story of the Time She Got the Pin-Cushion Stuck Inside She Bamsee, and My Grandmother Attempted to Operate and Almost Pulled out Her Whole Asshole', offers further evidence of the ways in which Antoni's comic strategies mobilise readers. In this story, jokes operate simultaneously on a number of levels, generating a split in the story's tone and purpose. In a study of bilingual communities, Doris Sommer explains how bicultural jokes allow people to "pass from one position to another" and "become agents of jokes where they had been objects". As a result, they are "double-barreled jokes that shoot off in more than one direction", breaking down "distinctions between inside and outside" (Sommer 1999, 101, 103). A similar kind of duality is at play in the narrator and Gregoria's farcical double-act; light-hearted jokes aimed at a fictional audience of visiting US soldiers have darker connotations to be picked up by a more critically aware audience beyond the text.

This duality is underscored by Antoni's allusions to Invader's 'Rum and Coca Cola' (1943). Neptune notes that Morey Amsterdam, "an American emcee who had come to work at the Port of Spain USO in late 1943", altered some of the lyrics of 'Rum and Coca Cola' and "presented Lord Invader's composition to the Andrews Sisters as his own" (Neptune 2007, 141). Rohlehr gives details of the court case following this, eventually won by Invader in 1947, where Amsterdam's lawyer claimed that Invader's song was folklore and therefore uncopyrightable (Rohlehr 1990, 362). Amsterdam's version of the calypso extended its popularity beyond Trinidad to a much wider audience. Selling at least 2.5 million copies (Rohlehr 1990, 21), the Andrews Sisters gave a local cultural form global prominence. A comparison of Morey Amsterdam's lyrics with Invader's indicates that this promotion of the calypso came at the cost of reduced topicality:

When the Yankees first came to Trinidad
Some of the young girls were more than glad

They said that the Yankees treat them nice
And they give them a better price
(Invader 1943, 239)

Since the Yankee come to Trinidad
They got the young girls goin' mad
Young girls say they treat 'em nice
Make Trinidad like paradise
(Andrews Sisters 1944)

Invader's first verse is barely changed by the Andrews Sisters, but a minor alteration is telling: in replacing "better price" with "paradise", the US version at once underplays the financial basis of liaisons between US soldiers and local women, and evokes the exoticist trope of the Caribbean as a "new Eden" (Sheller 2004, 180). This produces an image of the region which accentuates its physical beauty while disguising its social problems. In other verses, discrepancies between the two versions become more pronounced:

I had a little chica the other day
But her mother came and took her away
Self, her mother, and her sisters
Went in a cab with some soldiers
[...]
I know a couple who got married one afternoon
And was to go to Miami on their honeymoon
But the bride run away with a soldier lad
And the stupid husband went staring mad
(Invader 1943, 239)

From Chicachicaree to Mona's Isle
Native girls all dance and smile
Help soldier celebrate his leave
Make every day like New Year's Eve
(Andrews Sisters 1944)

These verses differ not only in lyrics and imagery, but also in point of view. Opening his verses with "I had a little chica" and "I know a couple", Invader clearly positions himself within the Trinidadian community suffering the consequences of the US wartime "occupation" of their home (Brereton 1981, 189): themes of loss and madness weigh down his words in a way which contradicts the levity of the song's title and melody. Conversely, the Andrews Sisters' version invites listeners to identify with the perspective of the US soldiers. The focus is on the effect of these liaisons on the soldiers, who are "help[ed]" to "celebrate" their leave and can enjoy Trinidad in an ephemeral way, as a source of perpetual entertainment rather than as a real place both economically dependent on and socially disrupted by their presence.[2]

It is possible to compare *Folktales* with the Andrews Sisters' calypso; in both cases, the writers employ exoticist tropes likely to entice a foreign audience. However, the narrator's use of Invader's lyrics distinguishes Antoni's text from the Andrew Sisters' calypso. The exoticist narrative which *Folktales* seems, on the surface, to present to foreign readers is undermined by Antoni's selection of the words "better price" (158) rather than "paradise"; this detail reminds us of the status of "paradise" as a commercialised image and its cost to local Trinidadians.

The pin-cushion story features a comic performance staged for a fictional audience of US soldiers, whose meal of numerous courses coincides with the increasingly spectacular stages of the operation. It is embedded within a longer narrative in which the same audience reappears, eating a similar meal and enjoying the performance indirectly as a story. This mirroring effect draws attention to correspondences between the meal, Gregoria's body and the narrator's story as consumables, collapsing the boundaries between viewing, listening and reading audiences. On all three levels, Gregoria's distress potentially heightens the enjoyment and amusement of consumers. The soldiers' laughter is often elicited through a reinforcement of racial and sexual stereotypes. For example, the narrator compares her act of operating upon Gregoria to "peering inside the deep dark hole of Calcutta" (160). Although she insists she is referring only to the bad lighting in the kitchen, the pun on "hole" depends upon an inaccurate association of Gregoria with a place she has neither been to nor is ancestrally linked to; as we have learned in an earlier story, she is descended from Amerindians. As such, the joke draws on the exoticist trope of replacing individuality and cultural specificity with a homogenising fantasy of otherness.

While the narrator's jokes certainly cater to the exoticist desires of the soldiers—just as she literally caters for them with her meals of many courses—they also contain the potential to undermine exoticist reading practices. On one level, it is possible for readers to share the laughter of the listening US soldiers. On another level, the near-rape of Gregoria by one of those soldiers reveals the dangers of this form of humour. The ridiculous image of the soldier Tanzania wearing the tattoo's shell "like as if he was trying to fulfil the fiction of *me* in my firechief hat" (168) allows the narrator to make a serious point regarding the active role that her entertaining story has played in Tanzania's subsequent assault of Gregoria. To quote David Rudder's comments on calypso humour, laughter at this point becomes a "cutting kind of laugh" which "cut[s] through everything" (Rudder 1991, 55), laying bare the exploitative nature of the soldiers' relations with the local women, as well as the complicity of the narrator in that exploitation. Two jokes therefore operate at the same time, as the demeaning laughter of the soldiers is set against the narrator's ironic reflections on that laughter. Antoni's humour, returning to Doris Sommer's words, is "double-barreled", shooting "off in more than one direction", and in doing so deliberately destabilising readers. The layering of different kinds of laughter invites us to "pass from one position to another", shifting between sharing in the soldiers' amusement and appreciating the narrator's joke against them.

Both in its depiction of consumer figures and in its nuanced interpellation of readers, *Folktales* intervenes in critical debates surrounding the marketing and reception of postcolonial cultural products, showing how theories of "the West"'s consumption of the Caribbean region encounter problems when placed in dialogue with discussions of contemporary reading cultures. Antoni's stories illustrate how theoretical models of a "metropolitan reading public" are becoming increasingly inapplicable in a twenty-first-century world characterised by a heightened mobility of people and cultural products. In this way, his fiction helps to reformulate conceptions of readerships and reading practices. Furthermore, by encouraging readers based outside the Caribbean region to position themselves as insiders, *Folktales* potentially influences the shaping of reading communities. Karin Barber considers the dynamic function of texts in the formation of reading constituencies, looking at how an address to readers can "play a part in constituting new forms of sociality" (Barber 2007, 139). *Folktales* performs such a role, contributing to the emergence of a Caribbean readership of permeable and negotiable borders.

Notes

1. The problems I encountered in my attempt to obtain sales figures for Antoni's text within the Caribbean region highlight the difficulty of identifying a local Caribbean readership in the twenty-first century. Antoni's book was most successful in the US, where 1,381 copies have been sold since its publication in 2000, and in the UK, where 1,258 copies have been sold (Nielsen BookScan 2011). However, bearing in mind the growing Caribbean diaspora in both of these locations, these figures do not necessarily represent a foreign audience.
2. Bridget Brereton describes the "tremendous socio-economic impact" of the construction of US bases in 1940s Trinidad, explaining how it led to a drastic rise in employment among Trinidadians, the abandonment of established industries and a sharp increase in prostitution and organised crime (Brereton 1981, 92).

References

Alsopp, Richard, ed. 1996. *Dictionary of Caribbean English Usage.* Jamaica: University of the West Indies Press.

Amsterdam, Morey, Al Stillman, Paul Baron and Jeri Sullavan. 1944. "Rum and Coca Cola." Reproduced by permission of EMI Music Publishing Limited, London W8 5SW. Canada Decca 10205.

Antoni, Robert. 2000. *My Grandmother's Erotic Folktales*. London: Faber & Faber.

Balliger, Robin. 2007. "The Politics of Cultural Value and the Value of Cultural Politics: International Intellectual Property Legislation in Trinidad." In *Trinidad Carnival: The Cultural Politics of a Transnational Festival*, edited by Garth L. Green and Philip W. Scher, 198–215. Bloomington: Indiana University Press.

Barber, Karin. 2007. *The Anthropology of Texts, Persons and Publics: Oral and Written Culture in Africa and Beyond*. Cambridge: Cambridge University Press.

Brennan, Timothy. 1990. "The National Longing for Form." In *Nation and Narration*, edited by Homi K. Bhabha, 44–70. London: Routledge.

Brereton, Bridget. 1981. *A History of Modern Trinidad 1783–1962*. Kingston: Heinemann.

Brouillette, Sarah. 2007. *Postcolonial Writers in the Global Literary Marketplace*. Basingstoke: Macmillan.

"Dorit Lombroso Bio." 2003. Dorit Lombroso Photography. http://www.lombrosophoto.com/bio/index.htm.

Fraser, Robert. 2008. *Book History through Postcolonial Eyes: Rewriting the Script*. London: Routledge.

Huggan, Graham. 2001. *The Postcolonial Exotic: Marketing the Margins*. London: Routledge.

Invader, Lord. 1943. "Rum and Coca Cola." Reproduced in *Calypso Calaloo: Early Carnival Music in Trinidad*, by Donald R. Hill, 239–40. Gainesville: University Press of Florida, 1993.

Lovelace, Earl. 2003. "Progress and Calypso." In *Growing in the Dark (Selected Essays)*, edited by Funso Aiyejina, 131–34. San Juan, Trinidad: Lexicon Trinidad.

Naipaul, V. S. (1962) 2001. *The Middle Passage: Impressions of Five Colonial Societies*. London: Picador.

Neptune, Harvey R. 2007. *Caliban and the Yankees: Trinidad and the United States Occupation*. Chapel Hill: University of North Carolina Press.

Nielsen BookScan data on sales of Robert Antoni, *My Grandmother's Erotic Folktales*. Email correspondence.

Rahim, Jennifer. 2006. "'A Quartet of Daffodils' Only: Negotiating the Specific and the Relational in the Context of Multiculturalism and Globalization." In *Caribbean Literature in a Global Context*, edited by Funso Aiyejina and Paula Morgan, 31–64. San Juan, Trinidad: Lexicon Trinidad.

Rohlehr, Gordon. 1990. *Calypso and Society in Pre-independence Trinidad*. Port of Spain, Trinidad: Gordon Rohlehr.

———. 1998. "'We Getting the Kaiso That We Deserve': Calypso and the World Music Market." *The Drama Review* 42(3): 82–95.

Rudder, David. 1991. "Trinidad." *New York Times*, March 31. Quoted in Cynthia Mahabir. 1996. "Wit and Popular Music: The Calypso and the Blues." *Popular Music* 15(1): 55–81.

Scher, Philip W. 2007. "When 'Natives' Become Tourists of Themselves: Returning Transnationals and the Carnival in Trinidad and Tobago." In *Trinidad Carnival: The Cultural Politics of a Transnational Festival*, edited by Garth L. Green and Philip W. Scher, 84–101. Bloomington: Indiana University Press.

Sheller, Mimi. 2003. *Consuming the Caribbean: From Arawaks to Zombies*. London: Routledge.

———. 2004. "Natural Hedonism: The Invention of Caribbean Islands as Tropical Playgrounds." In *Beyond the Blood, the Beach and the Banana*, edited by Sandra Courtman, 170–85. Kingston, Jamaica: Ian Randle.

Smith, Eric D. 2004. "Pandering Caribbean Spice: The Strategic Exoticism of Robert Antoni's *My Grandmother's Erotic Folktales*." *Journal of Commonwealth Literature* 39(3): 5–24.

Sommer, Doris. 1999. "Be-Longing and Bi-Lingual States." *Diacritics* 29(4): 84–115.
Sparrow, Mighty. (1965) 2007. "Congo Man." *Congo Man/Patsy.* 7" National NSP-052
   Reproduced by permission of "Dr. Slinger Francisco" aka Mighty Sparrow.

Part IV
Reading and Nationalism

10 Reading Gender and Social Reform in the *Indian Social Reformer*

Srila Nayak

Most histories of women's reform in late nineteenth-century India approach the subject through opposing counters of bourgeois nationalism and imperial ideology (Chatterjee 1989, 233–53). It is suggested that male reformers and nationalists imagined Indian womanhood in terms either of strict demarcation between domestic and public worlds or changing patriarchal ideologies, which sought a synthesis between modern colonial culture and Hindu nationalism in order to self-differentiate from reactionary patriarchy. However, centring attention on colonial readers of reform-centred periodicals such as the *Indian Social Reformer* (1890–1936) reveals that the periodical's middle-class audience attempted to think of a more pluralistic approach to women's reform beyond the hegemonic connections between women's rights and nationalist or imperial constructions of her subjectivity. Recent in-depth studies of the identities of colonial readers of fiction and journalism have been of seminal importance in challenging entrenched perspectives on the relations between empire and colony (Newell 2011; Joshi 2002). In place of the binary opposition between the local and global or a view of the colonial press as a unified site for nationalist sentiment, these studies of colonial readerships reveal variable and heterogeneous responses and relations with empire and new insights into colonial identities shaped by active engagement with and transformation of imperial modes of knowledge. My chapter too attempts to move beyond the binary of empire and nationalism by exploring how a form of educated Indian opinion in *ISR*, committed to drawing masses of illiterate or under-educated women and young widows into the ambit of colonial modernity, gave rise to a species of colonial liberalism. The latter ideology attempted to assimilate imperial culture as well as nationalist will and also recognised the limits of both imperial tutelage and cultural nationalism, as it attempted to define women's reforms by appropriating and reconfiguring imperial ideologies of reform.

The movement for social reform that *ISR* initiated and consolidated in the 1890s constructed readers' identities within the context of modernising colonial culture and its liberal possibilities of female education and marriage reforms, which were pitted against an orthodox Hindu revivalist-nationalism that upheld "gender and class hierarchies" (Tanika Sarkar 2001, 171). At the same time, reform-minded readers of the periodical framed women's reforms within multiple hermeneutical contexts of contestation, restructuring and assimilation of nationalism that presented women's emancipation as a prerequisite to nationalism's demand for self-government. In my chapter on the social reform–oriented periodical *Indian Social Reformer*, I suggest that Indian men and women read liberal reform journalism as a means of entry into reform-oriented public activities that fostered identities often counter to nationalism's attempt "to make modernity consistent with the nationalist project" (Chatterjee1989, 240). The reform movement in late nineteenth-century India, to which *ISR* devoted most of its issues, spawned an alternative public sphere in which literate women and men attempted to frame women's reforms as a form of sovereign liberalism that was striven for irrespective of whether the issue of women's rights fit the ideal requirements of a nineteenth-century public culture of synthesis between modern imperial ethos and Hindu tradition. *ISR*'s editorial content demonstrates an eagerness to appropriate the Indian woman from imperial ideologies of reform in order to open up channels for native agency and identification with the reformist legacy of empire. At the same time, male reformers faulted the colonial government for using the justification of Hindu orthodox ire to resist legislation on abolition of the marriage of minors. Indian women, on the other hand, wrote to *ISR* about their dissatisfaction with the overwhelming influence of male orthodoxy upon the social reform movement, which continued to discriminate between women and men. My chapter will focus on late nineteenth-century language of reform in *ISR* (1895–99), its dissemination and consumption in order to gain insights into the formation of a public sphere of male and female middle-class reformers.

There has generally been a lack of attention to the coexisting discourses of male and female readerships in studies of press in colonial India, and comparative studies in relation to the colonial press have most often dealt with intertwined Indian and British national identities (Codell 2003, 15–28; Burton 1994, 63–96). Moreover, a scholarly and critical recovery of female readerships in India has been undertaken primarily in relation to periodicals and literature written for a female audience (Burton 1994; Anagol 2005; Tharu and Lalitha, 1991), thus leaving room to explore the discontinuities and linked histories of male and female subject positions within a periodical that was initiated to largely reflect and encourage male reformist and philanthropic sympathies but also provided space for female readers to explore their changing identities as educated women, a new sense of their roles in the public space of the nation and the impact of reforms upon their personal and social lives. *ISR*'s own strategies of social pedagogy, persuasion and inclusion underscored its attempts to both differentiate and unify the genders in the battle for social reforms. Through responses to editors and journalists as well as independent opinion pieces, male and female readers of *ISR* demonstrate opposing, collaborative and intersecting perspectives on the periodical's social reform agenda. Textual forms such as letters to the editor, field notes, pledge forms, letter essays and speech manuscripts reveal not only burgeoning new identities that overstepped conventional gendered barriers of public communication, but also distinctive textual and discursive modes through which the periodical invoked the identities of its male and female readers, in relation to the different ideological registers of imperial liberalism, Hindu orthodoxy and anti-colonial nationalism.

The Indian Social Reformer's Male Readers: Towards a New Patriarchy

The *Indian Social Reformer*, founded in 1890 in Madras by Kamakshi Natarajan, quickly became a key instrument in revitalising, radicalising and consolidating the social reform movement in India in the 1890s. One of the primary reasons for founding this periodical was to invigorate and sustain Indian men's interest in the movement for women's reform to counter the growing prominence of conservative Hindu opinion in the arena of anti-colonial nationalism. The famous Bengali reformer nationalist Bipin Chandra Pal wrote in *ISR* that the decade of the 1860s saw the least number of widow marriages in Bengal as opposed to the previous two decades and that there was a palpable decline of interest in women's reforms in Bengal, once at the forefront of the widow marriage movement (Pal 1902, 140). Sumit Sarkar has demonstrated how the steady erosion of support for social reforms by Bengal's educated public in the face of massive conservative reaction against women's reforms from the 1870s can be attributed to the patriarchal conflation of religious orthodoxy and Indian nationalism (Sarkar 2000a, 256). As Natarajan pointed out decades later, "The need for a special journal to deal with social reform was felt acutely during the fierce Age of Consent agitation of 1890 when the *Reformer* was launched into existence" (1928, 11). The British government's Age of Consent Bill, finally written into law in 1891 as a result of the long and arduous campaign for marriage reforms by Parsi reformer Behramji Malabari, had raised the legal age of consent to sexual intercourse and, hence, marriage of girls in India from ten to twelve years of age, provoking a fierce reaction from conservative Hindus at the colonial state's attempted jurisdiction over the personal domains of family and marriage practices. *ISR* also originated to side with radical public opinion during a fierce controversy relating to widow marriage in the Madras presidency. Until 1890, the social reform party of the Madras presidency, operating on Shastraic principles, or the precepts found in ancient Hindu religious texts, could barely advance the cause of widow marriage. In 1890, the remarriage of the widowed daughter of G. Subrahmanya Iyer, founding editor of the Indian daily *Hindu*, scandalised the Hindu community in Madras, who felt betrayed by this act of remarriage of a Hindu widow. Thus, *ISR* was initiated by a faction of *Hindu*'s journalists as an exclusively reform-oriented periodical in order to mobilise and encourage the views of those sections of the public who supported the cause of widow marriage but found themselves outnumbered by angry reactionaries and older, enervated reformers subject to orthodox traditions and unable to give practical effect to their sympathies.

ISR's goal was to represent itself as a radical venue for a newly emerging segment of the Indian male populace who supported far-reaching female reforms and embolden them to discuss all aspects and implications of the issue in their capacity as subjects in a rapidly modernising world. *ISR* was started as the special organ of the Reform movement in Southern India and worked in close collaboration with the Madras Hindu Social Reform Association, which was established in 1892. In 1901, Natarajan moved the journal to Bombay, seeking larger, cosmopolitan and more sympathetic audiences within the most progressive metropolis of colonial India. One of the key reasons for a push to transfer to Bombay from Madras, as indicated by Natarajan in his editorial, was the belief that the journal would find a more enthusiastic readership supportive of radical female reforms because "Female education seems to be the most popular in Bombay" (Natarajan 1898, 372). *ISR* also developed close connections with the prominent reformer from Western India, M. G. Ranade's National Social Conference, which served as a national platform for all reform organisations. As the journalistic counterpart of the National Social Conference, the periodical devoted considerable space to speeches on social reform presented at the annual conferences and reached out to larger audiences in both Southern and Western India. While *ISR* promoted the activities of the Social Conference to its readers, it was by no means its propagandistic mouthpiece and the periodical encouraged readers' radicalisation and self-authorisation, by inviting them to respond to, criticise and improve the Conference's frequently timid resolutions on women's reforms.

The journal was also instrumental in the formation and sustenance of numerous social reform associations across India along the lines of the Reform Association in Madras, which turned the activity of reform into a vocation, and reformers into a class of citizens whose vision of female emancipation sufficiently distinguished them from the majority of Hindu men. *ISR*'s portrayal of the issues of widow marriage, female education and the struggle to make an increase in the age of marriage for minors socially acceptable created a space for readers to assume the initiative and publicly debate controversial issues of the day with nationalists reluctant to make women's reforms a part of their endeavour for political emancipation. These debates reported in opinion pieces in the newspaper and conducted in public meetings of reform associations throughout the country shaped the complex discourse of gendered reforms. *ISR*'s combative stance against orientalists, Hindu revivalists and conservative nationalists in Bengal and Pune (Maharashtra) profoundly influenced the manner in which the periodical framed the identities of its male readers as progressive and liberal national subjects who would battle for the liberties of women as a means to a fuller political enfranchisement. Recorded opinions of male reformers in letters and published speeches attest to their view of women's reforms as a product of the influence of empire and also of the necessity to conceive reform as a national movement that would eventually develop into political self-government. Recorded opinions in *ISR* show that while a small and eloquent minority of Indian men pushed for swifter and more extensive implementation of reforms for Indian women, a large section of older male reformers urged a more cautious approach to social reforms, arguing that conservative reaction was caused only by too "rapid a progress" (M.G. Ranade 1897, 310). Historians of social reform argue that both Indian male reformist and revivalist discourses are constitutive parts of the "Hindu patriarchal system", blurring boundaries among revivalist-nationalists, the broader category of revivalist thinkers and liberal nationalists who invariably dissolved all differences in their defence of Brahmanical patriarchy (Anagol 2008, 306; Tanika Sarkar 2008, 259–81). However, as mentioned earlier, a section of *ISR*'s male readers resisted assimilation to structures of religious Hindu orthodoxy and wrote to the periodical in support of a more independent and ambitious approach to women's reforms.

While *ISR* insisted upon the choice of marriage for virgin widows or those girls who had been married and widowed while still very young, in letters certain male readers, often writing pseudonymously, went even further and called for "the freedom of all widows to remarry," if they so wished (N.S. 1895, 412). Lay correspondents, who were ordinary members of local reform associations in South India and volunteered reports on regional statistics pertaining to female education and widow marriage, accused the national reform association of diluting the aims of female education by moving from the more rigorous objective of "higher female education" to one of "raising the standard of female education" (Dekhani 1899, 117). The latter meant that only "the reading and writing of one's vernacular" which a girl would have acquired by the age of ten became the new "ideal of female education" (ibid., 117). In fact, statistics on widow marriages, late marriages in which the bride had been above sixteen years of age and female education that were forwarded from various towns and districts by members of reform associations created an alternative to the colonial government's census and gave high priority to new aspects of female identity in India. Letters and correspondences by men highlight their differences with the weak and ineffectual resolutions to promote women's reforms passed by eminent social reformers at the helm of the National Reform Conference, prompting *ISR* to ask at one point, "Why should the Conference then take a narrower view of the question (widow marriage) than the masses?" (Natarajan 1897, 202). This multifaceted character of *ISR*'s male readership shows both a tendency to advance and cautiously delimit the sphere of women's reforms in relation to the discourse of cultural nationalism. Frequently, discussions of women's rights in relation to Hinduism, imperial liberalism, anti-colonial nationalism and social reform movements in *ISR* also had the unfortunate effect of eliciting a male reformist rhetoric that seemed more concerned with propagating the view of a rational, non-misogynistic Hinduism that supported women's freedom in the abstract than with addressing the actual conditions of women's lives or identifying women's rights as the defining issue.

Those readers of *ISR* who self-identified as liberal reformers found in the periodical a medium to combat what Chatterjee terms an impermeable nationalist division between a feminised private sphere and a masculine public domain (1993, 120). *ISR* actively tried to foster an enlightened paternalism that would enable women to step out of their domestic identities on a quest for education with the support of male family members. Reform journalism played a significant role in recasting its Indian male readers as agents of a softer and more enlightened form of authority that was favourably contrasted with orthodox, revivalist and nationalist versions of patriarchy. Male readers were urged to recognise themselves not as passive consumers of journalism but as active agents of progressive social change and equal collaborators in a representation of their new self-image as reformers. Besides strategies such as essay contests on the topic of widow marriage, to expand male readers' social and cultural horizons as reformers, the periodical also solicited and published essays under the rubric of "Autobiography of a Reformer," which contained self-portraits of educated, ordinary Indian men whose path to social reform was enabled by English education in mission schools and a thriving print culture of reform-oriented periodicals (Gadre 1896, 342). Some of the autobiographical sketches were by those who had themselves married widows with the help of Reform associations, missionary societies and widow marriage associations. These autobiographies, while attesting to the modernising influence of reformist discourses and colonialism on ordinary Indians, also carefully highlight the victory of morally empowered individual agency over orthodox social forces.

Perhaps the most distinctive way in which male readers of the periodical were encouraged to change their patriarchal practices was through a new kind of performance of their roles as fathers and guardians within the domestic space. It was endeavoured to achieve this by obtaining their signatures on pledge forms distributed by the periodical, which required interested individuals to commit to reforms, which they would be in a position to carry to fulfilment. The document gave readers the liberty to commit to one or all the reforms, which included pledges such as not to marry one's son or daughter below a certain age, to do the utmost to further the education of one's own daughters and to use one's influence whenever possible against restrictions on widow marriage. The first draft of the form had signatures of well-known public figures and included an additional form which the periodical requested be distributed widely to friends and families of readers. It was pointed out that the pledge did not constrain anyone's liberty and should be treated as a "free expression of individual opinion" based on the belief that existing marriage practices can be best changed by "the method of each individual pledging himself to carry out such reforms as meet with his conscientious approval, and associating with others who take similar pledges" (K. Natarajan 1897, 582). While *ISR* attempted to use social reform to usher in a new moral and cultural landscape based upon changes to gender practices, its male readers employed the discourse of reform to translate themselves into modernised authority figures and benefactors of middle-class Indian women.

As a genre that rendered most visible a sense of common identity shaped by the social reform movement, texts of speeches and resolutions from public meetings constituted a core segment of the periodical. Such meetings were ambitiously organised in different provinces with the stated aim to move the government to legislate on further increasing the minimum age of marriage of boys and girls. The speeches focused on the physical, emotional and financial costs of early marriage and how a learned interpretation of the *Shastras* would actually reveal that the practice of child marriage was incompatible with Hinduism. Public reform speeches as printed manuscripts were creatively used by *ISR* to connect the restricted social space of regional meetings in which they appeared with the political arena they sought to influence, thus offering readers greater impetus to participate in such gatherings. As can be clearly discerned from such speeches, male reformers and *ISR* journalists vigorously advocated legislative reforms that would transform marriage practices by abolishing practices such as child marriage, enforced lifelong widowhood, polygamy and unequal marriages between middle-aged or old men and female children. *ISR* charged that the colonial government's 1891 Age of Consent act raising the legal age of marriage for females from ten to twelve was hardly adequate, particularly considering the fact that it was hardly enforced and child marriages went on with impunity. The journalists of *ISR* tried to shape a late nineteenth-century discourse of women's reforms predominantly centred on tracking and debating legislation on child marriage. Interestingly enough, public meetings in South India called upon the colonial government to implement an act that would prohibit the marriage of boys below nineteen years of age. An increasing section of male readers wrote letters to the periodical asserting that early marriage was equally harmful to the male as family responsibilities at an early age disrupted his education and this widespread practice meant that higher education statistics for men were not much higher than they were for women. Thus, readers were transforming the orthodox domain of marriage into a form of public activism and a barometer by which social progress could be measured. Men's writings advocating legislative reforms in *ISR* showed a willingness to criticise the shortcomings of the imperial government, particularly the compromise struck by colonial authorities with orthodox Hindu opinion (Anagol 2008, 282–312). The widespread movement to fight for appropriate social legislation to improve the conditions of Indian marriage introduced to native readers the distinct possibility of effective self-determination in which the native population possessed the ability for rational critique and reform.

Female Readership and Social Reform

Indian female readers, as opposed to male readers, were more closely identified with the modernising influence of empire by the periodical and, in particular, were encouraged to mingle, collaborate and associate with English women and their various reform activities in India. Sumit Sarkar has argued that a view of "relentless colonial domination" in the influential aftermath of Edward Said's *Orientalism* (1978) has obscured the many variations of colonial authority and the manner in which movements by and on behalf of women "did try to utilize Western ideologies, and colonial law, justice and administration as major resources" (Sarkar 2000b, 247). The most telling example of *ISR*'s efforts to shape public opinion in favour of women's education in the colonial metropolis was its reports on London-based National Indian Association's drawing room meetings on women's reforms in India that were attended by English social reformers as well as upper-middle-class women and men of the Indian diaspora. *ISR* would often reproduce these reports from the British journal *Indian Magazine and Review* on its pages, interpellating its female readers in India as subjects of a liberal, pluralistic public sphere and fellow citizens in an international public sphere of reform. The editor of *Indian Magazine and Review* and president of the National India Association in London, Elizabeth Manning's schedule of speeches and appearances at different reform societies in India were announced in *ISR* prior to her arrival, and very often the speeches given by Indian women at public meetings attended by Manning made their way into *ISR*'s opinion columns. Thus, the alliance between Indian and English feminists was promoted as central to Indian women's self-determination and social agency. The most crucial difference between male and female readers of the periodical was the virtual absence of female opinion on relations among social reform, nationalism, Hindu tradition and spirituality. Unlike their male counterparts, female readers were far less bothered about the need to justify or adapt women's rights to national interests and were, instead, focused on the practical effects of liberal education and companionate marriage upon their lives and spoke insistently of the need to disentangle female education from the dogmatic views of patriarchy and Hindu traditionalism. *ISR* managed the discontinuous experiences of colonial culture on the part of its male and female readers by representing social reform both as a form of female awakening through colonial contact and indispensable to future national political freedom, as educated women with equal rights would expand the ambit of modern citizenship in India.

In an attempt to encourage educated Indian women to think of themselves as modern subjects within a liberal, sovereign and transnational sphere of reform, *ISR* highlighted the close rapport between exceptional Indian women such as the first female lawyer, Cornelia Sorabjee, pioneering social reformer Pandita Ramabai and imperial feminists. The periodical on more than one occasion reproduced the text of Sorabjee's talks in London at the National Indian Association's meetings on the subject of female education in India, alongside talks by Manning and British and Indian male reformers. Such essay speeches powerfully demonstrated to the periodical's middle-class female readers a prototype of an emancipated Indian woman who enjoyed the advantages of education, travel and social intercourse with both women and men in highly public venues, and, most importantly, was invested with the authority to speak on matters of national importance. Sorabjee and Ramabai as professional women and transnational citizens who studied, lived and worked in India, Britain and America presented new modes of understanding the objectives of women's social reforms that transcended a limited emphasis on improvement of women's domestic conditions, and a new model of female authority in the public sphere.

Female readers, more often than not, responded positively to the stimulus of contact with colonial education and with an international reformist enterprise, and expressed reservations about both nationalist and orientalist attempts to cast Indian womanhood in terms of the traditions of India's past. Antoinette Burton has pointed out that within British periodicals such as *Indian Magazine and Review*, "Indian women appeared as a colonial clientele that defined and authorized British feminists' imperial saving role" (Burton 1994, 101). Although Burton's argument rightly identifies the larger imperial framework of British reformist feminism, the diversity of affiliations, some of which were captured in *ISR*, between Indian women and Western feminists cannot be reduced just to the rubric of "feminist imperial domination" (Burton 1994, 102). Moreover, the female reading public of *ISR* predominantly identified the vast majority of Indian men as the primary obstructionists in their battle for reforms and sought the support of non-native networks which would not sacrifice women's reforms at the altar of Hindu tradition. In an essay-speech, delivered in Tamil on the occasion of Manning's visit to Madras, a female speaker repudiates the dominant male discourse of reform which primarily asserted parallels between female emancipation and Hindu tradition and demands her right to the modern education that the colonial government had introduced in India:

> Whatever the past may have been, of what use it to us of the present time to speak of past greatness? That some female scholars lived centuries before our days will not make us learned. It is only after the British took possession of our country that they included female education among the other benefits that they confer on the people. Even among

the English, the Christian missionaries have been the pioneers of female education in this country. (*ISR* 1897, 201)

Indian feminists pushed educational reforms for women in the direction of higher standards for female education beyond the basic level that male reformers and even British educationists deemed was necessary for them to be good wives and mothers. The foregoing example shows that female readers participated most frequently in *ISR*'s liberal reformist discourse through the form of public lectures or talks, and a representation of this form of female voice shows that the periodical's attempt to mobilise female identity through socio-political, extra-domestic and public modes of communication was seen as a far more effective way of drawing attention to the exercise of female self-expression than anonymous letters to the editor. While one might argue that this speech in the presence of Manning naively exaggerates the benevolent powers of empire, the fact remains that native female critique of male subservience to structures of Hinduism was a consistent theme in most writings and lectures by Hindu women, even when delivered in forums that were entirely Indian in context and composition. Thus, Indian women's association with imperial feminists, as Anagol puts it, "significantly reflects their loss of faith in Indian men" (Anagol 2008, 299). Female readers often criticised the enterprise of social reform as constitutive of a masculine public sphere in which the exchange of literature among male interlocutors confers a new respectability and identity upon educated male colonial subjects, but does little to uplift the condition of women in concrete terms.

Unlike male readers who approached female education by exploring its relations with Hindu scriptural texts, female readers eschewed abstract perspectives and were, instead, deeply interested in exploring how education would materially affect their lives as mothers and wives. Also unlike male reformers, letters and essays by female readers only on rare occasions considered the issue of marriage as the only means to relieve a widow's misery, instead, advocating a view that greater standards of female education and vocational training would ensure a better life for widows. Imperial feminists and organisations such as National Indian Association in an attempt to accommodate their advocacy of women's reforms in India with Hindu orthodoxy proposed a programme of social reform that "accepts the basis of existing institutions and merely tries to render the women of India more intelligent companions as the wives of educated husbands and more intelligent mothers of educated children" (*ISR* 1897, 372).

Female readers most enthusiastically engaged with this relationship between education and conjugal compatibility, asserting that with the increase in the numbers of English-educated Indian men, there was bound to be a gulf between them and their illiterate or semi-literate wives. In a piece titled "An Open Letter to My Hindu Sisters," a female writer characteristically says that English education for Indian women will "make the Hindu homes as bright and cheerful as the English homes, which are havens of rest and comfort to those around" (Kamala Sathianandan 1899, 314). Female opinion almost unanimously insisted that the unhappy conjugal unions in India were due to both lack of consent, as most marriages took place between minors at the will of parents, and the great disparity between the education of a man and his wife, preventing any genuine affection between the two. Women's perspectives and opinions in *ISR* testify to the progressive enlargement of the public roles of educated female readers and activists who articulated new ways of understanding women's reform, a move that endorsed British women's view of the centrality of female education to conjugal happiness and also transcended it to a consideration of women's lives outside domestic structures.

In letters and in public speeches at reform associations, women deplored the low standards of female education as barely adolescent girls had to cease or interrupt their education upon marriage and most were not educated beyond puberty, at which point they had to move to their husband's household and assume marital duties. In a Tamil lecture, delivered to the Madras Social Reform Association, an anonymous female speaker boldly emphasizes that higher education would enable an unmarried woman to live respectably and happily by adopting a profession: "And if she has no husband, is it not better that a woman should take to some useful calling like midwifery, nursing, medicine or teaching than that she should work like a slave under other people? If a girl is allowed to be at school till 12 at the utmost, how can we expect her to fit herself for such duties?" (*ISR* 1897, 233). In fact, higher standards for female education quickly became a part of *ISR*'s liberal discourse, underscoring limitations of the imperial domestic model of reform, as women readers insisted that their new message on education be incorporated into reform agendas across the country. *ISR* constantly solicited information from its readers and published reports on the progress of girls' schools in cities across India as well as euphoric accounts of Indian women who had stayed unmarried with the support of their families in order to complete their education, graduating with degrees in the arts, sciences and medicine.

ISR employed the voices of its educated middle-class female readers in articles such as the aforementioned "An Open Letter to My Hindu Sisters" to create and consolidate a bourgeois female subject position that attempted to find a middle ground between imperial models of womanhood and Indian women's self-authorisation as modern subjects. Written under a thinly disguised pseudonym, nineteenth-century novelist and editor of the *Indian Ladies Magazine*, Kamala Sathianandan's 'An Open Letter to My Hindu Sisters' in *ISR* sought to bridge the gap, as Sarah Chambers says of the genre, "between the public and the private, calling into question a strict division between political and domestic" (Chambers 2003, 59). This letter provoked responses from another female reader who, like Sathianandan, also identified herself as a Hindu lady ("An Open Reply to an Open Letter"). The genre of the feminist open letter had been inaugurated nearly two decades earlier, when Rakhmabai initiated her revolutionary campaign against child marriage by sending letters on the pernicious custom of pre-pubescent marriage to the *Times of India* under the name "A Hindu Lady" (Kosambi 2000, 127–130). The moniker of a "Hindu lady" as well as the format of the open letter of critique, protest and advocacy was thus adapted by female readers of *ISR* in an obvious attempt at identification with the feminist discourse of marriage and educational reforms that had been inaugurated by nineteenth-century female pioneers of the reform movement. In the first letter, Sathianandan concludes by stating that the education of Indian women in English "will be a principal instrument of social reform in India" (1899, 314). The prompt response to Sathianandan's missive issued a denial of the virtues of English language education. In "An Open Reply to An Open Letter," the female reader argues that Sathianandan's letter on female education written in English would not be understood by the vast majority of Indian women; such letters and lectures were implicitly aimed at a male audience, and for enlightening masses of Indian women other methods were required, such as "delivering lectures to women in the vernacular at social classes similar to those organized by the local Reform Association" (*ISR* 1899, 336). Notwithstanding the differing views about the benefits of colonial education, these "manuscript-letters" were remarkable for not adhering to narrow conceptions of Indian womanhood and for tying education to affective relationships with husband and family as well as espousing its absolute value vis-à-vis Hindu society and imperial culture.

My chapter attempts to offer a study of liberal reformist discourse through the participation of male and female readers with the most radical reformist periodical of nineteenth-century India. *ISR* invoked and elicited responses from its specific audience of educated Hindu males in order to give a new direction to their national and cultural identities vis-à-vis Western modernity and through the social context of gender reforms. The rich archive of male responses to imperatives of social reform demonstrates that reformist male discourses considerably complicate the portrait of a monolithic, conservative, nationalist Hindu male identity (Tanika Sarkar 1993, 259–81; Chatterjee 1989, 250). Undoubtedly there existed a section of male readers of *ISR* who viewed themselves as independent reformists, sufficiently distinguishable from Hindu revivalists and conservative nationalists, who prioritised female emancipation and women's expanded role in a modern colonial culture as germane to the conception of a modern Indian identity. Middle-class Indian female readers, while responding positively to *ISR*'s advocacy and promotion of alliances between Indian women and transnational socio-cultural reformist networks, also employed their identities as readers and writers to reinvent themselves as modern subjects in a colonial political culture. Women responded to the reformist press's new construction of their identities as reformers in a social movement with international dimensions by making arguments for and against aligning gender reforms with colonial education, thus demonstrating their own intervention in the shaping of public opinion about women's reform against the backdrop of imperial Western liberalism.

References

1897. "Woman's Duty in Regard to her Education." *Indian Social Reformer*, October 8: 201–202–203.
1897. "The National Indian Association." *Indian Social Reformer*, April 30: 372.
1897. "Early Marriage." *Indian Social Reformer*, April 11: 233.
1899. "An Open Reply to an Open Letter." *Indian Social Reformer*, June 25: 336.
Anagol, Padma. 2005. *The Emergence of Feminism in India, 1850–1920*. London: Ashgate.
Burton, Antoinette. 1994. *Burdens of History: British Feminists, Indian Women and Imperial Culture, 1865–1915*. Chapel Hill: University of North Carolina Press.
———. 2008. "Rebellious Wives and Dysfunctional Marriages." In *Women and Social Reform in Modern India*, edited by Sumit Sarkar and Tanika Sarkar, 282–312. Bloomington: Indiana University Press.
Chambers, Sarah. 2003. "Letters and Salons: Women Reading and Writing the Nation." In *Beyond Imagined Communities*, edited by Sara Castro-Klarén and John Charles Casteen, 54–83. Baltimore: Johns Hopkins University Press.
Chatterjee, Partha. 1989. "The Nationalist Resolution of the Women's Question." In *Recasting Women: Essays in Indian Colonial History*, edited by Kumkum Sangari and Sudesh Vaid, 233–53. New Brunswick: Rutgers University Press.
———. 1993. *The Nation and its Fragments: Colonial and Postcolonial Histories*. Princeton: Princeton University Press.
Codell, Julie, 2003. Introduction to *Imperial Co-histories: National Identities and the British and Colonial Press*, edited by Julie Codell, 15–28. London: Associated University Presses.
Dekhani. 1899. "Dekhan Notes: Education and Social Reform." *Indian Social Reformer, May 7: 117.*
Gadre, G. B. 1896. "Autobiography of a Reformer." *Indian Social Reformer*, September 17: 342–343.
Joshi, Priya. 2002. *In Another Country: Colonialism, Culture and the English Novel in India*. New York: Columbia University Press.
Kelkar, Umabai. 1899. "The Advantages of Having Educated Mothers." *Indian Social Reformer*, October 8: 41.
Kosambi, Meera. 2000. "Women, Emancipation and Equality." In *Ideals, Images, and Real Lives: Women in Literature and History*, edited by Alice Thorner and Maithreyi Krishnaraj, 104–144. Mumbai: Orient Longman.
Natarajan, Kamakshi. 1898. "Notes," *Indian Social Reformer*, July 14: 372.
———. 1897. "The Annual Social Reform Conference." *Indian Social Reformer*, January 24: 201–202.
———. 1897. "Letter from the Editor." *Indian Social Reformer*, February 28: 72.
———. 1928. *Miss Mayo's Mother India: A Rejoinder*. Madras: G. A. Natesan and Co.
Newell, Stephanie. 2011. "Articulating Empire: Newspaper Readerships in Colonial West Africa." *New Formations* 73.
N.S. 1895. "Correspondence." *Indian Social Reformer*, August 24, 1895, 412.
Pal, Bipin Chandra. 1902. "Anniversary Address by Mr. Bipin Chandra Pal." *Indian Social Reformer*, December 14: 139–141.

Ranade, Mahadev G. 1897. "Remarriage of Widows." *Indian Social Reformer*, May 30: 309–310.

Said, Edward. 1978. *Orientalism*. New York: Pantheon Books.

Sarkar, Sumit. 2000a. "Middle-Class Consciousness and Patriotic Literature in South Asia." In *A Companion to Postcolonial Studies*, edited by Henry Schwartz and Sangeeta Ray, 252–68. Massachusetts: Blackwell.

———. 2000b. "Orientalism Revisited: Saidian Frameworks in the Writing of Modern India History." In *Mapping Subaltern Studies and the Postcolonial*, edited by Vinayak Chaturvedi, 239–54. New York: Verso.

Sarkar, Tanika. 1993. "Rhetoric against Age of Consent: Resisting Colonial Reason and Death of a Child-Wife." *Economic and Political Weekly* 28(36): 1869–74.

———. 2001. *Hindu Wife, Hindu Nation*. Bloomington: Indiana University Press.

———. 2008. "Conjugality and Hindu Nationalism: Resisting Colonial Reason and the Death of a Child-Wife." In *Women and Social Reform in Modern India*, edited by Sumit Sarkar and Tanika Sarkar, 259–281. Bloomington: Indiana University Press.

Sathianandan, Kamala. 1899. "An Open Letter to My Hindu Sisters." *Indian Social Reformer*, January 18: 313–315.

Tharu, Susie, and K. Lalitha. 1991. *Women Writing in India*. Vol. 1, *600 B.C. to the Early Twentieth Century*. New York: Feminist Press.

11 Reading after Terror
The Reluctant Fundamentalist and First-World Allegory

Neelam Srivastava

A body of Anglo-American criticism on the fictional and filmic representations of 9/11 has recently begun to emerge, though few critics so far have dealt specifically with the role of readers and audiences in relationship to these texts. Images of Palestinians apparently celebrating the collapse of the Twin Towers circulated extensively around the globe in the immediate aftermath of the attacks, and became a popular stereotypical image representing certain responses from the Muslim world. These visual reproductions of the discrepant audience not only introduced the possibility of a polysemic reading of this event, but also provoked a general questioning that was conveniently condensed in George Bush's question to Congress in the days after September 11: "Why do they hate us?" Commentators suggested that trends in the US media which began in the 1980s, under the Reagan administration, had led to a reduction of foreign correspondents and of international news coverage; this became "a key factor in early media descriptions of 9/11 as a baffling, inexplicable and motiveless event" (Holloway 2008, 59). Bush's question also highlighted "the luxury of not having *had* to know, a parochialism and insularity that those on the margins can neither enjoy nor afford". Derek Gregory interpreted Bush's *Candide*-like question as imbued with the arrogance of the imperial gaze (Gregory 2004, 21). The baffled reaction of American political authorities and of some Western media commentators suggests that there was no readily available interpretative frame through which to view or understand this event.

After September 11, the need to know the answer to Bush's question began to dominate debates in the American public sphere, and more generally the Western public sphere. One consequence of this was an eager audience for fiction that focused on non-Western perspectives of the attacks against the Twin Towers. Mohsin Hamid's *The Reluctant Fundamentalist* (2007) went on to sell half a million copies in the first two years after its publication.[1] Along with other novels that focused on 9/11, Hamid's did not just attract a mainstream readership, it also turned insistently upon the wider question of "reading" (as interpretation) itself. But in what follows we will see that Hamid's novel functions to short-circuit the interpretive role of the reader. Everything sits on the surface of the text; even its allegorical elements (conventionally linked to latent and manifest, surface and depth meaning) stubbornly refuse to conceal themselves. The tale of a young Pakistani whose initial love for America becomes increasingly critical reads as an insistent allegory for the strained relationships between America and the Muslim world. This explicit allegorisation takes on interesting connotations when we look at readers' reviews of the novel on the Amazon website. Many readers picked up the text expecting a novel about Islamic fundamentalism, and indeed came away disappointed by the novel's apparent failure to deliver the "explanation" for why Muslims hated the US.

In what follows, I will examine how these various responses to the novel tend to adopt a symptomatic reading in the light of the "terror effect" that much 9/11 fiction seeks to explore. Symptomatic reading indicates a critical approach where we read texts for their ideological and "unconscious" meanings, with the assumption that we as critics can successfully plumb their interpretative depths, and "that the most interesting aspect of a text is what it represses" (Best and Marcus 2009, 3). It assumes that texts are shaped by questions they do not themselves pose and "contain symptoms that help interpreters articulate those questions, which lie outside texts as their absent causes" (Best and Marcus 2009, 5). My broader argument is that postcolonial reading has for a long time privileged a symptomatic approach. A pre-eminent example of this symptomatic postcolonial reading is Fredric Jameson's notion of the national allegory. While I argue against the reduction of postcolonial reading to symptomatic reading, I also suggest that the novel presents a counter-reading of 9/11 itself, an oppositional narrative to Eurocentric literary fictions about the fall of the Twin Towers.

Stephen Best and Sharon Marcus's notion of "surface reading", which they present as an alternative critical model to symptomatic reading, offers useful insights for tackling the peculiar veneers of Hamid's novel. Surface reading rejects symptomatic reading for its surface/depth structuration of the text's meaning. It sees symptomatic reading as outmoded, and also as leading to possible misapprehensions and inaccuracy with its predominant focus on political, or unconscious meanings, of the text. The text thus has no hidden meanings, no underneath: it is "the text as a constellation of multiple surfaces understood as concealing nothing" (Best and Marcus 2009, 9). The purpose of the critic should no longer be seen as that of the political activist, a charge that would be easily applicable to postcolonial theory. The function of criticism is a much more modest one: to indicate what the text says about itself. For Best and Marcus, "depth is continuous with surface and is thus an effect of immanence" (11). Thus the critic must show carefully, and with as much accuracy as possible, all of the meanings that are always already present at the surface of the text. In some sense, we could say that the text acts as its own reader. Surface reading resolutely rejects Frederic Jameson's notion that the meaning of texts is latent and concealed, and that the critic structures them all in terms of master-code or a meta-language that makes this latent content visible and conscious, thus making the critic the real author of the text (ibid., 5, 15).

The Reluctant Fundamentalist, I propose, renders symptomatic reading redundant in order to shift our attention to the postcolonial politics of the surface. More broadly, I will use surface reading in order to re-examine Fredric Jameson's notion of third-world literature as national allegory, and to move beyond this concept which has influenced the field so profoundly. Along the lines of Best and Marcus, I suggest that rather than reading politics into contemporary postcolonial writing, texts such as *The Reluctant Fundamentalist* present political critique in the very structure and surface of their text. In doing so, I argue that the novel's function as a form of political critique is enabled by an allegory at the surface of the text, rather than from the demystificatory operation of the critic (like Jameson's notion of third-world literature as national allegory).

A reading of the text from the point of view of surface reading also allows for a re-evaluation of the function of stereotype both as a mode of representation of otherness, and as a newly productive site for understanding the "framing" of Muslims in the aftermath of 9/11. The concept of "framing", as Peter Morey and Amina Yaqin argue, is central to the ways in which news and other media reproduce and structure dominant understandings of Muslim "reality" (146–147). If we read its narrative as a performance, then the reader might be construed as the audience of the dramatic monologue. The dramatization of this encounter between a mysterious Pakistani and a silent American in the streets of Lahore works to create a suspicion that Changez may be a terrorist, and forces the reader into a state of attentiveness to the complexity of its stereotypes and their workings in the text.

Stereotype retains a central space in narratives about the war on terror, and is thus activated by the implied reader of the text, mediated through the proliferating representations of Muslims and "terrorists" that circulate within the culture. A text with the title of *The Reluctant Fundamentalist* in some sense presents itself as "always-already-read" (Jameson 1981, 9 quoted in McGonegal 2005, 258), raising our expectations that this will be a story about religious fanaticism, most probably in a Muslim context; and this is how many readers approached it. Indeed some readers went so far as to persist in looking for "The Reluctant Fundamentalist" throughout their reading experience. Their disappointment at the apparent lack of such a figure was expressed in the titles of the reviews, such as "Where's the Fundamentalist?" (Qureshi 2007). If we take stereotype as a form of surface reading that relies upon a commonsense logic in which what others stand for is always manifest, automatically (self-)evident, then Hamid's novel presents us with deceptively recognizable images of Pakistan (and indeed, of America). In Changez's pre-emptive strategy of figuring Lahore as it might be seen through the eyes of an American, a threatening and sinister urban space is evoked, which at the same time contains the possibility of being interpreted in an entirely innocent way: "What bad luck! The lights have gone. But why do you leap to your feet? Do not be alarmed, sir; as I mentioned before, fluctuations and blackouts are common in Pakistan. Really, you are overreacting; it is not yet so dark" (Hamid 2007, 56).

Changez, the narrator, takes charge of the stereotypes evoked by his story, and maps both prejudice and allegory in all their complexity. In its contradictory, ambivalent dimension, Hamid's stereotyping is akin to his use of allegory, a mode of representation that has an unstable, shifting relationship to its referent. In much the same way, his text trains an allegorical gaze on America, and brings to consciousness the political implications of September 11, 2001.

The role of allegory in postcolonial texts was famously inaugurated in Jameson's 1986 essay, 'Third-World Literature in the Era of Multi-National Capitalism'. Jameson's theory that *all* third-world texts must necessarily be national allegories has helped to consolidate the enduring critical distinction between "Western" and postcolonial writing. I argue here that while Jameson's theory has been influential, it has also been misunderstood. Rather than a concept that structures the genre of what he calls "third-world" writing, we should understand national allegory as a method of *reading* non-Western literature on the part of a first-world critic. I pursue Julie McGonegal's assertion that for Jameson, allegory is activated by the subject-position of the *reader*, a notion that is implicit in Jameson's essay but is never explicitly stated as such. His implicit subject-position is that of the American critic reading a text which is not from his own cultural tradition. Jameson's approach is a method of reading "third-world texts" which takes into account the fact that these texts reach us as "always-already-read", (Jameson 1981, 9 quoted in McGonegal 2005, 258), mediated through prior readings and interpretations. By "always-already-read", McGonegal means that texts are read as "third-world" because the implied reader is from the *first* world.

Jameson's theory of "third-world" literature stems from his profound investment in the idea of symptomatic reading, and we might suggest, in allegorical reading: "*the story of the private individual destiny is always an allegory of the embattled situation of the public third-world culture and society*" (Jameson 1986, 69). The critic restores to interpretation the history that the text represses. For Jameson, as just noted, all readings are allegorical in that they enact the meaning of a text: "meaning is the allegorical difference between surface and depth" (Best and Marcus 2009, 5). Meaning is the allegorical significance that the critic assigns to the superficial effects of a text. This is why he assigns such an important function to allegory: in addition to seeing it as a genre, he sees it as a method of reading; as is exemplified in *The Political Unconscious* (1981), criticism is construed as a form of demystification. We might suggest that for Jameson, the genre of allegory is constituted by the very act of reading a text symptomatically.

While allegory can be seen as an overly simplified mode of construct-ing a narrative, "an unsophisticated, even perfunctory form of expression that merely reproduces a text's social and historical 'pretext' rather than envisioning it and transforming it anew", for Jameson it functions as a rhe-torical device that allows the unconscious to return to the surface of the text, and one that is activated by the reader herself (McGonegal 2005, 252). We now see why Jameson views allegory as a profoundly progressive genre, or a genre which has a politically emancipatory potential: it has the power to highlight the otherwise repressed content of social and political issues, unveiling hegemonic ideologies at work under the surface of the text. How-ever, for Jameson, Western literature is incapable of allegory in the way in which third-world writing is, because "in the west, conventionally, political commitment is recontained and psychologized or subjectivized by way of the public-private split I have already evoked" (Jameson 1986, 71). Jameson's method of reading Western literature saw it as a site of "placeless individual-ity", of "dying individual bodies without collective pasts or futures bereft of any possibility of grasping the social totality" (85). Hence, again, the role of the critic is presented as crucial for demystifying the unwritten capitalist ideology that underpins Western literature.

Hamid's novel invites a "surface reading" (as opposed to a symptomatic reading), because its allegory is so explicit: his narrator, Changez, reverses the gaze of the Western critic on the third-world text, by presenting us with his own "third world sensibility" on the first world, namely his migrant per-spective of America's reaction to 9/11 (Hamid 2007, 62). I use Hamid's text as an example of how surface reading offers a way to move beyond Jameson and his notion of national allegory, in order to sketch out a new significance to the allegorical genre.

In Hamid's text, allegorical stand-ins for America are multiple and obvi-ous: Changez's beloved, Erica, the valuation firm he works for, Underwood Samson, and the unnamed American interlocutor (though to be precise, one might suggest he stands in for the American *reader*). Each incarnation illus-trates a facet of America, an embodiment of a moral or economic quality: Underwood Samson represents the potency, efficiency and cut-throat compet-itiveness of American corporate culture, and Erica stands in for the wealthy, privileged and intellectual American upper-middle class to which Changez aspires to belong. At the same time, we take note of Changez's ambiguous subject-position in the text: is he "just" American or "just" Pakistani? In the course of the novel, he puts distance between himself and America; and yet, probably the most telling words about his sense of himself comes when he first arrives in New York to take up his job at Underwood Samson:

> I was, in four and a half years, never an American; I was *immediately* a New Yorker. What? My voice is rising? You are right; I tend to become sentimental when I think of that city. It still occupies a place of great

fondness in my heart, which is quite something, I must say, given the circumstances under which, after only eight months of residence, I would
later depart. (Hamid 2007, 31)

Changez's sense of multiple belonging, familiar to diasporic subjects, questions the notion of national allegory as inevitably situated *only* within third-
world culture and society, returning a political gaze onto the first-world
society he has lived in. Rather than being an allegory of his own embattled
Pakistan, Changez takes up the position of the Western critic as the privileged reader of third-world nationalism, and reverses his gaze, by allegoris-
ing America and its war on terror as a symptom of the country's malaise. It
is an allegory, but one which is visible on the surface of the text, and not as
the effect, or the production, of a symptomatic reading such as that of Jameson's. Allegory in *The Reluctant Fundamentalist* is located in the text itself,
rather than in the reader who imposes a meaning which becomes the end
result of his "deep" reading. Changez's almost relentless allegorisation of his
life in America as symptomatic of his shifting relationship to this country is
an explicit and *conscious* function of the text, which collapses the distinction
between the personal and the political. What Hamid produces is a "first-
world allegory" generated from a "third-world perspective". Though according to Jameson, in "third-world culture", the story of the personal is always
necessarily the story of the political, here the first world is revealed to be
capable of allegorisation, of having its repressed political content exposed,
on the part of a third-world gaze.

At the same time, Changez is knowingly self-contradictory about his relationship to America; even after he returns to Pakistan, in a conscious rejection of everything that America represents, he knows he has not made a
clean break: "I have been telling you earlier, sir, of how I *left* America. The
truth of my experience complicates that seemingly simple assertion; I had
returned to Pakistan, but my inhabitation of your country had not entirely
ceased. I remained emotionally entwined with Erica, and I brought something of her with me to Lahore—or perhaps it would be more accurate to say
that I lost something of myself to her which I was unable to relocate in the
city of my birth" (Hamid 2007, 160). This passage equates Erica, his American beloved, with America, thus registering the conscious discrepancies of
the text in terms of a lack of realistic connection between the two terms of
the allegory.

The novel's dramatic monologue is set in Lahore, where we find Changez
narrating the story of his "love affair" with America to an unnamed and
silent American interlocutor whom he meets in the market. The frame narrative spans a whole day, while the story Changez tells to the American spans
a period of almost five years, though it focuses mainly on the eight months he
spent as a consultant at the prestigious valuation firm, Underwood Samson,
located in the heart of corporate Manhattan. Thus the novel produces two

parallel plots that are strictly intertwined: the frame narrative and the chain of events that befall Changez. Clearly, we are being made to understand that the narrative is being structured in such a way as to be tailored to its interlocutor. Changez's story operates as an allegory of contemporary America seen from the point of view of a privileged Pakistani migrant who experiences a severe personal and ideological crisis after the collapse of the Twin Towers. Thus the text thematises a shifting allegory of reading; at one level, the reader inhabits the position of the American (the Model Reader), and the Pakistani constitutes the "text" to be read. At another level, however, it is the American who emerges as an allegorical text that Changez is interpreting; the Pakistani speaks for the other and imagines the other's reactions to the story he is telling, in an ironic reversal of orientalist discourse. In setting up this structure, the novel allegorises readers' responses to the novel, and what they might expect from it.

Hamid's novel represents an important literary intervention in recent discussions of "9/11 fiction" as writing that depoliticises the event it purports to narrate (Scanlan 2010; Eaglestone 2007). The privileging of trauma as the focus of narrative attention has been at the expense of a political engagement with the causes of terrorism. Pankaj Mishra is quite scathing of Don DeLillo's "retreat into domesticity" in *Falling Man*, and John Updike's unoriginal stereotyping in *Terrorist* (Mishra 2007). Jonathan Safran Foer's acclaimed novel *Extremely Loud and Incredibly Close* treats 9/11 as a mysterious and unmentionable event, a perspective made more believable by making the narrator of the novel a nine-year-old boy who has lost his father in the attacks. Trauma in this novel is presented as an intensely personal and emotional experience that never strays into the realm of political interpretation or contextualisation.

Hamid's novel can be seen to offer a form of literary redress to the ideological silences of this corpus of 9/11 fiction. It resolutely rereads the event in terms of a *lack* of trauma on the part of its narrator. Changez's story is told very much after the fact, a re-visiting of his former Americanised self before 9/11, and then of his subsequent awakening to the realities of his condition as a Pakistani migrant who was beginning to have divided loyalties. Changez finds himself in Manila on business when he hears about the Twin Towers. Manila produces a curious effect on him; it is here that for the first time, he actively tries to act like an American, though his unconscious starting point is the "third world sensibility" that he shares with the inhabitants (Hamid 2007, 62). This impulse is triggered by a very nationalistic sense of hurt pride; while Manila is ostensibly the "third world", its economic conditions and the architectural splendor of its skyline "were unlike anything I had ever seen in Pakistan" (Hamid 2007, 59). And it is in Manila that Changez watches the towers collapse on television. Here, in a foreign land, he first experiences the beginning of his self-transformation; in reaction to the Twin Towers, "I *smiled*. Yes, despicable as it may sound, my initial reaction was to be remarkably pleased" (Hamid 2007, 66). Changez preempts the reader's reaction when he swiftly follows up his remark with a direct address to his American interlocutor:

> Your disgust is evident; indeed, your large hand has, perhaps without your noticing, clenched into a fist. But please believe me when I tell you that I am no sociopath; I am not indifferent to the suffering of others. [. . .] But at that moment, my thoughts were not with the victims of the attack . . . no, I was caught up in the *symbolism* of it all, the fact that someone had so visibly brought America to its knees. (Hamid 2007, 66–67)

What is striking here is the way in which the narrative represents the absence of trauma relating to this event. While much 9/11 fiction focuses precisely on this moment of trauma—characterised by an almost obsessive re-examining of the time and place one found oneself at the time of the attacks—Changez experiences a sense of pleasure. For him, this is not a traumatic moment. Trauma, for him, relates to the moments—mediated through visual representation—when he sees Pakistan in danger of being bombed by America as part of its war on terror, and he fears for his family (Hamid 2007, 155–56). Changez's signal absence of trauma in his reaction to 9/11 is contrasted by the effect the event has on his beloved Erica. When he first sees her again after the attacks, he notes that "her lips were pale, as though she had not slept—or perhaps she had been crying" (ibid., 73). The experience of 9/11 has re-awakened her own latent memory of trauma, namely her sense of loss at the death of her boyfriend Chris. "The destruction of the World Trade Center had, as she had said, churned up old thoughts which had settled in the manner of sediment to the bottom of a pond; now the waters of her mind were murky with what had previously been ignored" (ibid., 76). Erica's depression is rekindled by the collapse of the Twin Towers: "It's kind of like I've been thrown back a year" (ibid., 74). This return of the repressed, and her subsequent inability to cope with her depression, is read by Changez as an allegory of America's inability to cope with this trauma in a vital and progressive way, falling back, instead, on nostalgia.

Erica gradually disappears into a powerful nostalgia for the dead Chris; and it seems to Changez that "America too, was increasingly giving itself over to a dangerous nostalgia at that time", characterised by a jingoistic patriotism of flags, uniforms, and "newspaper headlines featuring such words as *duty* and *honor*. I had always thought of America as a nation which looked forward; for the first time I was struck by its determination to look back" (ibid., 106). The equivalence is established by the narrative voice, and thus casts the story in an allegorical light. Both Erica and Underwood Samson (whose name suggests both the cut-throat business policies of the US, and emasculation) are allegorical signs of America– signs whose difference from the literal America come themselves to thematise the gap between the literal and the allegorical.

Changez's narrative contains within it a strong element of self-reflexivity and self-consciousness about the way in which his implied reader will receive his life story. Prejudice and stereotype deliberately haunt the text, daring readers to question the assumptions they have brought to the narrative, and to understand the partiality of Changez's views about America by enabling us to feel empathy with his situation. However, a (necessarily limited and partial) survey of readers' responses shows that Changez's position was often read in ideological terms, as is revealed by reviews posted on the Amazon website of the novel. The value of the Amazon site as a source for reader response to the novel is determined by the way the reviews are used as "guides" for future readers, or for potential readers debating whether to buy the book. Readers often respond to previous readers' comments, thus engendering a lively debate around the novel, a sort of online reading group. The site is also useful for a snapshot of immediate reactions to the novel, since a large number of them are dated shortly after its publication. The novel elicited strong reactions. Of the 180 reviews of the novel on the US Amazon website, many readers assumed a "we" being addressed in the text: "afloat on a sea of questions and new information about the people we have been attacking" (Grady Harp 2007). There is an assumption of an American national identity which finds an understandable parallel with Jameson's first-world reader of the third-world text. It was as if these readers almost unquestioningly inhabited the "you" of the text's dramatic monologue. They felt that the novel failed in its characterisation of Changez; it was not made sufficiently clear how and why Changez, after all the opportunities America had given him, suddenly turned so much against his adopted country (book-lover 2007). Such readers also misunderstood the title, and failed to find the "reluctant fundamentalist" in the novel. One reader even accused Changez of not being a good Muslim: "Throughout the novel I was looking for a fundamentalist who perhaps finds his true self after overcoming his insecurities and obstacles. Instead I found Changez to be a bad excuse for a Muslim who did better off with himself in the beginning of the novel and just went straight downhill from when 9–11 occurred. [. . .] He ended up getting fired due to his carelessness at work, lost his H-1 visa and had to go back to Pakistan" (Qureshi 2007). Many Indian readers objected to the way he presented politics between India and Pakistan. More than one reader also felt that it perpetuated stereotypes about Muslim men wanting revenge against America (Fried Green Chillies 2007). But there were also many positive and appreciative responses to the novel; indeed 107 out of 180 readers rated it four stars or five stars.

What is most remarkable about the readers' responses is their emphasis on a reading mediated by religious and national ideological perspectives. This is despite the fact that at no point in his narrative does Changez mention religion; this is not a story about belief, it is a story about competing nationalisms, which is part of the reason why its readership is so divided. (This is not to assume that all readers read within national discursive frameworks—I have commented earlier on the sympathetic and appreciative responses of many American readers—but some certainly did.) It is also an awakening of political consciousness, and an exhortation to the reader to do the same.

The novel makes stereotype a conscious function of the text, bringing to the fore the "latent content" of orientalist assumptions. The contradictory connotations and inherent instability of the stereotype as an interpretative frame for understanding reality are displayed, indeed theatricalised in the text's dramatic monologue. It is the ambivalence of the stereotype that both ensures its repeatability in different historical and political contexts, long past the end of formal colonisation, and "produces that effect of probabilistic truth and predictability which, for the stereotype, must always be in *excess* of what can be empirically proved or logically construed" (Bhabha 1994, 66). Changez's pleasure at the collapse of the Twin Towers reads at first as an ambiguous stereotype of Muslim reactions to 9/11, well codified within global media reports of the event. This is a stereotype that Changez is attempting to explain, not in terms of the poverty, violence and terrorism of the society where he comes from (as many readers might have expected), but rather from an uncovering of the very foundations of *American* society and nationhood.

Fundamentalism in the novel is represented by economic globalisation, not religion. Changez is a reluctant fundamentalist because he is wary and suspicious of economic globalisation as a hegemonic cultural narrative, as a success story for migrants like him: at Underwood Samson, "our creed was one which valued above all else maximum productivity" (Hamid 2007, 108). But he realises after a very short while that it is impossible for him to return to this single-minded pursuit of fundamentals. Changez soon begins to take on a "Muslim" identity quite aggressively, by appropriating stereotypes about the Muslim other, such as his almost mocking formality, his beard and his new role as an anti-American political activist, having made it his mission "to advocate a disengagement of your country from mine" (ibid., 166). Changez's performance appears as the unsettling aftermath of orientalism, when it obtains a new purchase among the very people it was meant to describe and fix. Stereotype is thus created, negotiated and subverted through narrative performance such as the one that Changez enacts with the American. Neo-orientalism aggressively reinforces the binaries of East versus West in such a way as to eschew cultural dialogue, but it also constitutes an appropriation of racist stereotype as a form of empowerment.

The novel, therefore, sets up stereotype as an unstable mode of representation. There is a psychoanalytic rhetoric of concealment leading to (self) revelation that Changez develops in relationship to the re-emergence of the political within the private and public life of America, and to the re-discovery of his own nationalism as a discourse of resistance. One of the most powerful metaphors that describe his relationship to America is that of the Janissaries,

"Christian boys . . . captured by the Ottomans to be soldiers in a Muslim army, at that time the greatest army in the world. They were ferocious and utterly loyal: they had fought to erase their own civilizations, so they had nothing else to turn to" (ibid., 140). Changez pounces on this historical reference to make it an allegorical vehicle for his own present condition:

> There could really be no doubt: I was a modern-day Janissary, a servant of the American empire at a time when it was invading a country with a kinship to mine and was perhaps even colluding to ensure that my own country faced the threat of war. (ibid., 141)

This image taken from history finally opens Changez's eyes to the imperialistic pretensions of America. He returns a postcolonial gaze to America, the "ex-Janissary's gaze—with, that is to say, the analytical eyes of a product of Princeton and Underwood Samson, but unconstrained by the academic's and the professional's various compulsions to focus primarily on parts, and free therefore to consider the *whole* of your society" (ibid., 145). Changez demonstrates to his listener/reader that the explanation for his return to Pakistan, his rejection of America and his emergent anti-Americanism is to be found within American society itself, not within the supposedly flawed or failed society of Pakistan, or the "third world". America, in response to the attacks, has retreated into myths of its own difference, and assumptions of its own superiority, "so that the entire planet was rocked by the repercussions of your tantrums, not least my family, now facing war thousands of miles away" (ibid., 156). America's rejection of any attempt to understand why the attacks happened is made the subject of an allegorical structure that seeks to render visible the political manoeuvrings of imperialist power. Effectively, we could say that Changez occupies the subject-position of Jameson as a first-world critic who reads third-world texts, and reverses the gaze on to a first-world situation, which "must be deciphered by interpretive mechanisms that necessarily entail a whole social and historical critique of our current first-world situation" (Jameson 1986, 79).

The novel contains within it a meta-fictional and intertextual reference to literary narratives about 9/11. After Erica's mysterious disappearance, Changez reads her (presumably posthumously) published novella, hoping to understand better why she has withdrawn from life and from him. But the story "was simply a tale of adventure, of a girl on an island that learns to make do", that "shimmered with hope"; while beautifully written, it offers no clues to Erica's tortured personality and most importantly, her relationship with Changez (Hamid 2007, 154). Changez's reading of Erica's novella shows that the political has been neatly recontained within the psychological in his friend's literary narrative, written while she was experiencing great depression and in the aftermath of the September 11 attacks. "I had begun to understand that she had chosen not to be part of my story; her own had proven too compelling" (ibid.,

155). There is no recognition of the other's presence or suffering; Changez, her Pakistani friend who loves her, has been written out of the narrative. Conversely, Changez's own story is told in a deliberately opposing style: highlighting the inevitable intersections between the political and the personal, and thus at the same time suggesting that contemporary literature needs to have its "libidinal dynamic" exposed. Immediately after his account of reading Erica's novella, Changez remarks angrily on America's attitudes after the attacks: "As a society, you were unwilling to reflect upon the shared pain which united you with those who attacked you" (ibid., 155). Like America, which has discarded any possible solidarity with other societies suffering from violence and terror, Erica (and here again, the allegory is deliberately overstated), has chosen to write a story without Changez in it, seeing her own trajectory as unique, "in splendid isolation".

My reading of *The Reluctant Fundamentalist*, using Best and Marcus's notion of surface reading, Jameson's notion of national allegory and readers' responses to the novel, has been partly to argue for a re-thinking of the concept of allegory in fiction, and to question the critical distinction between Western and postcolonial writing which Jameson's essay did so much to consolidate. If the construction of allegory in the novel may seem forced or artificial, I would argue it is asking the reader for a different sort of participation, an attention to the surface reading of the text: a reinscription of the political into the literary, as it were. The novel presents us with a "Third-World sensibility" (in Changez's own words) about the first world; a national allegory of America conveyed through the dramatic monologue of a Pakistani speaking to a silent American. A symptomatic reading of the text as "postcolonial" would be misleading here, and possibly reductive.

Notes

1.   The novel's sales were undoubtedly helped by its inclusion in the Booker Prize shortlist. Three hundred thousand copies were sold in the US, 150,000 in the UK, and the rest in other countries (Hamid 2009).

References

Best, Stephen, and Sharon Marcus. 2009. "Surface Reading: An Introduction." *Representations* 108: 1–21.
Bhabha, Homi. 1994. *The Location of Culture*. London: Routledge.
Booklover, 2007. "I Wanted to Love This Book". *Amazon* (USA). http://www.amazon. com/review/R3PMJNKIOHYCJ8/ref=cm_srch_res_rtr_alt_2
DeLillo, Don. 2007. *Falling Man*. London: Picador.
Eaglestone, Robert. 2007. "'The Age of Reason Is Over . . . An Age of Fury Was Dawning': Contemporary Anglo-American Fiction and Terror." *Wasafiri* 22(2): 19–22.
Fried Green Chillies, 2007. "Literary Laziness". *Amazon* (UK). http://www.amazon. co.uk/review/R3A0VMFRGDWBIO/ref=cm_aya_cmt?ie=UTF8&ASIN=024114 3659#wasThisHelpful

Gregory, Derek. 2004. *The Colonial Present: Afghanistan, Palestine, Iraq*. Oxford: Blackwell.

Harp, Grady. 2007. "A Brilliant Novel that Affords the Reader the Stance of an Outsider". *Amazon* (USA). http://www.amazon.com/gp/community-content-search/results/ref=cm_srch_q_rtr/?query=Grady+Harp&search-alias=community-reviews&Go.x=0&Go.y=0&idx.asin=0151013047.

Hamid, Mohsin. 2007. *The Reluctant Fundamentalist*. London: Hamish Hamilton.

———. 2009. E-mail message to author, June 22.

Holloway, David. 2008. *9/11 and the War on Terror*. Edinburgh: Edinburgh University Press.

Jameson, Fredric. 1981. *The Political Unconscious: Narrative as a Socially Symbolic Act*. Ithaca, NY: Cornell University Press.

———. 1986. "Third-World Literature in the Era of Multinational Capitalism." *Social Text* 15: 65–88.

McGonegal, Julie. 2005. "Postcolonial Metacritique: Jameson, Allegory, and the Always- Already-Read Third World Text." *Interventions: International Journal of Postcolonial Studies* 7(2): 251–65.

Mishra, Pankaj. 2007. "The End of Innocence." *The Guardian*, May 19. http://www.guardian.co.uk/books/2007/may/19/fiction.martinamis.

Morey, Peter, and Amina Yaqin. 2010. "Muslims in the Frame." *Interventions: International Journal of Postcolonial Studies* 12(2): 145–56.

Qureshi, Rabia. 2007. "Where's the Fundamentalist?". *Amazon* (USA). ttp://www.amazon.com/gp/cdp/member-reviews/A2DLLM7YQ74KA2/ref=cm_cr_pr_auth_rev?ie=UTF8&sort_by=MostRecentReview

Safran Foer, Jonathan. 2005. *Extremely Loud and Incredibly Close*. London: Penguin.

Scanlan, Margaret. 2010. "Migrating from Terror: The Postcolonial Novel after 9/11." *The Journal of Postcolonial Writing* 46(3–4): 266–78.

Updike, John. 2006. *Terrorist*. New York: Knopf.

Yaqin, Amina. 2008. "Mohsin Hamid in Conversation." *Wasafiri* 23(2): 44–49.

12 "Macaulay's Children"

Thomas Babington Macaulay and the Imperialism of Reading in India

Katie Halsey

Gauri Viswanathan's classic study, *Masks of Conquest*, asserts that "literary education" was "a major institutional support system of colonial administration". In British India, she argues, the study of English literature was never ideologically neutral, since, from its inception, it helped to sustain the colonial project (Viswanathan [1989] 2002, 4). Thomas Babington Macaulay's 'Minute on Indian Education' of 1835 sketched out the principles of the British imperial education system in India for the rest of the nineteenth century, and notoriously set up a cultural hierarchy of texts, within which indigenous Indian writing (and the cultures and traditions out of which it came) was dismissed as worthless, while the canon of Western literature, in particular English literature, was glorified. Although the extent of the influence of 'Minute' itself is sometimes debated (as in Evans 2002, 261–62), more broadly, critics such as Viswanathan, Priya Joshi and Robert Phillipson argue that the introduction of English as the medium of instruction in higher education in India in the nineteenth century had long-lasting and broadly negative cultural effects. Macaulay himself has become a metonym for the colonial project more generally in these accounts, often used to exemplify the cultural arrogance of the coloniser (see, for example, Joshi 2002, 229; Phillipson 1992, 110).

The term "Macaulay's children", referring to those Indians who have adopted Western cultural values, or who display attitudes influenced by their erstwhile colonisers, is almost always used pejoratively, and the connotation is one of disloyalty to nation and heritage. The term and its variants (such as "brown sahibs", "captive minds" and "Orientalized Orientals" (Sardar 1999, 85)) have been applied so widely in Indian political and social life as to have almost lost their specificity, but in fiction a notable example of its use is the scornful description of "Macaulay's Minutemen", who "would hate the best of India", in Salman Rushdie's *The Moor's Last Sigh* ([1995] 1996, 376). Rushdie has engaged explicitly and publicly with the question of whether an Indian writer can or should express himself in English. In *Imaginary Homelands* (1991), he writes:

> I hope all of us share the view that we can't simply use the language in the way the British did; that it needs remaking for our own purposes.

Those of us who do use English do so in spite of our ambiguity towards it, or perhaps because of that, perhaps because we can find in that linguistic struggle a reflection of other struggles taking place in the real world, struggles between the cultures within ourselves and the influences at work upon our societies. To conquer English may be to complete the process of making ourselves free. (Rushdie [1991] 1992, 17)

Rushdie's lexical choices are revealing: for the Indian writer in English, expressing oneself is a process of resistance, a constant "struggle", an attempt to "conquer" the language as part of the battle to overthrow the erstwhile conquerors to make oneself free. Such an attitude suggests that the policies laid out in Macaulay's 'Minute on Indian Education' have had far-reaching consequences for generations of Indian readers and writers, leading to an often troubling disjunction between experience and expression, a simultaneous resistance to and appropriation of the language of oppression.

In this chapter, I wish to advance the argument that it is impossible to understand the influence of 'Minute on Indian Education' without understanding not only the immediate political context of that document, but also Macaulay's own education and reading practices. In 'Minute', Macaulay argues for the value of English literature over vernacular literature, suggests that the medium of instruction of the "higher branches" of knowledge in India should be English, and calls, in an oft-quoted phrase, for "a class of interpreters between us and the millions whom we govern—a class of persons Indian in blood and colour, but English in tastes, opinions, in morals, and in intellect" (Macaulay [1835] 1935, 359). The attempt to impose the colonising force's tastes, opinions and morals on the colonised people by creating "mimic men" (Naipaul 1967) through education is one of the first strategies of cultural imperialism. Using Macaulay's 'Minute' as an example, Homi K. Bhabha suggests, however, that gestures of mimicry such as those demanded in 'Minute' are not simple attempts to become more like the people of the colonising power, but are in fact always complex, parodic and ambivalent, and thus point to the flaws in colonialist ideology and are part of the resistance of the colonised people (Bhabha 1994, 87). Bhabha suggests indeed, that the "absurd extravagance" of Macaulay's 'Minute' accidentally renders "the great tradition of European humanism . . . capable only of ironizing itself" (ibid., 87). Certainly Macaulay's pronouncements—"who could deny that a single shelf of a good European library was worth the whole native literature of India and Arabia" (Macaulay [1835] 1935, 349)—make him one of imperialism's most damning readers. But Macaulay's own attitude towards the tradition of European humanism was far from simple, and when we look at Macaulay's own reading practices we discover a crucial tension. I shall argue that there is a central conflict between Macaulay's own reading habits (resistant, oppositional, critical) and the ways in which he conceptualised the effects of reading on Britain's Indian subjects. A close consideration of

Macaulay's encounters with his own reading within the traditions of imperialism thus helps to re-contextualise the attitudes towards literature and the English language that shaped Indian educational policy, and hence reading practices and postcolonial audiences, in the nineteenth century and on into the twentieth.

'Minute on Indian Education' arose out of controversy and polemic, and intervened in what was, by 1835, a lengthy and bitter disagreement between the members of the General Committee of Public Instruction over the language of education in India. Some members, such as H. H. Wilson and H. T. Prinsep, still believed in orientalism, the educational policy established by Warren Hastings in the previous century, which encouraged learning in Sanskrit, Persian and Arabic on the grounds that such scholarship would "result in greater efficiency and economy in British administration and promote Indian loyalty to British rule in India" (Cutts 1953, 832). Others, supported by Lord William Bentinck, the governor general of British India, and backed financially by prominent Hindus such as Ram Mohun Roy, favoured English language education. Bentinck's espousal of English language instruction formed part of a raft of financial and judiciary reforms that were designed to destroy the remnants of Warren Hastings's influence in India and establish a new policy—Anglicism—in place of Hastings's focus on oriental scholarship. Hastings's policy had been based on the premise that British officials needed to have "knowledge and sympathetic understanding of Indian institutions, laws and customs", as well as of Indian languages and culture in order to "conciliate influential sections of the Indian community by demonstrating British respect and admiration for the indigenous languages and culture" (Evans 2002, 262). Elmer H. Cutts argues (1953, 825–29) that there were strong economic and political motives behind Bentinck's desire to do away with Hastings's policies, which Macaulay both recognised and understood. Influential British groups in favour of free trade and utilitarianism put pressure on the East India company to shift the emphasis of its policy away from appeasing influential Indians towards a more aggressive attempt to disseminate "useful" (i.e., Westernised) knowledge. Macaulay threw his considerable rhetorical skills behind this movement, producing 'Minute' in his role of president of the General Committee of Public Instruction.

Bhabha's characterisation of the "extravagance" of 'Minute' is accurate, but it does not take account of the precise context of the document's production, nor of its specifically *generic* characteristics. The "extravagance" of 'Minute', I would argue, is the result of genre as well as argument: it is a piece of deliberately crafted rhetoric, in the tradition of Cicero, designed to persuade not only through legitimacy of argument, but also through style and expression. In English schools of the nineteenth century, and in private homes where young men were educated by tutors, the curriculum focused heavily on teaching young men to engage with, criticise, translate and imitate the literature of the classical world, and was particularly directed towards the ability to construct, deploy and oppose argument. These paradigms of engagement, criticism, translation, imitation and opposition were, for Macaulay, as for others of his generation and those that succeeded him, the markers of intellectual achievement. Macaulay's nephew wrote that his uncle "placed Cicero's treatises on oratory altogether above anything that ever had been written in that department of literature" (Trevelyan [1876] 1978, 2: 425[1]), and Macaulay's annotations to such works as the *De Finibus*, the *Academic Questions* and the *Tusculan Disputations* suggestively point to his appreciation of the ways in which style sometimes triumphs over argument in Cicero's works. He described the Stoic theory, as expounded by Cicero, as "[b]eautifully lucid, though the system is excessively absurd" (ibid., 424). This is not to suggest that Macaulay did not believe in the arguments he sets forth in 'Minute on Indian Education' (classical rhetoricians such as Demosthenes are, after all, unanimous in recommending that the rhetorician believes in his own cause), but we should remember the generic conventions of rhetorical writing when attempting to understand the "extravagance" of the argument.

'Minute on Indian Education' begins by arguing that there is no legal reason why the money allocated "for the intellectual improvement of the people" should continue to be used to support Sanskrit and Arabic (as it had under the Hastings administration), posing the "simple question" (a question that is, in fact, far from simple, and which demonstrates the utilitarian agenda behind Macaulay's 'Minute'): "What is the most useful way of using it [the money]?" Macaulay then claims (wrongly) that the dialects commonly spoken in Bengal "contain neither literary nor scientific information" and are "moreover so poor and rude" that it will not be easy to translate works from other languages into them (Macaulay [1835] 1935, 348). Although the premise is false, this allows him to dismiss Bengali dialects without further discussion, and to take the next logical step in the construction of his argument: a non-vernacular language must therefore be necessary to disseminate such literary or scientific information. Having neatly, if erroneously, dismissed the possibility of instruction in Bengali, he turns to the question of whether the non-vernacular language should be English, Sanskrit or Arabic, and here he makes a statement that is both breathtakingly arrogant and astonishingly ill-informed. Admitting that "I have no knowledge of either Sanskrit or Arabic", Macaulay dismisses the poetry written in these languages, claiming that "I never met with any orientalist who ventured to maintain that the Arabic and Sanskrit poetry could be compared to that of the great European nations". He then passes on from "works of imagination" to scientific literature, in which "the superiority of the Europeans becomes absolutely immeasurable" (ibid., 349). All of this section of 'Minute' is the result of Macaulay's ignorance of the tongues in question, but his rhetorical engineering turns this ignorance into a position of cultural authority.

The part of 'Minute' relating most closely to Macaulay's own education and reading follows this. Arguing for the utility of the English language, he writes:

> the claims of our own language it is hardly necessary to recapitulate. It stands pre-eminent even among the languages of the West. It abounds with works of imagination not inferior to the noblest which Greece has bequeathed to us. . . . Whoever knows that language has ready access to all the vast intellectual wealth which all the wisest nations of the earth have created and hoarded in the course of ninety generations.
> (Macaulay [1835] 1935, 349–50)

For Macaulay, the English language functions as a sort of repository of knowledge (including that kind of knowledge which can be obtained from "works of imagination"), distilled from many other languages, which will be useful to all those who have access to it. Macaulay not only read the classical authors in Latin and Greek, and French, Italian, Portuguese and Spanish literature in those languages, but also analysed them, commented on them and, crucially, made them his own, in English. *Contra* the orientalist faction of the period, he did not think it too difficult for the Indian population to learn to read and understand another language, suggesting instead that Indian readers were "quite competent to discuss political or scientific questions with fluency and precision in the English language" (Macaulay [1835] 1935, 358). However, he also disingenuously sees no qualitative difference between, for example, a Bengali speaker reading in English, and he himself reading in Greek or Latin, failing to reflect on this proposed equivalence as a position which crucially depoliticises and dehistoricises linguistic acculturation, ignoring issues of India's and Britain's imperial histories and the cultural costs of hierarchies of knowledge. Furthermore, his assumptions of racial superiority are revealed in the next part of 'Minute':

> Nobody, I suppose, will contend that English is so difficult to a Hindoo as Greek to an Englishman. Yet an intelligent English youth, in a much smaller number of years than our unfortunate pupils pass at the Sanscrit College, becomes able to read, to enjoy, and even to imitate not unhappily the compositions of the best Greek authors. Less than half the time which enables an English youth to read Herodotus and Sophocles ought to enable a Hindoo to read Hume and Milton. (Macaulay [1835] 1935, 358–59)

While Macaulay's intention here is to suggest that Indian youths are as capable of learning to read as their English counterparts, his juxtaposition of "intelligent" English and "unfortunate" Indian youths undermines the analogy he is attempting to advance.

Macaulay frequently read in two languages simultaneously, deploying classical authors to criticise or comment on English writers. He uses Aeschylus to assess Shakespeare, for example: "The silence of Hamlet during the earlier part of this scene is very fine, but not equal to the silence of Prometheus and Cassandra in the Prometheus and Agamemnon of Aeschylus" (Trevelyan [1876] 1978, 2: 412); Horace to comment on Pope: "Horace had perhaps less wit than Pope, but far more humour, far more variety, more sentiment, more thought" (ibid., 403); and Cicero to criticise Ben Jonson (see ibid., 424 for Macaulay's reading of Jonson's *Catiline* in the light of Cicero's *De Divinatione*). Classical authors almost always came first to Macaulay's mind when he was engaged in the activity of reading and comparing authors; indeed often he seems to apply lessons from Greek or Latin texts to those written in English. Presumably he believed that the same model of cross-cultural reading would apply to students of writing in English and vernacular Indian languages. Macaulay's "class of interpreters" was destined to "refine the vernacular dialects of the country" and "to enrich those dialects with terms of science borrowed from the Western nomenclature" (Macaulay [1835] 1935, 359). What is clearly problematic about his assumption of Western superiority is that it gives no place to India's own history, culture and literature. Macaulay does not even consider the possibility that India's long tradition of writing in Sanskrit and Arabic could be considered to be equivalent to the Latin and Greek texts of his own education. It seems that he either could not or would not think beyond the cultural hierarchies set up earlier in 'Minute'.

Indeed he seeks to shore them up with further examples of East/West linguistic contact on the boundaries of Europe: he argues that the introduction of non-vernacular literature to Russia had "civilized" the Russian by making him compare the "old women's stories which his rude fathers had believed" with what he read in "those foreign languages in which the greatest mass of information had been laid up". Macaulay suggests that the same will be true for the Indian population: "The languages of Western Europe civilized Russia. I cannot doubt that they will do for the Hindoo what they have done for the Tartar" (ibid., 352). All of this deliberately ignores India's own long history of "civilisation", making the assumption that Indian readers were ignorant savages in need of the cultural enlightenment of the West. In refusing to acknowledge India's own civilised history, Macaulay also refuses to acknowledge the basis of Hastings's orientalist policy, which had believed that Britain's mission in India was "to reinvigorate rather than replace Indian civilization" (Evans 2002, 262), and hence makes a strongly political point within the context of the Anglicist/orientalist debates.

Here we must turn to a more detailed study of Macaulay's reading habits in order to elucidate further the problematic moments in 'Minute'. Macaulay's reading was first described in detail by his nephew, Sir George Otto Trevelyan, in his *Life and Letters of Lord Macaulay* (1876). William Chislett discussed Macaulay's classical reading in 1918; A. N. L. Munby catalogued

Macaulay's library in 1966, and more recent discussions of the subject include articles by Wynne Williams and Felicity Stimpson (1993 and 2007 respectively), and Robert E. Sullivan's *Macaulay: The Tragedy of Power* (2009). Critics agree that Macaulay was an astonishingly meticulous reader, with an almost encyclopaedic knowledge of Latin and Greek literature, and a photographic memory. The range and breadth of his reading were extremely wide, and attention to what he was reading was both intense and unwavering. As Frederic Myers told Trevelyan, "he seems habitually to have read as I read only during my first half-hour with a great author" (Trevelyan [1876] 1978, 2: 402). Macaulay read extensively for pleasure, but he also read with an eye to using his reading in his numerous literary, historical and political writings. At the end of the year 1835 (the year in which he drafted 'Minute on Indian Education' in Calcutta), Macaulay reckoned up his reading as follows:

> I have cast up my reading account, and brought it to the end of the year 1835. It includes December 1834; for I came into my house and unpacked my books at the end of November 1834. During the last thirteen months I have read Aeschylus twice; Sophocles twice; Euripides once; Pindar twice; Callimachus; Apollonius Rhodius; Quintus Calaber; Theocritus twice; Herodotus; Thucydides; almost all Xenophon's works; almost all Plato; Aristotle's Politics, and a good deal of his Organon, besides dipping elsewhere in him; the whole of Plutarch's Lives; about half of Lucian; two or three books of Athenaeus; Plautus twice; Terence twice; Lucretius twice; Catullus; Tibullus; Propertius; Lucan; Statius; Silius Italicus; Livy; Velleius Paterculus; Sallust; Caesar; and, lastly, Cicero. I have, indeed, still a little of Cicero left; but I shall finish him in a few days. I am now deep in Aristophanes and Lucian. (Pinney 1976, 3: 159–60)

The books he took with him to Calcutta in 1834 bear the evidence of his reading. Macaulay did not just read these works casually. They were read with great care, as shown by the pencil marks, single, double and treble lines, which mark passages of particular interest, and by the copious marginal notes in which Macaulay delighted. As seen earlier, he frequently read texts more than once, often recording his impressions on each reading. At the end of Xenophon's *Anabasis*, for example, are the words: "Decidedly his best work.–December 17, 1835. Most certainly.–February 24, 1837" and "One of the very first works that antiquity has left us. Perfect in its kind.– October 8, 1837" (Trevelyan [1876] 1978, 2: 443). Early in his Calcutta years, Macaulay made the decision to "go fairly through the whole literature of Greece and Rome before I return" (Pinney 1976, 3: 136). "Having acquired some knowledge of the literature of France, Italy, Spain, and Portugal, having seen something of the world, having been a spectator and an actor in politics," Macaulay wrote to his friend Richard Sharp, in February of 1835, "the ancient writers . . . appear quite new to me". He found in them "ten thousand things worthy of notice which never struck me in my college days," writing, "My admiration for Greek increases every day. It almost amounts to idolatry" (ibid., 137). The "ancient writers" became a renewed source of wonder, if not obsession, to Macaulay at the very time that he was beginning to draft 'Minute on Indian Education'.

In that document, Macaulay equates England's role in India to the humanist revival of the late fifteenth and early sixteenth centuries in Europe:

> The first instance to which I refer is the great revival of letters among the Western nations at the close of the fifteenth and the beginning of the sixteenth century. At that time almost everything that was worth reading was contained in the writings of the ancient Greeks and Romans. Had our ancestors acted as the Committee of Public Instruction has hitherto noted, had they neglected the language of Thucydides and Plato, and the language of Cicero and Tacitus, had they confined their attention to the old dialects of our own island, had they printed nothing and taught nothing at the universities but chronicles in Anglo-Saxon and romances in Norman French,—would England ever have been what she now is? What the Greek and Latin were to the contemporaries of More and Ascham, our tongue is to the people of India. (Macaulay [1835] 1935, 351)

Once again making use of rhetorical devices—here, in particular the rhetorical question—Macaulay makes the argument for English as a *lingua franca* for "the people of India" and explicitly suggests that the English language now deserves a similar status to Latin and Greek on the grounds that it has taken over the function of disseminating enlightenment and knowledge previously carried out by the ancient languages. The comparison with two leading humanists is carefully chosen. Roger Ascham did much to revive and popularise the Greek tongue in the sixteenth century, not least in his role as tutor to Queen Elizabeth I. Ascham writes that "only in the Greek and Latin Tongue" are "the true Precepts, and perfect examples of Eloquence" to be found (Ascham [1570] 1711, 172), so, by analogy, Macaulay's argument for the beauty of the English tongue is reflected here. Thomas More wrote and published *Utopia* in Latin in order to disseminate his vision of good government to the widest possible European readership, Latin being the *lingua franca* of the sixteenth century. Hence Macaulay's analogy: Latin and Greek disseminated humanist scholarship in the sixteenth century; English, the allusion implies, will complete the humanist project of encouraging human beings to become more responsible, sceptical, questioning and reasonable in the nineteenth. Most problematically, however, in this project India can be conceived only as a latecomer: Macaulay's comparison presupposes a primitive (or childlike) status for the Indian population in the present, not the distant or recent past (as in his example of the Anglo-Saxon or the Russian peasant). But Macaulay's referencing of the humanist project also provides an unintended subtext to 'Minute', as the heart of humanist endeavour was the desire to question received authority and to encourage all subjects to become citizens who were responsible for themselves, rather than to a higher authority. Such an intention runs directly counter to the paternalistic model of education proposed in 'Minute'.

Despite Macaulay's self-confessed "idolatry" of the Greeks, he, like More and Ascham, was in no sense a passive or uncritical reader, even of his favourite works. His reading of Plato is worthy of note, and his edition of Plato's works was particularly heavily annotated. Of the *Euthydemus*, he writes critically, "it seems incredible that these absurdities of Dionysodorus and Euthydemus should have been mistaken for wisdom, even by the weakest of mankind. I can hardly help thinking that Plato has overcharged the portrait. But the humour of the dialogue is admirable". His reading of the *Gorgias* is more complicated. At the beginning of the *Gorgias*, Macaulay notes, "This was my favourite dialogue at College. I do not know whether I shall like it as well now. May 1, 1837" (Trevelyan [1876] 1978, 2: 436). Reading this work, Macaulay engages with the controversy, seeming to have been particularly interested in the philosophical battles between Socrates and his opponents. He begins as a commentator on the literature, but he gradually loses himself and seems almost to imagine himself present, and an auditor to the dialogue: "Polus is much in the right. Socrates abused scandalously the advantages which his wonderful talents, and his command of temper, gave him". He moves into the second person, as he becomes more involved: "You have made a blunder and Socrates will have you in an instant." "*Hem! Retiarium astutum!*" And, at the conclusion, he writes ironically, "There you are in the Sophist's net. I think that, if I had been in the place of Polus, Socrates would hardly have had so easy a job of it" (ibid., 437). Macaulay's appropriation of Polus's place for himself is an example of his intense engagement with a philosophical dialogue, and suggests that Macaulay saw reading as, to some extent, a confrontational or oppositional activity, in which the reader pits his wits against either the characters within the work or the work itself. For Macaulay, admiration of a text did not preclude resistance, opposition or even mockery. This model of engaged, energetic, oppositional reading was second nature, even when he was reading the works that he most esteemed. Tellingly, in his account of Macaulay's relationship with his books, Trevelyan wrote that for his uncle, a book was not only a "companion", "counsellor" or "friend", but most importantly, "an adversary to stimulate his combativeness" (ibid., 388).

This kind of critical reading clearly has strong political resonances within the colonial context. In 'Minute' itself, Macaulay suggests that education can teach opposition: "If there should be any opposition among the natives to the change which I recommend, that opposition will be the effect of our own system" (Macaulay [1835] 1935, 356). And, in a speech to the House of

Commons in July of 1833, just before he left for Calcutta, Macaulay argued powerfully for the necessity of educating Britain's Indian subjects in such a way as to fit them for their eventual independence:

> We are told that the time can never come when the natives of India can be admitted to high civil military office. We are told that this is the condition on which we hold our power . . . Against that proposition I solemnly protest as inconsistent alike with sound policy and sound morality. We are free, we are civilized, to little purpose, if we grudge to any portion of the human race an equal measure of freedom and civilization. Are we to keep the people of India ignorant in order that we may keep them submissive? Or do we think that we can give them knowledge without awakening ambition? Or do we mean to awaken ambition and to provide it with no legitimate vent? Who will answer any of these questions in the affirmative? . . . It may be that the public mind of India may expand under our system till it has outgrown that system; that by good government we may educate our subjects into a capacity for better government; that, having become instructed in European knowledge, they may, in some future age, demand European institutions. Whether such a day will ever come I know not. But never will I attempt to avert or to retard it. Whenever it comes, it will be the proudest day in English history. To have found a great people sunk in the lowest depths of slavery and superstition, to have so ruled them as to have made them desirous and capable of all the privileges of citizens, would indeed be a title to glory all of our own. (Macaulay [1833] 1935, 152–55)

Macaulay evidently believes that it is impossible to educate people without awakening their critical faculties and "ambition", and for him, this is worthwhile, even if it means the end of Britain's "most profound schemes of policy" (ibid., 155). In his account, an education in "European knowledge" not only creates, but also demands, the desire for the "European institutions" of "freedom and civilization", and the craving for "all the privileges of citizens". Macaulay's use of the term "citizen" is telling here, suggesting that he envisages European freedoms as those of ancient Athenian or Roman citizens rather than contemporary British and Indian *subjects*. Macaulay's political position as articulated here is entirely consistent both with his support for the humanist project, and with his own practices of careful, critical and resistant reading. His own education had taught him these reading practices. Hence, the assumptions and allusions that underpin Macaulay's conception of the very nature of education implicitly undermine any attempt to keep an educated people "submissive", by teaching them the skills of criticism and resistance along with imitation. Of course, this is liberatory with limits: the "freedom" conceptualised here remains dependent on the Indian population wishing to imitate European institutions, and to continue to be part of the "empire" of Western arts, morals, literature and laws, rather than envisaging their own institutions and empires, and for Macaulay it significantly erases Indian agency: "it would be a glory all of our own". Nonetheless, once subjects have learned to read critically, to evaluate, to resist and to oppose, there is nothing to stop them turning these critical skills on their colonisers. As Harish Trivedi argues, "what began as a form of colonial imposition was soon turned around to be deployed as an effective instrument of resistance to colonial rule" (Trivedi 2009, 27–28).

Macaulay's deep love and profound knowledge of the canon of Western literature influenced the arguments he makes in 'Minute on Indian Education' for the value of that canon, and the simplistic assumptions he makes about "the intrinsic superiority of the Western literature" (Macaulay [1835] 1935, 349). Macaulay was either unable or unwilling to think outside the frame of reference provided for him by his own education and his subsequent reading and rereading habits, outlined earlier. To some extent, he appears to have believed that Indian readers would read in the same kinds of critical and resistant ways that he himself did, but simultaneously to have believed in a top-down model of reading, in which the ideals of Western literature would have been assimilated uncritically by thousands of Indian readers. Bhabha's assertion that the "gestures of mimicry" of postcolonial writers point to the flaws in colonialist ideology and the imperial project itself can thus be seen in a new context: that of the reading practices of the nineteenth-century colonisers and subsequent generations of Indian readers and writers. The postcolonial practice of resistance through mimicry might be reconceptualised therefore as *already present* in (but, of course, not limited to) the educational model that underpinned the imperial project itself. We have seen the humanist paradigms of engagement, criticism, translation, imitation and opposition in the reading practices of one of imperialism's most notorious readers. It is because all readers are, in Michel de Certeau's memorable formulation, to some extent active "poachers" rather than passive sponges (de Certeau [1984] 1988, 165–76) that this imperialist educational model carried within it some of the seeds of its own eventual downfall.

Notes

1. In representing Macaulay's marginal annotations, I have relied heavily on his nephew's account of these, first published in *Marginal Notes by Lord Macaulay*, ed. G. O. Trevelyan (London: Longman, Green & Co, 1907) and reproduced as Chapter XVI (2: 401–40) and Appendix II (2: 443–50) in Trevelyan's *Life and Letters of Lord Macaulay* (London: Oxford University Press, 1978). I have cited the latter work as it is much more easily accessible and available than *Marginal Notes*.

References

Ascham, Roger. (1570) 1711. *The Schoolmaster; Or, a Plain and Perfect Way of Teaching Children to Understand the Latin Tongue*. London: Benjamin Tooke.

Ashcroft, Bill, Gareth Griffiths and Helen Tiffin, eds. 1989. *The Empire Writes Back: Theory and Practice in Post-Colonial Literatures.* London: Routledge.

Bhabha, Homi K. 1994. *The Location of Culture.* London: Routledge.

Chaudhuri, Nirad C. (1951) 1971. *Autobiography of an Unknown Indian.* Bombay: Jaico.

Chislett, William Jr. 1918. *The Classical Influence in English Literature in the Nineteenth Century.* Boston: The Stratford Company.

Cutts, Elmer H. 1953. "The Backgound of Macaulay's Minute." *The American Historical Review* 58(4): 824–53.

de Certeau, Michel. (1984) 1988. *The Practice of Everyday Life.* Berkeley: University of California Press.

Evans, Stephen. 2002. "Macaulay's Minute Revisited: Colonial Language Policy in Nineteenth-Century India." *Journal of Multilingual and Multicultural Development* 23(4): 260–81.

Fanon, Frantz. (1952) 1967. *White Skin, Black Masks.* Translated by Charles Lam Markmann. New York: Grove Press.

Joshi, Priya. 2002. *In Another Country: Colonialism, Culture and the British Novel in India.* New York: Columbia University Press.

Macaulay, Thomas Babington. (1833) 1935. "A Speech Delivered in the House of Commons on the 10th of July, 1833." In *Speeches by Lord Macaulay with His Minute on Indian Education,* edited by G. M. Young, 114–55. London: Oxford University Press.

———. (1835) 1935. "Minute on Indian Education." In Young, 345–61.

McLeod, John. 2000. *Beginning Postcolonialism.* Manchester: Manchester University Press.

Munby, A. N. L. 1966. *Macaulay's Library.* Glasgow: Jackson.

Naipaul, V. S. 1967. *The Mimic Men.* London: Andre Deutsch.

Phillipson, Robert. 1992. *Linguistic Imperialism.* Oxford: Oxford University Press.

Pinney, Thomas, ed. 1974–81. *The Letters of Thomas Babington Macaulay.* 6 vols. Cambridge: Cambridge University Press.

Rakhit, Maanoj. 2003. *Christianity in a Different Light: Face behind the Mask.* Bombay: Ideal Press.

Rushdie, Salman. (1991) 1992. *Imaginary Homelands.* London: Penguin.

———. (1995) 1996. *The Moor's Last Sigh.* London: Vintage.

Sardar, Ziauddin. 1999. *Orientalism.* Buckingham: Open University Press.

Stimpson, Felicity. 2007. "'I Have Spent My Morning Reading Greek': The Marginalia of Sir George Otto Trevelyan." *Library History* 23(3): 239–50.

Sullivan, Robert E. 2009. *Macaulay: The Tragedy of Power.* Boston: Harvard University Press.

Trevelyan, George Otto. (1876) 1978. *The Life and Letters of Lord Macaulay.* 2 vols. Oxford. Oxford University Press.

———. 1907. *Marginal Notes by Lord Macaulay.* London: Longmans, Green & Co.

Trivedi, Harish. 2009. "The 'Book' in India: Orality, Manu-Script, Print (Post) Colonialism." In *Books without Borders,* edited by Mary Hammond and Robert Fraser, vol. 1, 12–33. Basingstoke: Palgrave Macmillan.

Viswanathan, Gauri. (1989) 2002. *Masks of Conquest: Literary Study and British Rule in India.* Oxford: Oxford University Press.

Williams, Wynne. 1993. "Reading Greek like a Man of the World: Macaulay and the Classical Languages." *Greece and Rome* 40(2): 201–16.

Part V
Reading and Postcolonial Ethics

13 Theorising Postcolonial Reception

Writing, Reading and Moral Agency in the *Satanic Verses* Affair[1]

Daniel Allington

It is difficult to engage with the ethics of writing within the mainstream of literary studies, because since the New Criticism, that discipline has overwhelmingly tended to conceive its object of enquiry as an abstract structure of pure language: "text". Moreover, the hiving off of critical editing from critical interpretation and the theoretical and institutional privileging of the latter (see McGann 1983) have encouraged the text of pure language to be treated as a given. One knows that books come into being through human agency (see Darnton 1990). And yet, once one accepts that enquiry into the agency behind text is guided by an "intentional fallacy" (Wimsatt and Beardsley 1946), one seems to have little alternative but to treat text as if it were only an ineffable that-which-is-to-be-interpreted. Indeed, such an approach is celebrated by those who place literary critics at the centre of the textual universe, "writing" the texts that they interpret (e.g., Fish 1980). However, a more politically inclined theorist might be inclined to see in "the . . . maxim that it is the method that the reader brings to bear upon the text that enables it to be heard and seen" only a form of "false consciousness" (Pearce 1997, 42). That being so, false consciousness is difficult to escape within literary studies, since the institution of academic criticism obliges its practitioners endlessly to manufacture new interpretations, and since the agentless text of pure language can endlessly be reinterpreted (see Allington 2006). And if the critic is the producer of the meanings that he or she critiques, then criticism would seem a rather solipsistic and apolitical enterprise. How can it address the traumas of colonisation, decolonisation and globalisation?

Fortunately, there are other ways in which to conceive of literature. One such is provided by speech act theory, developed by the philosopher J. L. Austin (1962). Austin analysed the social conventions that permit the issuing of a text or utterance to count as a recognisable kind of action (technically, to carry a particular "illocutionary force"), and sometimes also to yield a particular result in the social world (thus coming to constitute a "perlocutionary act"). For example, an utterance or text might constitute the illocutionary act of an order (provided, of course, that the speaker holds the requisite authority; a point emphasised by Bourdieu (1992, 75)) as well as the perlocutionary act of getting the recipient of the order to do something (provided, of course, that he or she chooses to obey). This can provide a useful way in which to conceive writing other than as linguistic structure, although the theory may require a degree of elaboration before it can be applied to literary writing (see Allington 2008). In particular, a notable problem with Austin's work is a tendency to treat his (mostly invented) examples as possessing an obvious and definitive illocutionary force, which may not always be the case in the messier realm of real-world speech and writing. In this respect, scholars of reading and reception can learn from the rhetorical study of genre (Miller 1984), which draws on speech act theory and treats written genres as conventional social actions (see also Grafton 2010 for application to reception study). Some recent studies in this tradition (e.g., Miller and Shepherd 2004) have taken an "ethnomethodological" approach, rejecting the idea that texts can be definitively assigned to genres, and studying instead the ways in which notions of genre are appealed to in discussions of writing. And as we shall see, ethnomethodologists have analysed accounts of human action in a way that may shed considerable light on the things people say about books.

The notion that one should focus on writing as a form of action rather than on text as an object of endless reinterpretation is far from unusual outside the academy, as the example of Salman Rushdie's controversial novel, *The Satanic Verses* (1988), reveals. Popular discussion of this work has never focused on how its text can be interpreted, nor on the degree of support that the text offers for one interpretation or another. Rather, it has revolved around such questions as whether Rushdie had intended to cause offence to Muslims, whether he could have anticipated the geopolitical incident sometimes called the "*Satanic Verses* affair", and to what extent he can be held responsible for the violence of that incident. These are ethical questions. The scholar who studies *The Satanic Verses* in terms of human action can attempt not only to clarify those questions but also to understand the ways in which they have been posed and answered throughout the *Satanic Verses* affair itself. In doing so, he or she must conceive *The Satanic Verses* not as a linguistic structure to be interpreted this way and that, but as a complex and unfolding history of writing, publication and reception.[2]

Though such study may seem alien to the mainstream of literary criticism, it is of key importance if we are to understand a work like *The Satanic Verses* as it exists within our culture. If "production" can be taken to include not only the composition of a linguistic text and the manufacture of the material documents that embody (or imply) it, but also its "symbolic production" (Bourdieu 1993)—that is, the production of belief about the text (in particular, belief that it is or is not a great work of literature)—then the actions of those who pronounced upon *The Satanic Verses* are as central to an understanding of the work as are the actions of those who wrote and published it. For their legacy has been the production of the *Satanic Verses* that Muslims and non-Muslims know today (regardless of whether they have read it).

In this chapter, I try to understand how public commentators construed the agentive and moral character of actions involved in the linguistic, material and symbolic production of *The Satanic Verses*: construals that I consider to participate as contributions in their own right to the symbolic production of *The Satanic Verses*. To do this, I employ ethnomethodologist Lena Jayyusi's argument that accounts of human action are constructed by reference to ideas of "intention", "knowledge" and "outcome" (Jayyusi 1993, 452). According to Jayyusi, an ordinary description of human action "depends on and projects a particular 'composite' or 'conjuncture' of these three action parameters" (ibid.). Jayyusi refers to this as a "logical grammar" (ibid.), although I would argue that "moral grammar" might be more appropriate, given that the purpose of such descriptions is so often to apportion praise or blame. As we shall see, media texts on *The Satanic Verses* employ Jayyusi's three action parameters in different ways in order to apportion varying degrees of blame to Rushdie and other agents—and in order to justify or condemn particular courses of answering action. Importantly, these agents include the readers of *The Satanic Verses*, who are in some cases regarded simply as the locus of the outcome of the author's action, and in others accorded responsibility for their own reading and its consequences. Thus, what might at first glance seem to be straightforward statements about readers' responses and feelings turn out to play a role in advancing a particular moral vision of events, and in producing *The Satanic Verses* as a symbolic object of a particular type.

The Satanic Verses as British and World Event

Today, Salman Rushdie is a member of the literary "jet set" (Kovac and Wischenbart 2010, 17): a high-profile international media personality whose works are published in multiple languages. As such, he has aptly been dubbed "by all means, the most consecrated, successful, and 'denationalised' post-colonial writer" (Brouillette 2007, 80). Born in India, educated in the UK, and now residing in the US, Rushdie holds a unique place in the British cultural scene. This is demonstrated not only by his 2007 knighthood but also by his unparalleled success with the UK's most prestigious literary award, the Booker Prize (now the Man Booker Prize): his second novel, *Midnight's Children* (Rushdie 1981), won the Booker itself in its year of publication; in 1993, it won the special Booker of Bookers award, created to celebrate the Booker Prize's twenty-fifth anniversary; and in 2008, it won the Best of the Booker award, which celebrated the prize's fortieth anniversary. In Britain and elsewhere, however, public perceptions of Rushdie remain dominated by the controversy over his fourth novel, *The Satanic Verses*. The controversy is well documented (Netton 1996; Pipes 2003), and can with hindsight be seen to have constituted a key moment in the evolving relationship between political Islam and the West.

When *The Satanic Verses* was published in the UK on September 26, 1988, it appears to have seemed innocuous enough. By that time, Rushdie was established as one of the country's leading left-wing intellectuals. His two previous novels had been critical and commercial successes, and his non-fictional writing made regular appearances in the national media.

Despite this, *The Satanic Verses* received relatively little publicity to begin with, and was reviewed only in the three most intellectual British national newspapers (the centrist *Independent*, the right-leaning *The Times* and the left-leaning *Guardian*). Just one of these reviews discussed the novel with reference to Islam—and somewhat tellingly, it did so only with bafflement, wondering "why exactly are we being treated to a fanciful recreation of selected aspects of Muhammad's story?" (Tomalin 1988, 28). With hindsight, this seems incredible. But that is because the text as it is knowable to us today has been irrevocably shaped by the history of its reception as an attack upon Muslims.

That history began in India. There, pre-publication release of extracts from *The Satanic Verses* led to immediate allegations of blasphemy against Islam and offensiveness to Muslims, and the novel was officially banned on October 5. Numerous other states, mostly Muslim-majority countries, followed suit with bans of their own. This transnational reception was not, it should be noted, the combined result of thousands of individuals encountering the book as a whole and responding with spontaneous anger. Rather, it was a political campaign that gathered force as Muslim organisations around the globe notified one another of the book's content and encouraged one another to take action within their respective local contexts. Few of those who protested against *The Satanic Verses* at that stage would have had the opportunity to read the book as a whole—assuming that they wished to. The architect of the book's Indian ban disavowed any intention of reading it, for example (Shahabuddin 1989).

British protests were most strongly associated with urban South Asian Muslim communities in the north of England: copies of the book were publicly burned in Bolton on December 2, 1988 and Bradford on January 14, 1989. The presence of the media at the January burning made Bradford the symbolic centre of British Muslim anger against the book, with some non-Muslim commentators making far-fetched comparisons with the book burnings of Nazi Germany. In Asia, matters took a more serious turn. Thousands of anti-Rushdie protestors had attacked the American Cultural Centre in Islamabad on February 12, 1989, with five dying (as Brouillette (2007, 85) notes, *The Satanic Verses* was frequently linked to the US by those who attacked it, despite the fact that Rushdie was then resident in the UK). The following day, a major riot in India led to the death of one anti-Rushdie protestor, and the Supreme Leader of Iran, the Ayatollah Khomeini, issued a fatwa, or legal ruling, calling on all Muslims to assassinate both Rushdie and his publishers. The following week, Khomeini issued the additional ruling that it would be acceptable for Muslims to arrange for the assassination of Rushdie at the hands of a non-Muslim. Rushdie was given police protection by the British state, and went into hiding for the next decade.

Protest and violence continued sporadically for several years, and a number of attempts were made on the lives of individuals involved in the novel's international publication—most famously, the Japanese translator, who was murdered in 1991. The appearance of a British paperback edition of *The Satanic Verses* in 1992 led to renewed controversy, and the following year, up to forty people died in a related arson attack in Turkey. Rushdie's knighthood in June 2007 led to fresh expressions of Muslim outrage, particularly in Pakistan, where news of the honour was met by government condemnation, anti-British street protests and the (subsequently retracted) statement from the minister for religious affairs that "[i]f somebody has to attack by strapping bombs to his body to protect the honour of the Prophet, then it is justified" (Ijaz-ul-Haq, quoted in Hoyle 2007, 3). Twenty-first century condemnation came no slower from the right wing of the British press: a journalist writing in the *Telegraph* opined that a knighthood "should never have been offered" to Rushdie, as "[h]e is an appalling writer, and seems to despise the country honouring him" (Heffer 2007, 25).

One of the lingering consequences of the Rushdie affair is a tendency for many within the South Asian Muslim diaspora to despise Rushdie as a traitor and reject all of his works. This is well illustrated by the following exchange, which was fortuitously collected in a sociological study of cultural consumption. Here, a member of a focus group of working-class British Pakistani women explains the "very, very bad experience" she had on a rare visit to the theatre, accompanying her husband to a production of a Rushdie novel whose name she has forgotten:

Zahra: The one by the writer. Then I know which writer but before I know . . . a crazy guy his name is Salman Rushdie and I really hated this guy but my husband already bought the tickets. I said for me this is enemy I don't like this guy because he is crazy . . .
Kamran: I don't think that we people go to theatres.
Moin: He wrote the book *The Satanic Verses*.
Zahra: No, I didn't read it.
               (UK Data Archive, Study Number 5832, document ID: 5832fg011)

As Moin's response suggests, it was as the author of *The Satanic Verses* that Zahra is likely to have known and "hated" Rushdie the "enemy" and "crazy guy". Yet none of the women in the focus group claim to have read *The Satanic Verses*, and in fact Zahra explicitly claims not to have read it. One does not have to read *The Satanic Verses* in order to know the social meaning that it has acquired in relation to the British Pakistani community—any more than Zahra had to see the play to which she refers in order to know that she would loathe it. To attempt to understand this state of affairs by analysing the words printed in an edition of *The Satanic Verses* would clearly be futile.

The Actions of Writing and Reading *The Satanic Verses*

I shall now turn to examples of statements on *The Satanic Verses* that appeared in 1989. For reasons of space, these are limited to four extracts from British print sources broadly critical of Rushdie and/or his publishers. The first is from a book by Shabbir Akhtar, a member of the Bradford Council for Mosques, which played a prominent role in the British campaign against *The Satanic Verses*:

> The life of the Arabian Prophet is of great interest to many thinkers and historians . . . It is also valid territory for imaginative reconstruction . . . But neither historical nor fictional exploration of his biography can, with impunity, lapse into abuse and slander. Rushdie relishes scandalous suggestion and pejorative language. His account is uniformly self-indulgent, calculated to shock and humiliate Muslim sensibilities. It is unwise to ignore the role of provocation and polemic in exciting hatred and anger to the point of physical confrontation. (Akhtar 1989, 12)

Here, Akhtar insists that Rushdie *calculated* the book to hurt Muslims, implying not only intention but also a degree of foreknowledge on Rushdie's part. Where an act is deemed to be wrong, the allegation of calculation on the part of the actor implies pronounced culpability; it was also emphasised by Khomeini, whose initial ruling declared *The Satanic Verses* to be "a calculated move aimed at rooting out religion and religiousness, and above all, Islam and its clergy" (al-Khomeini 1989, 90).

In Akhtar's version of events, physical confrontation occurred because of Rushdie's *premeditated* infliction of shock and humiliation. On the same page, Akhtar matter-of-factly discusses a murder that took place many years earlier in Lahore, reinforcing the idea that the illocutionary act of slandering Muhammad is invariably the perlocutionary act of causing a Muslim to assassinate the slanderer: Akhtar thus accords agency (and therefore moral responsibility) only to the slanderer. Such an interpretation was also implied by the literary theorist Sandy Petrey, who argued that the novel and the fatwa were "bound as cause and effect" (Petrey 1990, 55), and saw in this relation the confirmation of his speech act theory of literature: "The language of *The Satanic Verses* is as immediately persuasive an example of words that do things as you can imagine. To set uncounted numbers of people on an assassin's task is a linguistic performance of titanic proportions" (Petrey 1990, 54). This account of events is confused: it was Khomeini's speech act, not Rushdie's, that called for assassinations, and there is little reason to suppose that "uncounted numbers of people" ever seriously set out to fulfil it. But it usefully exemplifies a rhetorical tendency on the part of Muslims and non-Muslims alike to attribute agency solely to Rushdie, and to see the unfolding violence as an outcome of Rushdie's action, rather than as a complex of actions in its own right.

A strategy intriguingly similar to Akhtar's is pursued in the following account, written by Yakub Zaki, a British convert to Shi'a Islam. This account was published in that most established of British newspapers, *The Times*, its author's credentials further established by the accompanying description of him as "a visiting professor at Harvard University":[3]

> The ravings of the popular press may be discounted, but when the *Independent* says that Khomeini's verdict on Salman Rushdie is acceptable only to the 10 per cent (really 12 per cent) of the Muslims in the world who are Shi'ite, it is time for scholarship to enter the fray. . . .
>
> To the medieval mind . . . Islam was nothing less than a satanic conspiracy and the Koran a satanic fabrication. Satan had pulled off the greatest religious fraud of all time, producing a scripture purporting to come from God while all the time being the work of the Devil. Only satanic intervention in world history could explain Islam's phenomenal success.
>
> Rushdie's use of the name of the devil responsible for the fraud is intended to indicate that the whole Koran is fraudulent and Muhammad a mean impostor: not a question of the two verses spotted as such but all the 6236 verses making up the entire book. In other words, the title is a *double entendre* . . . .
>
> On the penalty for apostasy, there is complete unanimity between all five schools of law in Islam (four in Sunnism, one in Shi'ism). . . .
>
> Imam Khomeini, simply by articulating what every Muslim feels in his heart, has recouped at one stroke everything lost in the war with Iraq and emerged as the undisputed moral leader of the world's one billion Muslims. Meanwhile, the silence from such Islamic capitals as Riyadh, Cairo, and Islamabad is deafening.
>
> (Zaki 1989, 14)

This article presents Khomeini's "verdict" as an inevitability, given the content of *The Satanic Verses*. It accords Khomeini a speech act, but makes this no more nor less than the act of articulating what all Muslims know to be the case (i.e. that Rushdie should be killed): thus, Khomeini has no moral responsibility for Rushdie's fate, since he did no more than speak the obvious truth—and yet because, in speaking it, he was the only Islamic authority to state what "every Muslim" already knows, he thereby established for himself a moral authority that transcends the Shi'a / Sunni divide. That this was a fantasy of Zaki's should hardly be doubted: the idea "that somehow Khomeini spoke for all Muslims" was a point of concern for many Muslims at the time (Hussain 2002, 17). And Zaki's invocation of "complete unanimity between all five schools of law in Islam" is also highly misleading, as it implies that Khomeini's pronouncement was unambiguously in accordance with all forms of Islamic law. As Bernard Lewis observes, there exists a (primarily Sh'ite) view that a Muslim must immediately kill anyone who insults Mohammad *in his presence*, but "even the most rigorous jurists . . . say nothing about an arranged killing for a reported insult in a far place" (1991, 194).

As a response to *The Satanic Verses*, Zaki's article bears a certain superficial resemblance to a work of academic literary criticism, in that the interpretation (expressed in the form of a claim as to Rushdie's intentions in writing) is anchored both in a linguistic feature of *The Satanic Verses* (ie., the name "Mahound") and in an assembled mass of contextual information. It should be noted, however, that this is a very great weight to place on a single piece of textual evidence, and that the omniscient narrator of the novel states that the name is actually adopted "[t]o turn insults into strengths" (Rushdie 1988, 93). Zaki does not attempt to argue against this alternative interpretation. Indeed, since his article is *not* a work of "scholarship" but an opinion piece in a newspaper, he does not really have to; addressing a general audience proportionally few of whose members are likely to have read *The Satanic Verses*, he can quote as selectively as he pleases. Perhaps the most interesting thing about this piece is that, although Zaki uses *The Satanic Verses* to make his case, his main purpose is clearly to praise the Ayatollah: the article announces itself as having been occasioned by a slight on the latter's authority, and it concludes with scorn for Sunni leaders and hyperbolic aggrandizement of Khomeini himself.

The next account, written by a right-wing historian but published in a supplement to a national newspaper identified with the political centre, recognises both Rushdie and Khomeini as agents, and criticises both of them:

> I wonder how Salman Rushdie is faring these days, under the benevolent protection of British law and the British police, about whom he has been so rude. Not too comfortably, I hope. Of course, we must protect him against holy murder, and in general I admit to some sympathy for heretics; but I cannot extend it to him. After all, he is well versed in Islamic ideas: he knew what he was doing, and could foresee the consequences.
>
> If an expert entomologist deliberately pokes a stick into a hornet's nest, he has only himself to blame for the result. . . .
>
> I would not shed a tear if some British Muslims, deploring his manners, should waylay him in a dark street and seek to improve them. If that should cause him thereafter to control his pen, society would benefit and literature would not suffer. If caught, his correctors might, of course, be found guilty of assault; but they could then plead gross provocation and might merely, if juvenile, be bound over. Our prisons are, after all, overcrowded. This would seem more satisfactory, in the long run, than extending the law against blasphemy.

> If only it had not been for the Ayatollah in Iran! . . . Once the late Ayatollah, for his own internal political purposes . . . had called on the faithful to despatch the heretic, the whole situation was transformed.
>
> (Trevor-Roper 1989, 14)

The first point to note here is the way in which Rushdie's knowledge of "Islamic ideas" is used to establish his moral responsibility for his own sufferings ("he has only himself to blame"). This was a common theme in non-Muslim criticism of Rushdie: a similar assertion was, for example, made by the popular children's author Roald Dahl (1989). Rushdie responded to such assertions by challenging those who endorsed them to apply their underlying axiom to other cases than his own: "when Osip Mandelstam wrote his poem against Stalin, did he 'know what he was doing' and so deserve his death?" (Rushdie 1991, 407).[4]

Agency is denied to Muslims by Trevor-Roper in a different way to that in which they are denied it by Akhtar: Muslims are, in Trevor-Roper's version of events, only hornets into whose nest a stick has been poked (a familiar metaphor for needless provocation, and one that distinctly implies mindlessness on the part of the provoked), and it is even suggested that this viewpoint should be adopted by a court of law, in the event of Rushdie's being physically assaulted. Interestingly, however, Khomeini is accorded agency (and indeed blame) for making the situation worse, and for doing so hypocritically, i.e., not because he was provoked, but "for his own internal political purposes". Furthermore, Trevor-Roper implies that the main cause for regret ("If only it had not been . . . !") is that, in calling for Rushdie's murder, Khomeini has obliged the British state to protect Rushdie, and thus prevented the latter's would-be "correctors" from giving him the beating that might otherwise have seemed such a "satisfactory" resolution to the controversy.

Although there is not space here to examine arguments in support of Rushdie, it is worth contrasting all the foregoing with the views of an Arab Muslim resident in Britain: the Islamic scholar, Zaki Badawi. In an interview with the *Guardian*, Badawi combined criticism of Rushdie with criticism of calls for violence against Rushdie, stating that he would offer shelter to the author from those who would carry out Khomeini's fatwa. As Badawi explains:

> The book, which I've read from cover to cover, is a confused surrealistic jumble: a hurling of insults and mockery rather than a concerted argument or campaign against Islam. It does make Islam look ridiculous and less than holy and it violates the Prophet's person. That's a very deep wound to those who read it—but the remedy was for Muslims not to read it. (Badawi, interviewed by Martin 1989, 39)

The speech acts with which Badawi identifies the book—"hurling of insults and mockery" etc.—are similar to those of Akhtar's account, and elsewhere in the same interview, Badawi expresses the pain of reading *The Satanic Verses* in hyperbolic terms ("far worse . . . than if he's raped one's own daughter . . . an assault on every Muslim's inner being . . . like a knife being dug into you—or being raped yourself" (39)). However, he states that *The Satanic Verses* is not "a concerted argument or campaign against Islam". Badawi also accords agency to the reader of *The Satanic Verses*, so that the responsibility for the pain is shared by the individual Muslim who chooses to let it be inflicted on him or herself—as Badawi had to in order to speak as an authority ("The book, which I've read *from cover to cover*"). His account thus breaks the "cause and effect" link that many commentators constructed between blaspheming and becoming the object of violence. Later in the interview, Badawi presents a detailed argument to the effect that killing Rushdie would be against Islamic law, and expresses sympathy for the author, whom he describes as "a tortured soul, whose loss of faith appears to have stemmed in part from the disgust he felt at some Islamic rulers" (39).

It is tempting to position Badawi simply as a voice of reason. But his argument relies on the assumption that reading is an individual and volitional encounter with a single, closable book—an assumption with limited application to real acts of reading, especially where *The Satanic Verses* is concerned. Aamir Mufti argues that, if we are to understand the *The Satanic Verses* affair, "[c]onceptions of reception based on an almost Victorian image of the solitary bourgeois reader" must be abandoned in favour of a "reconceptualisation of reception" that will "account for forms of mass 'consumption' other than 'reading' in the narrower sense of that word" (1991, 97). Muslims who did not read *The Satanic Verses* as a *book* will have encountered it as a *work* in the form of rumours, quotations and misquotations that amplified its potential to offend. This was why response was able to precede publication in many international contexts. But similar processes occurred where the book was easily available: in Bradford, for example, the *Telegraph & Argus* newspaper printed an article purporting to explain the causes of "Islam anger" but filled with inaccurate statements designed to provoke that anger (Siddique 1989). Moreover, public readings of the very passages from *The Satanic Verses* that Muslims could be expected to find most offensive were organised by protest leaders such as Shabbir Akhtar (see above), who insisted that "[a]nyone who fails to be offended by Rushdie's book *ipso facto* ceases to be a Muslim" (quoted in Mufti 1994, 323). Thus, at the same time that some Muslims were attempting to protect their co-religionists from being offended by *The Satanic Verses*, others were attempting to turn such offence into a universal Muslim experience.

Conclusions

The Satanic Verses is not a typical novel. But the typicality or exceptionality of a novel is no more a given than the goodness or badness of its author's intentions: rather, it is a shared belief that must be brought into being through social processes of agreement, negotiation and challenge. Multiple viewpoints collided throughout the Rushdie affair, and in their collisions contributed to the production of the symbolic object that we call *The Satanic Verses*. Yet outside academia, few commentators imagined this work primarily as a linguistic structure. It is as a sequence of actions (real and alleged) that any work becomes—and remains—a part of the social world.

Notes

1. Some of this chapter's content was previously published in Allington 2008.
2. In this chapter, "history" means a train of real-world events (see Oxford English Dictionary, "history", sense 4b) rather than a textual or spoken account of such events.
3. As of 2010, the Harvard University press office was unable to confirm or deny that Zaki had held such a position.
4. In fact, Pipes shows that Rushdie cannot (in this sense) have known what he was doing: there is a long history of apostasy, blasphemy and freethinking in the Muslim world, but the response to *The Satanic Verses* was unprecedented and could not have been foreseen by anyone (2003, 70–93).

References

Akhtar, Shabbir. 1989. *Be Careful with Muhammad: The Salman Rushdie Affair*. London: Bellew.

al-'Azm, Sadik Jalal. 1994. "The Importance of Being Earnest about Salman Rushdie." In *Reading Rushdie: Perspectives on the Fiction of Salman Rushdie*, edited by M. D. Fletcher. Amsterdam: Rodopi, 255–293.

al-Khomeini, Ruhollah al-Musavi. 1989. "Rushdie and the 'World Devourers.'" In *The Rushdie File*, edited by Lisa Appignanesi and Sara Maitland, 89–91. London: Fourth Estate.

Allington, Daniel. 2006. "First Steps towards a Rhetorical Psychology of Literary Interpretation." *Journal of Literary Semantics* 35(2): 123–44.

———. 2008. "How to Do Things with Literature: Blasphemous Speech Acts, Satanic Intentions, and the Uncommunicativeness of Verses." *Poetics Today* 29(3): 473–523.

Austin, J. L. 1962. *How to Do Things with Words: The William James Lectures Delivered at Harvard University in 1955*. Oxford: Clarendon Press.

Bourdieu, Pierre. 1992. "Price Formation and the Anticipation of Profits." In *Language and Symbolic Power*, edited by John B. Thompson, translated by Gino Raymond and Matthew Adamson, 66–89. Cambridge: Polity.

———. 1993. "The Market of Symbolic Goods." In *The Field of Cultural Production: Essays on Art and Literature*, translated by R. Swyer, 112–44. Cambridge: Polity Press.

Brouillette, Sarah (2007). *Postcolonial writers in the global literary marketplace*. Basingstoke: Palgrave Macmillan.

Dahl, Roald. 1989. Letter to the editor. *The Times*, February 28.

Darnton, Robert. 1990. "What Is the History of Books?" In *The Kiss of Lamourette: Reflections in Cultural History*, 107–35. London: Faber & Faber.

Fish, Stanley. 1980. *Is There a Text in This Class? The Authority of Interpretive Communities*. Cambridge: Harvard University Press.

Grafton, Kathryn. 2010. "Paying Attention to Public Readers of Canadian Literature: Popular Genre Systems, Publics, and Canons." PhD diss., University of British Columbia.

Heffer, Simon. 2007. "His Lordship Should Stick to Fish and Chips." *Daily Telegraph*, June 23.

Hoyle, Ben. 2007. "Muslim World Inflamed by Rushdie Knighthood." *The Times*, June 19.

Hussain, Amir. 2002. "Misunderstanding and Hurt: How Canadians Joined Worldwide Muslim Reactions to Salman Rushdie's The Satanic Verses." *Journal of the American Academy of Religion* 70(1): 1–32.

Jayyusi, Lena. 1993. "Premeditation and Happenstance: The Social Construction of Intention, Action, and Knowledge." *Human Studies* 16(4): 435–54.

Kovac, Miha, and Rudiger Wischenbart. 2010. *Diversity Report 2010: Literary Translation in Current European Book Markets. An Analysis of Authors, Languages, and Flows* http://www.wischenbart.com/diversity/report/Diversity-Report_2010.pdf.

Lewis, Bernard. 1991. "Behind the Rushdie Affair." *The American Scholar* 60(2): 185–96.

Martin, Paul. 1989. "Face to Faith: Spurn the Book, Spare the Man." *Guardian*, February 27.

McGann, Jerome J. 1983. *A Critique of Modern Textual Criticism*. Chicago: University of Chicago Press.

Miller, Carolyn R. 1984. "Genre as Social Action." *Quarterly Journal of Speech* (70): 151–76.

Miller, Carolyn R., and Dawn Shepherd. 2004. "Blogging as Social Action: A Genre Analysis of the Weblog." In *Into the Blogosphere: Rhetoric, Community, and Culture of Weblogs*, edited by Laura Gurak, Smiljana Antonijevic, Laurie Johnson, Clancy Ratliff and Jessica Reyman. University of Minnesota. http://blog.lib.umn.edu/blogosphere/blogging_as_social_action_a_genre_analysis_of_the_weblog.html.

Mufti, Aamir. 1991. "Reading the Rushdie Affair: An Essay on Islam and Politics." *Social Text* (29): 95–116.

———. 1994. "Reading the Rushdie Affair: "Islam", Cultural Politics, Form." In *The Administration of Aesthetics*, edited by Richard Burt, 307–49. Minneapolis: University of Minnesota Press.

Netton, Ian R. 1996. *Text and Trauma: An East-West Primer*. Richmond: Curzon.

Pearce, Lynne. 1997. *Feminism and the Politics of Reading*. London: Arnold.

Petrey, Sandy. 1990. *Speech Acts and Literary Theory*. New York: Routledge.

Pipes, Daniel. 2003. *The Rushdie Affair: The Novel, the Ayatollah, and the West*. 2nd ed. New Brunswick, NJ: Transaction Publishers.

Rushdie, Salman. 1981. *Midnight's Children*. London: Jonathan Cape.

———. 1988. *The Satanic Verses*. London: Penguin.

———. 1991. "In Good Faith." In *Imaginary Homelands: Essays and Criticism, 1981–1991*, by Rushdie, 393–414. London: Granta Books.

Shahabuddin, Syed. 1989. "You Did This with Satanic Forethought, Mr Rushdie." In *The Rushdie File*, edited by Lisa Appignanesi and Sara Maitland, 45–49. London: Fourth Estate.

Siddique, Mohammed. 1989. "Why Islam Anger Goes on Burning." *Telegraph & Argus*, June 16, 6.

Tomalin, Claire. 1988. "The Wheel That Would Not Turn." *Independent Weekend Books*, September 28, 28.

Trevor-Roper, Hugh. 1989. "Hugh Trevor-Roper Refuses to Forgive Salman Rushdie." *Independent Magazine*, June 10, 14.

Wimsatt, M. K., and M. C. Beardsley. 1946. "The Intentional Fallacy." *The Sewanee Review* (54): 468–88.

Zaki, Yakub. 1989. "Rushdie's Real Crime." *The Times*, February 28.

14 Reading before the Law*
Melville's 'Bartleby' and Asylum Seeker Narratives

David Farrier

The measure of reception is a crucial index of literary postcolonial ethics. The chapters in *Postcolonial Audiences* look to shed light on the "shadowy figure" of the reader in postcolonial literary studies; this chapter argues that, concomitantly, asylum seekers can be thought of as contemporary incarnations of Spivak's enshadowed subaltern: insistent presences hovering on the margins of society but effectively silenced within popular and academic discourse (Spivak 1999, 198–311). Furthermore, as postcolonial studies in general responds to the neo-imperialisms of the twenty-first century, it is compelling to think of asylum seekers in the West as embodying one of the key traits of the field since the decolonising literature of the 1950s: the creation of subjecthood through narrative. Asylum seekers' narratives are central in asylum determinations. They are the currency of sanctuary, subject to the devaluing effect of credibility determinations and "compassion fatigue".[1] In effect, asylum seekers are charged with narrating themselves into a place of safety. As the subject seeking sanctuary moves from the provisional (asylum seeker) to the permanent (refugee) by the relaying of traumatic experiences, textuality and the contexts for narration remain as vital postcolonial concerns as ever.

The reception of asylum narratives is thus imbricated with the question of an ethical postcolonial reading practice. The discrepancy between acts of reading in the (legal) context of an asylum determination, and literary reading, is also pertinent; J. Hillis Miller's deconstructive ethics posits reading as a constantly deferred, "undecideable" activity (Miller 1977, 441), which contradicts the requirement in asylum determinations for a definite outcome. As Audrey Macklin has observed, however, where ambiguity prevents a definite positive or negative ruling, *de facto* decisions to refuse on the basis of credibility can be taken via a refusal to decide (Macklin 1999, 134–41). In this chapter I consider the ethical relationship between reading and hospitality in the reception of asylum seekers and their narratives, via a calibrated reading of the acts of refusal depicted in Herman Melville's 'Bartleby' (1853).

Some initial qualifications are necessary. First, and most obviously, 'Bartleby' is neither a postcolonial text nor a narrative of asylum. It is important to establish that I am not interested in analogies; key details in 'Bartleby' make any attempt to describe him as the archetypal refugee impossible (even if an "archetypal" reading were desirable). I am also mindful that contextual pressures can shape asylum seeker testimonies: in juridical and therapeutic forums, asylum accounts will inevitably be organised after differing criteria; and that, furthermore, literary writing by asylum seekers often has a testimonial function. To mediate these pressures, I will proceed according to Ato Quayson's sense of a calibrated reading of the literary for the social. "The social" here is distinct from society in that it resists particularity; rather, Quayson argues that literary works reveal their value in the way in which the variegated "thresholds" which constitute literary structure replicate and are replicated in the "articulated encapsulation of transformation, processes, and contradictions" which defines the social (Quayson 2003, xv). His sensibility is founded on an inherent relationality, which permits "local" insights offered by particular texts to be translated into other times and settings (Quayson 2003, xxxi). Bearing in mind, then, the proliferation of recent interpretations of Bartleby's idiosyncratic expressions of resistance, reading him as one who is both literally and hermeneutically displaced presents an opportunity to reflect on the politics of representing the displaced person.[2] I contend that reading Melville's story for the thresholds it reveals in itself can also reveal something of the social worlds of asylum seeker narratives, where the difference between text and the social is blurred by the degree to which life depends on the *reception* of narrative.

In addition to his many critical appropriations, Bartleby has also been "read" in a recent literary work. Abdulrazak Gurnah's *By the Sea* (2001) features a Zanzibari asylum seeker, Saleh Omar, who conceals his ability to speak English in the hope of making himself more plausibly deserving (later, the novel's other migrant character, Latif, acknowledges that, "Without English you are even more a stranger, a refugee, [. . .] more convincing [. . .]. You're just a condition, without even a story" (Gurnah 2001, 143)). Saleh in effect makes himself nameless, in order to claim the new name of refugee who, as Liisa Malkki has said, is commonly constituted as speaking through silence (Malkki 1996, 390). When challenged by his caseworker, Saleh says that he declined to reveal he speaks English because, "I preferred not to", a deliberate invocation of Bartleby (Gurnah 2001, 65). What links the two is the expression of agency in apparent passivity: both employ a strategy of refusal in order to declare an interest in refuge. Saleh gains entry by withholding his narrative, and thus his own narratability. All that remains is the condition of need he is seen to represent. Bartleby also makes a *de facto* demand for hospitality by ostensibly refusing to make a decision (at most, a negative decision). He imposes himself while seeming to efface himself (it is significant that Melville's narrator observes that Bartleby is a man about whom nothing could be known). The narrator provides an account of that which cannot be accounted for; Bartleby is a "loss to literature" whose story is nonetheless told (Melville 1986, 3).

The condition of sanctuary to which each appeals is *asylos*, in Greek, the inviolable. In a manner that recalls the etymological investigations behind Derrida's neologism, "hostipitality", *asylos* has its root in a seemingly antithetical term, the verb *asylao*, meaning to violate or lay waste (Derrida 2000, 3–18; Plaut 1995, 11).[3] Both Bartleby and Saleh subvert the norms of conditional hospitality by making the host hostage to an impossible demand for a hospitality without limits (i.e., one that is not subject to the host's discretion), making the hospitable decision the prerogative of the guest. Following Derrida's suggestion that every responsible decision contains within it the (undecidable) decision of the Other (Derrida [2001] 2006, 102), and J. Hillis Miller's notion that reading is both parasitic and undecidable (Miller 1977, 441), I contend that reading Melville's 'Bartleby' can point to an ethical postcolonial reading response to asylum seeker narratives. In what follows, I argue that Bartleby's refusal (to verify his copy; to defer to the authority of his host) can be read, after Giorgio Agamben, as an articulation of potentiality through impotentiality (Agamben [1993] 2007, 37). Similarly, there is a trend in much writing by asylum seekers to employ, in protest and as a call on the host to responsibility, a vocabulary of self-effacement and bare life. I therefore consider how a parasitic reading practice, after Miller, both undermines legal restrictions on belonging, and reveals the nature of responsibility for the Other as undecidable—that is, determined by "the Other's decision in me" (Derrida [2001] 2006, 103).

Parasite, like hospitality or *asylos*, is, for Miller, "one of those words which calls up its apparent 'opposite' [. . .] signifying at once proximity and distance". A parasite occupies, simultaneously, both sides of a boundary line, and moreover, is also "the boundary line itself, the screen which is at once a permeable membrane connecting inside and outside, [. . .] dividing them but also forming an ambiguous transition between one and the other" (Miller 1977, 441). Parasitic reading is therefore concerned with what might be called "threshold utterances". It is notable that, as well as "in front of", "against" and "near", Miller also lists "before" among the meanings of "para-"; he imagines reading as a chain, to which "there is always something earlier or something later [. . .] which [. . .] keeps the chain open, undecidable" (Miller 1977, 441). Bartleby incarnates the threshold character of the parasite and its undecidability: he is both the "intolerable incubus" and someone for whom the narrator has an ineluctable responsibility (Melville 1986, 36, 38). Melville's tale is, as Miller has identified, principally about the impossibility of assuming responsibility without first being able to explain Bartleby. It is plausible therefore to connect the undecidability of Bartleby with the undecidable in reading (and as, shall be seen, the undecidable figure of the asylum seeker).

To speak of coming "before the law" introduces a chain of potentially undecideable relations. To come before can mean to appeal to an authority; or to precede, which has a significant resonance with the condition of the refugee who, on entering the host country, becomes an asylum *seeker*, made to wait on the validation of his or her refugee status. The parasitic resonance of "before", where "para-" signifies the boundary, connects the parasite with the figure of the sovereign in Agamben—the one who, within the suspension of law that is the state of exception, is defined as "being-outside and yet belonging" (Agamben 2003, 35). For Agamben, the sovereign is positioned in symmetry with the *homo sacer*, who in Roman law could be killed but not sacrificed: "the sovereign is the one with respect to whom all men are potentially *homines sacri*, and *homo sacer* is the one with respect to whom all men act as sovereign" (Agamben 1998, 84). Parasite, sovereign and *homo sacer* all find their place in the social order defined by their place on a boundary. The figure of the parasite, then, before the law, is a permeable membrane through which extremes of power and powerlessness are transferred.

As Matthew Gibney has observed, it is now virtually impossible to claim asylum legally in the UK (Gibney 2004, 129). The nature of what makes people flee their homes means that few asylum claimants are able to leave openly; consequently, the 2004 Asylum and Immigration Act, which made it an offence to enter the UK without a valid passport, and also stipulated that destroying such documents on the advice of the agent who facilitated their travel was not a reasonable defence, in effect criminalised both many asylum seekers and the stories they tell. The AIA 2004 also demonstrates asylum seekers' complex relationship with *paper*. Paper facilitates entry into citizenship: it is first, says Derrida, "the place of the self's appropriation of itself, then of becoming a subject in law" (Derrida 2005, 56). Although Derrida has in mind the French *sans papiers*, irregular migrants who in the mid-1990s protested at their unrecognised status by adopting the name of undocumented or paperless person (*sans papier*), the implications of paperlessness also apply to the AIA 2004.

Furthermore, Derrida's assertion that "the war against 'undocumented' or 'paperless' people testifies to [the] incorporation of the force of law [. . .] in paper" extends to the relationship between law and literature (Derrida 2005, 60). Both enact a similar kind of paper-based guarantee of self; Derrida describes a passport (a parasitic document which facilitates the transfer between outside and inside) as "the juridical personality of 'here I am'", a statement that recalls his earlier assertion in 'Before the Law' that the literary *text* has "its own legal personality" (Derrida 2005, 61; Derrida 1992a, 184). For Derrida, law and literature intersect at a point of différance, where readability does not oppose unreadability; both encompass a simultaneous "possibility and impossibility" (of reaching a final decision, or definitive reading) (Derrida 1992a, 196). Law implies enforceability and the possibility of making a calculable decision. In contrast, justice (or "natural law") and literature are each, as Derrida has said, "an experience of the impossible [and] incalculable" (Derrida 1992b, 16). In Derridean terms, a decision is such only by virtue of the presence of the undecidable—without "the ordeal of the undecideable", there is simply a mechanical process (Derrida 1992b, 24).

Aligning the aporia necessary for a just decision with the undecidable or unreadable in literature has a direct bearing on how to read both 'Bartleby' and asylum narratives. According to Deleuze, Bartleby is "the man without references" (Deleuze [1993] 1998, 74); the narrator observes that, "[w]hile of other law-copyists I might write the complete life, of Bartleby nothing of that sort can be done." That is, he is both paperless and entirely occupied by paper. He arrives, "one morning [. . .] upon [the] office threshold" and proceeds to do "an extraordinary quantity of writing" (Melville 1986, 11, 12). Bartleby's relationship with the documents he produces is fundamental to his unsettling effect. The first instance of his famous "I would prefer not to" occurs when he is asked to "verify the accuracy of his copy" (Melville 1986, 12). Bartleby thus unsettles paper's legitimising function, creating a devastating imprint of doubt in a system absolutely dependent on verification. He undermines the entire edifice of paper as a support to a legitimised existence; all his copy potentially contains a fault, or, to return to one of the various meanings of "para-", is *irregular.* The paperless parasite thus makes irregular the system of regularisation that is founded on paper.

Furthermore, there is a striking resonance with Melville's text in legal discourse on the infamous section 55 (s 55) of the 2002 Nationality, Immigration and Asylum Act, which absolved the state of responsibility for providing support for an asylum claimant deemed not to have made their claim "as soon as reasonably practicable after the person's arrival in the United Kingdom" (Nationality, Immigration and Asylum Act, s55 1(b) 2002). In one of the first test cases for the NIAA 2002, the attorney general argued that, should asylum seekers be "entitled to pray in aid what they have been told by facilitators [i.e., the agents they had paid to facilitate their entry to the UK] in order to justify failure to seek asylum at the port of entry, s 55 would become a *dead letter*" (*R vs. Secretary of State for the Home Department*, par 39, emphasis mine). The resonance with 'Bartleby', who we are told in a postscript once worked as clerk in a dead letter office, is immediate, and compounded by the fact that each very different text is concerned with the question of responsibility for a stranger who would otherwise be at risk of vagrancy. One consequence of s55 was a spike in cases of asylum destitution in 2003.[4] The central question it raised was thus one of responsibility for the potential destitution of the stranger, which is the central moral problem facing Melville's narrator. Both texts are also concerned with defining legitimate and illegitimate forms of representation. S55, and the argument of the attorney general in support of it, demanded that asylum seekers engage legitimate grounds for the manner in which they arrive. To arrive clandestinely, to be, like Bartleby, "without references", is to be contrary to the law. Although Bartleby is not impeded by his lack of references, his unyielding expressions of preference also raise the question of self-representation. Bartleby does not actively refuse anything, yet his passivity effects the total negation of the enforceability of the law, if not its abrogation. The narrator, although legally right, is powerless to impose upon Bartleby, who is ultimately subject to the law (as his incarceration in the Tombs demonstrates) but also undoubtedly outside it. Thus, although it remains intact, the law is, in a sense, made a dead letter.

Bartleby's prior employment among dead letters has an important relation to his occupation as scrivener; as Miller has observed, "an unverified copy is a dead letter. It is of no more use than a blank sheet of paper. By refusing to proofread what he has copied, Bartleby renders all his work of copying null and void" (Miller 1990, 157). Bartleby's preference not to verify his copies makes them resemble a key aspect of the parasite, and thus, curiously, to resemble himself. Miller comments that the effect is to make each copy "into words that have meaning but have been drained of their efficacy [. . .]—neither words nor nonwords" (Miller 1990, 159). The description recalls the parasite, which straddles the boundary of inside and outside, meaning and non-meaning, so as to in fact incarnate that border. Bartleby also brings the law, as he is charged with reproducing it, into a parasitic condition. Just as he neutralises the law by remaining immoveable before it, he negates the apparatus of the law by introducing the worm of doubt—of irregularity—into the arena of the scrivener.

Bartleby's conjuring with the incalculable resonates with the legal reception of asylum seeker narratives. Asylum seekers' testimonies are framed by a need to make a calculable decision. Yet in cases where asylum applications are rejected but the applicant is not removed, the figure of undecideability persists. In a short film by Nick Broomfield and Marc Hoeferlin, for Amnesty's campaign on behalf of destitute asylum seekers, Ashfin, a destitute refused asylum seeker, describes his liminal existence:

> [I]f you don't have acceptance paper from Home Office then you do not exist anymore as human being, your existence is gone. [. . .] They put me to death without committing any crime. Nobody seemed to care and it was like my life is meaningless because my name is asylum seeker. (*Still Human* 2007)

Like that of Bartleby, the narratives of many failed asylum seekers who have not been returned to their home country also in a sense account for what cannot be accounted for; describing the impossible situation of those who cannot remain but cannot be returned, who have no acknowledgeable presence yet are nonetheless *present*.

As one who "calls upon [his] apparent opposite[s]", Bartleby also resembles the Iranian poet Mohsen Soltany-Zand, who was detained for four years in Villawood detention centre in Australia. In 'Don't Cry for Me' Soltany-Zand writes:

> Don't cry for me
> let me remain alone
> Don't cry for me

allow me my destitution
Don't cry for me
let me become the echo of a name to you. (Soltany-Zand 2008)[5]

Soltany-Zand insists that he should be recognised as existing in "para", at a threshold of proximity and distance (from the reader; from full citizenship) that he himself incarnates. His demand to be allowed his destitution recalls the perversity of Bartleby, whose refusals provoke the narrator to greater offers of hospitality, culminating in the invitation to share his home. Like Soltany-Zand, by the end of the tale Bartleby has become no more than "the echo of a name" to the narrator; however, in this case as a remedy to the latter's sense of thwarted responsibility. His final exclamation, "Ah Bartleby! Ah humanity!", enfolds Bartleby in a sense of pathos; casting him as "a valid synecdoche for all mankind", as if "to say the one thing is to say the other" (Melville 1986, 46; Miller 1990, 163, 173). However, as Miller asserts, the attempt to account for Bartleby signifies the narrator's failure to take responsibility, connecting the impossibility of describing Bartleby with the impossibility of making a decision about him. Rather, Bartleby's name becomes an echo of his undecidable condition as a *para*-site, transmitted between the poles of his identification as the "intolerable incubus" and the object of responsibility.

Nonetheless, this kind of strategy of negation *is* concerned with potentiality. Agamben follows Aristotle's notion that potentiality is defined most purely by its negation; the potential to act is distinguished from actuality by the potential not to act. In other words, the object of pure potentiality contains within itself and is articulated by impotentiality. Aristotle's image for this is the writing tablet on which nothing is written, which for Agamben directly connects it with Bartleby: "a scribe who does not simply cease writing but 'prefers not to', is the extreme [example] that writes nothing but its own potentiality to not-write" (Agamben [1993] 2007, 37; see Aristotle 1986, 203). Bartleby possesses the capacity to write, but most completely inhabits that capacity by refraining from doing so—he is, as Agamben says, "in full possession of the act of writing in the moment in which he does not write". (Agamben [1993] 2007, 37). When related to Miller's assertion that unverified copies resemble blank sheets of paper (or *dead letters*), Agamben's reading brings Melville's narrative into proximity with Soltany-Zand, who also articulates being and belonging through their opposite. Just as Bartleby's "I prefer not to" encapsulates his potentiality in a negation, Soltany-Zand exemplifies a trend in asylum seeker narratives of working with motifs of silence and effacement—of speaking through not speaking, presence configured as absence—which becomes a vocabulary of (im)potentiality in relation to belonging.

Postcolonial reading ethics are determined, largely, by the nature of the reader's response to an undecidable question: how to engage with representations of other(ed) experiences, without replicating in the reading act worldly structures of power. Properly ethical postcolonial reading is thus a process of crossing thresholds: between the literary and the social, as Quayson advocates; between a projected here and elsewhere, then and now; between decision and indecision. Spivak employs Derrida's notion of *teleopoiesis*—"imagining yourself, really letting yourself be imagined (experiencing that impossibility) without guarantees"—to describe reading as an exchange of subject positions: reading is "the imagination made ready for the effort of othering, however imperfectly" (Spivak 2003, 52, 13). For Spivak, reading acts involve crossing multiple thresholds that resist complete transition. "Active teleopoiesis," she says, "in all moments of decision makes the task of reading imperative and yet indecisive" (Spivak 2003, 31). It is this same *para-siting* of the reading subject that Soltany-Zand initiates in his poetry. Although his poetry does not change his position before the law, by introducing the aporia of the undecidable into a discourse predicated on making a calculable decision, he facilitates a reading practice which opens up an ethical experience of undecidability. Soltany-Zand's poetry frequently addresses a visitor who comes to stand for the state that is detaining him. This recalls the more elaborate slippage in Derrida's ethics of hospitality, which on occasion conflates the nation-state's responsibility towards immigrants with the host's responsibility towards a guest. Soltany-Zand also, however, addresses a *reader* (situating the reader who receives his narrative in the place of the visitor whom he receives as guest); as such, his writing can be seen to bring together an ethics of reading and an ethics of hospitality. In another poem, 'True Freedom', he writes:

> You, who are reading this,
> Come with me,
> Me and you make 'we'
> Together we can all escape. (Soltany-Zand 2008)

Here we have in effect a statement of Levinasian ethics: "me and you make 'we'" recalls Levinas's references to the *third*, that element of the encounter with the other (itself, according to Levinas, a relation of infinite responsibility) that looks outwards to a relation to humanity as a whole in which the ethical is inherent in the political (see Levinas [1974] 2004). By representing the ethical within the political, Soltany-Zand draws upon a concept of responsibility, in which the encounter with the other provokes wider questions of justice and its relation to humanity. He brings together the citizen-reader and non-citizen asylum seeker in a relationship of solidarity—a we—that occurs through the agency of Soltany-Zand himself. It is his invitation that allows the citizen-reader to escape, inverting the terms of a conditional hospitality which Derrida has called "the hospitality of the invitation", where "the host remains the host" (Derrida [2001] 2006, 98). His inversion of the invitation remakes this relation between migrant and citizen into one that is in "para"—no longer merely subject to the sovereign decision in the flux of a political exception, but oriented rather around the simultaneity of proximity and distance which the parasite incarnates.

The place of the reader within such a gesture in *para* is at the point where the act of reading is, in Miller's words, "undecidable". Soltany-Zand exhorts the reader to adopt Derrida's statement that, "we are responsible for something Other than us." Paradoxically, this responsibility casts the reader in much the same passive role as Saleh Omar in Gurnah's novel, and the *sans papiers*: in this case, as hostage to the requirement to acknowledge the obligation to the other. The nature of this responsibility is, in effect, the undecidable: for a decision to be distinguishable from mere automation, "my decision should not be mine, it should be, as impossible, the decision of the Other, my decision should be the Other's decision in me, or through me, and I have to take responsibility for the decision which is not mine" (Derrida [2001] 2006, 102). A responsible decision, therefore, occurs in the *invitation* of the other, which, in terms of an ethical reading practice, places the reader in the position of a parasite, at a threshold between decision and indecision. In keeping with the sense of the threshold inherent in "parasite", the reader of asylum narratives (as parasite) resembles both Bartleby and the narrator of Melville's tale. Like Bartleby, s/he "prefers not to" produce a definitive reading, deferring instead to the other and their narrative. Like Melville's narrator, reading asylum seeker narratives is to receive an invitation from the other to make a responsible decision, but one that also recognises the impossibility of doing so. Possible only insofar as impossible, decidable only insofar as undecidable; asylum seeker narratives present the other whose decision resides within the ethical decision.

Notes

*   This chapter is an extract from a more detailed discussion in David Farrier's *Postcolonial Asylum: Seeking Sanctuary Before the Law*, published by Liverpool University Press, 2011. I am grateful to the publishers for their permission to reproduce some of this material.

1.   Frequently, the emphasis on narrative in asylum determinations creates a market for horror; increasingly devastating accounts of traumatic experience are required to achieve the desired effect, a process that also forces an individual claiming asylum to collude in his or her positioning as victim. As Anthony Good has said, "'[m]erely' to have a spouse or parent killed before one's eyes [. . .] counts for little on the prevailing scale of persecution assessment" (Good 2007, 3–4). See also Fassin and d'Halluin (2005, 597–608).

2.   See Hardt and Negri (2000, 203–4); Deleuze ([1993] 1998, 68–90); Žižek (2006, 330–86); Agamben (1999, 243–71); Miller (1990, 141–78).

3.   Derrida builds on the observations of Emile Benveniste, that the root of 'hospitality', the Latin *hospes* meaning guest-master, contains the more ancient

hostis, signifying 'enemy'. Thus, Derrida says, hospitality "remains forever on the threshold of itself", at the point where host and guest, and friend and enemy, become one another. See Benveniste (1969, 71, 74, 78); Derrida (2000, 14).

4. In 2003, of 14,760 applications for support to mitigate the effects of s55, 9,410 were rejected. See Refugee Action (2006, 18); Refugee Council (2004, 12).

5. Please note that the website originally provided the texts of the poems cited here, but no longer does so.

References

Agamben, Giorgio. (1993) 2007. *The Coming Community*. Translated by Michael Hardt. London: University of Minnesota Press.

———. 1998. *Homo Sacer: Sovereign Power and Bare Life*. Translated by Daniel Heller-Roazen. Stanford: Stanford University Press.

———. 1999. *Potentialities: Collected Essays in Philosophy*. Translated and edited by Daniel Heller-Roazen. Stanford: Stanford University Press.

———. 2003. *State of Exception*. Translated by Kevin Attell. Chicago: University of Chicago Press.

Aristotle. 1986. *De Anima (On The Soul)*. Translated by Hugh Lawson-Tancred. London: Penguin.

Benveniste, Émile. 1969. *Indo-European Language and Society*. Translated by Elizabeth Palmer. London: Faber and Faber.

Deleuze, Gilles. (1993) 1998. *Essays Critical and Clinical*. Translated by Daniel W. Smith and Michael A. Greco. London: Verso.

Derrida, Jacques. 1992a. "Before the Law." In *Acts of Literature*, edited by Derek Attridge, translated by Avital Ronell and Christine Roulton, 181–220. London: Routledge.

———. 1992b. "Force of Law: The 'Mystical Foundation of Authority.'" In *Deconstruction and the Possibility of Justice*, edited by Drucilla Cornell, Michael Rosenfeld and David Gray Carlson, 3–67. London: Routledge.

———. 2000. "Hostipitality." *Angelaki* 5(3): 3–18.

———. (2001) 2006. "Hospitality, Perfectibility, Responsibility." In *Deconstruction Engaged: The Sydney Seminars*, edited by Paul Patton and Terry Smith, 93–104. Sydney: Power Publications.

———. 2005. *Paper Machine*. Translated by Rachel Bowlby. Stanford: Stanford University Press.

Derrida, Jacques, and Anne Dufourmantelle. 2000. *Of Hospitality*. Translated by Rachel Bowlby. Stanford: Stanford University Press.

Fassin, Didier, and Estelle d'Halluin. 2005. "The Truth from the Body: Medical Certificates as Ultimate Evidence for Asylum Seekers." *American Anthropologist* 107(4): 597–608.

Gibney, Matthew. 2004. *The Ethics and Politics of Asylum*. Cambridge: Cambridge University Press.

Good, Anthony. 2007. *Anthropology and Expertise in the Asylum Courts*. New York: Routledge-Cavendish.

Gurnah, Abdulrazak. 2001. *By the Sea*. London: Bloomsbury.

Hardt, Michael, and Antonio Negri. 2000. *Empire*. Cambridge: Harvard University Press.

Levinas, Emmanuel. (1974) 2004. *Otherwise the Being, or Beyond Essence*. Translated by Alphonso Lingis. Pittsburgh: Duquesne University Press.

Macklin, Audrey. 1999. "Truth and Consequences: Credibility Determination in the Refugee Context." In *Realities of Refugee Determination on the Eve of the New Millennium*, edited by Jordan, Nesbitt and Associates Ltd., 134–41. Haarlem: Association International des Judges aux Affaires des Réfugiés.
Malkki, Liisa H. 1996. "Speechless Emissaries: Refugees, Humanitarianism and Dehistoricization." *Cultural Anthropology* 11(3): 377–404.
Melville, Herman. (1853) 1986. "Bartleby." In *Billy Budd and Other Stories*. London: Penguin.
Miller, J. Hillis. 1977. "The Critic as Host." *Critical Inquiry* 3(3): 439–47.
———. 1990. *Versions of Pygmalion*. Cambridge: Harvard University Press.
Nationality, Immigration and Asylum Act, s55 1(b). 2002. HM Government. http://www.opsi.gov.uk/Acts/acts2002/ukpga_20020041_en_1
Plaut, W. Gunther. 1995. *Asylum: A Moral Dilemma*. Westport, CT: Praeger.
Quayson, Ato. 2003. *Calibrations: Reading for the Social*. Minneapolis: University of Minnesota Press.
R (on the application of Q and others) vs. Secretary of State for the Home Department. 2003 EWCA Civ 364.
Refugee Action. 2006. Report. *The Destitution Trap: Research into Destitution among Refused Asylum Seekers in the UK*. Refugee Action.
Refugee Council. 2004. Report. *Hungry and Homeless: The Impact of the Withdrawal of State Support on Asylum Seekers, Refugee Communities and the Voluntary Sector*. Refugee Council.
Soltany-Zand, Mohsen. n.d. "Don't Cry for Me." http://stickylabel.com.au/mohsen.html.
———. n.d. "True Freedom." http://stickylabel.com.au/mohsen.html.
Spivak, Gayatri Chakravorty. 1999. *A Critique of Postcolonial Reason*. Cambridge. Harvard University Press.
———. 2003. *Death of a Discipline*. New York: Columbia University Press.
Still Human, Still Here. 2007. Nick Broomfield and Marc Hoeferlin, dirs. Amnesty.
Žižek, Slavoj. 2006. *The Parallax View*. Cambridge: MIT Press.

15 Sympathetic Shame in J. M. Coetzee's *Disgrace* and *Diary of a Bad Year*

Katherine Hallemeier

The potential of literature for cultivating sympathy has been a subject of ongoing debate since the novel's inception. Recent scholarship has offered an alternative to sympathy, however, by articulating an ethics of reading centred on the circulation of shame. In this chapter, I offer brief genealogies of theories of sympathy and shame as they have related to novel reading since the eighteenth and nineteenth centuries. Whereas sympathy is felt for an other, and so risks denying the other's significant difference, the argument goes, shame is felt before an other, and so inaugurates an experience of self-difference. I trouble this seemingly clear contrast, however, by attending to how shame and sympathy might be understood as mutually constitutive. Through a reading of J. M. Coetzee's *Disgrace* (1999) and *Diary of a Bad Year* (2007), I conclude with a caution against an ethics of reading that elevates shame as a productive response to legacies of empire.

The rise of the novel in the eighteenth century coincides with the rise of sympathy as a moral sentiment: ever since, novel reading has been upheld as a potential means of developing individual and civic virtue. Adam Smith's construction of sympathy as a social good in *The Theory of Moral Sentiments* (1759) draws upon a literary culture in which immensely popular epistolary novels—notably those by Samuel Richardson—were understood as instilling in their readers a "refined sense" of fellow feeling (Woessner 2010, 235). Smith's theory of sympathy reflects this culture in its suggestion that novels can develop a reader's "sense of propriety" ([1759] 2006, 137): specifically, "the propriety of resigning the greatest interests of our own for the yet greater interests of others; and the deformity of doing the smallest injury to another in order to obtain the greatest benefit to ourselves" (ibid., 133). Novel reading as an exercise of the sympathetic imagination is a means of furthering not only individual moral development, but also the common welfare. Smith's connection between individual sympathy and public virtue continues to resonate. As Sophie Ratcliffe demonstrates in *On Sympathy* (2008), arguments as to the moral beneficence of sympathy are ubiquitous in contemporary arguments supporting the value of a literary education: "In the last decade, there have been many general claims made in relation to literature and its power to evoke sympathy, and about the relations between the idea of sympathy and empathy and the idea of goodness" (225). These arguments are united by their suggestion that sympathetic reading can enhance "the achievement of political peace and unity" (227).

However, even as arguments that conceive of reading literature in terms of enhancing community have had enduring appeal, scholars have just as often critiqued these arguments for obfuscating the self-centredness that arguably structures the sympathetic impulse. Ratcliffe, for example, warns that "much of the desire for emotional exchange comes from a ghostly desire for some sort of salvation" (2008, 232). Amit Rai similarly questions the purportedly selfless quality of sympathetic feeling, positing that, "[f]or modern readers [. . .] to sympathize with the oppressed seems hopelessly quaint [. . .] bearing connotations of a patronizing, even colonizing benevolence" (2002, xii). These writers issue compelling arguments that individual sympathy does not necessarily translate into public good. On the contrary, sympathy's propagation, as Rai suggests, can work to uphold "the project of colonialism" as easily as the "justice in abolitionism" (xiv). An ethics of sympathy dictates the relinquishment of self-interest in favour of the greater good. The relinquishment of self-interest is significantly qualified, however, and the potential for injustice heightened, by the assumption that it is the extension of one's own sympathy that strengthens community.

Interrogating the connection between individual feeling and social well-being from a different angle, Daniel Born offers an alternative genealogy of the relations between reading and moral sentiment to that suggested by Enlightenment accounts of literature and sympathy. In *The Birth of Liberal Guilt* (1995), he argues that recognition of the frequent disjunction between individual and societal interests assumed "crisis proportions" in the late Victorian period, giving rise to a new kind of novel (13). Works by Dickens, Eliot and Conrad are distinctive, he claims, because they "show a sense of collective guilt about the very poor and the sins of empire" (16). More than inviting sympathy for another's suffering, these novels, Born suggests, solicit shame for one's complicity in that suffering.[1] As in the case of sympathy, however, shame emerges as a moral sentiment that is cultivated in the individual reader: "Literature of liberal guilt invites [. . .] that we assess ourselves in light of the work" (165). This self-assessment in turn holds the potential for public virtue, insofar as it prompts introspection, which is, Denis Donoghue argues, "not the puny, self-regarding act as it is commonly said to be but an act of ethical and moral bearing" (quoted in Born 1995, 165).

While Born's argument concerns literature written during the height of the British Empire, his suggestion as to the centrality of shame to reading persists in contemporary studies of postcolonial literatures. Timothy Bewes offers the strongest articulation of this centrality, arguing that "postcolonial literature has, since its inception, been engaged in a thinking and materialization of the relation between shame and form" (2011, 47). Postcolonial literature, suggests Bewes, is "writing that comes into existence always already aware of its reflection in the eyes of the other" (42); it is writing that foregrounds both its privilege and presumption, as well as its complicity in colonial modes of thought. Postcolonial literature, Bewes concludes, is "particularly suited to a reading" that attends to the shame of the text—that is, to the text's "representational and ethical inadequacy" (47). Bewes stresses that this shame "is not an ethics predicated upon the obligation of the 'self' towards the 'other'" (29)—such an ethics, as we have seen, is the purview of sympathy. Rather, shame "is an experience of the subject's dissolution" (28): it is a figure of "the very discontinuity of the self, its otherness to itself" (23). "A work that affects us with shame," by this account, is an "event" wherein "the object of shame coincides with the experiencing subject" (22). Literary shame, Bewes argues, foregrounds "the ethical necessity" to "think in the absence of forms," including those of "subject" and "object" (46).

While Bewes's concern is postcolonial literature in general, other authors have examined the implications of reading shame in specific national contexts where the legacy of colonisation continues to be negotiated through projects of reconciliation. Like Bewes, these authors highlight shame's "quality of intersubjectivity" (Bewes 2011, 41). Elspeth Probyn, for example, contends that attentiveness to "the necessarily intertwined and intersubjective production of shame" through narratives can produce the opportunity for "using and relating to shame" in ways that "make our history more humane" (2005, 114–15). Specifically, Probyn argues that shame in Australia "provides a way of navigating the complexity of everyday life in a postcolonial milieu," insofar as it "demonstrates both the singularity of Aboriginal and non-Aboriginal cultures and their deep interconnection" (2004, 329). While proponents of sympathetic reading tend to highlight literature's potential for extending mutuality, Probyn argues that shameful stories can potentially lead to the recognition of extant differences that constitute community.

Caitlin Charos similarly maintains the potential value of shame for negotiating reconciliation, but in this instance refers to "the question of writing the postapartheid nation" in South Africa (2009, 278). "[T]he call to nation-building in South Africa," suggests Charos, "is one that [. . .] must not demand an eradication of shame but acknowledge its persistence in the postapartheid moment" (2009, 302). Charos cites specifically the "unique possibilities" in fiction "for exploring ambiguities and elusive feelings like shame" (284). Focusing on Zoë Wicomb's *David's Story* and Phaswane Mpe's *Welcome to Our Hillbrow*, Charos argues: "Acknowledging that shameful feelings are still with South Africans after apartheid, and that they might not go away, these writers [. . .] move us to consider what it might mean to live in an indefinite state of shame" (284–85). Shame, Charos suggests, is a way of "indicating our *interest* in communing with one another" (302), even while acknowledging past and present failures to fully do so. Once again, whereas sympathetic reading purports to extend community through the cultivation of a "refined sense" of fellow-feeling, readings grounded in shame arguably reveal the limits of sympathy within a community.

Insofar as accounts of reading shame stress the potential for experiencing the limits of sympathy by rendering the self an object of feeling, they resonate, I suggest, with prominent literary theories in the "ethical turn." For example, a literary education in Gayatri Spivak's formulation is valuable insofar as "the effort of reading is to taste the impossible status of being figured as object in the web of the other" (2002, 18). Reading, in other words, offers the opportunity to render the self an object of the imaginative, creative "gaze of others" (2003, 45). This description mirrors Sartre's account of shame, wherein by virtue of the gaze of the "Other," "I am put in the position of passing judgment on myself as an object, for it is as an object that I appear to the Other"; in shame, "I recognize that I am as the Other sees me" (1956, 222). Spivak describes reading not in terms of shame, however, but as *teleopoiesis*: the act of "imagining self, letting yourself be imagined (experience that impossibility) without guarantees, by and in another culture" (2003, 50). As an exercise of the imagination, reading is here not a means of extending collectivity, but rather of being taught collectivity's indeterminable character. It is, like the experience of shame, a challenge to self-complacent sympathy.

Derek Attridge also frames an ethics of reading as an encounter with alterity that can be understood as evocative of theoretical descriptions of shame. For Attridge, "[a] reading that does justice to what is literary in a literary work" is one that "is fully responsive to its singularity, inventiveness, and otherness" (2004, 11). This responsiveness, he suggests, is an "experience of transformation" of "familiar norms and habits" that introduces "new possibilities for thought and feeling" (11). Insofar as Attridge understands reading as a re-negotiation of the boundaries of the self, his theory bears comparison with shame as Jennifer Biddle describes it, as that which "arises as an impossible and yet necessary imperative of the continuously emergent self, bound to the very other it is equally bound to fail in order for its very identity" (Biddle 2009, 117). The work of Spivak and Attridge helps to clarify how reading with shame—as articulated by Bewes, Probyn and Charos—differs from reading with sympathy. If sympathy presumes the separation of "self" and "other" that it then purports to bridge, shame presumes the relational "self" that is always already constituted before the "other."

In the contemporary postcolonial moment, I have suggested, there is a certain scholarly consensus that the ethical promise of literature seems to lie in its shame—in its disruption of an ethics of sympathy through apprehension of singular difference that yields an experience of self as object. However, following the work of American psychologist Silvan Tomkins (1911–91), I am intrigued by the ways in which shame might be conceived not only as a disruption of, but also as a continuation of, sympathetic feeling. Tomkins positions shame as central to the operation of sociality by defining it as "a specific inhibitor of interest and enjoyment" that is yet an "*incomplete* reduction of interest or joy" (1995, 134, emphasis mine). In this definition, interest or enjoyment in another is integral to the condition of shame; if shame denotes a disruption of sympathy, it also depends upon sympathy for its inception. What is more, shame suggests a continuation of sympathy in the desire that "a relationship of mutuality" *fully* be restored (Tomkins 1995, 138). While Tomkins prefers "mutuality" to "sympathy," the latter is generally compatible with Smith's definition of the emotion as "our fellow-feeling with any passion whatever" ([1759] 2006, 5): sympathy, as opposed to say, "disgust" (ibid.), is precisely the emotion that marks an experience of "mutuality." Following Tomkins, then, it is possible to highlight how shame requires sympathy, even as sympathy produces the conditions for shame. How might recognition of this imbrication affect our understanding of what it means to read with shame? With this question in mind I turn to the author J. M. Coetzee, whose writing has been integral to Bewes's account of the shame of postcolonial literature, and to both Spivak's and Attridge's accounts of reading. I focus on two works by Coetzee, *Disgrace* and *Diary of a Bad Year*, respectively set in South Africa and Australia–two countries where, as Charos and Probyn contend, ongoing projects of reconciliation have meant grappling with the relation between personal and national shame.

The writing of J. M. Coetzee has been central to literary critical studies of shame and sympathy, and significant work exists on shame or sympathy in *Disgrace* alone. Within this body of scholarship, shame tends to be upheld as Coetzee's ethical endpoint, while sympathy is that which must be reconfigured as disrupted and incomplete in order to constitute an ethical position– that is, sympathy must be reconfigured, to be more like shame.[2] Along these lines, Mike Kissack and Michael Titlestad argue that *Disgrace* protagonist David Lurie achieves an "ethical disposition" of "secular humility" (2003, 137). Mike Marais, discussing the limits of the sympathetic imagination in *Disgrace* as they pertain to reading, suggests that Coetzee's narrative strategy of incompletion provides the reader with an opportunity for ethically encountering an "excess of closure" that imparts to reading the humility implicit in mourning (2006, 89).[3] Sam Durrant (2006) similarly argues that Coetzee's writing represents how an ethical relationship with difference occurs through the failure of the willful sympathetic imagination. Insofar as these readings proffer the ethical value of an interrupted sympathy, they embrace the ethical value of something akin to a posture of shame. While work on shame and sympathy in *Diary of a Bad Year* is relatively scarce, Jonathan Lear argues that the form of the novel– including its sympathetic representation of "JC"–works to suggest to (implicitly American) "liberal intellectual" readers a complicity in torture "we do not yet recognize" (2008, 93), so that "we" come to "see that our own reason has been implicated in a motivated structure of not-seeing" torture, in order to avoid the shame of having tolerated it. The novel thus promotes, argues Lear, "genuine ethical thought" in the reader (71). Lear, like critics of *Disgrace*, finds in shame, especially, the ethical kernel of Coetzee's work.

While this scholarship articulates how Coetzee's writing operates as a critique of self-complacent sympathy, I argue that his novels also caution against the elevation of shame as an ethical relation to suffering and therefore as an ethical mode of reading. By reading scenes of shame in *Disgrace* alongside those in *Diary of a Bad Year*, I show that the texts foreground how sympathy operates through shame and shame operates through sympathy in such a way that categories of subject and object can be reinforced, as easily as they can be dissolved. Shame, in Coetzee's writing, not only disrupts habits of sympathy, but also produces new sympathetic attachments that are problematically premised on a shared state of shame.

Disgrace and *Diary of a Bad Year* offer parallel relationships in which the dynamics of shame in a world full of suffering are debated. In *Disgrace*, Lucy refuses to tell the police that she has been raped by three men. Her decision distresses her father, David Lurie. He urges Lucy to reconsider: "There is no shame in being the object of a crime. You did not choose to be the object. You are an innocent party" (Coetzee [1999] 2000, 111). For her part, Lucy consistently refuses such identifications. Exasperated by her father's continued attempts to sympathise, Lucy writes him a letter: "You have not been listening to me. I am not the person you know. I am a dead person and I do not yet know what will bring me back to life" (161). Lucy is clear: Lurie cannot know how she feels.

In *Diary of a Bad Year*, Anya tells the police that she has been raped by three men. The police captain, "a very nice man, very sympathetic," is distressed, and asks Anya if she is sure she wants to report the crime: "You know, dishonour, *infamia*, is like bubble gum, wherever it touches it sticks" (Coetzee 2007, 100). Anya summarily rejects this view of things: "In the twentieth century, when a man rapes a woman, it is the man's dishonour" (101). Despite Anya's dismissal, the captain's assessment of how shame works is voiced again by Señor C, the modestly famous author to whom Anya relays the story of the rape: "Your three American boys—I [Señor C] have never laid eyes on them, but they dishonour me nevertheless. And I would be very surprised if in your inmost depths they did not continue to dishonour you" (109–11). Señor C implies that one cannot know that Anya is *not* ashamed.

Lurie and Señor C offer different but complimentary accounts of the "stickiness" of shame. In asserting Lucy's innocence, Lurie works to soothe the shame he imagines she feels as "the object of a crime" (Coetzee [1999] 2000, 111). He again seeks to mitigate what he imagines to be Lucy's shame when he reads Lucy's refusal to report the rape to the police as a sign of liberal guilt before the history of South African apartheid: "Do you think you can expiate the crimes of the past by suffering in the present?" (112). Lurie's framing of Lucy's rape in broad historical terms is particularly ironic, as Lucy Graham notes, given that "Coetzee demonstrates very clearly that Lurie is blind to the history of his own actions" (2003, 437): in the first half of the book, Lurie rapes one of his students and seeks to "justify" his actions in terms of an ahistorical Romantic desire. Whether considering either his own violent actions or Lucy's response to violence, however, Lurie simultaneously imagines and renounces the experience of shame as an appropriate response to ongoing histories of colonisation and apartheid. Señor C is both more encompassing and more accepting in his attribution of shame: "When you live in shameful times, shame descends upon you, shame descends upon everyone" (Coetzee 2007, 96). He believes that the disgrace that falls on Americans because of the actions of their state is greater than that which falls on Australians for the actions of theirs (43). And it is his "strong opinion" that "[t]he generation of white South Africans to which I belong, and the next generation, and perhaps the generation after that too, will go bowed under the shame of the crimes that were committed in their name" (44). Both men propose that the women feel shame by virtue of their membership in a particular national or international community, even as Lurie disavows this shame and Señor C insists upon it.

Lucy and Anya, for their part, refute this theory of sentiment. Lucy is tersely dismissive of Lurie's suspicion that she is acting to "expiate the crimes of the past": "I don't act in terms of abstractions" (Coetzee [1999] 2000, 112). She insists, rather, that "in this place, at this time"—"[t]his place being South Africa"—what happened to her is "my business, mine alone" (112). Lucy shifts the discussion away from her feelings and towards the particular circumstances that inform her actions. These circumstances include a culture in which, as both Rosemary Jolly and Meg Samuelson have argued, the rape of women has come to symbolise national shame. Within this context of stigmatisation, the representation of rape as shameful "potentially reiterates the primary violation" (Samuelson quoted in Charos 2009, 284); it raises "the spectre or the reality of re-victimizing" women who have been raped "as shamed" (Jolly 2010, 92). Jolly's and Samuelson's arguments resonate with Kathleen Woodward's insistence that there are "many models of shame," and that the experience of shame for the masculine moral subject, the feminine objectified subject and the racialised traumatised subject can be radically different experiences, particularly in their relation to moral knowledge (2000, 213). Lucy's refusal of shame (as Jolly suggests) might be read as a refusal of the re-victimisation inhering to the objectification of feminised bodies as shameful. At the same time, however, her refusal also gestures towards an acknowledgement of the complex racial politics inhering in post-apartheid South Africa. Lucy implies that the public arrest and prosecution of her three black attackers would do very little to ensure justice—"I am not just trying to save my skin," she says (Coetzee [1999] 2000, 112). Lucy's decision not to report the rape is informed, in part, by a desire not to reinforce white privilege ("my skin") in a country cleaved by racial inequality. Lucy suggests that she does not so much feel guilty for the past as aware of how current cultural and political structures represent and exploit rape. "Shame" inadequately describes her considered response to these structures.

Anya, like Lucy, questions the theorising of shame that produces a grand historical narrative. She turns "quite flinty" after Señor C reasserts his theory of pervasive shame (Coetzee 2007, 113): "From her eyes beamed a ray of pure cold rage. *Don't you tell me how I feel!* she hissed [. . .] *What do you know!*" (115). What Señor C does not know, Anya implies, is very similar to what Lurie does not know—the gender and racial politics that are particular to the circumstances surrounding a specific rape. Señor C elides the fact that Anya defies the police captain and files a report with her friend (who has also been raped)—"we had all the names, all the particulars" (99)—because she is reasonably confident that the report of three rich Americans raping two racialised women (she describes herself, tongue in cheek, as "the little Filipina" (29)) will result not in further suffering, but some measure of justice. And indeed, "they issued a warrant and those boys were arrested," and "the story hit the papers back in Connecticut or wherever and they were in deep shit" (99). Señor C theorises a shame similar to that which Sara Ahmed aptly describes in her discussion of reconciliation in Australia: "a collective shame that does not affect individuals in the present, even as it surrounds and covers them, like a cloak or skin" (2004, 102). This notion of collective shame, however, once again appropriates a woman's considered response to rape, refiguring it as a feeling which promotes a sympathetic response. Like Lucy, Anya suggests that sympathy for her "shame" is misplaced. Claims to know how she feels as an ostensible member of an international liberal community elide discussion of the cultural and political circumstances that materially affect whether the victim-survivor of rape is re-victimised, or the racialised subject re-stigmatised, in her search for justice within that community.

It is possible to read Lurie and Señor C's attribution of shame to Lucy and Anya as simply repeating the objectifying work of sympathy. Yet, if these men attribute shame to others, they also feel shame—intensively and immediately. Before urging Lucy to report the rape, Lurie imagines her attackers learning that they are "being sought for robbery and assault and then nothing else": "It will dawn on them that over the body of the woman silence is being drawn like a blanket. *Too ashamed*, they will say to each other, *too ashamed to tell*, and they will chuckle luxuriously, recollecting their exploit" (Coetzee [1999] 2000, 110). The passive voice in the first sentence reveals that Lurie does not imagine that Lucy will be thought of by others as the prime actor in silencing the rape, though it is her body that is figured as the source of shame that must be covered. Rather, the passage implies that Lurie, who is already ashamed by his failure to protect Lucy—"I did nothing. I did not save you," goes his "confession" (157)—will be further shamed if the rapists are not prosecuted as rapists, if they are not shamed in turn. Lurie's shame, while marking Lurie's imbrication in patriarchal and racist ideology, also denotes a sense of complicity in and responsibility for violence: his shame marks his failure to protect "*his people*" (201; emphasis in original). Señor C's shame likewise signals his sense of complicity with and responsibility for suffering. Anya briefly exposes the visceral closeness of this shame: "'Dishonour descends upon one's shoulders,' she repeated softly. That sounds like the inmost depths to me. I sat shaken, speechless" (92). Through her repetition of Señor C's proclamation of shameful times and shameful states (40), Anya implies that the generalised shame of which Señor C writes and speaks is a displaced articulation of his own sense of shame: "So what is going to save you from dishonour, Senor C? she said" (92). In his shakiness and speechlessness, Señor C betrays shame—he is "lost" and shame is his "lot" (96).

Lurie and Señor C feel shame in their inability to adequately respond to violence and suffering. In his "failure" to prevent or ameliorate this violence, each experiences himself as "other" than "himself": shame disrupts an ethics of sympathy in which the masculine "self" is empowered to sacrifice for and protect the feminised "other." At the same time as the protagonists experience shame as an attenuation of mutuality, however, their shame also arguably creates new occasions for sympathy—namely, for the shame that Lurie and Señor C imagine the women feel for having been raped. As Lurie and Señor C experience a shame that renders them more like passive objects than active subjects, they sympathise with women who have been treated as objects. For these two men, shame both disrupts *and extends* feelings of sympathy.

Coetzee's writing can itself be read in terms of this paradoxical relation between sympathy and shame. In an oft-quoted interview in *Doubling the Point* (1992), Coetzee describes his work in terms that echo Lurie's and Señor C's sense of impotency before violence:

> Let me add [. . .] that I, as a person, as a personality, am overwhelmed, that my thinking is thrown into confusion and helplessness, by the fact of suffering in the world, and not only human suffering. These fictional constructions of mine are paltry, ludicrous defenses against that being-overwhelmed, and, to me, transparently so. (248)

The passage suggests a potent connection between shame and sympathy in Coetzee's fiction. On the one hand, Coetzee describes the shame of his "confusion and helplessness": the boundary between subject and object blurs in the author's account of being "overwhelmed" by human and nonhuman suffering. The self is rendered an object to itself, yielding authority in the declension from "I" to "a person" to "a personality." On the other hand, shame is nonetheless located within a particular "self." Carol Clarkson concisely describes how this sense of a "self" affected by others persists through Coetzee's writing: "[E]ven in the moment of exposing the contingency of cultural or personal beliefs (or, differently put, *because* of the responsiveness to countervoices), the singularity of an authorial voice is affirmed" (2009, 105). This singular authorial voice consistently demonstrates, as Heather Walton phrases it, an ongoing sympathy "with those subjects which are gendered feminine in our culture" (2008, 288). The acts of sympathy that are manifest in "[t]hese fictional constructions of mine" are themselves potentially shameful, however, insofar as they function as "paltry, ludicrous defenses" against the "being-overwhelmed" that describes shame before other suffering beings. Unlike his protagonists, Coetzee sympathises with culturally objectified "others," while locating the shame that potentially informs this work within a particular, albeit overwhelmed "self."

Disgrace and *Diary of a Bad Year* similarly contain, limit and qualify shame as that which potentially engenders acts of sympathy that are yet shameful and shaming. In these texts, Coetzee dramatises how the experience of objectification that Lurie and Señor C undergo through their shame is different from the objectification that constitutes the feminised body as shameful. In the former case, shame potentially marks a transformation of the "subject"; in the latter, shame potentially marks a reinscription of an experience of the self as "object." Coetzee lays bare how being overwhelmed by the objective fact of suffering in the world is different from having suffered in the world as an "object" of violence. In light of these different and highly gendered effects of shame, the apprehension or prescription of a shared shame in the postcolonial moment, though arguably borne of shame, is also an act of sympathy: an act of sympathy that potentially reinforces the objectification of others and occludes broader discussions of social justice. By insisting on the ambiguity of Lucy and Anya's feelings, *Disgrace* and *Diary of a Bad Year* resist the objectification inhering to both sympathy and shame: these texts imagine victim-survivors of violence as acting subjects. The shame in and of Coetzee's writing, concomitantly, does not demand a sympathetic, shame-filled reading. Rather, *Disgrace* is constructed such that it will "necessarily produce diverse effects" on readers (Peter McDonald 2002, 330),[4] even as the structure of *Diary of a Bad Year* "ensures a whole multiplicity of readings" (Iddiols 2009, 195).

The mutually constitutive quality of sympathy and shame in these texts serves to qualify arguments that uphold reading postcolonial literature as that which potentially disrupts sympathy—the objectification of the "other"—by enacting a state of shame that renders the self an "object." The construction of such a mode of reading assumes that shame will not re-enact and reinforce objectification, but rather transform a self-complacent subject. For some privileged readers, reading with shame may enact a dissolution of the reading "subject" and the literary "object," but this transformation is qualified insofar as the humbled subject comes to feel sympathy for others through a state of shame. For some readers, in contrast, particularly those constituted as cultural "others," invocations to read with shame may reiterate past and present experiences of objectification. Postcolonial readers, like texts and their authors, are differently circumscribed in their relations to shame. An ethics of reading that suggests the transformative potential of shame does not fully account for those differences. Through the figures of Anya and Lucy,

Coetzee's work suggests how reading and writing that disseminate shame may, at times, be the proper object of rage.

Acknowledgement

I am grateful to Chris Bongie and Rosemary J. Jolly for commenting on earlier versions of this essay, although I alone am responsible for its errors. This research was supported by the Social Sciences and Humanities Research Council of Canada.

Notes

1. I deliberately use "shame" interchangeably with "liberal guilt." Given that guilt commonly describes "what I have done," while shame describes "who I am" (Abdel-Nour 2003, 707), the "guilt" that Born delineates is more akin to the latter: "Liberal guilt carries distinctiveness chiefly on account of its inability to find for the problem of guilt a consolatory response" (Born 1995, 166). There is no particular act that could be performed in order to atone for particular actions. On the contrary, liberal guilt is generalised to "every level of human social institutions and relations" (Born 1995, 167). It is, in fact, shame in what the system *is*.
2. Notable exceptions to this argument include Geoffrey Baker, who suggests that interpersonal sympathy is "Coetzee's middle road—a practical agenda for transformative action that occurs on a seemingly non-political plane" (2005, 29), and Hania Nashef, who argues that Coetzee's characters experience an "excruciating and overwhelming sense of shame" (2009, 1), for which they can often find no justification (6). Discussions of shame, gender and race in *Disgrace* likewise tend to stress the agony of shame; these are brought to bear later in this chapter.
3. Tomkins on shame in mourning: "Another major source of shame in interpersonal relationships is the loss of the love object, through separation or death" (1995, 153).
4. For a comprehensive account of the reception of *Disgrace*, which generated notable controversy among different sets of readers, see Andrew van der Vlies's *J. M. Coetzee's* Disgrace: *A Reader's Guide* (2010).

References

Abdel-Nour, Farid. 2003. "National Responsibility." *Political Theory* 31(5): 693–719.

Ahmed, Sara. 2004. *The Cultural Politics of Emotion*. New York: Routledge.

Attridge, Derek. 2004. *J. M. Coetzee and the Ethics of Reading*. Chicago: The University of Chicago Press.

Baker, Geoffrey. 2005. "The Limits of Sympathy: J. M. Coetzee's Involving Ethics of Engagement." *ARIEL: A Review of International English Literature* 36(1–2): 27–49.

Bewes, Timothy. 2011. *The Event of Postcolonial Shame*. Princeton: Princeton University Press.

Biddle, Jennifer. 2009. "Shame." In *Emotions: A Cultural Studies Reader*, edited by Jennifer Harding and E. Deidre Pribram, 113–25. London: Routledge. Originally published in *Australian Feminist Studies* 12(26): 227–39.

Born, Daniel. 1995. *The Birth of Liberal Guilt in the English Novel.* Chapel Hill: University of North Carolina Press.

Charos, Caitlin. 2009. "States of Shame: South African Writing after Apartheid." *Safundi: The Journal of South African and American Studies* 10(3): 273–304.

Clarkson, Carrol. 2009. *J. M. Coetzee: Countervoices.* Basingstoke: Palgrave Macmillan.

Coetzee, J. M. 1992. *Doubling the Point: Essays and Interviews.* Edited by David Attwell. Cambridge: Harvard University Press

———. (1999) 2000. *Disgrace.* London: Vintage.

———. 2007. *Diary of a Bad Year.* London: Harvill Secker.

Durrant, Sam. 2006. "J. M. Coetzee, Elizabeth Costello, and the Limits of the Sympathetic Imagination." In *J. M. Coetzee and the Idea of the Public Intellectual*, edited by Jane Poyner, 118–34. Athens: Ohio University Press.

Graham, Lucy Valerie. 2003. "Reading the Unspeakable: Rape in J. M. Coetzee's *Disgrace.*" *Journal of Southern African Studies* 29(2): 433–44.

Iddiols, Katy. 2009. "Disrupting Inauthentic Readings: Coetzee's Strategies." In *J. M. Coetzee in Context and Theory*, edited by Elleke Boehmer, Katy Iddiols and Robert Eaglestone, 185–97. New York: Continuum.

Jolly, Rosemary. 2010. *Cultured Violence: Narrative, Social Suffering, and Engendering Human Rights in Contemporary South Africa.* Liverpool: Liverpool University Press.

Kissack, Mike, and Michael Titlestad. 2003. "Humility in a Godless World: Shame, Defiance and Dignity in Coetzee's *Disgrace.*" *Journal of Commonwealth Literature* 38(3): 135–47.

Lear, Jonathan. 2008. "The Ethical Thought of J. M. Coetzee." *Raritan* 28(1): 68–97.

Marais, Mike. 2006. "J. M. Coetzee's *Disgrace* and the Task of the Imagination." *Journal of Modern Literature* 29(2): 75–93.

McDonald, Peter D. 2002. "Disgrace Effects." *Interventions* 4(3): 321–30.

Nashef, Hania A. M. 2009. *The Politics of Humiliation in the Novels of J. M. Coetzee.* New York: Routledge.

Probyn, Elspeth. 2004. "Everyday Shame." *Cultural Studies* 18(2–3): 328–49.

———. 2005. *Blush: Faces of Shame.* Minneapolis: University of Minnesota Press.

Rai, Amit S. 2002. *Rule of Sympathy: Sentiment, Race, and Power 1750–1850.* New York: Palgrave.

Ratcliffe, Sophie. 2008. *On Sympathy.* Oxford: Oxford University Press.

Sartre, Jean-Paul. 1956. *Being and Nothingness: An Essay on Phenomenological Ontology.* Translated by Hazel E. Barnes. New York: Philosophical Library.

Smith, Adam. (1759) 2006. *The Theory of Moral Sentiments.* Mineola, NY: Dover Publications, Inc.

Spivak, Gayatri Chakravorty. 2002. "Ethics and Politics in Tagore, Coetzee, and Certain Scenes of Teaching." *Diacritics* 32(3–4): 17–31.

———. 2003. *Death of a Discipline.* New York: Columbia University Press.

Tomkins, Silvan. 1995. *Shame and Its Sisters: A Silvan Tomkins Reader.* Edited by Eve Kosofsky Sedwick and Adam Frank. Durham: Duke University Press.

van der Vlies, Andrew. 2010. *J. M. Coetzee's* Disgrace: *A Reader's Guide.* London: Continuum.

Walton, Heather. 2008. "Staging John Coetzee/Elizabeth Costello." *Literature & Theology* 22(3): 280–94.

Woessner, Martin. 2010. "Coetzee's Critique of Reason." In *J. M. Coetzee and Ethics: Philosophical Perspectives on Literature*, edited by Anton Leist and Peter Singer, 223–47. New York: Columbia University Press.

Woodward, Kathleen. 2000. "Traumatic Shame: Toni Morrison, Televisual Culture, and the Cultural Politics of the Emotions." *Cultural Critique* 46: 210–40.

16 Responsible Reading and Cultural Distance

Derek Attridge

When Alaa al-Aswany's Arabic novel *Imarat Ya'qubyan* was published in 2002, it quickly established itself as a runaway popular success. It was the Arab world's bestselling work of fiction for 2002 and 2003, and listeners to the Middle East Broadcasting Service voted it the best novel of 2003.[1] A highly successful Egyptian film and mini-series followed. By 2007 the work was in its ninth edition.

In 2006 in the US and 2007 in the UK, an English translation by Humphrey Davies with the title *The Yacoubian Building* appeared to great critical acclaim—the British paperback includes two pages of glowing tributes from the country's leading newspapers and magazines—and achieved substantial sales. English is far from being the only language in which a version of the novel has appeared: in conversation with Pamela Nice in 2006, al-Aswany noted that it had been translated into nineteen languages, and in 2010 he responded angrily when the Israel-Palestine Centre for Research and Information made an unauthorised Hebrew translation freely available. Samia Mehrez, in her 2008 study of cultural conflict in the Egypt of the Mubarak era (i.e., after 1981), calls the novel's global triumph "mind-boggling and overwhelming," and cites nearly two hundred thousand sales world-wide at the time of writing (Mehrez 2008, 56). This figure has undoubtedly risen considerably since then.

What is the relation between these two sets of facts? To what degree do the reasons for the success of the Arabic original overlap with the reasons for the success of the various translations—and the English translation in particular? And what would constitute a responsible reading of one of the translated versions by a reader without Arabic, a reading that could be said to do justice to al-Aswany's work?

I'm using this very specific example to raise the much broader question of cultural distance as a factor in reading. Inevitably, when a work crosses geographical and linguistic boundaries, the cultural context within which it was produced and within which it was first read (for simplicity's sake, I shall assume for the time being that these are the same) differs from the cultural contexts within which it is received. If, then, the work that I encounter strikes me as remarkable, how do I know whether that remarkableness is a direct response to the author's achievement in his or her own milieu, or is generated by the cultural difference between that milieu and my own? And how much does it matter which of these it is?

To get to grips with these questions, it's necessary to consider what "remarkable" might mean when used in this way. Literary works that achieve high status in Western culture are characterised by their *singularity*; those that are seen as merely following out a formula, and are thus barely distinguishable from other examples of the genre in question, are accorded low standing and may not, in fact, be dignified with the title "literature". The same is probably true of most of the cultures that now rub shoulders in the global arena. This singularity is the result of *inventiveness*: the inventiveness of the work, reflecting the inventiveness of its creator (though not necessarily in any straightforward way). And the singular, inventive work can be thought of as one that introduces into the field of the same—the habitual, the taken-for-granted, the normal—something *other*, something that can't be exhaustively explained within existing norms of thinking and feeling.[2] While the uninventively formulaic work can achieve a degree of popularity, global and enduring success is more likely to spring from an author's capacity to invent new forms and discover new subject-matter, particularly when what is offered to the reader is glimpses of ideas, emotional complexes or factual realities upon whose occlusion the persistence of the status quo has depended. It can be no accident that the canonical works in the European literary tradition are those that have broken new ground in form or content, or, very often, both. A reading that can be said to do justice to such a work is one that responds to its singularity, inventiveness and alterity with an active, creative reading, bringing to bear on it the reader's own singular existence as the product of a variety of cultural and other forces—what I have called the individual subject's *idioculture* (Attridge 2004, 20–21; 82–83). At the same time, a creative reading of this kind involves a certain kind of passivity, of being hospitably open to the otherness of the work, of being ready to be changed by what it has to offer.

Using these terms to rephrase our question, we can ask how to account for the experience of inventiveness, singularity and alterity that a reader may have when encountering a work that arises from, and on its initial publication spoke to, a significantly different cultural context from his or her own. To what extent does a responsible reading of such a work imply a project of countering any sense of inventiveness (from now on I'll use just one of the three interlocking terms to imply all of them) that arises *solely* from the cultural distance between the contexts of production and of reception? If so, how can this be achieved? How can we know if it has been achieved? If, on the other hand, it is legitimate to capitalise on effects of inventiveness that arise from cultural difference, how can we avoid reducing the work to an example of pleasurable exoticism?

The first point to make in tackling these questions is that this problem is not unique to the situation in which a work is read in a different part of the world, and thus a different cultural context, from that in which it was created. Exactly the same question arises when the work being engaged with was written in the same place in which it is being read, but at an earlier period; here too there are likely to be significant differences between the two contexts that in themselves could account for an experience of inventiveness, and here too it is not easy to say just what a responsible reading would consist of. Is the best reading the one that most successfully shears off modern assumptions and utilises historical knowledge to approach the work with the habits and predispositions of the earlier period? Or is it legitimate to allow the effects of historical change to enhance the experience of inventiveness? If a work is *both* historically and geographically distant, of course, these questions—which have been mulled over repeatedly in many different literary theoretical discourses—become even more acute.

To begin to suggest answers, we need to banish any notion that there is a real possibility that a literary work could be read without any cultural distance between reader and work, the idea that there exist instances of the perfect matching of context of production and context of reception against which we can measure other (necessarily inferior) kinds of reading. Cultural difference is not a matter of black and white, but of degree: there can never be total accord between the moment of creation and the moment of reading. Even a work written by someone extremely like myself and published very recently at the heart of the culture which has formed me will speak from a different place: variations of class, experience, personality, background, profession, family, and many other attributes will always have an impact. Here we can see the inadequacy of my earlier working assumption that the cultural contexts within which a work is produced and within which it is first read are identical; they can be very similar, but some differences will always necessarily make themselves felt. This complicates any attempt to measure the effects of cultural distance between "the work" and the situation of the reader, as it's not clear whether we are referring to the author's own context or that of its first readers. There may be later readers, or readers in other places, who, in terms of their situation and assumptions, actually come closer to the author than those original readers. Moreover, the "first readers" do not constitute a homogeneous and clearly defined group any more than "later readers." Another problem is that it's never a simple matter to say what the author's cultural context actually *is*; it remains a matter of interpretation, as does the cultural context of those "first readers." Our access to them is largely a mediated one, through other texts.

A second, complementary point that equally deserves attention is that there will nearly always be *some* degree of overlap between the context of production and the context of reception, stemming from shared historical and cultural conditions or, sometimes, arising out of sheer coincidence. If there were no such overlap, the work in question would be incomprehensible, a complete blank to the reader. The only case in which this would not be so is where chance factors grant the work an intelligibility in its new context that has absolutely nothing to do with its original meanings, a situation that is hard to imagine. A museum-goer in twenty-first-century Britain may enjoy many features of a Mayan figurine that would have had absolutely no value to the original viewers (or users) of the object; nevertheless, the fact that the figurine implies a certain valorisation of the human body provides a minimal degree of overlap. We are almost always, then, operating in a realm of cultural distance, somewhere between complete coincidence and total difference.

Given this inevitable in-betweenness, what constitutes a responsible reading? One extreme position is that the ideal reading situation is an encounter, as Raymond Williams sarcastically puts it, of "naked reader with naked text" (Williams 1986, 11): the question of the original context and readership is held to be irrelevant, as is the question of the reader's own formation and the biases and blind spots that have resulted from it. This argument would be valid only if it were possible to encounter works of art in a vacuum, having jettisoned everything one has absorbed about one's own culture and that from which the work has sprung. But it is out of one's own cultural inheritance, one's idioculture, that one responds to art, and that inheritance includes knowledge (accurate or otherwise) about the work being engaged with and about the matrix of its production. If I am familiar with Yoruba religion, I will read Ben Okri's *The Famished Road* differently from someone who is not; and if I do possess that knowledge, I'm not able to discard it while reading. It's part of not only the book's formation, but also my own. There is no such thing as a pure reading of the words on the page: even if I know nothing about the text's origins, I am seeing through the highly determined lenses bestowed upon me by my particular background—and these will lead me to infer an origin, regardless of whether I am conscious of this deductive process. This is why even an argument that one should take into account one's own formation, as far as possible, but not that of the work, is implausible: there is no way of separating the two. The context of the work is something I bring to my reading, not something out there to which I have unmediated access and can choose to ignore if I wish; it's part of my mental world as the product of my earlier reading and other experiences I have had.

The argument at the other extreme is analogous to the demand for a wholly historicised engagement I alluded to earlier: it would allow a reading to be responsible only if it wholly eradicated the effects of the context of reception and was entirely absorbed into a reconstructed context of production. According to this view, I would be able to do justice to Satyajit Ray's *Pather Panchali* only if my idioculture was transformed, for the duration of the film, into an identical copy of that of a moviegoer in West Bengal in the 1950s. Put like this, the argument is clearly fallacious; no amount of research would enable me to achieve this transformation. But it is implicitly present in any claim that the closer one gets to the original matrix of a work (and by the same token, the more one sheds one's own culture's assumptions) the better one's reading. Perhaps a responsible reading is one that, *as far as possible*, invokes the original context of the work? We've already seen that "the original context" is a problematic notion, and it's equally difficult to know what "as far as possible" means. Does responsible reading hinge on the time and money one has available to carry out the research needed to establish that context? The elitist implications of this conclusion are unsatisfactory in themselves; fortunately, there is little theoretical justification for such a position, which would discredit most of the actual reading that takes place.

If we are to abandon both the idea that a pure engagement with the text "itself" offers the best reading and the idea that the paradigm towards which one should be striving is complete recovery of the original context, we find ourselves occupying a rather messy, but perhaps more realistic, middle position. One possible stance that suggests itself would be that as long as the reader experiences the work as inventive it *is* inventive, and that there is no need to worry about whether this experience is the result of the reader's distance from the original cultural matrix or is really a response to the author's inventive act; it will, in any case, *feel* like the latter if no thoughts about the original context are allowed to interfere. Yet most of us, I think, would be unhappy with this position. One's readings are, surely, usually improved by increasing one's knowledge about the cultural context of the work and at the same time scrutinising one's own assumptions for cultural biases. What needs to be rejected is the notion that there is one ideal reading towards which all empirical readings strive, or even that—since our readings are all mediated by our own specific cultural histories and situations—there is one ideal reading for a particular reader at a particular time.

If we return the verbal noun "reading" to the verb, and remember that the literary work has its existence as an *event* rather than an *object*, we can come closer to an understanding of the multiple possibilities that a concept of responsible reading encompasses. I am reading responsibly if I am simultaneously referring the words back to what I know about the various contexts that are relevant—the literary traditions out of which the work emerges, the conditions under which it was written, the aims of the writer and those of his or her peers, the social, historical, economic and political backgrounds to the act of writing and the earliest readings, the discussions of the work that may have taken place in print or other media since publication—and referring my own responses to what I am able to access of my own culturally derived ways of thinking and feeling. Certainly, if I carry out some detailed research, I may be able to improve my knowledge of the relevant contexts, and there may be some payoff in my reading (though this can never be guaranteed), but I should not be under the illusion that I will eventually be able to read in just the same way as those "first readers."

Let us return now *The Yacoubian Building* and our question about the variety of readerships, and let us simplify that question as one about Egyptian readers, or perhaps even urban Egyptian readers, for whom the depicted events would have had a highly familiar ring, and British or American readers, for the large majority of whom they would not be at all familiar. Al-Aswany's novel uses the building named in the title—a grand apartment block in downtown Cairo that has seen better days—as a microcosm of Egyptian society, following the interlinked stories of several of its occupants as they deal with the challenges of their personal lives and those thrown at them by Egypt's social, economic and political systems and processes. It is set in the late 1980s and early 1990s, though readers of the English translation are told in a translator's note not to pay too much attention to this fact as "the novel reflects the Egypt of the present," thus providing them with some extra-textual information which readers of the original version presumably did not need. (Humphrey Davies's "present" must be around 2006–7, when the translation was published, whereas al-Aswany started the novel in 1998, much closer to the period in which it is set, and the initial publication was in 2002; we are left to conclude that nothing much changed between 1990 and 2006—and the novel certainly conveys the impression that the Egypt it reflects is not in any imminent danger of being transformed.) The picture of urban Egyptian life painted in the novel is not a pretty one: the gap between rich and poor is vast (symbolised by the contrast between the lives of the wealthy occupants of the largest apartments in the building and those of the indigent group who inhabit the small rooms on the roof originally built for storage); corruption flourishes at all levels; advancement is dependent not only on being able to afford the necessary bribes but also on having the right family background; women are routinely abused; the democratic machinery is a sham; torture is an accepted part of police methods; prejudice against homosexuality is widespread. As a result, every character is engaged in a struggle to achieve fulfilment, whether it be sexual, financial, political or professional; and most fail.

As one indication of the type of response to *Imarat Ya'qubyan* that has emerged from the Arab critical world we can take Samia Mehrez's comment:

> Within the Egyptian literary field, al-Aswany, a dentist by profession, is perceived as a writer of "popular" and not avant-garde fiction; his first novel, *Imarat Ya'qubyan,*is considered "scandal literature" that appeals to the literate masses but not the literary elite. (Mehrez 2008, 56)

Merhez clearly speaks for the "literary elite" to which she refers (she has served as a member of the Naguib Mahfouz Award, a rough equivalent of the Booker Prize for Arab writing, which conspicuously failed to honour *Imarat Ya'qubyan* when it was published), and her comments hint that a dentist

writing his first novel could hardly be expected to produce important literature (hence her words about its "mind-boggling and overwhelming global
success" cited earlier). But she is well aware that the translated version was
treated with much more respect by the "literary elite" in the West: she notes
that *Le Monde* referred to it as a "chef-d'oeuvre du roman arabe contempo-
raine," and adds, now distancing herself somewhat from the elite,

> Much to the venerable scribes' dismay, al-Aswany's spectacular success
> came to confirm that the way into the international republic of letters
> may depend not on the scribes' local status in the alley but rather on the
> global village and what *it* deems to be a "classic." (56)

No doubt Mehrez is correct when she says that one explanation for the success
of al-Aswany's novel compared to others regarded more highly by the "vener-
able scribes" is its relatively conventional form; whereas a novel like *Dhat* by
Sonallah Ibrahim "requires, in fact demands, the active creative participation
of its readers . . . *Imarat Ya'qubyan* navigates within the boundaries of classical
realism that appeals to a much wider spectrum of uninitiated readers in the
global village" (57). But this, of course, does not explain why many another
novel written in a traditionally realist style has had nothing like the success of
al-Aswany's novel. We will need to re-visit the question of the novel's form in
due course.

It is Mehrez's epithet "scandal literature" that points to another, perhaps
more important, aspect of the novel's appeal to its readers in the Arab world.
It was shocking in two different ways: in its frank portrayal of sex, including
homosexual sex, and in its unflinching depiction of the endemic corruption
of Egyptian society. Pamela Nice, interviewing people in Cairo in 2006 about
the novel and the film, which had just been released, found both of these
being given as reasons for reading the book. "Few could deny," she comments, "that both the book and the film created a phenomenon in Cairene
culture because of the many taboos broken in the name of freedom of artistic
expression," and she goes on to list both torture, exploitation and bribery on
the one hand and sexual explicitness on the other (Nice 2006). The director
of the film, Marwan Hamed, focuses on the same qualities:

> The book is very, very bold. . . . It addresses some of the issues people
> don't even dare to talk about. The amount of realism in the book and the
> amount of honesty Alaa Al-Aswany had for the characters is something
> I admired very much. (Salama 2005)

Imarat Ya'qubyan, then, struck Egyptian readers, and perhaps readers more
widely in the Arab world, with the force of truth: it exposed realities which both
officialdom and most media kept hidden. Al-Aswany himself seems less than
happy that this aspect of his work is the one that readers in his own country

repeatedly focus on; Nice records him as saying, "People say 'Yacoubian Building' was popular because of the sex, exposed corruption, police brutality, etc., but won't acknowledge that, perhaps, it was a good piece of literature."

The sympathetic portrayal of homosexuality was clearly an important element in the book's shock value in the Arab world. No doubt for many readers this aspect was hard to accept, given the extent of anti-gay prejudice in Arab culture; for others, it must have been a positive expansion of mental and emotional horizons; for yet others, a welcome endorsement of their own attitudes and convictions. One of the novel's central characters, Hatim Rashid, the gay editor of a French-language newspaper in Cairo, falls passionately in love with a young police officer from northern Egypt, and the novel tracks the highs and lows of the relationship with the same attention as it does the heterosexual exploits of the aging playboy Zaki Bey or the secret second marriage of the businessman and drug-dealer Hagg Azzam. Sex is also prominent in the story of Busayna, the beautiful roof-dweller who finds that she can't keep a job in a store without granting sexual favours to the proprietor, but finally catches the eye of Zaki Bey and agrees to a marriage that gives the novel a conventional happy ending.

To most Western readers of the translation, the power of the book could not be said to lie in its revelation of unspoken truths. Some readers will have already been aware of Egypt's rampant corruption, heavy-handed political rule and gross disparity between the rich and the poor; others will have been surprised to learn of these problems; in neither case would the content have come over with the shock of unspoken but widely known truth frankly revealed.[3] The book's depiction of sex is tame in comparison with much Western fiction, and its willingness to include gay relationships hardly startling to a Western reader. We need to look elsewhere, then, for an explanation for its success in the West. Perhaps al-Aswany's faith in his own work as "a good piece of literature" has something to do with it.

The *Daily Telegraph* reviewer, Tash Aw, notes the "rich mixture of characters", the "wry delivery" and the way in which the narrator refrains from making judgements, in "this superbly crafted feat of storytelling" (Aw 2007). Rachel Aspden, in the *Observer*, while describing al-Aswany's prose as "resolutely affectless" (another way, perhaps, of describing its reluctance to offer judgements), praises his treatment of religious extremism as "without sensationalism or irony" and admires his eye for details (Aspden 2007). For Alev Adil, in the *Independent*, this "addictively readable" novel combines "the humanist realism of Balzac with the hyperbolic momentum of Egyptian soap opera" (Adil 2007). The *San Francisco Chronicle*'s John Freeman likes the fact that *The Yacoubian Building* doesn't close neatly: "Some plotlines end abruptly, in tragedy, while others simply vanish into the noise of the street" (Freeman 2006). Lorraine Adams, in the *New York Times Book Review*, comments that "Aswany's empathy combines with perceptive narrative detail" (Adams 2006). In their various ways, these reviewers, and others, praise not just the boldness with which al-Aswany portrays the injustices and injuries inflicted on his characters and describes practices usually concealed, but also the skill with which the stories are told—a creative achievement which is part and parcel of the enjoyment readers experience. Al-Aswany's inventiveness, to which these readers are responding, lies partly in his continuous interweaving of the various plots—there are no chapters, just a series of short episodes, sometimes continuous, sometimes jumping in time and place—and in the use of a style capable of dealing with a great range of behaviours without judging or moralising. This is not to say there are no villains, for there are plenty; but they are minor players, and the main characters, whatever their weaknesses, are treated with understanding and frequently with generous humour. The handling of Taha, the roof-dweller who dreams of becoming a policeman and who turns his anger at rejection into radical Muslim activism, is particularly deft; while there is no suggestion that his faith-inspired violence is to be lauded, its origins are convincingly detailed, and the blame is laid as much on the secular establishment as on the Muslim fundamentalists who indoctrinate him.

Al-Aswany's handling of sex is an area where Arab and Western responses are visibly distinct. Whereas in the Egyptian context, what seems most striking to readers is the openness with which sexual, especially gay, relations are described, Western reviewers often find al-Aswany's treatment of the subject wanting. Adil's view is that "the depiction [of male homosexuality] is often uncomfortable because it seems prejudiced rather than permissive . . . At times, the voice is culturally as well as sexually conservative"; while Aw extends his critique to the depiction of heterosexual relations as well, citing clichés—homosexuals bear a "sad, mysterious, gloomy look," for instance—that "create a sense of bathos and risk puncturing the believability of the novel." Cultural distance is clearly at work to produce two different novels here.

If Arabic-speaking and English-speaking readers are not reading the same novel—beyond the fact that translation inevitably introduces differences—what are the implications for the question of responsible reading? If I, as a member of the latter group, find the novel inventive for its handling of narrative, its tonal subtlety, its reworking of the canonical nineteenth-century realist novel, its moral stance and its sheer informativeness, how concerned should I be to learn that these are not central to responses by the former group? My answer is that I should not be concerned, just as I should not withdraw a negative judgement of some of al-Aswany's (or his narrator's) sweeping generalisations about women and homosexuals if I become convinced that Egyptian readers don't share my view. I cannot not read the novel in the context of the tradition of the European novel, to which it in part belongs, both through translation but also through its evident affinities with that tradition; and to do so is to be alerted to some of the details of its technique that might seem unimportant to someone at home in the traditions of Arabic literature. (At the same time, as I have read Naguib Mahfouz's

Cairo novels, I am in a position to complicate that response by appealing to a local antecedent, at least as mediated by English translations.) In other words, *The Yacoubian Building*, entering the space of Western literature, offers itself to readers in a new context, one which downgrades certain aspects but heightens others. This doesn't represent a betrayal of the novel, but a new exploitation of its potential. Exoticism does, inevitably, play a role, and the strangeness of some of the scenes depicted in the novel provides Western readers with certain pleasures not granted those who are familiar with them; but if this strangeness is understood as part of the novel's subtle challenge to our habitual ways of thinking, although not part of the novel's original effectiveness, there is no reason for it to be dismissed.[4]

The ethics of reading literary works from other cultures is not, it turns out, significantly different from the ethics of reading works from one's own culture, which are always distanced to some degree or other. That distance is part of what makes the work valuable, and a responsible reading is one that will take full account of it rather than one that undertakes the impossible task of abolishing it. I'm not speaking here of the value of such works when treated as documents that may convey important information about other cultures, a valid function but one which literary texts share with other kinds of documents; I'm speaking of the value of a certain kind of *experience*, a pleasurable opening up to new possibilities that only art can produce. There's no guarantee that this opening up will be beneficial, though it usually is; it's the opening itself that is valuable. *The Yacoubian Building* is a useful repository of knowledge, and thanks to its popularity it has no doubt helped to spread awareness of the problems Egypt faces well beyond the Arab world; less fortunately, it may have reinforced prejudices about Arab culture and society. But its value as a literary work lies in the multiple readings through which it has come to life over and over again, dislodging old attitudes and shifting old configurations of feeling by means of its subtly interlaced tracings of imagined lives and passions, achieving this differently in its Arabic version from the way it does in its English version, but memorably and productively in both.

Notes

1. Translator's note, al-Aswany (2007, xi).
2. I elaborate on this interlocking and interdependent trinity in Attridge (2004).
3. For a survey of Egypt's political, social and economic conditions, see Rodenbeck (2010). This chapter was written before the popular uprising of January 2011, which has made non-Egyptian readers much more fully aware of the crimes, and the unpopularity, of the Mubarak regime. What these events confirmed was just how widely the injustices depicted in al-Aswany's novel were felt among Egypt's citizens, and how central this aspect of the novel was to its original success.
4. Many of the reviews on Amazon's UK website (submitted by "ordinary" readers) reflect a preoccupation with cultural difference—e.g., "The Yacoubian

Building offers western readers like myself a fascinating glimpse at how life might be lived at different social levels in Cairo"; "I didn't open it looking for a masterpiece of style or psychological depth, but for a window into another society's values, types, behaviors and problems"; "Western readers coming to this novel will find it an exciting reading experience and a vibrant and descriptive primer illuminating the various forces in contemporary Egypt that affect its current political climate"; "When travelling I always try to read a book based on the country being visited . . . this was a great insight into Egyptian society which gave our visit much 'background colour.'" The American website has similar comments, such as, "I was able to relate it to what I know of Egyptian culture, and it opened my eyes to aspects of the culture which I have not personally seen" and "It is an eye-opener, and one assumes the depictions of social, political, and religious conditions are authentic."

References

Adams, Lorraine. 2006. "Those Who Dwell Therein." *New York Times Sunday Book Review*, August 27. http://www.nytimes.com/2006/08/27/books/review/Adams.t.html.

Adil, Alev. 2007. "Home Truths in Egypt's Multi-story Saga." Review of *The Yacoubian Building*, by Alaa al-Aswany. *Independent*, February 16. http://www.independent.co.uk/arts-entertainment/books/reviews/the-yacoubian-building-by-alaa-al-aswany-trans-humphrey-davies-436484.html.

Al-Aswany, Alaa. 2007. *The Yacoubian Building*. Translated by Humphrey Davies. London: Harper Perennial.

Aspden, Rachel. 2007. "Sex and the City, Egyptian-Style." Review of *The Yacoubian Building*, by Alaa al-Aswany. *Observer*, February 18. http://www.guardian.co.uk/books/2007/feb/18/fiction.features/print.

Attridge, Derek. 2004. *The Singularity of Literature*. London: Routledge.

Aw, Tash. 2007. "Upstairs, Downstairs." Review of *The Yacoubian Building*, by Alaa al-Aswany. *Daily Telegraph*, January 28. http://www.telegraph.co.uk/culture/books/3662789/Upstairs-downstairs.html.

Freeman, John. 2006. "A Window into Rich Life of Cairo Apartments." *San Francisco Chronicle*, August 13. http://www.sfgate.com/cgi-bin/article.cgi?f=/c/a/2006/08/13/RVGROK9TJ91.DTL.

Mehrez, Samia. 2008. *Egypt's Culture Wars: Politics and Practice*. London: Routledge.

Nice, Pamela. 2006. "A Conversation with Alaa al-Aswany on *The Yacoubian Building*." *Al Jadid* 12(56/57). http://www.aljadid.com/interviews/Alaa-al-Aswany-interview.html.

Rodenbeck, Max. 2010. "The Long Wait: A Special Report on Egypt." *The Economist*, July 17.

Salama, Vivan. 2005. "As *Yacoubian Building* Sets to Head West, The Author Discusses the Story's Message." *Daily News Egypt*, December 8. http://www.dailystaregypt.com/article.aspx?ArticleID=157.

Williams, Raymond. 1986. Foreword to *Languages of Nature: Critical Essays on Science and Literature*, by L. J. Jordanova, 10–14. London: Free Association Books.

Contributors

Daniel Allington worked in publishing and education before moving into academia, now working as a lecturer at the Open University. He has published extensively on the history and sociology of reading. His first book, *Communicating in English: Talk, Text, Technology* (edited with Barbara Mayor), is forthcoming from Routledge in 2012. Together with David Brewer, Stephen Colclough, and Kathleen Tonry, he is currently writing a monograph on the history of the book in Britain, forthcoming from Blackwell in 2014.

Derek Attridge is Professor of English at the University of York, and a fellow of the British Academy. He has published widely on James Joyce, including *How to Read Joyce* (2002), *Joyce Effects: On Language, Theory, and History* (2000), and *Peculiar Language: Literature as Difference from the Renaissance to James Joyce* (1988), and four edited or co-edited volumes on Joyce. He edited *Jacques Derrida's Acts of Literature* (Routledge, 1992), and his theoretical study, *The Singularity of Literature* (Routledge, 2004), won a European Society for the Study of English Book Award in 2006. Other books include *J. M. Coetzee and the Ethics of Reading: Literature in the Event* (Chicago, 2004) and *Writing South Africa* (Cambridge, 1998; co-edited with Rosemary Jolly). His latest books are *Reading and Responsibility: Deconstruction's Traces* (Edinburgh University Press, 2010) and *Theory after "Theory"* (Routledge, 2011; co-edited with Jane Elliott). He is currently co-editing *The Cambridge History of South African Literature*.

Shakuntala Banaji lectures in international media and film in the Media and Communications Department at the LSE. She has published widely on Hindi cinema, audiences, creativity, news reception and online civic participation; her 2010 edited collection, *South Asian Media Cultures*, is currently available from Anthem Press, and her forthcoming book about the Internet and youth civic participation, co-authored with David Buckingham, is out from MIT Press in 2012.

Bethan Benwell is a Senior Lecturer in the Division of Literature and Languages at the University of Stirling. She has published chapters and articles

on discursive approaches to reading and reception, discourses and representations of masculinity in popular culture and (with Elizabeth Stokoe,
Loughborough University) tutorial discourse and student identity. She is the
editor of *Masculinity and the Men's Lifestyle Magazine* (2003, Blackwell) and
co-author (with Elizabeth Stokoe) of *Discourse and Identity* (2006, EUP). She
was co-investigator (with Kay, Procter and Robinson) on an AHRC-funded
project (2007–10) examining the relationship between readers, location and
diaspora literature: http://www.devolvingdiasporas.com/.

Lucy Evans is a Lecturer in postcolonial literature at the University of
Leicester. She has published articles on E. A. Markham, Mark McWatt,
Dionne Brand, V. S. Naipaul and Paul Gilroy. She has also co-edited (with
Emma Smith and Mark McWatt) a collection of essays, *The Caribbean
Short Story: Critical Perspectives* (Peepal Tree Press, 2011). Her monograph,
Communities in Contemporary Caribbean Short Stories, will be published by
Liverpool University Press in 2013.

David Farrier is a Lecturer in modern and contemporary literature at the
University of Edinburgh. He is the author of monographs on nineteenth-century and early twentieth-century Pacific travel writing (*Unsettled Narratives:
The Pacific Writings of Stevenson, Ellis, Melville and London*, Routledge, 2007),
and on representations of asylum seekers and refugees in contemporary literature, visual art and film (*Postcolonial Asylum: Seeking Sanctuary before the
Law*, Liverpool University Press, 2011). He has also published on the work
of Derek Walcott, Michael Ondaatje, Robert Louis Stevenson, Abdulrazak
Gurnah, Caryl Phillips, the filmmaker Michael Winterbottom and asylum
theatre. He is currently editing *Asylum Accounts*, a special issue of *Moving
Worlds: A Journal of Transcultural Writings* on asylum, due out in 2012.

Katherine Hallemeier is a PhD candidate at Queen's University in
Kingston, Canada. Her research interests include the relationship of ethics, emotions and reading in the novels of J. M. Coetzee. She has published 'Ethics and the Nonhuman: J. M. Coetzee's *Lives of Animals* and
Disgrace' in *Proteus: A Journal of Ideas* (Spring 2007). Two forthcoming
articles respectively examine the humanities and suffering in Coetzee's
Elizabeth Costello and hybridity in Brian Castro's *Shanghai Dancing*.

Katie Halsey is a Lecturer in the literature of the long eighteenth century
at the University of Stirling. She has published widely on print culture in
the eighteenth and nineteenth centuries. Recent publications include *The
Concept and Practice of Conversation in the Long Eighteenth Century* (2007),
edited with Jane Slinn, *The History of Reading* (2010), edited with Rosalind
Crone and Shafquat Towheed, and *The History of Reading: Evidence from
the British Isles 1750–1950* (2011), edited with Bob Owens. She has just

completed a monograph, entitled *Jane Austen and her Readers* (forthcoming with Anthem Press in 2012).

Graham Huggan is Chair of Commonwealth and Postcolonial Literatures at the University of Leeds, and also directs the university's cross-disciplinary Institute for Colonial and Postcolonial Studies (ICPS). He is the author of many books and articles, mostly in the field of comparative postcolonial studies. Recent published work includes a co-written book on postcolonial ecocriticism (Routledge 2010, with Helen Tiffin).

Michelle Keown is a Senior Lecturer in English literature at the University of Edinburgh. She has published widely on Maori and Pacific writing and is the author of *Postcolonial Pacific Writing: Representations of the Body* (Routledge, 2005) and *Pacific Islands Writing: The Postcolonial Literatures of Aotearoa/New Zealand and Oceania* (Oxford University Press, 2007). She is co-editor (with David Murphy and James Procter) of *Comparing Postcolonial Diasporas* (Palgrave, 2009) and co-editor of *The Edinburgh Introduction to Studying English Literature* (Edinburgh University Press, 2010). Current research projects are focused on the relationship between British and US imperialism in the Pacific; postcolonial translation studies; settlement studies; and the postcolonial short story.

Elizabeth le Roux lectures in Publishing Studies at the University of Pretoria. She has worked for more than a decade in the field of scholarly publishing, most recently as director of the University of South Africa Press. She is currently working on her doctoral studies, focusing on the social history of university presses in South Africa. She has also worked as a freelance translator and editor, and has published several articles on publishing history, literature and the media in Africa.

Lucienne Loh is a Lecturer in English Literature at the University of Liverpool. Her first book, *Postcolonial Dislocations: Politics of the Country in Contemporary Literature*, will be published by Palgrave Macmillan in 2012. She has previously published on contemporary postcolonial writing in *Wasafiri* and *Journal of Postcolonial Writing*, and has forthcoming articles in *Interventions* as well as in a special issue of *Textual Practice* on "Postcolonial Literature and Challenges of the New Millennium," which she is also co-editing. She helped to establish the Postcolonial Studies Association in 2008 and served on its executive committee till 2011. She is currently embarking on a research project on Black British heritage, funded in part by the British Academy.

Gail Low teaches Book History and Contemporary Literatures in English at the University of Dundee. She is the author of *Publishing the Postcolonial:*

West African and Caribbean Writing in the UK 1948–68 and *White Skins/ Black Masks: Representation and Colonialism*, and has co-edited *A Black British Canon?* with Marion Wynne Davies.

Srila Nayak has a Ph.D. in Literary and Cultural Studies from Carnegie Mellon University. She was formerly an assistant professor in the Department of English at UNC-Charlotte, and is currently an independent researcher, residing in Chicago. Her articles have appeared or are forthcoming in *Modern Philology* and *Conradiana*. She is presently working on her monograph, *Calling a Nation by Another Name: Transnational Imagination in Postcolonial and Modernist Writings*.

James Procter is a Reader in the School of English at Newcastle University. He is the author of *Dwelling Places: Postwar Black British Writing* (Manchester University Press, 2003) and *Stuart Hall* (Routledge, 2004), and the editor of *Writing Black Britain 1948–1998: An Interdisciplinary Anthology* (Manchester University Press, 2000) and (with Keown and David Murphy) *Comparing Postcolonial Diasporas* (Palgrave, 2009). Recent articles include the 'The Postcolonial Everyday' (*New Formations* Number 58) and 'Reading Taste and Postcolonial Studies' (*Interventions* 11(2)). He was the principal investigator (with Benwell, Kay and Robinson) on an AHRC-funded project (2007–10) examining the relationship between readers, location and diaspora literature: http://www.devolvingdiasporas.com/.

Gemma Robinson is a Senior Lecturer in English studies at the University of Stirling. She is the editor of *University of Hunger: The Collected Poems and Selected Prose of Martin Carter* (Bloodaxe, 2006) and *Over Seas: A Transnational Caribbean: Special Issue of The Arts Journal*, 2(2) (2006), and co-editor (with Carla Sassi) of *Caribbean-Scottish Passages: Special Issue of The International Journal of Scottish Literature*, 4 (2008). Her research on postcolonial writing and bibliography has appeared in *Small Axe* and *Moving Worlds*. She was co-investigator (with Benwell, Kay and Procter) on an AHRC-funded project (2007–10) examining the relationship between readers, location and diaspora literature: http://www.devolvingdiasporas.com/.

Claire Squires is the Director of the Stirling Centre for International Publishing and Communication at the University of Stirling. Her publications include *Marketing Literature: The Making of Contemporary Writing in Britain* (2007) and *Philip Pullman: Master Storyteller* (2007). She is co-volume editor for the forthcoming *Cambridge History of the Book in Britain Volume 7: The Twentieth Century and Beyond*, and is on the judging panel for the Saltire Literary Awards. Previously she worked at Hodder Headline publishers.

Neelam Srivastava is a Senior Lecturer in Postcolonial Literature at Newcastle University (UK). She is the author of S*ecularism in the Postcolonial Indian Novel: National and Cosmopolitan Narratives in English* (Routledge, 2007), and has recently co-edited *The Postcolonial Gramsci* (Routledge, forthcoming). She is the coordinator of a Leverhulme Research Network, "Postcolonial Translation: The Case of South Asia".

Florian Stadtler is a Research Associate at the Open University. From 2008 to 2010 he has been working on the major AHRC project 'Making Britain: South Asian Visions of Home and Abroad, 1870–1950'. He has published articles and essays on South Asian literature in English, British Asian history and literature, and Indian popular cinema. His monograph *Fiction Film and Indian Popular Cinema: Rushdie's Novels and the Cinematic Imagination* is forthcoming with Routledge. He is reviews editor for the magazine of international contemporary writing *Wasafiri.*

Index

C

CAIPSA (Consortium of Academic and Independent Publishers of South Africa), 78

Cairo, impact of *The Yacoubian Building*, 240

Calder, Liz, 117

Cambridge University Press, 83

Campbell, Roy, 88

Canada. *See also* Kingston, Ontario

Canadian Aboriginal Peoples Television Network (APTN), 38

Canadian literary texts, Plomer's consideration of, 92

Cape (publisher). *See* Jonathan Cape

Cape Town International Book Fair (CTBK), 77

Caribbean culture: and consumption in Antoni's stories, 15, 142, 143–144, 145–146, 148, 150, 151; impact of globalisation, 143

Caribbean writing: diverse readership, 143, 151; selection for publication, 86–7

Caribbeanness: and Diaz's *Oscar Wao*, 46; and Levy's *Small Island*, 46–47, 49–50, 52, 54

Carter, David, xiii, 7, 8

Casanova, Pascale, 50–51

Castaway, The (Walcott), 95

censorship: of *The Satanic Verses*, 119; under apartheid in South Africa, 3

Certeau, Michel de, 4, 194

Chak de, India (film), 62, 63, 66

Chakava, Henry, 75–76

Chakravarty, Sumita, 123

Chambers, Claire, 103, 106, 107

Chambers, Sarah, 167

Chandra, Bipin, 159

Charles, Prince of Wales, 30

Charles II, King of Great Britain and Ireland, 6

Charos, Caitlin, 224–225, 225

Chartier, Roger, 4

Chatterjee, Gayatri, 123

Chatterjee, Partha, 162

children's books, produced by black British publishers, 108

Chislett, William, 189

Chomondeley, Lady Sybil, 95

Cicero, importance in nineteenth-century English education, 186–187

cinema. *See* Hindi films; Indian popular cinema

Clark, Helen, 30

Clark, Steve, 129

Clarkson, Carrol, 230

class: attitudes in Mishra's travel narrative, 131, 133, 135–136; in publishing industry, 106; representations in Hindi cinema, 57, 58, 59, 65, 65–67

classical literature, importance in Macaulay's reading, 187, 189, 190–191, 192

classical realism, *Imarat Ya'qubyan*, 240

Coetzee, J. M., 74; *Diary of a Bad Year*, 18, 222, 226–227, 227–232; *Disgrace*, 18, 222, 226–232; *Doubling the Point*, 230

Cole, Desmond, 82

Colenso, William, 6

colonial period: flow of cultural production and distribution, 73, 83; readers of reform-centred publications, 157–158; and women's reform in India, 164, 165–166. *See also* British Empire; empire

colonial project: imposition and resistance, to 194; Macaulay and his view of education, 184, 185–186, 192–193

colonialism: legacy of hierarchies in India, 137–138; Plomer's view, 88, 91; and social inequalities in New Zealand, 39

colonisation: and experience of shame in *Diary of a Bad Year*, 228; reconciliation and legacy of, 224

Colsen, Kurt, 82

comedy: in *bro'Town*, 29–30, 31–32, 35; using ethnic/cultural stereotypes, 27–28

commodification: and concerns about culture, 143; in marketing of postcolonial literature, 107, 130, 142

Connor, Steven, 100

Conrad, Joseph, 223

consumer culture/consumption: audiences and readers, 3–4; and Caribbean culture in Antoni's *Folktales*, 15, 142, 143–144, 145–146, 148, 150, 151; and reception theory, 7. *See also* American consumer culture

Cope, Jack, 92

Corelli, Marie, 4

cosmopolitanism: Mishra's readers, 15, 130–131; Plomer's reading, 14, 87, 92; postcolonial readers 43; readers of Indian writing in English, 128; Rushdie, 116

crime/thrillers, in surveys of multicultural readers, 101, 102, 103

criticism. *See* literary criticism

.